MEASURING NONCOGNITIVE SKILLS IN SCHOOL SETTINGS

Also Available

The Early Education Leader's Guide:
Program Leadership and Professional Learning
for the 21st Century
*Nonie K. Lesaux, Stephanie M. Jones,
Annie Connors, and Robin Kane*

Making Assessment Matter:
Using Test Results to Differentiate Reading Instruction
Nonie K. Lesaux and Sky H. Marietta

Teaching Advanced Literacy Skills:
A Guide for Leaders in Linguistically Diverse Schools
*Nonie K. Lesaux, Emily Phillips Galloway,
and Sky H. Marietta*

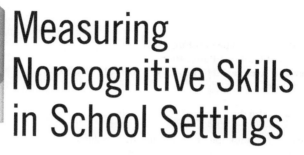

Measuring
Noncognitive Skills
in School Settings

Assessments of Executive Function
and Social–Emotional Competencies

edited by
Stephanie M. Jones
Nonie K. Lesaux
Sophie P. Barnes

Foreword by Timothy P. Shriver

THE GUILFORD PRESS
New York   London

Copyright © 2022 The Guilford Press
A Division of Guilford Publications, Inc.
370 Seventh Avenue, Suite 1200, New York, NY 10001
www.guilford.com

Printed in the United States of America

This book is printed on acid-free paper.

Last digit is print number: 9   8   7   6   5   4   3   2   1

Library of Congress Cataloging-in-Publication Data is available
from the publisher.

ISBN 978-1-4625-4866-8 (paperback)
ISBN 978-1-4625-4867-5 (cloth)

About the Editors

Stephanie M. Jones, PhD, is the Gerald S. Lesser Professor in Child Development and Education at the Harvard Graduate School of Education, where she also serves as director of the Ecological Approaches to Social and Emotional Learning (EASEL) Lab. Anchored in prevention science, Dr. Jones's research focuses on the effects of poverty and exposure to violence on social, emotional, and behavioral development from early childhood through early adolescence. Over the past 15 years, her work has centered on evaluation research addressing the impact of social and emotional learning (SEL) interventions at the preschool and elementary levels on behavioral and academic outcomes and classroom practices, as well as new curriculum development, implementation, and testing. With Nonie K. Lesaux, Dr. Jones is codirector of the Saul Zaentz Early Education Initiative and coprincipal investigator of the Early Learning Study at Harvard. She serves on numerous national advisory boards and expert consultant groups related to social–emotional development, early childhood education, and child and family antipoverty policies, including recently as a member of the Council of Distinguished Scientists for the Aspen National Commission on Social, Emotional, and Academic Development. Her research is published in academic and educational journals as well as trade publications, and she regularly presents her work to national academic and practitioner audiences.

Nonie K. Lesaux, PhD, is the Juliana W. and William Foss Thompson Professor of Education and Society at the Harvard Graduate School of Education. Her developmental and experimental research on school-age children and youth investigates language, reading, and social–emotional development; classroom quality and academic growth; and strategies for accelerating language and reading comprehension. This research is conducted largely in urban and semiurban school districts and settings. With Stephanie M. Jones, Dr. Lesaux is also codirector of the Saul Zaentz Early Education Initiative and coprincipal investigator of the Early Learning Study at Harvard. She is a recipient of the William T. Grant Scholars Award and the Presidential Early Career Award for Scientists and Engineers, the highest honor given by the United States government to young professionals beginning their independent research careers. Dr. Lesaux has served on the Institute of Medicine and National Research Council's Committee on the Science of Children Birth to Age 8, and is the author of a widely circulated state literacy report, *Turning the Page: Refocusing Massachusetts for Reading Success*, that forms the basis for a Third Grade Reading Proficiency bill passed in Massachusetts. Her research appears in numerous scholarly publications, and its practical applications are featured in four books.

Sophie P. Barnes, EdM, is a doctoral candidate in the Human Development, Learning, and Teaching concentration at the Harvard Graduate School of Education. Her research centers on understanding the setting- and individual-level mechanisms that support children's social, emotional, and behavioral skill development in school contexts, with a focus on executive function and self-regulation. She is also interested in adding nuance and precision to the measurement of SEL and partnering with schools and districts to develop feasible, responsible, and actionable assessment plans. Prior to beginning her doctoral studies, Ms. Barnes worked in the EASEL Lab led by Stephanie M. Jones on a number of evaluations of school-based interventions that target children's SEL growth and development, as well as research and translational writing projects.

Contributors

Rachel M. Abenavoli, PhD, Institute of Human Development and Social Change, New York University, New York, New York

Sophie P. Barnes, EdM, PhD candidate, Graduate School of Education, Harvard University, Cambridge, Massachusetts

Daniel Berry, EdD, College of Education and Human Development, University of Minnesota, Minneapolis, Minnesota

Amy M. Briesch, PhD, Department of Applied Psychology, Northeastern University, Boston, Massachusetts

Mary H. Buckingham, PhD, Eliot-Pearson Department of Child Study and Human Development, Tufts University, Medford, Massachusetts

Sandra M. Chafouleas, PhD, Department of Educational Psychology, University of Connecticut, Storrs, Connecticut

Paul A. Chase, PhD, Eliot-Pearson Department of Child Study and Human Development, Tufts University, Medford, Massachusetts

Laura A. Davidson, PhD, Director of Research and Evaluation, Washoe County School District, Reno, Nevada

Lise Fox, PhD, Department of Child and Family Studies, University of South Florida, Tampa, Florida

Patricia Gansert, MA, School of Social Work, Boston College, Chestnut Hill, Massachusetts

Carolina Goncalves, MA, Eliot-Pearson Department of Child Study and Human Development, Tufts University, Medford, Massachusetts

Rachel A. Gordon, PhD, Cecil J. Picard Center for Child Development and Lifelong Learning, University of Louisiana Lafayette, Lafayette, Louisiana

Laura S. Hamilton, PhD, Educational Testing Service, Princeton, New Jersey

Mary Louise Hemmeter, PhD, Department of Special Education, Vanderbilt University, Nashville, Tennessee

Stephanie M. Jones, PhD, Graduate School of Education, Harvard University, Cambridge, Massachusetts

Keira B. Leneman, MA, PhD candidate, College of Education and Human Development, University of Minnesota, Minneapolis, Minnesota

Richard M. Lerner, PhD, Eliot-Pearson Department of Child Study and Human Development, Tufts University, Medford, Massachusetts

Nonie K. Lesaux, PhD, Graduate School of Education, Harvard University, Cambridge, Massachusetts

Clark McKown, PhD, Division of Behavioral Sciences, Rush Medical College, Rush University, Chicago, Illinois

Dana Charles McCoy, PhD, Graduate School of Education, Harvard University, Cambridge, Massachusetts

Deborah Moroney, PhD, American Institutes of Research, Arlington, Virginia

Samantha Neiman, MA, American Institutes of Research, Arlington, Virginia

Jessica Newman, MA, American Institutes of Research, Arlington, Virginia

Jelena Obradović, PhD, Graduate School of Education, Stanford University, Stanford, California

David Osher, PhD, American Institutes of Research, Arlington, Virginia

Richard Palumbo, PhD, MIT Media Lab, Massachusetts Institute of Technology, Cambridge, Massachusetts

Yerin Park, MA, Eliot-Pearson Department of Child Study and Human Development, Tufts University, Medford, Massachusetts

Abbie Raikes, PhD, College of Public Health, University of Nebraska Medical Center, Omaha, Nebraska

Kimberly A. Schonert-Reichl, PhD, Department of Psychology, University of Illinois Chicago, Chicago, Illinois

Lily Steyer, BA, PhD candidate, Graduate School of Education, Stanford University, Stanford, California

Jonathan M. Tirrell, PhD, Eliot-Pearson Department of Child Study and Human Development, Tufts University, Medford, Massachusetts

Myrna Veguilla, MSMS, MPH, Department of Child and Family Studies, University of South Florida, Tampa, Florida

Oliver Saunders Wilder, PhD, MIT Media Lab, Massachusetts Institute of Technology, Cambridge, Massachusetts

Dian Yu, PhD, Eliot-Pearson Department of Child Study and Human Development, Tufts University, Medford, Massachusetts

Foreword
Measure for Change

For the better part of a century, education in the United States and in many other countries has been dominated by a model of human functioning that is much like mechanical assembly-line thinking. Our schools are still mired in a long since debunked assumption that children are generally blank or receptive machines who enter a school building in which information-rich adults mechanically transfer information kernels into brains in sequenced and linear steps. Notwithstanding enormous changes in our collective understanding of how children grow, develop, and learn, success in schools is still largely defined as large amounts of information being transferred into the child so that the child can recall it. The means of achieving success remain rooted in this same assembly-line thinking: the child is a product assembled in stages, made capable by adding components resulting in effective performance.

Of course, this is not the professed belief of the vast majority of educators or families. Most know that for children to flourish many non-mechanical qualities are necessary: strong attachment to adults, healthy physical activity, relationships rich in empathy and confidence, high levels of trust, a clear sense of purpose, and a valued identity. But for the most part, attention to these core developmental needs—attachment, trust, purpose, identity, and more—has not been the focus of most schools. These *social and emotional* factors in development have been treated as idiosyncratic—dependent on the individual effort of teachers or, worse, irrelevant to the rigors of learning. "Enter to learn" one sign read in the school where I taught, "and leave your problems at the door." To some, this captures the goal: to remove emotional and social factors from the brain so it can receive information. There's only one problem with it: it's impossible.

The current volume is part of a massive and critically important shift in our most foundational concepts of teaching and learning and in the basic assumptions underpinning how we structure the educational process itself. Of central importance in this volume is the relationship between the complex social and emotional elements of child development and the ways in which schools support and respond effectively to those needs. Importantly, the volume is not primarily theoretical, though it is grounded in theory. It is what educators urgently need: practical guidance about what needs to be taught, what needs to be infused into the culture of schools, and, most dauntingly, how to measure what matters. Educators have long labored under the assumption that "not all that matters can be measured," and while the current volume doesn't suggest that everything can be measured, it offers major strides in how to think about, design, and implement an effective measurement approach. We can measure more than we think. And we must.

It's impossible to overestimate the importance of measurement in the larger shift educators, families, and children are so hungry for. We know we can teach valuable skills like self-regulation, empathy, active listening, and agency, but without tools that enable teachers to measure outcomes, the teaching is suspect and vulnerable to being eliminated. We know we can offer restorative techniques in how we manage behavior and discipline, but without tools that enable administrators to measure the impact of these techniques, they are likely to be shelved. We know we can improve the training of adults to help them manage their own social and emotional needs while also pushing them to remove bias and negative assumptions from their expectations and practices, but without tools to assess the impact of these training protocols, teachers will question their utility. In short, great strides in new strategies that promote the healthy belonging, motivation, and full development of children are vulnerable to being dismissed without clear measurement strategies.

For all these reasons, Stephanie M. Jones and her colleagues have created a significant contribution to the advancement of the education of all our children. At a time when educators are increasingly aware of the extent of mental health problems in children, this volume is urgently needed if we are to respond. At a time when families and communities are increasingly aware of the challenges of motivating and inspiring children, this volume is urgently needed. At a time when employers are increasingly demanding social and emotional skills in the workplace, this volume is urgently needed. And finally, at a time when countries around the world are recognizing the pervasive, destructive, and unconscionable racism and bias that infect our treatment of children, this volume is urgently needed. Although it may seem daunting, schools really can be institutions that strengthen mental health, inspire motivation, prepare children for the complexities of work, and treat all children equitably. But all that won't happen without significant effort and leadership. And both of those will require sophisticated and reliable measurement.

The hope of our time is that we might educate our children in the deepest meaning of the term: to draw them out and to awaken them to the possible. The challenges of our time—widespread fear, loneliness, loss of trust, group antagonism—are like a summons to our schools to equip children with the purpose and inspiration necessary to create something new. We want them to flourish, to be strong, to make a difference. We know enough to realize a new model is needed for a new future to emerge. And we know the need is urgent. This volume will help bring that new model to reality. It can't happen soon enough.

TIMOTHY P. SHRIVER, PhD
*Board Chair, Collaborative for Academic,
Social, and Emotional Learning
Chairman of the Board, Special Olympics*

Contents

Introduction

Stephanie M. Jones, Nonie K. Lesaux, and Sophie P. Barnes

The labor market is changing. The work force of the future will need "people skills"—meaning they will need the sophisticated emotional, interpersonal, and cognitive skills necessary for working in teams, managing complex tasks, sifting and sharing information, and collaborating. With decades of accrued knowledge about the importance of these skills to success and growing information about effective practices and interventions, it is now increasingly the role of the education sector to ensure children and youth have them. A cornerstone of that effort is measurement and assessment,[1] and in particular the development and use of tools in classrooms and schools that enable educators to make decisions about how to best cultivate and support such skills among children and youth. This edited volume brings together leaders and innovators in the fields of human development and neuroscience, social and emotional learning (SEL), character development, special education, and behavior and discipline to (1) share their cutting-edge research and development work focusing on designing tools to capture a wide array of noncognitive skills, and (2) reflect on the applicability and use of these tools to improve teaching and learning in school settings. In this Introduction, we begin by briefly addressing the complex issue of what the broad domain of *noncognitive skills* actually means and includes. We then turn to the current state of measurement and assessment in this field, and we present a set of key considerations important to the task of using these tools to improve the conditions for and practice of teaching and learning.

---

[1] We operationalize *measuring* as a research-oriented term that refers to capturing a phenomenon and *assessing* as a practice-oriented term referring to the collection of information one might then act on.

1

● What's Noncognitive?

What are we talking about when it comes to noncognitive skills? Researchers, educators, and policymakers alike have trouble agreeing on exactly what's included in this broad domain—and what isn't (Jones & Doolittle, 2017). The popular press has highlighted a wide array of concepts, such as grit, empathy, growth mindset, social skills, and more. The research and practice communities similarly use a broad set of terms to organize and categorize this body of skills, including *SEL, character education, 21st-century skills, life skills, soft skills,* and *noncognitive skills,* just to name a few. Each label draws from a slightly different theoretical perspective, draws upon a different set of research, and has its own related fields and disciplines (Jones & Doolittle, 2017). In this edited volume, we refer to the domain as "noncognitive skills" for two reasons. First, the term *noncognitive* resonates with stakeholders outside of and across the specific fields noted above, speaking to policymakers, practitioners, and parents alike. Second, it is an umbrella term that covers the wide range of ideas, skills, competencies, and approaches captured in this book. However, we also note there is some discomfort with this name, as we know from decades of research and practice in human development, neuroscience, educational psychology, and teaching and learning that *noncognitive* actually includes a diverse and interrelated set of cognitive, emotional, and social skills as well as a body of beliefs and ideas about the self and the world that are linked to success in the academic domains and to a wide variety of life outcomes well into the future (Jones, McGarrah, & Kahn, 2019).

Generally, the noncognitive domain comprises specific skills and competencies that students need in order to set goals, manage behavior, build relationships, and process and remember information. Importantly, as with other foundational domains of learning and development, this area is fundamentally tied to characteristics of settings that can be intentionally structured to nurture these skills and competencies. Looking across a variety of disciplines, organizing systems, and correlational and evaluation research, the recent Aspen Institute Commission on Social, Emotional, and Academic Development (2019) described the domain as representing three broad areas: (1) social, emotional, and cognitive skills and competencies; (2) attitudes, beliefs, and mindsets; and (3) character and values.

Cognitive skills and competencies underlie the ability to focus and pay attention; set goals, plan, and organize; and persevere and problem solve. Social and interpersonal skills and competencies enable children and youth to read social cues and navigate social situations; negotiate and resolve conflicts with others; demonstrate respect toward others; and cooperate and work effectively on a team. Emotional skills and competencies help children and youth recognize and manage their emotions; understand the emotions and perspectives of others; and demonstrate empathy. Attitudes, beliefs, and mindsets include children's and youth's attitudes and beliefs about themselves, others, and their own circumstances. Finally, character and values represent ways of thinking and habits that support children and youth to work together as friends, family, and community and encompass understanding, caring about, and acting on core character traits such as integrity, honesty, compassion, diligence, civic and ethical engagement, and responsibility.

While there is growing agreement as to what elements are included in the domain, and there is a robust body of evidence about their role in learning and development as well as effective strategies to promote them, what continues to bedevil the field is how to measure them in a way that captures their depth (from individual to setting), their breadth (from physiological to behavior to beliefs and dispositions), and their relevance to the practical concern of teaching and learning. Measurement is not "simply" a matter of documenting the skills and competencies for research purposes (e.g., the study of human development, the evaluation of key practices), but is also about capturing them in a manner that enables those doing the work of fostering and supporting them to make strategic decisions about what to do, how to do it, and when to do it (e.g., Lesaux, Galloway, & Marietta, 2016).

The State of Measurement and Assessment

Measurement can be a powerful tool to aid practice—it can inform both moment-to-moment and higher-level decision making about priorities, approaches, and specific directions for a variety of education stakeholders including educators, administrators, and policymakers. In the noncognitive domain, a large body of work over the past 5 years has addressed important, though largely logistical or administrative, questions about measurement including pros and cons of various measure types (e.g., direct assessment, observational tool, survey), reporters (e.g., self, caregiver, teacher report), level of measurement (e.g., individual, setting), and specific skills or features to assess (Assessment Work Group, 2019; Bailey & Jones, 2019; McKown, 2019). What has become apparent in this literature, and is reflected in the chapters in this volume, is that the field of noncognitive skill development, and assessment more broadly across learning domains, is approaching a new frontier that shifts away from debates about logistical or administrative questions to focus on issues of assessment use and responsibility, ethics, and preparedness to assess. However, there remains a wide range of views on *what, where,* and *how* the noncognitive domain is assessed. Before turning to key considerations important to the task of using tools in service of improved teaching and learning, we describe some of the variation in the field that ultimately shapes measurement and assessment in this area.

- *What is measured?* Above, we noted the range of perspectives and theoretical approaches captured in this broad domain. But beyond the breadth reflected in terminology, we also see breadth in the disciplines and approaches engaged in the work of developing measurement and assessment tools that can drive teaching and learning. The focus of the chapters included in this book reflects the wide array of noncognitive skills that are important, ranging from executive function and self-regulation, to social skills and relationships, to character and values such as gratitude.

- *Where are skills measured?* In addition to capturing the skills and competencies of individuals, there is a focus in this volume on how to operationalize and foster skills and competencies within and across settings—and on the multiple, often complementary, contexts where children grow, learn, and play (e.g., home, school). Expanding beyond a child's immediate context, authors emphasize the importance of capturing patterns and trends at other levels of the ecosystem and in settings, including the classroom, school, district, and population levels.

- *How are skills measured?* The "what" described above represents a wide range of targets, and the tools presented in this volume reflect the diversity of ways to capture them, from physiological markers (e.g., heart rate) and tablet-based individual assessments to setting (e.g., classroom observation) and population-level measurement approaches (e.g., surveys of whole populations of students and adults).

Grounded in the core idea that measurement and assessment are a key link between what we know and what we do, the chapters in this volume all make connections between the tools presented and teaching, learning, and classroom practice. Broadly, our intention is to bring together research evidence with practical application to provide concrete, actionable solutions to practitioners. There are good examples from other fields where progress at this intersection has been made. In their 2016 volume, *Teaching Advanced Literacy Skills: A Guide for Leaders in Linguistically Diverse Schools*, Lesaux, Galloway, and Marietta, grapple with the challenge of the revolving door literacy-related programs, policies, and initiatives. At the core of their recommendations is the need to use data to both align choices with setting-specific needs and to guide instructional practices. The noncognitive field now faces a similar challenge, with multiple practical options (curricula, standards, initiatives) for schools, districts, and other stakeholders to choose from. What's needed is information about measurement and assessment tools that can guide decisions about approaches and practices that align with the specific needs of a setting or population.

• Key Considerations for Measurement and Assessment in Service of Teaching and Learning

Measurement and assessment are complicated and depending on their purpose require different things. Below are a set of features to consider when thinking about measuring and assessing noncognitive skills in a manner that supports teaching and learning.

1. *Relevant.* Measurement and assessment should capture the child or youth in the relevant context. This means that the child deserves to be understood in relation to their ecological system, and measurement and assessment should be tied to the distinct demands of a particular setting.

2. *Contextual.* Measurement and assessment should capture aspects of the ecology. There is a tendency to focus exclusively on measurement of the child and what he or she can do, but it is equally important to consider contexts and experiences. In education, measures that provide more information about the setting can provide another point of intervention and help us better understand the child's behavior in context.

3. *Actionable.* Measurement and assessment should be tied to actionable, evidence-based practices and strategies that schools and educators can adopt and implement in their setting, and these should include actions that are directed to features of the setting itself.

4. *Developmentally salient.* Measurement and assessment should align with what is realistic to expect of children and youth at specific ages and should represent features of developmentally salient contexts.

5. *Sensitive and nuanced.* Measurement and assessment must be both sensitive and nuanced enough to capture variation that exists within and between children and youth over time as well as meaningful variation that exists within and between contexts, such as different classrooms within the same school.

6. *Psychometrically sound.* Importantly, psychometric soundness is not a property of a measure itself, rather it reflects the reliability and validity of a measure for a specific purpose. Psychometric issues in measurement tend to fall into two big categories:

    a. The first is *reliability,* or the internal consistency of the scores.

    b. The second is *validity,* which primarily focuses on whether the measure captures what it is designed to measure, evidence for the use of a measure in a certain way or context, and inferences that can be responsibly drawn from the findings.

To effectively drive change, measurement and assessment efforts cannot address only one or two of the criteria listed above. Doing so may result in measures that are not used properly, that neglect important conceptual or psychometric features, or importantly are not actionable or relevant to practitioners.

• This Volume

This book focuses on the myriad ways that measuring and assessing noncognitive skills can improve teaching and learning. We chose this focus for several reasons. First, we bring together a diverse set of tools, approaches, and perspectives that often exist primarily in their own disciplines (e.g., developmental and school psychology, ambulatory technology, special education, measurement and assessment). By putting these perspectives in conversation with one another, we highlight that across disciplines and measurement types, a core set of issues, questions, and considerations exist (see above). Second, measurement and assessment in the noncognitive domain is experiencing rapid growth and implementation in school contexts. Matching the excitement of stakeholders who are eager to employ these measures in practice, this volume provides guidance around using these tools with care, rigor, and alignment with the goals and features of the setting.

We've brought together a group of scholars who represent the frontiers of measurement and assessment in this broad domain. Across the chapters, authors raise and grapple with complex issues of the purpose of measurement and assessment, ecological and contextual variation and validity, developmental growth and change, and the challenge of designing tools that link research to practice and drive change in the settings where children and youth learn and grow. The chapters are organized into broad substantive and conceptual categories. The book begins with individual measurement approaches, moves to chapters focused on settings and behaviors, then novel physiological measurement approaches, broader settings—districts and populations—and finally, global perspectives on measurement and assessment. Also included are chapters that address cross-cutting policy and methodological challenges and opportunities.

The chapters in Part I address creative and thought-provoking ways to approach individual measurement, while keeping context in mind. The first three chapters cover assessments at scale. Jelena Obradović and Lily Steyer propose a new approach to direct assessment using a group-based scalable approach. Clark McKown discusses the possibility of using high-quality assessment to sustain and scale the use of evidence-based SEL programs, and Dana McCoy addresses scalable measurement in a global context.

The next two chapters focus on children's physiology. Keira Leneman and Daniel Berry explore the multiple physiological systems in the body that influence and support children as they navigate their ever-changing worlds. Oliver Wilder and Richard Palumbo discuss practical considerations and examples of measuring psychophysiology in real-world educational settings to capture noncognitive skills in young children. Finally, Paul Chase and colleagues explore a person-centered approach to measuring character that examines variability in individual pathways of development over time based on context and experiences.

The chapters in Part II emphasize setting- and behavior-focused measurement approaches. Measures of child behavior are used in the chapters by Sandra Chafouleas and Amy Briesch (Direct Behavior Ratings) and by Lise Fox, Myrna Veguilla, and Mary Louise Hemmeter (the Behavior Incident Report System) with an eye toward using data to reduce exclusionary discipline practices and policies and to look carefully at setting-level features that influence children's behavior. Abbie Raikes explores noncognitive measurement and assessment at a global level and addresses a number of key challenges with operationalizing and measuring noncognitive skills to drive improvements in teaching, learning, and child development, many of which parallel key challenges in U.S. settings related to deciding what to measure and how, and the responsible use of findings. In their chapter, Sophie Barnes, Rachel Abenavoli, and Stephanie Jones make the case that setting-level measurement is critical for understanding the social processes (i.e., teacher practice) that shape children's development.

The chapters in Part III present novel measurement tools that focus on broader settings. Rachel Gordon and Laura Davidson address cross-cutting issues related to measurement in district contexts, using a self-report measure developed in a research-practice partnership as an illustration. Kimberly Schonert-Reichl applies these ideas to an even broader context, focusing on population-level measurement to gain a better understanding of broad trends and patterns in middle childhood development at the population level.

Part IV addresses cross-cutting methodological and policy issues. In their chapters, both Laura Hamilton (on methodological considerations) and Jessica Newman and colleagues (on policies and assessment that foster equity and thriving) highlight the promise of measurement tools as well as the need for careful, clear, and responsible use.

• What's Next for Measurement and Assessment in the Noncognitive Domain?

The chapters in this volume bring to light novel measurement approaches, and also cautions for the future as we seek to build on the momentum around capturing noncognitive skills to improve teaching and learning. The emphasis across chapters on responsible use of assessment is promising. At the same time, we acknowledge (and at times, share) the general worry and anxiety related to implications of measurement in this area in particular. However, as measurement is now common practice in educational contexts, what we need is to use our knowledge and experience to approach measurement with care, responsibility, and attention to detail, salience, and scientific rigor.

REFERENCES

Aspen Institute National Commission on Social, Emotional, & Academic Development. (2019). *From a nation at risk to a nation at hope.* Retrieved from *http://nationathope.org/wp-content/uploads/2018_aspen_final-report_full_web-version.pdf.*

Assessment Work Group. (2019). *Student social and emotional competence assessment: The current state of the field and a vision for its future.* Collaborative for Academic Social and Emotional Learning.

Bailey, R., & Jones, S. M. (2019). An integrated model of regulation for applied settings. *Clinical Child and Family Psychology Review, 22*(1), 2–23.

Jones, S. M., & Doolittle, E. J. (2017). Social and emotional learning: Introducing the issue. *Future of Children, 27,* 3–11.

Jones, S. M., McGarrah, M., & Kahn, J. (2019). Social and emotional learning: A principled science of human development in context. *Educational Psychologist, 54*(3), 129–143.

Lesaux, N. K., Galloway, E. P., & Marietta, S. H. (Eds.). (2016). *Teaching advanced literacy skills: A guide for leaders in linguistically diverse schools.* Guilford Press.

McKown, C. (2019). Challenges and opportunities in the applied assessment of student social and emotional learning. *Educational Psychologist, 54,* 205–221.

PART I

FROM PHYSIOLOGY
TO CHARACTER VIRTUES

Creative, Contextually Relevant Approaches
to Capturing Individual Functioning

Direct Assessment of Students' Executive Functions and Motivation in Elementary Classroom Settings

Jelena Obradović and Lily Steyer

Social and emotional learning (SEL) is an umbrella term for malleable skills and beliefs that help children set and achieve learning goals, persist in the face of challenges, understand and manage emotions, engage in positive social interactions, and make responsible decisions (Weissberg et al., 2015). Since this involves the interplay of numerous social, emotional, and cognitive skills whose application is influenced by contextual factors, it is difficult to get a "true" measure of children's SEL. Adult reports provide a subjective assessment of children's SEL-related behaviors in a given environment, while direct assessments using performance-based tasks add insight into children's SEL skills as they are developed and applied across various contexts, independent of observer biases. Indeed, scholars in this volume have created and validated novel direct assessments of elementary school students' emotion understanding and emotion regulation skills in the context of social interactions (see McKown, Chapter 2, this volume), showing the value of a multimethod approach to measuring SEL.

This chapter focuses on direct assessments of skills that help elementary school students set, maintain, and achieve learning goals, including those skills that underpin the established psychological construct of self-regulated learning (McCombs & Marzano, 1990; Schunk & Zimmerman, 2012; Zimmerman, 1990) and the more recent SEL construct of self-management (Weissberg, Durlak, Domitrovich, & Gullotta, 2015). Researchers studying both constructs have shown that students' goal-directed behaviors are supported by their ability to plan, organize, sustain attention, and exercise self-discipline, as well as their initiative and agency. Accordingly, this chapter highlights direct assessments of executive functions (EFs), a well-studied set of cognitive skills that support goal-directed behaviors, as well as aspects of student motivation that reflect the choice and effort involved in pursuing learning-related goals.

First, we review recent efforts to directly measure EF skills and relevant aspects of student motivation. Recognizing that a comprehensive review of the extensive scholarship in these areas is beyond the scope of this chapter, we emphasize direct assessments that can be used at scale to assess entire classrooms of students with minimal disruption to teaching. Further, we highlight tasks that can be used in elementary schools, since young students are not able to reliably report their own behaviors and beliefs and, historically, motivation processes have been understudied during this important developmental period. In the second part of the chapter, we discuss the need for assessments to be ecologically valid and applicable to classroom instruction and supports. We call for more research into the many contextual factors influencing the development, application, and evaluation of these skills, shifting the focus away from individual children's differences and toward identifying environments that nurture EFs and motivation in all children. We conclude by noting cultural and equity concerns that must be addressed in future work.

• Assessment of Executive Function Skills

Advantages of Direct Assessments

EFs are cognitive skills that support goal-directed behaviors by helping students to control impulses and stay focused amid daily distractions (i.e., inhibitory control), mentally manipulate verbal and nonverbal information (i.e., working memory), and flexibly shift between competing task rules or environmental demands (i.e., cognitive flexibility). In recent decades, researchers have identified key methodological advantages of directly assessing children's EFs using standardized performance tasks, rather than relying on observer reports (for detailed reviews, see McCoy, 2019; Zelazo, Blair, & Willoughby, 2016). For example, direct assessment of working memory may involve asking a child to reverse numeric or visual sequences of increasing length, whereas observer report of working memory may rely on adults' perceptions of how well a child can remember and complete multistep activities.

Tasks administered and scored according to consistent procedures yield a degree of "objectivity" compared to adults' subjective ratings of EF-related behaviors, which may be biased by impressions of children's overall behavior, appearance, or demographic characteristics (e.g., Brandmiller, Dumont, & Becker, 2020; Fitzpatrick, Côté-Lussier, & Blair, 2016; Garcia,

Sulik, & Obradović, 2019), and may reflect adults' own well-being (e.g., Joyner, Silver, & Stavinoha, 2009; Silver, 2014) or beliefs and identities (Yoder & Williford, 2019). Direct assessments also allow for more precise evaluation and differentiation of specific EF skills, compared to adult reports that often show a halo effect (i.e., the rating of one skill influences the rating of another skill; McCoy, 2019).

The relative objectivity of direct assessments is supported by associations between children's performance on EF tasks and markers of neurocognitive development, including chronological age and the structure and activation of underlying brain areas (Diamond, 2013; Fiske & Holmboe, 2019; Moriguchi & Hiraki, 2013). However, this does not mean that direct assessments are perfectly objective. Children may experience differently the assessment format, administrative setting and procedures, or specific task stimuli and task instructions, which may seem unfamiliar, irrelevant, or discouraging to certain groups. In the last section of this chapter, we suggest ways to address such disparities.

Standardized performance tasks can be designed to have strong psychometric properties. Notably, many EF tasks demonstrate good test–retest reliability (e.g., Beck, Schaefer, Pang, & Carlson, 2011), internal reliability and convergent validity (e.g., Willoughby, Pek, Blair, & Family Life Project Investigators, 2013; Zelazo et al., 2013), and measurement invariance across ethnic/racial groups (e.g., Daneri, Sulik, Raver, & Morris, 2018; Willoughby, Blair, Wirth, & Greenberg, 2012). These properties increase researchers' confidence that studies of how EF skills change over time or vary by group are appropriate and meaningful.

Further, children's scores on age-appropriate EF tasks tend to approximate a normal distribution, indicating that the performance data offers better differentiation of skill levels than adult reports of EF-related behaviors, which can be susceptible to social desirability and tend to be positively skewed (i.e., many children receive high scores). Since performance scores on EF tasks capture greater variability in students' skill levels, they are well suited to examining the growth of EF skills over different time periods and identifying contextual factors that explain this growth (e.g., Finch, Garcia, Sulik, & Obradović, 2019; Hackman et al., 2014).

Using scores from different EF tasks, researchers have studied how distinct EF skills are correlated across developmental periods (e.g., Karr et al., 2018; Wiebe, Espy, & Charak, 2008) and how distinct EF skills uniquely contribute to the growth of academic skills (e.g., Allan, Hume, Allan, Farrington, & Lonigan, 2014; Lan, Legare, Ponitz, Li, & Morrison, 2011; Purpura, Schmitt, & Ganley, 2017). This can help practitioners understand which EFs are more or less relevant for different school behaviors and academic skills, informing the design of appropriate and effective classroom supports. For example, evidence that children's working memory plays a central role in math skill development (Friso-van den Bos, van der Ven, Kroesbergen, & van Luit, 2013) has spurred the development of working memory training interventions that improve elementary and middle school aged children's math capabilities (Bergman-Nutley & Klingberg, 2014).

And yet, performance on EF tasks does not capture how EF skills are applied in real-life settings. This decontextualization can be useful, insofar as it provides insights into students' capacities independent of some concurrent situational factors. Nevertheless, we must be careful not to confuse decontextualization with objectivity, as children's performance on these tasks is never independent of the history of supports and challenges they have experienced, nor the immediate context in which they are situated. Direct assessments should complement, not replace, adult reports of children's EFs in elementary settings; together, these measures can provide a more comprehensive view of how children regulate their attention and behavior to support learning-related goals. Importantly, direct assessments are also critical tools in evaluating practices and policies aimed at improving student supports, especially when adult reporters such as teachers are aware or part of the intervention efforts in ways that may affect their ratings of students' postintervention outcomes.

Ecological Validity and Scalability of EF Assessments

EF skills are typically assessed in a quiet, controlled space, such as the researcher's university laboratory or a designated room in the student's school. A highly trained assessor works closely with one child to explain the task instructions, provide feedback during practice trials, and ensure focused completion of the task. The physical proximity, monitoring, and praise that children receive during this individual assessment do not resemble the real-world conditions in which they are expected to apply EF skills every day, thus limiting the ecological validity of the data. Moreover, removing children from the classroom one at a time for individual assessment reduces instructional time and disrupts other students. Since this is costly and impractical for large-scale research studies or routine assessments by school districts, most direct assessments of EF skills in the United States employ small-to-medium samples lacking in socioeconomic and racial/ethnic diversity. (For notable exceptions, see the Family Life Project and the Early Childhood Longitudinal Study, Kindergarten Class of 2010–2011, as well as the Early Learning Study at Harvard, ongoing.)

In an effort to address these shortcomings, we developed a novel approach to simultaneously assess the EF skills of all students in a classroom (Obradović, Sulik, Finch, & Tirado-Strayer, 2018). We adapted three developmentally appropriate and widely used EF tasks for administration on tablet computers in an elementary classroom setting. The tasks were designed to measure students' ability to control impulsive or dominant responses, to flexibly shift between two competing task rules, to ignore distracting information, and to mentally reverse and recall sequences of numbers (see Obradović et al., 2018, for details). The lead research assistant delivered the task instructions to the entire classroom and facilitated group practice of each task rule by soliciting students' verbal responses. Students also read simplified task rules on their tablet screens and received automated feedback on their practice trials before the test trials. The lead research assistant paced the assessment, while two other research assistants provided technical help as needed.

This resource-efficient, minimally disruptive approach enabled us to assess over 800 third-, fourth-, and fifth-grade students ($N = 451$) across 33 classrooms in two public school districts in the San Francisco Bay Area. Since the assessment was structured similar to a classroom activity, we were able to include all students who assented and whose parents did not opt out of the study, thus ensuring high coverage and representative diversity. Moreover, this group-assessment process typically took no more than 30 minutes to administer to a full classroom of students. By contrast, individual assessments would require 30 minutes *per student* and involve repeated disruptions to classroom activities as individual children leave the classroom to be assessed one-by-one. Classroom-based studies that employ EF assessments in an inclusive way can help address equity concerns identified in developmental science research, including the historic underrepresentation of students of some racial/ethnic, gender, and cultural identities (Brown, Mistry, & Yip, 2019).

To validate this novel group-assessment approach, we had a subset of students ($N = 269$) complete the same three tablet-based EF tasks in an individualized setting before or after the group assessment (counterbalanced to account for practice effect). In this subsample, group-assessment and individual-assessment performance scores for the same tasks were highly related, equally reliable, and showed similar associations with demographic characteristics, including gender and parent education. They were also similarly related to teachers' reports of self-regulated classroom behaviors and standardized achievement test scores (see Obradović et al., 2018). Notably, only the children's group-assessment scores predicted longitudinal gains on standardized academic achievement tests. This study demonstrated that the direct assessment of EF skills in more ecologically valid classroom settings, with naturally occurring distractors, demands, and incentives, can yield data that is psychometrically comparable to one-on-one assessment and has greater predictive validity for children's academic growth. These findings should be replicated and extended to investigate if the greater predictive power is related to structural inequities shared between the group assessment and standardized achievement testing. For example, experiences of psychological stress (e.g., stereotype threat) and physiological stress (e.g., elevated stress hormones) documented among students of marginalized racial/ethnic and gender identities during standardized testing (Heissel, Levy, & Adam, 2017; Inzlicht & Schmader, 2012) could be similarly activated during group assessments of EF and related SEL skills. Although we found no evidence that overall student performance was lower in the group setting than the individual setting, future work should interrogate how student stress and related factors may vary across assessment contexts.

In recent years, many tabletop EF performance tasks have been digitized (e.g., Mueller & Piper, 2014; Zelazo et al., 2013). Computerized versions of EF tasks minimize the training needed to administer EF assessments and increase the standardization of scoring children's performance. Further, the portability and ease of tablet-based EF tasks have enabled researchers to scale up EF assessments outside the laboratory context and study larger and more diverse samples of children, who were previously excluded from EF research. Specifically, tablet-based tasks have been crucial for studying children's EFs in low- and middle-income countries, where portable assessments can be adapted to various field sites and where digitized protocols help assessors who have less formal training in test administration (Obradović & Willoughby, 2019).

Nevertheless, not all computerized EF tasks are conducive to group assessment. Individual administration of digitized assessments is also necessary when the target age group (e.g., preschoolers) is too young to understand the task directions without individual screening or assistance (e.g., the Minnesota Executive Function Scale [MEFS]; Carlson & Zelazo, 2014; the Head-Toes-Knees-Shoulders computerized version [HTKS-c]; Spiegel & Lonigan, 2018). Future studies should investigate the feasibility of administering EF assessments to small groups of younger elementary school students. Although group-assessment procedures can advance EF research by increasing the feasibility of working with large, diverse samples, these new approaches may also obscure some children's comprehension of and compliance with assessment instructions, which are easier to monitor when assessing an individual child. Thus, children's performance on both practice and test trials obtained through large-scale assessments need to be rigorously scrutinized on an ongoing basis to ensure the validity of collected data (see Obradović & Willoughby, 2019, for specific analytic recommendations). Future research should examine systematic differences in elementary school students' comprehension, compliance, and performance across various assessment settings and approaches.

Current Applications of EF Assessments

Extant research has used direct EF assessment as an outcome measure to identify contextual factors that affect the development of EF skills. Most of this work has focused on the home environment, linking EF skills to family economic resources, home stimulation, and parenting behaviors (e.g.,

Fay-Stammbach, Hawes, & Meredith, 2017; Hackman et al., 2014; Haft & Hoeft, 2017; Obradović et al., 2019; Raver, Blair, Willoughby, & Family Life Project Key Investigators, 2013). More recent research has probed EFs in the school environment. Some studies have shown a positive association between students' performance on EF tasks and the overall quality of classroom supports and instructions (Choi et al., 2016; Hamre, Hatfield, Pianta, & Jamil, 2014; Hatfield, Burchinal, Pianta, & Sideris, 2016; Pianta et al., 2020; Piccolo, Merz, & Noble, 2019), while others have found null or curvilinear links (Fuhs, Farran, & Nesbitt, 2013; Guerrero-Rosada et al., 2021; Weiland & Yoshikawa, 2013). Notably, the majority of studies examining relations between EF and classroom-level factors have used preschool samples (Cumming, Bettini, Pham, & Park, 2020), highlighting the need for similar work with elementary and middle school populations.

To study how specific teacher classroom behaviors relate to students' EF skills, we developed a novel classroom observation measure, Teachers' Displays and Scaffolding of Executive Function (T-DASEF; Bardack & Obradović, 2019). In a sample of 813 elementary school students who completed direct EF assessments in a classroom setting, we used this observation protocol across four 1-hour classroom visits during a single school year. We found that teachers' displays of impulsivity, distraction, or disorganization were negatively linked to students' directly assessed EFs in the fall, whereas teachers' scaffolding of cognitive flexibility (e.g., by encouraging students to adopt different perspectives) and organization (e.g., by helping students plan their work time) were positively linked to students' directly assessed EFs in the spring (Bardack & Obradović, 2019). Since we had high coverage of direct EF assessments across 33 classrooms, thanks to the group-assessment procedure (see Obradović et al., 2018), we were also able to investigate peer effects on individual students' EF skills (Finch et al., 2019). We found that classmates' average EFs were associated with improvements in individual students' performance on EF tasks from fall to spring. More work is needed to understand how different aspects of the classroom experience contribute to the growth of EF skills in elementary school students.

Direct assessments of EF skills have been consistently linked to academic achievement (Allan et al., 2014; Fuhs, Farran, & Nesbitt, 2015; Nguyen & Duncan, 2019; Yeniad, Malda, Mesman, van IJzendoorn, & Pieper, 2013) as well as longitudinal change in academic achievement (Blair, Ursache, Greenberg, Vernon-Feagans, & Family Life Project Investigators, 2015; Fuhs et al., 2015; Obradović et al., 2018). Our work has shown that fall-to-spring change in elementary school students' performance on four widely used EF tasks predicted 2-year change in students' achievement test scores (Finch & Obradović, 2017b). Researchers have also linked student performance on EF tasks to teacher and observer reports of self-regulated classroom behaviors that support school readiness and classroom engagement (Ciairano, Visu-Petra, & Settanni, 2007; Finch & Obradović, 2017a; Mann, Hund, Hesson-McInnis, & Roman, 2017; Nelson et al., 2017; Rimm-Kaufman, Curby, Grimm, Nathanson, & Brock, 2009; Sasser, Bierman, & Heinrichs, 2015).

Given the relevance of EFs for school success and the sensitivity of direct assessment to capturing longitudinal change in EF skills, performance on EF tasks has been used to measure the effectiveness of school-based intervention programs (Diamond & Ling, 2016). Indeed, studies of programs that target children's mindfulness, self-regulation, and general cognitive skills have revealed that EFs can be improved in both preschoolers and elementary school students (e.g., Blair & Raver, 2014; McClelland et al., 2019; Riggs, Greenberg, Kusché, & Pentz, 2006; Wenz-Gross, Yoo, Upshur, & Gambino, 2018). Moreover, students' performance on EF tasks has been used as a key child outcome in evaluating interventions that focus on improving overall classroom quality or teacher–student relationship quality (e.g., McCoy, Zuilkowski, Yoshikawa, & Fink, 2017; Pianta et al., 2017; Willoughby, Piper, Oyanga, & Merseth King, 2019). Future work should examine the impact of school-based interventions on the EFs of larger, more representative student samples—an effort that can be aided by scalable group-assessment protocols.

• Beyond EFs: Assessment of Students' Motivation

Studies of skills supporting self-regulated learning (McCombs & Marzano, 1990; Zimmerman, 1990; Zimmerman & Schunk, 2011) and self-management (Weissberg et al., 2015) need to go beyond EF assessment to capture differences in students' choices and effort in terms of selecting and persisting on challenging tasks. A review of the extensive conceptual and empirical work on different aspects of student motivation and their relevance for academic achievement and general school success is beyond the scope of this chapter (see Ryan & Deci, 2020; Schunk & Zimmerman, 2012). We focus here on assessments of students' challenge-seeking choices and their effort and persistence in completing challenges. We chose these aspects of student motivation as they can be directly measured via performance on tasks, without relying on children's report of their own beliefs and mindsets, which can be unreliable in younger elementary school students. However, due to the limited availability of scalable direct assessments of challenge-seeking and persistence behaviors, we open this section with a brief review of two related constructs, grit and growth mindset, which partially reflect differences in students' effort and are commonly measured via student self-report. We then describe our work surveying elementary school students, before discussing new efforts to develop direct assessments of challenge-seeking and persistence behaviors. While we discuss research that draws on different theoretical frameworks, we conceptualize student motivation to engage and persist on challenging learning tasks not as a character or personality trait, but rather as a product of various socialization processes and situational factors that are cognitively and emotionally internalized by students and further reinforced by their environmental experiences and opportunities.

Student Report

Over the past 15 years, there has been great interest in understanding how student motivation contributes to educational outcomes. Two constructs in particular—grit and growth mindset—have resonated with educators, spurring a prolific body of school-based research that employs student report on survey questionnaires. Although conceptually distinct, both grit and growth mindset emphasize the importance of student effort. Grit surveys were originally designed to capture both *consistency of interest* (sample items: "I often set a goal but later choose to pursue a different one"; "I have difficulty maintaining my focus on projects that take more than a few months to complete") and *perseverance of effort* (sample items: "I finish whatever I begin"; "Setbacks don't discourage me"; "I am diligent") (Duckworth & Quinn, 2009). However, a large meta-analysis revealed that only the effort component of the grit survey is reliably associated with academic performance and, moreover, that the relation is modest (Credé, Tynan, & Harms, 2017). Meanwhile, growth mindset surveys capture students' beliefs about whether intelligence is malleable and can be changed with one's effort (sample item: "No matter who you are, you can significantly change your intelligence level") (Dweck, 2008). This construct has also been scrutinized by a large meta-analysis, which found that the overall association between growth mindset and academic achievement is weak, and that the effectiveness of mindset interventions varies, with the greatest benefits for disadvantaged students (Sisk, Burgoyne, Sun, Butler, & Macnamara, 2018).

While this survey research has been conducted primarily with adolescent and young adult participants, it has had a profound impact on educational policy and practice for kindergarten through twelfth grade (K–12). For example, the collaborative of CORE Districts in California has developed a system of school accountability and continuous improvement that includes student report of growth mindset on an annual survey. However, a recent field test study of 378,465 students across five districts revealed issues with elementary school students' self-report (West, Buckley, Krachman, & Bookman, 2018). Specifically, the internal and test–retest reliabilities of the growth mindset composite score were lowest among the four

SEL domains measured, meaning that elementary school students' reports on different growth mindset questions were not as interrelated or consistent over time as their report on self-management, social awareness, and self-efficacy questions. Further, this study did not employ teacher report of growth mindset, as it was deemed not externally observable. These findings point to the need to develop assessment tools that can yield reliable and valid insights into K–5 students' challenge-seeking behaviors.

Conceptualized as an aspect of intrinsic motivation, high challenge preference is associated with mastery-oriented learning goals and a willingness to risk failure to learn new skills because the process of engaging with a challenging task is internally rewarding (Elliott & Dweck, 1988; Harter, 1981). In contrast, low challenge preference is linked to performance-oriented learning goals; students avoid challenges that may make them look incompetent and pursue easier tasks that maximize their performance outcomes and external recognition. Our recent work has focused on studying elementary school students' challenge-seeking preferences using a five-item, binary response survey that asks students to choose between easy/familiar and challenging/novel scenarios (sample item: "I like a puzzle that is easy to solve"/"I like a puzzle that takes hard work to solve"; Developmental Studies Center, n.d.). Our survey was informed by laboratory-based puzzle tasks used in original studies of young children's challenge preference (Smiley & Dweck, 1994; Stipek, Recchia, McClintic, & Lewis, 1992), but its brief and simple format enables group administration to an entire classroom of elementary school students. The use of concrete and developmentally salient scenarios, such as completing a puzzle or playing a game with peers, increases young students' comprehension of the survey questions as well as the ecological validity of this instrument. Further, the focus on students' behavioral choices rather than the reasons behind those choices enhances the reliability of responses from young students who may not have developed metacognitive skills to reflect on their motives.

Indeed, in a diverse sample of 707 third-, fourth-, and fifth-grade students attending public schools in the San Francisco Bay Area, the reliability of this short scale was high (ordinal alpha = .82). In a subsample of 334 students for whom we also obtained teacher report, we showed that student report of challenge preference was uniquely related to teacher ratings of task orientation, assertiveness, peer social skills, and frustration tolerance over and above the significant contribution of directly assessed EF skills (Finch & Obradović, 2017a). Further, challenge preference significantly moderated the association between students' EFs and assertive classroom behaviors (e.g., is comfortable as a leader, defends own views under group pressure, questions rules that seem unfair/unclear), in that EF skills were less strongly associated with students' assertiveness among students with higher levels of challenge preference. Among students with lower EF skills, those who reported higher challenge preference were seen by their teachers as being more assertive. These findings suggest that classroom practices that genuinely encourage and support choosing and persisting through challenging learning opportunities may contribute to students' adaptive classroom behaviors regardless of their EF skills and may promote confident classroom participation, especially among students whose EFs are still developing.

In a follow-up study of a subsample of 569 students for whom we obtained school records, we showed that challenge preference was positively associated with math and ELA achievement performance over and above demographic covariates, directly assessed EFs, and teacher report of EF-related classroom behaviors (Sulik, Finch, & Obradović, 2020). Despite focusing on nonacademic scenarios, students' reports of challenge preference continued to explain a small amount of unique variance in mathematics while also controlling for the strong contribution of prior achievement scores. This work demonstrates the feasibility of using self-report surveys at scale to measure 8- to 12-year-olds' perceptions of their own behavioral tendencies in the context of challenging nonacademic learning activities. It also underscores the importance of examining the unique and interactive effects of student motivation and EFs for elementary school students' educational outcomes (e.g., Howse, Lange, Farran, & Boyles, 2003). Such examinations can inform our understanding of how students' challenge-seeking tendencies support their learning, independently or in conjunction with cognitive skills that enable the pursuit of chosen or relevant learning goals.

Direct Assessments

Researchers have called for more objective, performance-based measures of student SEL to support improvements in daily education practice and enable rigorous program evaluation (Duckworth & Yeager, 2015). Analogous to EF research, adult reports of students' effort, persistence, and challenge preference are subjective and can be biased by adults' well-being and mindsets as well as adults' overall perceptions of children's classroom behaviors or academic track records (Kozlowski, 2015). Direct assessments of students' effort and challenge-seeking behaviors can enable researchers to identify systematic differences in these behavioral tendencies and inform educators of ways in which inequitable social expectations and environmental supports contribute to these disparities. Further, researchers can study whether there is divergence between students' challenge-seeking behaviors during decontextualized, nonacademic performance tasks, compared to adult reports of student classroom behaviors, and whether that divergence can be explained by classroom experiences of stereotype threat or discriminatory pedagogical practices. A recent study of adolescents revealed that teachers may ignore or even respond adversely when girls of color raise their hands or seek help in class, suggesting that contextual factors like teachers' adverse responses may undermine student motivation to seek and persist on challenging tasks (Annamma, Handy, Miller, & Jackson, 2020). Systematic discrepancies across direct assessment and teacher reports of these behaviors can be used to improve teachers' SEL mindsets, expectations, and practices through professional development opportunities designed to promote educational equity. Below, we highlight three examples of recent innovative approaches to directly assessing students' effort, persistence, and challenge-seeking behavior.

Response Time Effort Measures

Leveraging students' engagement metrics during digitized academic assessments, researchers can identify students whose quick response patterns suggest that they did not carefully consider the test items. Soland and colleagues have conceptualized such rapid responding as an index of low effort (response time effort [RTE]) and linked it to lower levels of student-reported self-efficacy and self-management among middle and high school students (Soland, Zamarro, Cheng, & Hitt, 2019; Soland & Kuhfeld, 2019). Despite adequate reliability and construct validity of some RTE measures (Wise & Kong, 2005), more work is needed to understand the added value of this assessment approach in explaining variability in students' academic achievement or classroom engagement. Further, the utility of these "stealth" assessments for elementary school students has not been examined and may be complicated by the evidence that reaction time measures may represent different processes in younger and older learners (Domingue et al., 2020).

Challenge-Seeking and Effort Tasks for Older Students

In a small study of undergraduate students, time spent on unsolved anagrams and riddles during a task that allowed participants to skip difficult word problems was correlated with self-report of persistence (Ventura, Shute, & Zhao, 2013). Some studies have aimed to model real-life scenarios that distract students from completing boring or challenging tasks by offering high school seniors a choice between watching entertaining YouTube videos, playing Tetris, or completing simple math exercises that were said to improve problem-solving skills (Galla et al., 2014). The percentage of time spent solving math problems and the total number of correctly solved math problems were related to academic outcomes over and above demographic characteristics and intelligence test scores.

Minimizing the overlap between students' academic skills and the assessment of their effort, Meindl and colleagues (2019) offered college and high school students a choice between a challenging mirror-tracing activity and engaging with entertaining videos and games. The tracing activity was said to build valuable hand–eye coordination skills, but the trials were made nearly impossible, due to random drift of cursor movements. Time spent tracing was conceptualized as students' frustration tolerance and was linked to academic outcomes over and above student demographics, self-reported grit and self-control, and direct assessment of intelligence. Together, these studies show that the time students choose to spend on challenging tasks is uniquely predictive of academic outcomes, independent of their demographic differences, academic aptitude, and perceptions of their own learning-related behaviors. As such, these simple assessments can be used to evaluate practices aimed at fostering students' engagement.

Other researchers have evaluated adolescents' challenge-seeking behaviors by asking them to select very challenging, somewhat challenging, and not very challenging problems to create a personalized math worksheet (Yeager et al., 2016). A study of 7,501 ninth-grade students showed that their selections were related to their academic mindsets and were affected by a growth mindset intervention. However, selection tendencies were also correlated with students' math interest and anxiety, confounding the assessment of challenge-seeking behaviors with students' attitudes toward math. In addition to measuring students' choice of puzzle difficulty and time spent solving puzzles, Porter and colleagues (2020) designed a new task that measured how long students spent reading tips and their accuracy on easy puzzles following a difficult block. In a validation study of high school students, a composite performance score was related to grade point average, after controlling for student-reported mindsets and demographic characteristics (Porter et al., 2020). Collectively, these studies—which show that students' performance on tasks that assess challenge-seeking and persistence behaviors uniquely predict academic outcomes—underscore the importance of further understanding how these behaviors can be nurtured and supported in younger students. To more equitably assess student motivation, researchers should identify measures of effort and challenge-seeking behavior that are less strongly linked to students' problem-solving abilities.

Challenge-Seeking and Effort Tasks for Younger Students

Since most performance-based measures of motivation are designed for use with high school and college students, our recent work has focused on directly assessing challenge-seeking behaviors in elementary school students using a tablet-based puzzle task. The portability of tablet devices and elementary school students' familiarity and ease with using the touch-screen interface makes tablet-based tasks an ideal choice for scalable direct assessments (Obradović & Willoughby, 2019). To solve the puzzles, students must continuously trace a linear shape with their fingers, a task that does not rely on prior academic knowledge and minimizes recruitment of fluid cognitive skills. After trying an easy puzzle with few line segments (e.g., a diamond) and a more difficult one resembling a random web of lines, they are asked to select how challenging their next puzzle will be on a six-level difficulty meter. The task is modifiable in that the experimenter can set (1) how many line segments each difficulty level has; (2) the time limit for solving each puzzle; (3) whether it is possible to quit a puzzle; (4) whether puzzles are solvable or unsolvable; and (5) separate blocks of different puzzle types. Puzzles are randomly generated to reduce the practice effect, and including unsolvable puzzles allows researchers to assess challenge preference irrespective of children's ability to solve them.

We tested a version of this task where the first three levels comprised solvable puzzles of increasing size and the second three levels comprised unsolvable puzzles of increasing size. We chose this setting to minimize the confounding effect of student ability. We pilot-tested the task with a small group of second- and third-grade students ($N = 101$; 94% Latinx) attending an after-school literacy program. Students' challenge preference score, calculated as the average challenge level students selected across seven puzzles, was correlated with students' self-report on the challenge preference survey ($r = .33$, $p = .001$) and associated with greater performance on a delay of gratification task ($r = .28$, $p = .005$). The fact that student report and direct assessment of challenge preference behaviors were only moderately correlated suggests that these two assessment approaches capture related and unique aspects of student motivation and should be used as complementary approaches. Moreover, the directly assessed challenge preference score was not correlated with direct assessments of EFs in this sample, implying that challenge preference and EF may be two distinct constructs. This work offers preliminary evidence that challenge preference can be directly assessed in elementary school students, enabling future research into how these behaviors contribute to educational outcomes.

• Future Directions: Implications for Scalable Assessments

Despite widespread recognition among educators that EF skills and motivation are relevant for classroom engagement and learning, data from SEL performance tasks is typically not designed to be interpreted or used by teachers and school administrators (McKown, 2019). To address this challenge, some EF assessment tools include percentile scores or color-coded categories that compare individual students' performance to established norms (e.g., NIH Toolbox, MEFS). However, these comparisons can obscure important differences in assessment settings, procedures, and samples. Future research should investigate the intraindividual variability of students' EF task scores and the validity of research assessment tools for diagnostic or screening purposes.

Normed scores also do not help teachers understand how to support an individual student's EF development or use of EFs in the classroom. Thus, there is a need for translational partnerships to help educators make sense of assessment data. Our research group, for example, met with after-school literacy instructors to discuss their second- and third-grade students' performance on a visual working memory task. Knowing that a high percentage of students were unable to remember and mentally manipulate two pieces of visual information prompted instructors to consider how to support their students in completing activities that require multistep procedures and how to promote students' working memory skills within a literacy program. Future research–practice collaborations could investigate how teachers can routinely use students' SEL task performance to inform instructional approaches.

Translating EF and motivation assessments into actionable classroom supports could also contribute to the development of more educationally relevant SEL tasks. Our whole-classroom approach to EF and motivation assessment may have greater ecological validity than conventional procedures (Obradović et al., 2018), but it still employs standardized tasks that do not resemble everyday classroom activities. Responding to this limitation, researchers have designed game-based assessments in which students employ EF skills to accomplish a concrete task. For example, DeRosier and Thomas (2018) included an inhibitory control task in their Zoo U assessment module; students were instructed to feed an elephant by following a series of steps before the virtual class could go to recess. The percentage of time students spent on the task, rather than engaging with a distractor object, was conceptualized as a measure of impulse control and linked to teacher report of impulse control (DeRosier, Craig, & Sanchez, 2012). However, platforms such as Zoo U and SELweb (McKown, Allen, Russo-Ponsaran, & Johnson, 2013; see McKown, Chapter 2, this volume) tend to aggregate students' performance on multiple tasks, creating a single metric of SEL skills from tasks designed to measure social competence, emotion understanding, and self-regulation. While a single SEL composite may have greater reliability and predictive validity than individual task performance scores (and be easier for practitioners to consider), it obscures an understanding of distinct skills and students' unique strengths and areas of growth.

The pace at which app-based assessments are being developed and marketed to schools is not matched by empirical research demonstrating the reliability and validity of these assessments across different ages and diverse populations (see Day, Freiberg, Hayes, & Homel, 2019). While app-based, educator-administered assessments can provide practitioners with rapid data visualization and data aggregation that may inform their concurrent practice, it is important to continuously evaluate the psychometric properties and applicability of game-based tasks in classroom settings. Gamified assessments may appeal to students, but they introduce additional factors that need to be better understood. For example, we do not know if game-based tasks are equally motivating to all students, if they can be used repeatedly to understand longitudinal change, and if they indeed have stronger real-life implications than more conventional tasks.

Integrating SEL assessments and supports into academic curricula will increase the relevance of such skills for academic achievement. One promising avenue for developing ecologically valid EF assessments is the EF+Math Program, which funds projects that embed EF scaffolding and assessment within a math curriculum (see *www.efmathprogram.org*). Nevertheless, it is important not to confound students' EFs, which can support any goal-directed behavior, with their academic interests and skills. Researchers should engage practitioners not only in building school district capacities to administer, score, and interpret the SEL assessments on a routine basis, but also in developing direct assessments that maximize educational relevance and minimize biases.

• Cultural and Equity Considerations

As discussed above, a key strength of direct assessment is that it yields a scalable, standardized measure of a given set of skills that does not rely on subjective adult reports. However, before direct assessments are employed at scale, it is crucial that researchers identify sources of bias in direct assessment that systematically privilege or undermine the performance of certain groups. Further, standardized assessments should be used and interpreted in ways that do not reproduce or exaggerate existing inequities in educational systems; they should be seen as tools to evaluate the effectiveness of efforts to minimize disparities in learning opportunities. In this section, we provide suggestions for future work to enhance equity in both the implementation and the interpretation of direct assessments.

Direct Assessment Procedures

Children's performance on EF tasks can be confounded with their knowledge of the pictures, concepts, and rules that compose such tasks. For example, assessments of EF skills that rely on sorting pictures by color require that the child knows those colors. To address this limitation, researchers have worked with cultural experts to adapt EF task stimuli, instructions, and procedures for administration with young children in low- and middle-income countries (for examples, see Fernald, Prado, Kariger, & Raikes, 2017; Obradović et al., 2019; Prado et al., 2010). This work has advanced understanding of early EF development and its correlates across diverse cultures (Obradović & Willoughby, 2019). However, more work is needed to identify situational factors that can affect children's performance on direct assessments of SEL skills, including the assessor's demeanor, positionality, and framing of tasks as well as broader classroom dynamics. As an example of how researchers can scrutinize the performance of elementary school students on direct assessments of SEL, we highlight studies that have examined contextual factors affecting the assessment of delay of gratification, which is an emotionally salient aspect of impulse control. We do so while acknowledging that delay of gratification tasks are not universally relevant and fail to capture variability in children's skills in low- and middle-income countries (Fernald et al., 2017; Obradović et al., 2019; Prado et al., 2010).

First, researchers should understand the role of the assessor's demeanor and positionality in tacitly communicating expectations or producing discriminatory experiences. For example, studies conducted with small samples of preschoolers found that children's ability to delay gratification could be influenced by experimental manipulation of the assessor's trustworthiness; children promised a second, delayed treat by a trustworthy adult waited significantly longer than those tested by an unreliable adult (Kidd, Palmeri, & Aslin, 2013; Michaelson & Munakata, 2016; Moffett, Flannagan, & Shah, 2020). Future research should investigate how students' perceptions of assessors and their behavior, as well as demographic match between assessors and students, may affect students' performance.

Second, research should examine how classroom dynamics affect direct assessments conducted in that setting. Young children's delay of gratification skills are sensitive to their perceptions of their own group membership and group norms (Doebel & Munakata, 2018; Munakata et al., 2020). For example, after being told they were part of the "green" group whose members wait longer for marshmallows than the members of the "orange" group, children waited longer to receive a delayed treat and placed a higher value on delaying gratification, compared to children in the control condition (Doebel & Munakata, 2018). Future research should investigate how experiences of stereotype threat, as well as classroom-based discrimination by teachers and peers, may affect students' performance on standardized SEL assessments. A recent study found that Spanish-speaking preschool teachers may foster classroom environments that are less physiologically stressful for Spanish-speaking Latinx children (Miles et al., 2018). Since physiological arousal can affect children's testing performance (Adam et al., 2017), contextual factors should be examined across multiple levels of analysis (Obradović & Armstrong-Carter, 2020).

Third, there is a need to investigate how the intentional and unintentional framing of direct assessments may affect performance, especially on assessments of effort, persistence, and challenge preference in elementary school students. In a small sample of preschoolers, experimental exposure to storybook characters who learn that willpower is energizing was linked to longer wait times and a greater number of delay strategies (Haimovitz, Dweck, & Walton, 2020). Further, experimental manipulations of self-distancing—asking children to take a third-person perspective or pretend to be an exemplar other (e.g., Batman, Dora the Explorer) in role play—are associated with higher frustration tolerance and perseverance on performance tasks (Grenell et al., 2019; White et al., 2017) and improvements in EF (White & Carlson, 2016).

Studies like these can reveal ways to address systemic inequities that contribute to disparities in student performance on direct assessments. Future research should interrogate these processes using different tasks to disentangle skill-specific (e.g., EFs vs. compliance), task-specific (e.g., de-contextualized neurocognitive task vs. practical real-life task), and context-specific (e.g., differences in positionality of assessors) biases. Qualitative work is also needed to better understand how different students experience these assessments and the choices they make to engage or not engage. Identifying factors that can affect students' performance on direct assessments may also help us understand disparities in how students apply EF skills, effort, and challenge-seeking behaviors in real-world contexts. More importantly, this work can help identify new classroom supports for students' EF skills and motivation, which might include having teachers of similar cultural and linguistic backgrounds or harnessing the power of group belonging and classroom rituals (Rybanska, McKay, Jong, & Whitehouse, 2018).

Assessment Applications and Interpretations

Scalable direct assessments of SEL can enable researchers and educators to assess larger and more diverse groups of students, improving our understanding of how these skills develop and contribute to well-being and educational outcomes. Scalable assessments can also help school districts track whether policies, classroom supports, and teacher practices are effective in promoting SEL in all students. Future work will need to identify inequities in SEL supports and examine student experiences that hinder the development and expression of EF skills, effort, and challenge-seeking behaviors. To that end, researchers and educators need to combine direct assessments of SEL with assessments of contextual factors, so that they can routinely investigate the links between skills and context. It is important that the application of scalable SEL assessments illuminate deficits in educational settings rather than place a burden on individual students to improve their SEL skills.

Students' EF-related behaviors are sensitive to their social experiences with peers and adults, and direct assessments do not capture the application of these skills in real-life situations. Teachers are an obvious source of information about students' use of SEL skills in the classroom (e.g., Fuhs et al., 2015; Toplak, West, & Stanovich, 2013). However, because teachers are not trained to systematically differentiate between and evaluate the numerous components of SEL, their reports often reflect a general impression of the child's behavior. For example, temperamentally exuberant or extroverted children may be erroneously perceived as having greater social awareness skills than more behaviorally inhibited or introverted children. A second limitation is that teachers' reports are frequently tainted by demographic biases—biases that can be explored by comparing direct assessments and teacher ratings. For example, we found that teachers' reports of student EFs rated boys worse than girls, African American students worse than white students, and students with limited English proficiency worse than English-dominant students, beyond the differences shown in direct assessments of EFs (Garcia et al., 2019). We also found that these discrepancies did not lessen from fall to spring, even as teachers spent more time with students. There is also evidence of socioeconomic and racial/ethnic biases in teacher ratings of student effort (Kozlowski, 2015). This work should inform scaffolds that encourage teachers to reflect on implicit bias.

The format, data procedures, and content of conventional SEL surveys can exacerbate problems with teacher report. Educators are asked to complete many questions per student, for all students in their classrooms, in rapid succession, and they may take various shortcuts to relieve the mental overload of this burdensome task. Reducing adult reporters' stress may lead to more objective ratings of students' behavior (Herbers, Garcia, & Obradović, 2017). SEL surveys should also be revised to honor different cultural norms about what constitutes desirable and adaptive behavior. Extant survey items overemphasize behaviors that exemplify compliance with teachers' instructions and classroom rules (e.g., sitting still, not speaking out of turn), while presuming to measure EFs. We need to create more equitable, culturally sensitive classroom settings that accept and celebrate diverse applications of EF skills and expressions of motivation and effort, and design SEL survey items to match.

As researchers test new approaches to obtaining less burdensome and more scalable teacher reports of student SEL, it will be important to simultaneously employ direct assessments of SEL skills to investigate sources of convergence and divergence between the two assessment modalities. Future research should test the feasibility of hybrid assessments that include both teacher report and teacher-administered SEL tasks. Teachers' knowledge of their students' performance on direct assessments may challenge some of their preconceptions and prejudices. In one of our research–practice partnerships, teachers engaged in meaningful reflections after learning that boys who selected more challenging puzzles on a direct assessment were rated as more impulsive. Discussions focused on how to more effectively engage and support these students rather than dismissing them as restless or disruptive troublemakers. Hybrid assessment approaches should be tested only after addressing the concerns noted above about the potential effects of the assessors, in this case teachers, on students' performance.

Future work should also grapple with the concept of "self" that has shaped SEL assessments and the SEL field more broadly, as seen in domains such as self-management. Western researchers and educators tend to assume that measures of student knowledge, beliefs, and skills reflect a degree of independence from past and current contexts. However, this independence is overstated. Researchers should recognize the dynamic nature of coregulation in educational settings (akin to parent–child coregulation) and examine students' abilities to manage their attention, behavior, and emotions in light of the relational and instrumental supports available to them. We advocate that future research investigate how socialization processes and contextual experiences affect students' effort, persistence, and challenge-seeking behaviors, rather than conceptualize motivation and related choices as character traits. We further acknowledge the need for differentiated supports to ensure that children of diverse temperaments and personality characteristics, in addition to cultural backgrounds, thrive in mainstream schools.

• Conclusion

At its best, SEL rejects narrow definitions of student achievement and promotes a whole-child educational approach, fostering the cognitive, social, and emotional skills that students need to thrive in the 21st century. Direct assessments of all students in the classroom are needed to examine the effects of SEL policies and programs and to identify existing structural barriers and inequities. In this chapter, we have outlined the distinct benefits of classroom-based direct assessments of elementary school students' EFs, effort, and challenge-seeking behaviors—benefits that include scalability, representativeness and inclusivity, relative objectivity and precision, ecological validity, and potential utility to educators. We have also outlined concerns that standardized SEL assessments may replicate or exacerbate existing educational inequities, and we have provided recommendations for future work to address these concerns. These concerns are not new, but they need to be thoroughly investigated and addressed to realize the promise of SEL assessments.

REFERENCES

Adam, E. K., Quinn, M. E., Tavernier, R., McQuillan, M. T., Dahlke, K. A., & Gilbert, K. E. (2017). Diurnal cortisol slopes and mental and physical health outcomes: A systematic review and meta-analysis. *Psychoneuroendocrinology, 83*(1), 25–41.

Allan, N. P., Hume, L. E., Allan, D. M., Farrington, A. L., & Lonigan, C. J. (2014). Relations between inhibitory control and the development of academic skills in preschool and kindergarten: A meta-analysis. *Developmental Psychology, 50,* 2368–2379.

Annamma, S. A., Handy, T., Miller, A. L., & Jackson, E. (2020). Animating discipline disparities through debilitating practices: Girls of color and inequitable classroom interactions. *Teachers College Record, 122*(5).

Bardack, S., & Obradović, J. (2019). Observing teachers' displays and scaffolding of executive functioning in the classroom context. *Journal of Applied Developmental Psychology, 62,* 205–219.

Beck, D. M., Schaefer, C., Pang, K., & Carlson, S. M. (2011). Executive function in preschool children: Test–retest reliability. *Journal of Cognition and Development, 12*(2), 169–193.

Bergman-Nutley, S., & Klingberg, T. (2014). Effect of working memory training on working memory, arithmetic and following instructions. *Psychological Research, 78*(6), 869–877.

Blair, C., & Raver, C. C. (2014). Closing the achievement gap through modification of neurocognitive and neuroendocrine function: Results from a cluster randomized controlled trial of an innovative approach to the education of children in kindergarten. *PLOS ONE, 9*(11), e112393.

Blair, C., Ursache, A., Greenberg, M., Vernon-Feagans, L., & Family Life Project Investigators. (2015). Multiple aspects of self-regulation uniquely predict mathematics but not letter-word knowledge in the early elementary grades. *Developmental Psychology, 51*(4), 459–472.

Brandmiller, C., Dumont, H., & Becker, M. (2020). Teacher perceptions of learning motivation and classroom behavior: The role of student characteristics. *Contemporary Educational Psychology,* 101893.

Brown, C. S., Mistry, R. S., & Yip, T. (2019). Moving from the margins to the mainstream: Equity and justice as key considerations for developmental science. *Child Development Perspectives, 13*(4), 235–240.

Carlson, S. M., & Zelazo, P. D. (2014). *Minnesota Executive Function Scale: Test manual.* Reflection Sciences.

Choi, J. Y., Castle, S., Williamson, A. C., Young, E., Worley, L., Long, M., & Horm, D. M. (2016). Teacher–child interactions and the development of executive function in preschool-age children attending Head Start. *Early Education and Development, 27,* 751–769.

Ciairano, S., Visu-Petra, L., & Settanni, M. (2007). Executive inhibitory control and cooperative behavior during early school years: A follow-up study. *Journal of Abnormal Child Psychology, 35*(3), 335–345.

Credé, M., Tynan, M. C., & Harms, P. D. (2017). Much ado about grit: A meta-analytic synthesis of the grit literature. *Journal of Personality and Social Psychology, 113*(3), 492–511.

Cumming, M. M., Bettini, E., Pham, A. V., & Park, J. (2020). School-, classroom-, and dyadic-level experiences: A literature review of their relationship with students' executive functioning development. *Review of Educational Research, 90*(1), 47–94.

Daneri, M. P., Sulik, M. J., Raver, C. C., & Morris, P. A. (2018). Observers' reports of self-regulation: Measurement invariance across sex, low-income status, and race/ethnicity. *Journal of Applied Developmental Psychology, 55,* 14–23.

Day, J., Freiberg, K., Hayes, A., & Homel, R. (2019). Towards scalable, integrative assessment of children's self-regulatory capabilities: New applications of digital technology. *Clinical Child and Family Psychology Review, 22*(1), 90–103.

DeRosier, M. E., Craig, A. B., & Sanchez, R. P. (2012). Zoo U: A stealth approach to social skills assessment in schools [research article]. *Advances in Human-Computer Interaction.*

DeRosier, M. E., & Thomas, J. M. (2018). Establishing the criterion validity of Zoo U's game-based social emotional skills assessment for school-based outcomes. *Journal of Applied Developmental Psychology, 55,* 52–61.

Developmental Studies Center. (n.d.). Scales from student questionnaire, Child Development Project for elementary school students (grades 3–6). Retrieved from *www.collaborativeclassroom.org/resources/scales-from-student-questionnaire-child-development-project-for-elementary-school-students-grades-3-6.*

Diamond, A. (2013). Executive functions. *Annual Review of Psychology, 64,* 135–168.

Diamond, A., & Ling, D. S. (2016). Conclusions about interventions, programs, and approaches for improving executive functions that appear justified and those that, despite much hype, do not. *Developmental Cognitive Neuroscience, 18,* 34–48.

Doebel, S., & Munakata, Y. (2018). Group influences on engaging self-control: Children delay gratification and value it more when their in-group delays and their out-group doesn't. *Psychological Science, 29*(5), 738–748.

Domingue, B., Kanopka, K., Stenhaug, B., Sulik, M. J., Beverly, T., Brinkhuis, M. J., . . . Yeatman, J. D. (2020). *Speed accuracy tradeoff? Not so fast: Marginal changes in speed have inconsistent relationships with accuracy in real-world settings* [Preprint]. *PsyArXiv.*

Duckworth, A., & Quinn, P. D. (2009). Development and validation of the Short Grit Scale (Grit–S). *Journal of Personality Assessment, 91,* 166–174.

Duckworth, A. L., & Yeager, D. S. (2015). Measurement matters: Assessing personal qualities other than cognitive ability for educational purposes. *Educational Researcher, 44*(4), 237–251.

Dweck, C. S. (2008). *Mindset: The new psychology of success.* Ballantine Books.

Elliott, E. S., & Dweck, C. S. (1988). Goals: An approach to motivation and achievement. *Journal of Personality and Social Psychology, 54,* 5–12.

Fay-Stammbach, T., Hawes, D. J., & Meredith, P. (2017). Child maltreatment and emotion socialization: Associations with executive function in the preschool years. *Child Abuse & Neglect, 64,* 1–12.

Fernald, L. C. H., Prado, E., Kariger, P., & Raikes, A. (2017). *A toolkit for measuring early childhood development in low- and middle-income countries* (p. 128). World Bank.

Finch, J. E., Garcia, E. B., Sulik, M. J., & Obradović, J. (2019). Peers matter: Links between classmates' and individual students' executive functions in elementary school. *AERA Open, 5*(1), 1–14.

Finch, J. E., & Obradović, J. (2017a). Independent and compensatory contributions of executive functions and challenge preference for students' adaptive classroom behaviors. *Learning and Individual Differences, 55,* 183–192.

Finch, J. E., & Obradović, J. (2017b, March). *Executive functioning skills mediate associations between classroom quality and academic achievement in elementary school.* Society for Research on Educational Effectiveness.

Fiske, A., & Holmboe, K. (2019). Neural substrates of early executive function development. *Developmental Review, 52,* 42–62.

Fitzpatrick, C., Côté-Lussier, C., & Blair, C. (2016). Dressed and groomed for success in elementary school: Student appearance and academic adjustment. *The Elementary School Journal, 117*(1), 30–45.

Friso-van den Bos, I., van der Ven, S. H., Kroesbergen, E. H., & van Luit, J. E. (2013). Working memory and mathematics in primary school children: A meta-analysis. *Educational Research Review, 10,* 29–44.

Fuhs, M., Farran, D. C., & Nesbitt, K. T. (2013). Preschool classroom processes as predictors of children's cognitive self-regulation skills development. *School Psychology Quarterly, 28*(4), 347–359.

Fuhs, M., Farran, D. C., & Nesbitt, K. T. (2015). Prekindergarten children's executive functioning skills and achievement gains: The utility of direct assessments and teacher ratings. *Journal of Educational Psychology, 107*(1), 207–221.

Galla, B. M., Plummer, B. D., White, R. E., Meketon, D., D'Mello, S. K., & Duckworth, A. L. (2014). The Academic Diligence Task (ADT): Assessing individual differences in effort on tedious but important schoolwork. *Contemporary Educational Psychology, 39*(4), 314–325.

Garcia, E. B., Sulik, M. J., & Obradović, J. (2019). Teachers' perceptions of students' executive functions: Disparities by gender, ethnicity, and ELL status. *Journal of Educational Psychology, 111*(5), 918–931.

Grenell, A., Prager, E. O., Schaefer, C., Kross, E., Duckworth, A. L., & Carlson, S. M. (2019). Individual differences in the effectiveness of self-distancing for young children's emotion regulation. *British Journal of Developmental Psychology, 37*(1), 84–100.

Guerrero-Rosada, P., Weiland, C., McCormick, M., Hsueh, J., Sachs, J., Snow, C., & Maier, M. (2021). Null relations between CLASS scores and gains in children's language, math, and executive function skills: A replication and extension study. *Early Childhood Research Quarterly, 54,* 1–12.

Hackman, D. A., Betancourt, L. M., Gallop, R., Romer, D., Brodsky, N. L., Hurt, H., & Farah, M. J. (2014). Mapping the trajectory of socioeconomic disparity in working memory: Parental and neighborhood factors. *Child Development, 85*(4), 1433–1445.

Haft, S. L., & Hoeft, F. (2017). Poverty's impact on children's executive functions: Global considerations. *New Directions for Child and Adolescent Development, 2017,* 69–79.

Haimovitz, K., Dweck, C. S., & Walton, G. M. (2020). Preschoolers find ways to resist temptation after learning that willpower can be energizing. *Developmental Science, 23*(3), e12905.

Hamre, B. K., Hatfield, B., Pianta, R. C., & Jamil, F. (2014). Evidence for general and domain-specific elements of teacher-child interactions: Associations with preschool children's development. *Child Development, 85,* 1257–1274.

Harter, S. (1981). A new self-report scale of intrinsic versus extrinsic orientation in the classroom: Motivational and informational components. *Developmental Psychology, 17,* 300–312.

Hatfield, B. E., Burchinal, M. R., Pianta, R. C., & Sideris, J. (2016). Thresholds in the association between quality of teacher–child interactions and preschool children's school readiness skills. *Early Childhood Research Quarterly, 36,* 561–571.

Heissel, J. A., Levy, D. J., & Adam, E. K. (2017). Stress, sleep, and performance on standardized tests: Understudied pathways to the achievement gap. *AERA Open, 3*(3), 1–17.

Herbers, J. E., Garcia, E. B., & Obradović, J. (2017). Parenting assessed by observation versus parent-report: Moderation by parent distress and family socioeconomic status. *Journal of Child and Family Studies, 26,* 3339–3350.

Howse, R. B., Lange, G., Farran, D. C., & Boyles, C. D. (2003). Motivation and self-regulation as predictors of achievement in economically disadvantaged young children. *The Journal of Experimental Education, 71*(2), 151–174.

Inzlicht, M., & Schmader, T. (2012). *Stereotype threat: Theory, process, and application.* Oxford University Press.

Joyner, K. B., Silver, C. H., & Stavinoha, P. L. (2009). Relationship between parenting stress and ratings of executive functioning in children with ADHD. *Journal of Psychoeducational Assessment, 27*(6), 452–464.

Karr, J. E., Areshenkoff, C. N., Rast, P., Hofer, S. M., Iverson, G. L., & Garcia-Barrera, M. A. (2018). The unity and diversity of executive functions: A systematic review and re-analysis of latent variable studies. *Psychological Bulletin, 144,* 1147–1185.

Kidd, C., Palmeri, H., & Aslin, R. N. (2013). Rational snacking: Young children's decision-making on the marshmallow task is moderated by beliefs about environmental reliability. *Cognition, 126*(1), 109–114.

Kozlowski, K. P. (2015). Culture or teacher bias? Racial and ethnic variation in student–teacher effort assessment match/mismatch. *Race and Social Problems, 7*(1), 43–59.

Lan, X., Legare, C. H., Ponitz, C. C., Li, S., & Morrison, F. J. (2011). Investigating the links between the subcomponents of executive function and academic achievement: A cross-cultural analysis of Chinese and American preschoolers. *Journal of Experimental Child Psychology, 108*(3), 677–692.

Mann, T. D., Hund, A. M., Hesson-McInnis, M. S., & Roman, Z. J. (2017). Pathways to school readiness: Executive functioning predicts academic and social–emotional aspects of school readiness. *Mind, Brain, and Education, 11*(1), 21–31.

McClelland, M. M., Tominey, S. L., Schmitt, S. A., Hatfield, B. E., Purpura, D. J., Gonzales, C. R., & Tracy, A. N. (2019). Red light, purple light! Results of an intervention to promote school readiness for children from low-income backgrounds. *Frontiers in Psychology, 10*, 2365.

McCombs, B. L., & Marzano, R. J. (1990). Putting the self in self-regulated learning: The self as agent in integrating will and skill. *Educational Psychologist, 25*(1), 51–69.

McCoy, D. C. (2019). Measuring young children's executive function and self-regulation in classrooms and other real-world settings. *Clinical Child and Family Psychology Review, 22*(1), 63–74.

McCoy, D. C., Zuilkowski, S. S., Yoshikawa, H., & Fink, G. (2017). Early childhood care and education and school readiness in Zambia. *Journal of Research on Educational Effectiveness, 10*(3), 482–506.

McKown, C. (2019). Challenges and opportunities in the applied assessment of student social and emotional learning. *Educational Psychologist, 54*(3), 205–221.

McKown, C., Allen, A. M., Russo-Ponsaran, N. M., & Johnson, J. K. (2013). Direct assessment of children's social-emotional comprehension. *Psychological Assessment, 25*(4), 1154–1166.

Meindl, P., Yu, A., Galla, B. M., Quirk, A., Haeck, C., Goyer, J. P., . . . Duckworth, A. L. (2019). A brief behavioral measure of frustration tolerance predicts academic achievement immediately and two years later. *Emotion, 19*(6), 1081–1092.

Michaelson, L. E., & Munakata, Y. (2016). Trust matters: Seeing how an adult treats another person influences preschoolers' willingness to delay gratification. *Developmental Science, 19*(6), 1011–1019.

Miles, E. M., Dmitrieva, J., Hurwich-Reiss, E., Badanes, L., Mendoza, M. M., Perreira, K. M., & Watamura, S. E. (2018). Evidence for a physiologic home–school gap in children of Latina immigrants. *Early Childhood Research Quarterly, 52*, 86–100.

Moffett, L., Flannagan, C., & Shah, P. (2020). The influence of environmental reliability in the marshmallow task: An extension study. *Journal of Experimental Child Psychology, 194*, 104821.

Moriguchi, Y., & Hiraki, K. (2013). Prefrontal cortex and executive function in young children: A review of NIRS studies. *Frontiers in Human Neuroscience, 7*, 867.

Mueller, S. T., & Piper, B. J. (2014). The Psychology Experiment Building Language (PEBL) and PEBL Test Battery. *Journal of Neuroscience Methods, 222*, 250–259.

Munakata, Y., Yanaoka, K., Doebel, S., Guild, R. M., Michaelson, L. E., & Saito,

S. (2020). Group influences on children's delay of gratification: Testing the roles of culture and personal connections. *Collabra: Psychology, 6*(1), 1.

Nelson, T. D., Nelson, J. M., James, T. D., Clark, C. A. C., Kidwell, K. M., & Espy, K. A. (2017). Executive control goes to school: Implications of preschool executive performance for observed elementary classroom learning engagement. *Developmental Psychology, 53*(5), 836–844.

Nguyen, T., & Duncan, G. J. (2019). Kindergarten components of executive function and third grade achievement: A national study. *Early Childhood Research Quarterly, 46*, 49–61.

Obradović, J., & Armstrong-Carter, E. (2020). Addressing educational inequalities and promoting learning through studies of stress physiology in elementary school students. *Development and Psychopathology, 32*, 1899–1913.

Obradović, J., Finch, J. E., Portilla, X. A., Rasheed, M. A., Tirado-Strayer, N., & Yousafzai, A. K. (2019). Early executive functioning in a global context: Developmental continuity and family protective factors. *Developmental Science, 22*, e12795.

Obradović, J., Sulik, M. J., Finch, J. E., & Tirado-Strayer, N. (2018). Assessing students' executive functions in the classroom: Validating a scalable group-based procedure. *Journal of Applied Developmental Psychology, 55*, 4–13.

Obradović, J., & Willoughby, M. T. (2019). Studying executive function skills in young children in low- and middle-income countries: Progress and directions. *Child Development Perspectives, 13*, 227–234.

Pianta, R. C., Hamre, B., Downer, J., Burchinal, M., Williford, A., LoCasale-Crouch, J., . . . Scott-Little, C. (2017). Early childhood professional development: Coaching and coursework effects on indicators of children's school readiness. *Early Education and Development, 28*(8), 956–975.

Pianta, R. C., Whittaker, J. E., Vitiello, V., Ruzek, E., Ansari, A., Hofkens, T., & DeCoster, J. (2020). Children's school readiness skills across the pre-K year: Associations with teacher-student interactions, teacher practices, and exposure to academic content. *Journal of Applied Developmental Psychology, 66*, 101084.

Piccolo, L. R., Merz, E. C., & Noble, K. G. (2019). School climate is associated with cortical thickness and executive function in children and adolescents. *Developmental Science, 22*(1), e12719.

Porter, T., Catalan Molina, D., Blackwell, L., Roberts, S., Quirk, A., Duckworth, A. L., & Trzesniewski, K. (2020). Measuring mastery behaviours at scale: The Persistence, Effort, Resilience, and Challenge-Seeking (PERC) Task. *Journal of Learning Analytics, 7*(1), 5–18.

Prado, E. L., Hartini, S., Rahmawati, A., Ismayani, E., Hidayati, A., Hikmah, N., . . . Alcock, K. J. (2010). Test selection, adaptation, and evaluation: A systematic approach to assess nutritional influences on child development in developing countries. *British Journal of Educational Psychology, 80*(1), 31–53.

Purpura, D. J., Schmitt, S. A., & Ganley, C. M. (2017). Foundations of mathematics and literacy: The role of executive functioning components. *Journal of Experimental Child Psychology, 153*, 15–34.

Raver, C. C., Blair, C., Willoughby, M., & Family Life Project Key Investigators. (2013). Poverty as a predictor of 4-year-olds' executive function: New perspectives on models of differential susceptibility. *Developmental Psychology, 49*(2), 292–304.

Riggs, N. R., Greenberg, M. T., Kusché, C. A., & Pentz, M. A. (2006). The mediational role of neurocognition in the behavioral outcomes of a social-emotional prevention program in elementary school students: Effects of the PATHS curriculum. *Prevention Science, 7*(1), 91–102.

Rimm-Kaufman, S. E., Curby, T. W., Grimm, K. J., Nathanson, L., & Brock, L. L. (2009). The contribution of children's self-regulation and classroom quality to children's adaptive behaviors in the kindergarten classroom. *Developmental Psychology, 45*(4), 958–972.

Ryan, R. M., & Deci, E. L. (2020). Intrinsic and extrinsic motivation from a self-determination theory perspective: Definitions, theory, practices, and future directions. *Contemporary Educational Psychology,* 101860.

Rybanska, V., McKay, R., Jong, J., & Whitehouse, H. (2018). Rituals improve children's ability to delay gratification. *Child Development, 89,* 349–359.

Sasser, T. R., Bierman, K. L., & Heinrichs, B. (2015). Executive functioning and school adjustment: The mediational role of pre-kindergarten learning-related behaviors. *Early Childhood Research Quarterly, 30,* 70–79.

Schunk, D. H., & Zimmerman, B. J. (Eds.). (2012). *Motivation and self-regulated learning: Theory, research, and applications.* Routledge.

Silver, C. H. (2014). Sources of data about children's executive functioning: Review and commentary. *Child Neuropsychology, 20*(1), 1–13.

Sisk, V. F., Burgoyne, A. P., Sun, J., Butler, J. L., & Macnamara, B. N. (2018). To what extent and under which circumstances are growth mind-sets important to academic achievement? Two meta-analyses. *Psychological Science, 29*(4), 095679761773970.

Smiley, P. A., & Dweck, C. S. (1994). Individual differences in achievement goals among young children. *Child Development, 65,* 1723–1743.

Soland, J., & Kuhfeld, M. (2019). Do students rapidly guess repeatedly over time? A longitudinal analysis of student test disengagement, background, and attitudes. *Educational Assessment, 24*(4), 327–342.

Soland, J., Zamarro, G., Cheng, A., & Hitt, C. (2019). Identifying naturally occurring direct assessments of social-emotional competencies: The promise and limitations of survey and assessment disengagement metadata. *Educational Researcher, 48*(7), 466–478.

Spiegel, J. A., & Lonigan, C. J. (2018). A head-to-toes approach to computerized testing of executive functioning in young children. *Early Childhood Research Quarterly, 44,* 15–23.

Stipek, D., Recchia, S., McClintic, S., & Lewis, M. (1992). Self-evaluation in young children. *Monographs of the Society for Research in Child Development, 57*(1), i–95.

Sulik, M. J., Finch, J. E., & Obradović, J. (2020). Moving beyond executive functions: Challenge preference as a predictor of academic achievement in elementary school. *Journal of Experimental Child Psychology, 198,* 104883.

Toplak, M. E., West, R. F., & Stanovich, K. E. (2013). Practitioner review: Do performance-based measures and ratings of executive function assess the same construct? *Journal of Child Psychology and Psychiatry, 54*(2), 131–143.

Ventura, M., Shute, V., & Zhao, W. (2013). The relationship between video game use and a performance-based measure of persistence. *Computers & Education, 60*(1), 52–58.

Weiland, C., & Yoshikawa, H. (2013). Impacts of a prekindergarten program on children's mathematics, language, literacy, executive function, and emotional skills. *Child Development, 84,* 2112–2130.

Weissberg, R. P., Durlak, J. A., Domitrovich, C. E., & Gullotta, T. P. (2015). Social and emotional learning: Past, present, and future. In J. A. Durlak, R. P. Weissberg, C. E. Domitrovich, & T. P. Gullotta (Eds.), *Handbook of social and emotional learning: Research and practice* (pp. 3–19). Guilford Press.

Wenz-Gross, M., Yoo, Y., Upshur, C. C., & Gambino, A. J. (2018). Pathways to kindergarten readiness: The roles of second step early learning curriculum and social emotional, executive functioning, preschool academic and task behavior skills. *Frontiers in Psychology, 9,* 1886.

West, M. R., Buckley, K., Krachman, S. B., & Bookman, N. (2018). Development and implementation of student social-emotional surveys in the CORE Districts. *Journal of Applied Developmental Psychology, 55,* 119–129.

White, R. E., & Carlson, S. M. (2016). What would Batman do? Self-distancing improves executive function in young children. *Developmental Science, 19*(3), 419–426.

White, R. E., Prager, E. O., Schaefer, C., Kross, E., Duckworth, A. L., & Carlson, S. M. (2017). The "Batman effect": Improving perseverance in young children. *Child Development, 88*(5), 1563–1571.

Wiebe, S. A., Espy, K. A., & Charak, D. (2008). Using confirmatory factor analysis to understand executive control in preschool children: I. Latent structure. *Developmental Psychology, 44*(2), 575–587.

Willoughby, M. T., Blair, C. B., Wirth, R. J., & Greenberg, M. (2012). The measurement of executive function at age 5: Psychometric properties and relationship to academic achievement. *Psychological Assessment, 24*(1), 226–239.

Willoughby, M. T., Pek, J., Blair, C. B., & Family Life Project Investigators. (2013). Measuring executive function in early childhood: A focus on maximal reliability and the derivation of short forms. *Psychological Assessment, 25*(2), 664–670.

Willoughby, M. T., Piper, B., Oyanga, A., & Merseth King, K. (2019). Measuring executive function skills in young children in Kenya: Associations with school readiness. *Developmental Science, 22*(5), e12818.

Wise, S. L., & Kong, X. (2005). Response time effort: A new measure of examinee motivation in computer-based tests. *Applied Measurement in Education, 18*(2), 163–183.

Yeager, D. S., Romero, C., Paunesku, D., Hulleman, C. S., Schneider, B., Hinojosa, C., . . . Dweck, C. S. (2016). Using design thinking to improve psychological interventions: The case of the growth mindset during the transition to high school. *Journal of Educational Psychology, 108*(3), 374–391.

Yeniad, N., Malda, M., Mesman, J., van IJzendoorn, M. H., & Pieper, S. (2013). Shifting ability predicts math and reading performance in children: A meta-analytical study. *Learning and Individual Differences, 23,* 1–9.

Yoder, M. L., & Williford, A. P. (2019). Teacher perception of preschool disruptive behavior: Prevalence and contributing factors. *Early Education and Development, 30*(7), 835–853.

Zelazo, P. D., Anderson, J. E., Richler, J., Wallner-Allen, K., Beaumont, J. L., & Weintraub, S. (2013). II. NIH Toolbox Cognition Battery (CB): Measuring executive function and attention. *Monographs of the Society for Research in Child Development, 78*(4), 16–33.

Zelazo, P. D., Blair, C. B., & Willoughby, M. T. (2016). *Executive function: Implications for education* (Research Report NCER 2017-2000; pp. 1–148). National Center for Education Research, Institute of Education Sciences, U.S. Department of Education. Retrieved from *https://files.eric.ed.gov/fulltext/ED570880.pdf.*

Zimmerman, B. J. (1990). Self-regulated learning and academic achievement: An overview. *Educational Psychologist, 25*(1), 3–17.

Zimmerman, B. J., & Schunk, D. H. (Eds.). (2011). *Handbook of self-regulation of learning and performance.* Routledge.

CHAPTER 2

The Fidget Spinner Effect

Social and Emotional Assessment and the Healthy Evolution
of the Social and Emotional Learning Field

Clark McKown

Social and emotional learning (SEL) refers to the competencies children use to interact successfully with each other, to participate constructively in group activities, and to form and deepen relationships. SEL includes competencies like self-awareness, self-management, social awareness, relationship skills, and responsible decision making (*www.casel.org*). We know from extensive research that the better students' social and emotional competencies are developed, the better they do in relationships, in school, and in life (McKown, 2017).

Social and emotional competencies are also teachable: Done well, structured curricula that focus on explicit instruction of student social and emotional competencies (referred to in this chapter as "SEL programs") can produce desirable outcomes as diverse as improved behavior, mental health, and academic outcomes (Mahoney, Durlak, & Weissberg, 2019). The best evidence of SEL's promise comes from well-constructed experimental or quasi-experimental field trials (Durlak, Weissberg, Dymnicki, Taylor, & Schellinger, 2011). Outside of explicit instructional programs, we know that the quality of teacher–student interactions and children's relationships with their teachers (referred to here as "SEL practices") have long-term academic, social, and emotional consequences (Hamre & Pianta, 2001). It is this foundation in rigorous research that places SEL in the realm of the "evidence-based." Although SEL programs and SEL practices are both key components of school-based SEL initiatives, the focus of this chapter is on SEL programs, and the role of assessment in supporting their effective use.

Evidence that SEL programs are beneficial has ushered in a new era in which SEL programs are being adopted at a rapid clip. In two national surveys, 70% or more of elementary principals indicated that they had developed or implemented a plan to address student social and emotional competence. More than half reported that they had adopted an SEL program or curriculum (Atwell & Bridgeland, 2019; Hamilton, Doss, & Steiner, 2019).

End of story? Not by a long shot.

One of the key challenges that will soon face the field is the same challenge facing any field in which an evidence-based practice (EBP) is adopted on a massive scale. Specifically, how do we ensure that the SEL programs used in a large and growing number of schools in the United States contain the elements that made them effective in carefully executed studies such as those summarized in influential meta-analyses? On the one hand, we have learned that evidence-based SEL programs, implemented with sufficient intensity and quality, support positive student outcomes. On the other hand, if we assume that with the meta-analyses, we have all the evidence we need, and no more data are needed to scale up programs with fidelity and effectiveness, it is highly unlikely that SEL will maintain quality and impact at scale.

Without some way of measuring what is happening and whether it is making a difference, the field may find itself in trouble. What might happen, you ask? SEL programs that are effective in the context of well-resourced studies could be implemented too inconsistently or with insufficient fidelity to produce a benefit. I have spoken with many school administrators who reported that their district adopted an SEL program, and whether, how much, and how well that curriculum is being used varies from one classroom to the next. Many of those administrators do not know precisely who is using the curriculum or how well, so they do not know where to direct instructional coaching resources. Without assessment—of implementation, for example—it is impossible to know.

There is another problem that can arise from going to scale without assessment. Practices that are not known to benefit teaching, learning, or student outcomes may be marketed as SEL and adopted without evidence that they are beneficial. This is not always a problem because some well-designed programs may in fact benefit students even though a rigorous study has not yet demonstrated their efficacy. If educators use assessment—of student competencies, for example—they can monitor whether and how much students are acquiring the skills an "unproven" program is designed to nurture. However, unless educators assess student social and emotional growth, it is impossible to distinguish beneficial programs from ineffective programs.

When effective programs are not implemented well, and ineffective programs are marketed as evidence-based SEL, as the field grows, and student outcomes do not improve, this could lead to the erroneous conclusion that SEL is a waste of time, money, and energy. Critics will say SEL does not work when in fact, it is *ineffective* SEL that does not work. The risk of either or both of these problems increases with scale. Assessment can help educators use data to guide practice, measure progress, and ultimately, maintain the integrity and impact of SEL programs at scale. With assessment, educators can know how much and how well they are using an evidence-based program as intended, and how much those actions are contributing to student competence and other important outcomes. With assessment, educators can also know how much promising but unproven programs are helping.

• A Study in Contrasts

What does this all look like on the ground? Let's consider three teachers who heartily agree that SEL matters and who report they are engaged in practices that support student social and emotional development. One teacher's district adopted an evidence-based SEL program after reviewing a number of options, including reviewing evidence of their efficacy. District and school leadership strongly support SEL and expect all educators to use the program, and use it well, and they provide resources to support effective program use. The teacher has participated in professional development workshops with the program provider and ongoing structured coaching from the district to learn to use the program resources proficiently. Her goal is to teach students the social and emotional competencies they will need to succeed in school and life. At the beginning of the year, she administers a benchmark social and emotional competence assessment to all students. Each day, she teaches SEL lessons, following the scope and sequence, but adapting the lessons expertly as opportunities to connect to student experiences permit. During literacy, she reinforces social and emotional competencies by integrating intentional probes and questions. The benchmark assessment reveals that many of her students struggle with social problem solving, a key skill in conflict resolution. To address this need, she provides students opportunities to problem-solve hypothetical interpersonal conflicts. During literacy, when there are conflicts between characters, she encourages students to think through the nature and possible resolutions of the problem. Through her questioning during conflict resolution exercises and literacy, she formatively assesses student progress. Periodically, she administers a more formal assessment to measure student progress in response to her efforts.

A second teacher works in a district that has purchased an SEL program that was identified by a cabinet-level administrator at a conference. After a surprise announcement, the teacher participated in a 1-day workshop on using the program. No one has communicated expectations for program use. After the workshop, district and school leaders rarely mention the program. The teacher sees the SEL program as "one more thing" she has to do. After 3 months, in response to some social conflict between students, she reviews the first lesson plan, having forgotten most of what was covered in the workshop. She teaches the lesson but it does not go well and she decides that the program does not work and does not use it again.

A third teacher is concerned about student misbehavior. Several of his students are frequently off-task, out of their seats, and impulsive. His goal is to reduce the frequency of problem behaviors in these students. He heard from a colleague that fidget spinners support self-management, and this is his primary SEL "intervention."[1] Fidget spinners are a handheld manipulative widely marketed as a way to support greater focus. To support student self-management, he provides fidget spinners to his students who he has observed most frequently interrupting or engaging in off-task behavior. The students spin their fidget toys frequently during class, and other students tell the teacher they find them distracting. The teacher informally observes all students' behavior and develops an overall impression of how things are going. When asked by a colleague whether the fidget spinners work, he indicates his impression is that he is not sure, but he thinks so. He indicates that grades and test performance among the students who use the fidget spinner have not changed, but his overall impression is that they are less disruptive.

I would wager students in the first teacher's class will benefit from her efforts. The first teacher uses a program for which there is evidence of efficacy. She has engaged in systematic training on how to use the program skillfully. She uses assessment to guide SEL instruction for all students. Throughout the day, she creatively integrates multiple SEL touchpoints so the whole class can practice social and emotional competencies, particularly in areas of need identified in a whole-class assessment. In that way, SEL becomes part of the fabric of instruction. Will these efforts result in student academic, social, and emotional development? There are of course no guarantees. However, she is using approaches that have been shown to work and she is using them skillfully, with data and professional learning supports to guide her. In addition, she is measuring student growth, so she will be able to use data to see how much her students are acquiring social and emotional competencies.

I would also wager that students in the second teacher's class will not benefit from the SEL program, because it barely made it out of the proverbial shrink wrap.

My final bet: Students in the third teacher's class will benefit minimally, if at all, from his "SEL" intervention. The third teacher is using a very specific tool to reduce problem behaviors in a small number of students. His social and emotional goal is not to build strengths, but to

---

[1] Fidget spinners are not evidence-based.

extinguish problems. There is no evidence that fidget spinners can accomplish this goal beyond word of mouth and anecdotes. Outside of the fidget spinner, he does not change instruction to support the self-management skills of students, and he receives no professional-learning support to guide his practice. Furthermore, he has little evidence to know whether students' use of the fidget spinner changed behavior. He does, however, have evidence that other students find them distracting.

● DWI: Doing (SEL) without (Good) Information

The problem here is that all three teachers call what they are doing "SEL," but their approaches are very different in their likelihood of benefiting students. As the field grows, it seems likely that many activities will be described as "SEL," a phenomenon I refer to as "the fidget spinner effect." Although the fidget spinner example is rather extreme, it is highly likely that unproven but seemingly credible (often more credible than fidget spinners) SEL initiatives and effective but poorly implemented SEL approaches could also all be called "SEL." As SEL begins to unwittingly assimilate ineffective practices, and those practices predictably produce no measurable benefit, educators and the public could easily dismiss SEL as another fad. The proverbial baby could easily go the way of the bathwater.

To be clear, educators need a great range of tools to address their students' needs and they will need to adapt "out-of-the-box" programs to the local community—programs reflect only one such tool. They may, for example, adopt practices such as restorative justice or circle time or other kernels of social and emotional practice (Jones, Bailey, Brush, & Kahn, 2017) that reflect adult behaviors and processes rather than structured programs, and that is an important part of what educators should do. The key point is that when an educator implements a program or a practice with the aim of producing a social and emotional benefit, it is preferable that the program or practice has been demonstrated in the context of rigorous research to achieve the intended social and emotional benefit. In addition, whether or not such evidence exists, it is critical that educators use assessment to guide programs and practices, and measure the outcomes those programs and practices produce. In doing so, they can determine what is working, and let go of what is not.

● Bringing Evidence-Based Programs to Scale
(and Maintaining Impact)

The field of education, and SEL within it, is not alone in struggling with the challenge of bringing evidence-based practices (EBPs) to scale, by which

I mean taking practices that were originally used in a limited number of locations and implementing them in a massive number of settings. This is happening with SEL—as mentioned previously, more than half of U.S. school districts are implementing some form of SEL program. Right now, SEL programs are going to scale, often without a coordinated effort to assess social and emotional learning.

We can learn a great deal from other fields that have worked to bring evidence-based programs to scale. Alongside education, fields such as behavioral health, child welfare, juvenile justice, and public health all face the challenge of bringing evidence-based programs to scale (Fagan et al., 2019). Recognizing this challenge, the Society for Prevention Research (SPR) convened a task force to consider ways to bring evidence-based programs to scale in each of the five public systems mentioned. The rationale for doing so is perhaps obvious, but so it does not go unstated, bringing effective programs to scale in public systems has great potential to support population health.

The SPR task force identified specific factors that affect the scale-up of EBPs in public systems. One key factor is "statutory endorsement," which includes laws and regulations supporting the use of EBPs, and the flexibility to use funds to support their adoption. In that, the field of SEL has made strides, with 18 states (and counting) having adopted policies that indicate what social and emotional competencies students should know and be able to demonstrate (Dusenbury, Yoder, Dermody, & Weissberg, 2020). Another critical component to scaling effectively includes what the task force described as "data monitoring and evaluation capacity." That includes the routine collection of data on implementation and the outcomes EBPs are expected to produce and the use of those data to engage in practice improvements.

What should be assessed? In my view, educators will ideally assess SEL program implementation, student social and emotional competence, and climate. *Implementation* refers to the extent to which educators are using an SEL program as intended, and with sufficient intensity and quality. *Student competence* refers to the social and emotional knowledge, skills, and dispositions that are the targets of instruction in SEL programs, and that are described by the Collaborative for Academic Social and Emotional Learning (*www.casel.org*). *Climate* refers to the conditions of learning as students perceive it, and includes things like how safe students feel, how connected they feel to adults and peers, and how supported they feel as learners (Thapa, Cohen, Guffey, & Higgins-D'Alessandro, 2013). By assessing these three elements, educators can know what adults are doing, and how those actions are affecting student competencies and the conditions of learning. Assessing program implementation helps educators direct support for high-quality program use where it is needed most. Assessing student social and emotional competence early in the year can help guide what to teach to whom; assessing competence after a period of instruction can quantify growth. Similarly, assessing climate can help adults take actions to create a warm and inclusive learning environment, and monitor whether those actions are improving the climate.

In practice, what might an assessment system look like that reflects the kind of data monitoring and evaluation needed to support SEL at scale? My colleagues and I have developed one such system. We started by developing SELweb, a performance-based direct assessment of student social and emotional competencies for the elementary grades (McKown, Allen, Russo-Ponsaran, & Johnson, 2013). SELweb is a nationally normed web-based application that includes illustrated and narrated media that takes about 30 minutes for children to complete. Children interact with a series of tasks in which they demonstrate their ability to read others' feelings and perspectives, to solve social problems, and to manage their emotions. It is not a traditional self-report survey in which children rate their own competencies—rather, by using performance tasks, children have to show what they know and understand. Educators use SELweb to benchmark skills early in the year, make decisions about SEL instruction, and measure progress after a period of instruction.

Recognizing that a complete data-monitoring and evaluation system requires more than student competence assessment, we recently added a brief student climate survey measuring students' perceptions of safety, belonging, and instructional support. In addition, we added a brief teacher SEL program adherence survey to measure program implementation. SELweb is designed to measure dimensions of competence that are commonly the targets of instruction in SEL programs, and so it reflects a program-agnostic approach to measurement. Districts can flexibly adopt the assessment components that meet their needs, and can measure implementation, competence, and climate within a simple and unified assessment and reporting system.

SELweb, and other emerging SEL assessment systems (Assessment Work Group, 2019; Thapa et al., 2013), give hope that if the field moves fast, it can maintain the kind of commitment to data that elevated it to prominence in the first place, as reflected in meta-analyses and the studies they summarized (Durlak et al., 2011; Mahoney et al., 2019). This time, however, assessment data are not gathered and presented to establish initial evidence of efficacy (see meta-analyses). Instead, assessment data collection and use becomes an integral part of SEL program use—educators use assessment data to benchmark student competence and climate, to decide what to do to foster student competencies and create a positive climate, to monitor what teachers are doing so that coaching resources can be deployed based on need, and to measure change in student competence and climate. By intentionally collecting and reviewing strategically selected assessment data, educational decision makers—from superintendents to classroom teachers—have information about what is happening, how well it is happening, and what outcomes are associated with these activities. The regular availability of assessment data supports cycles of reflection and practice improvement.

The field of SEL will benefit greatly from adopting usable and feasible methods to measure SEL program implementation and the social–emotional competencies and dimensions and climate factors those programs are intended to influence. Building on educational traditions of data use, what if the field of SEL could measure SEL program implementation and outcomes? What would happen if policymakers, educators, and program developers committed to implementing assessment systems to support high-quality SEL program implementation? What might that look like? What should be assessed? How should the data be used? Next, I consider two models for the SEL field to consider. The first model, improvement science, is a method of conducting cycles of assessment, reflection, and action to address locally defined programs of practice. The second, positive behavioral interventions and supports, or PBIS, is a school-based systems intervention designed to support reductions in problem behaviors and increases in positive behaviors. Notably, PBIS integrates assessment and reflection on data to continuously improve practice.

Model 1: Improvement Science

What It Is

Improvement science (Bryk, Gomez, Grunow, & LeMahieu, 2017) offers a helpful framework for considering how assessment data might be used to support the healthy evolution of the field. This framework makes several important assumptions about systems change that can be instructive to efforts to scale up SEL. First, it assumes that systems change requires a strong understanding of the system, its routines, work processes, resources, and demands. Second, it assumes that to succeed in efforts to change systems requires input from the participants in the system. Third, it implies that systems change is essentially a locally managed phenomenon—in the case of scaling SEL, for example, the needs and pressures in which the SEL initiative is to be executed will vary from district to district and school to school. From an implementation science perspective, to succeed, local needs must be understood, accounted for, and addressed. Fourth, it assumes that successful change efforts will create and use a model or theory of the factors that need to be addressed to produce change in work processes (such as SEL implementation) and the outcomes they produce (such as student social and emotional competence). Finally, improvement science assumes that those in the system, in collaboration with experts in the field and others, should use data to monitor intended (and unintended) changes in work processes and the outcomes they are designed to produce. Data should be regularly collected to show successes and failures. Failures are acceptable as long as they guide modifications to the systems change effort and continued testing of those efforts. Improvement science is a way to clearly define local problems of practice and develop a rigorous plan for iteratively testing and evaluating approaches to solving the problem. A key premise of implementation science is that by developing work processes focused on data-informed cycles of practice improvement, positive systems change is more likely to take root.

What the Field of SEL Can Learn

What can those of us who want to see SEL scale with quality learn from improvement science? First, understanding what problem SEL programs solve for educators—from the point of view of educators—is key. When, for example, educators see an SEL program as a compliance requirement handed down from district leadership or beyond, the level of motivation and interest in implementation may be different than when they see an SEL program as a core element of their professional identities and a central driver of student success. An improvement science perspective might therefore suggest that success at scale requires us to assess and address educators' level and kind of motivation to adopt SEL programs.

Second, improvement science suggests that it is important to understand and account for local contexts, particularly the resources, work processes, and pressures endemic to a particular setting. For example, a district that has launched several new curricular initiatives may be at a different level of readiness to implement an SEL program than one that has been studying SEL, socializing its work force, and otherwise preparing to launch for 2 years. A district that has well-established data systems may be in a better position to use SEL assessment to support implementation than one that is grappling with data use. Broadly, therefore, an improvement science perspective might lead us to systematically assess readiness, capacity, and competing pressures within a district and plan implementation in a way that accommodates these factors. Such an assessment would ideally lead to a theory of the key drivers that influence the degree to which SEL programs can be successfully and deeply integrated into practice.

Third, an improvement science perspective suggests that the formulation of key drivers should guide targeted efforts to change the system. For example, a district might identify the following drivers of consistent high-quality SEL program implementation: (1) principal leadership and advocacy for SEL programs, (2) teacher skill in teaching the curriculum,

(3) teacher belief that SEL is important, (4) time for planning and instruction, and (5) teachers' own social and emotional wellness. Each of these hypothesized drivers has constituent elements that can be easily operationalized and measured. For example, teacher social and emotional wellness might include: (1) teachers' level of job-related burnout, (2) teachers' stress-management knowledge and skill, and (3) perceived support from principals. District leadership might decide that this is the most important driver to focus on and that they will invest in teacher wellness workshops and supporting positive teacher–principal relationships. The broad hypothesis might be that improvements in teacher wellness will lead to increased belief that SEL is important, paving the way for implementation.

Fourth, improvement science suggests that a district's hypotheses about the drivers are testable and therefore possibly wrong, and the district's decision to focus on a particular driver is an experiment. To test and refine the district's strategy requires assessment related to the strategy in question. In this case, that might involve assessing: (1) attendance at wellness workshops, (2) teacher ratings of workshop quality, (3) teacher and principal ratings of whatever intervention is designed to improve teacher–principal relationships, (4) teacher wellness as defined above, and (5) teacher beliefs about the importance of SEL. These data would be gathered at the onset of the initiative and frequently enough throughout to monitor what is happening, how well it is going, and whether the key outcome of interest (teacher attitudes about SEL) are moving in response. Where the data suggest that something is not working, this might precipitate a change in strategy.

Note that the above example did not include any assessment of student social and emotional competence. This highlights the importance of considering multiple forms of SEL assessment that can accomplish a variety of goals, all in service to consistent and high-quality programs. Student competence assessment is a key tool in that portfolio, along with measures of classroom practices. From an improvement science perspective, classroom practice is a key hypothesized driver of growth in student social and emotional competence. To test this hypothesis would require measuring program implementation *and* the student outcomes the program is hypothesized to produce using assessments such as SELweb.

Limitations

Improvement science does not provide a perfect solution to SEL's problem of scale. First, improvement science is designed to solve local problems of practice that are largely defined in the field. In this chapter, we presume *a priori* that implementing SEL programs consistently and well is a relevant problem of practice across many educational settings. In addition, improvement science appears to require a level of expertise, intellectual dexterity, and institutional culture that may be difficult to implement in practice without first engaging in significant systems change initiatives to accommodate the methods and habits of improvement science themselves. In light of these two limitations, it may be useful to consider models of continuous improvement that are more prescriptive and therefore may be easier for school districts to adopt and successfully implement. We consider one such model next.

Model 2: Positive Behavioral Interventions and Supports

What It Is

Positive behavioral interventions and supports, or PBIS, is a form of systems intervention that is adjacent to and complements SEL programs (*www.pbis.org*). PBIS is a system of daily practices and strategies aimed at setting clear positive behavioral expectations, reinforcing positive behaviors, and dealing constructively with behavioral infractions. The aim of PBIS is to improve student behavior, academic outcomes, and school climate, and reduce punitive disciplinary practices. From its inception, PBIS has integrated regular assessment data collection and review as a part of PBIS itself. Assessment elements that are routinely collected as part of PBIS include implementation data to understand how PBIS practices are being executed and student outcome data to understand the impact of those practices on behavioral and other outcomes. In addition, PBIS provides guidance about creating school-based teams to review and make decisions based on assessment data. Built into the PBIS practice model, therefore, are guidelines about what kinds of assessment data to collect to support practice, who to convene to collect and review those data, and how to structure teams and meetings to make data-based practice decisions.

One of the benefits of integrating assessment with PBIS is that we have a rich body of evidence about (1) supports required to obtain implementation fidelity (Barrett, Bradshaw, & Lewis-Palmer, 2008), (2) the impact of implementation on behavioral and other outcomes (Bradshaw, Mitchell, & Leaf, 2010), and (3) the impact and benefits of PBIS implementation on the organizational climate of schools (Bradshaw, Koth, Bevans, Ialongo, & Leaf, 2008). The published literature suggests that when PBIS is well implemented, it results in improved student behavior and reductions in disciplinary referrals (Bradshaw et al., 2010), improved climate (Bradshaw et al., 2008), and sometimes improved academic outcomes (Bradshaw et al., 2010). Those conclusions are helpful to decision makers who are considering adopting PBIS—they can weigh high-quality evidence of its impact in deciding whether it is right for them. This body of evidence is equivalent to meta-analyses of SEL programs, and the studies they summarize.

By integrating assessment into practice, PBIS continues its commitment to rooting practices in data. Integrating assessment with PBIS practice drastically reduces the chances that PBIS will be conflated with ineffective practices, or that watered down PBIS will lead to the incorrect blanket conclusion that PBIS does not work. Deeply integrated intentional assessment and data review practices reduce the chances that PBIS will fall prey to the "fidget spinner effect." This is because PBIS practices and outcomes are well-measured, so it is much less likely that an ineffective practice or poorly implemented PBIS will be confused with a potent form of PBIS. For example, if PBIS were implemented in an elementary school and the PBIS team, in reviewing implementation and student outcome data, learned that implementation was inconsistent and that student outcomes were not moving in the right direction, they would have a basis for supporting changes in adult practice, a way to measure progress as adults adopted new ways of doing PBIS, and a way to see whether student outcomes were moving in the right direction. In short, the PBIS team and their colleagues at this school would be able to tell how well they were "doing PBIS," what difference it was making, and whether changes in adult behavior were in order.

In addition, the continual use of data means that the field—including educators and scientists—will have useful information about how much and how well PBIS is practiced and how that changes student outcomes. When implementation is low or inconsistent, or outcomes are not moving in the right direction, this provides opportunities for reflection to diagnose the problem and approach intervention in new ways designed to improve practices and their downstream benefits to students. Integrating data systems into PBIS has supported a healthy growth and evolution of the field.

What the Field of SEL Can Learn

PBIS as a field of practice has integrated the kind of data surveillance systems that prevention scientists and others have identified as crucial to bringing effective interventions to scale while maintaining fidelity and impact. Because the target of PBIS is behaviors that are adjacent to, and overlap, the kinds of outcomes SEL programs seek to influence, it may therefore serve as an important model for integrating SEL assessment and its use into the practice of SEL. PBIS therefore has several important guideposts for the field of SEL.

First, the PBIS practice model is clear about what kinds of assessment data to collect, in ways that can be helpful to the field of SEL. PBIS practices include assessing (1) implementation, which includes what and how well PBIS practices are being put into practice, (2) climate, which involves student and teacher perceptions of the conditions of learning such as sense of safety and connectedness, and (3) student outcomes, including administrative data reflecting disciplinary practices such as office discipline referrals. Although the goals and tactics used in SEL programs are distinct from PBIS, as I have suggested earlier, these general forms of assessment data stand to support the field of SEL in the same manner and magnitude that they support the field of PBIS. PBIS therefore provides a model of the *kinds* of assessments that might be helpful. SELweb and the associated measures of climate and program implementation include these elements, with the goal of providing the kind of data educators can use to reflect on what they are doing, and how it is affecting changes in student competence and the school climate. In creating a system that integrates measures of implementation, student competence, and climate, we hope to support the field of SEL in the ways that PBIS's integrated assessment practice supports high-quality PBIS.

Second, PBIS provides a model of *how* assessment data can be used effectively to support practice. Specifically, PBIS has developed a specific model for data use called "team-initiated problem solving." This involves a standardized process of problem identification, goal clarification, solution generation and evaluation, implementation monitoring, and impact evaluation. This fits nicely into the response to intervention (RTI) approach to special education (*www.pbis.org/pbis/tiered-framework*). To support PBIS educators in implementing this system, free resources are available such as meeting agenda templates and other guidance (e.g., *www.pbis.org/ resource/tips-meeting-minutes-template*). Like the PBIS assessment, the Behavioral Incident Report System (BIRS), described by Fox, Veguilla, and Hemmeter (Chapter 8, this volume), offers a system for early childhood settings for assessing and addressing student behavior problems in a continuous improvement framework.

The field of SEL, in contrast, does not have a model of data review to guide educators in using whatever SEL assessment data they collect to make decisions, although some efforts have been made to articulate such a model (McKown, 2019a). A key lesson from PBIS, therefore, is that, beyond the kinds of SEL assessment data that are collected, for educators to use SEL assessment data constructively, they will benefit from support to develop an effective process for reviewing, reflecting on, and making decisions based on assessment data. Educators who use our teacher implementation survey, SELweb, and the student climate survey largely follow the PBIS way. That is, they assess periodically, review the data in teams, identify points to celebrate and areas of concern (in adult practices, climate, and student competence), and make specific plans intended to build on strengths and address needs. After a period of implementation, they reassess to see how student competence and climate are changing. They may also reassess teacher implementation to see how things have changed. The field of SEL has much to do to develop a robust data-monitoring and evaluation capacity, but such systems are emerging and available to educators who understand how assessment can support effective practices.

Third, the PBIS assessment practice model articulates specific assessment goals. That is, in the PBIS framework, the goal of assessment is to provide the data needed to continuously improve PBIS practices and the impact they are having on the climate and student behavior. This is distinct from other assessment goals such as assessing to determine school quality, diagnose students, or screen and identify students for extra support.[2] The major emphasis of assessment in the PBIS framework is therefore continuous practice improvement. Such a focus places assessment squarely in service to supporting high-quality practice and avoids the potential political pitfalls of using social and behavioral data for accountability purposes. Similarly, and consistent with the recommendations of recent reports (Assessment Work Group, 2019; National Practitioner Advisory Group, 2019), the field of SEL would do well to be clear about the assessment goals that will (and will not) best support consistent and high-quality program implementation. As states adopt standards, it seems likely that SEL assessment will be called on to meet accountability goals. However, in my view, and the view of the Assessment Work Group and National Practitioner Advisory Group, using SEL assessment for accountability purposes poses some risks. If funding and other high stakes are attached to test results, SEL practices and assessment results may become distorted and become a source of resentment and resistance. If, on the other hand, assessment is used to support educators and students to achieve their goals, without the threat of negative consequences, it seems more likely that assessment will be able to fulfill the goal of supporting consistent, high-quality program use.

Limitations

There is a key difference between PBIS and SEL. Specifically, PBIS is a flexible set of principles and practices that can be adapted to the realities of different schools and districts. In contrast, SEL includes a loose confederation, bound by evidence of efficacy and the goal of promoting student social and emotional competence, of programs that are provided by different companies, program providers, nonprofits, and universities. Although there is some overlap between programs, each is somewhat distinct in terms of instructional approach, method, content focus, and intended outcomes. Because of this, from one program to another, what constitutes high-quality implementation, and the expected impact on climate and specific student outcomes, may not be the same. If the field of SEL were to adopt an

---

[2]Note, however, that one component of PBIS practice does involve screening and identification of students who need extra support.

assessment practice model akin to that of PBIS, then an important issue to resolve would be the extent to which a single assessment system (combining assessment tools and data use practices) could support the diversity of program types. At one extreme lies a single program-agnostic assessment system designed to measure implementation, student competence, and climate regardless of the specific SEL program in use. At the other extreme, each program would need a specific and distinct set of assessments to measure implementation, competence, and climate. Given the large number of SEL programs in the field, it is important to work out how best to develop, integrate, or adopt assessments and data use practices to support the field.

• A Vision for Assessment Integrated with SEL

A key premise of this chapter is that high-quality assessment is necessary for evidence-based SEL programs to successfully go to scale. In this case, success means that massively adopted SEL programs continue to measurably benefit student outcomes. Improvement scientists recognize the importance of assessment and evaluation systems to monitoring the implementation and impact of evidence-based programs as they go to scale. Improvement scientists recognize the importance of assessment in monitoring the implementation and impact of systems change efforts in schools and other systems. PBIS recognizes the importance of assessment in monitoring the implementation and impact of PBIS. In both cases, the purpose of assessment is to provide feedback to decision makers, including teachers, so they know what is happening and how much difference it is making. In these instances, the point of assessment is to provide data that decision makers can use to make decisions about how to modify and improve practice and the outcomes it is intended to produce.

Building on the good work that has been done to develop social and emotional competence and climate assessments, what would an assessment system look like that can support SEL at scale? What should it measure? How should educators use the assessment data? What purpose should SEL assessment serve that is valuable to educators and the field? We have described our assessments, and they serve as one example of what such a system might look like. More specifically, next, I develop a vision for the elements of an SEL assessment system that could serve to support the health of the SEL enterprise.

Data Elements

As I have suggested previously, for SEL assessment to support the field of SEL as it "goes big," two broad kinds of assessment should be assessed in an integrative way, much as it is in PBIS. First, SEL assessment needs to include the measurement of implementation, broadly defined as the extent and quality with which SEL programs are being executed in classrooms and schools. Second, SEL assessment needs to include the measurement of outcomes that SEL programs are intended to produce, including improvements in student social and emotional competence and improvements in school climate.

Intended Uses

What should the goal of SEL assessment be? How should assessment data be used? How should they not be used? The goal of SEL assessment is to provide information to decision makers—from superintendents to teachers—about SEL programs and key outcomes so that they can make decisions about how to support consistent, high-quality programs, and the positive outcomes those programs are intended to nurture. A superintendent or principal, for example, might use implementation data to identify schools or classrooms with low-frequency implementation and then guide coaching resources to those settings to support greater implementation. Pairing implementation and outcome data can provide important information about the extent to which engaging in SEL programs is associated with improvements in student competencies and climate in ways that suggest the program is working. The broad goal of SEL assessment is therefore continuous improvement— the use of data gathered at strategic points in the year to guide consistent, high-quality SEL program implementation to produce positive student outcomes. The goal of SEL assessment is *not* to measure school quality, to evaluate teacher performance, or to screen, diagnose, or label students.

Technical Requirements

What technical properties should these assessments have? It is beyond the scope of this chapter to offer an in-depth treatment of psychometrics. However, it is important that assessments focused either on implementation or outcomes should have adequate technical properties where *adequate* means that the evidence of the assessments' score reliability, internal structure, association with other variables, and the like support their intended uses (Kane, 2013; McKown, 2019a). Imagine, for example, that a district opts to measure SEL implementation through a quarterly teacher survey asking teachers to report how many SEL lessons they taught, and how well the lessons went. To be confident in such an assessment, it would be helpful to have evidence that scores on this assessment are associated with other implementation assessments such as direct observation. Alternatively, it would help to know how strongly scores on the implementation assessment are associated with student outcomes such that higher teacher-reported implementation is associated with greater improvement in student social and emotional competencies.

Assessment Requirements

Implementing any initiative at scale is hard. That includes SEL assessment. Several things need to be true for SEL assessment to stand a reasonable chance of being used in the field. Assessments must be usable and feasible to administer. *Usable* means that with minimal or no training, an educator can administer an assessment and produce usable data in an informative reporting format. For example, a Web-based assessment is most usable if it offers single sign-on and is integrated with a district's data-management system. Scoring and reporting is most usable if it is automated and does not require toilsome hand scoring. *Feasible* means that administering the assessment and using the assessment data can be accomplished within the resource constraints of the school. A particularly important resource is time. For example, an assessment should consume as little instructional or planning time as possible. Similarly, data use meetings, to the extent possible, should be incorporated into existing standing meetings so that no additional time needs to be "found."

Practice Model

Beyond these minimal, though critical, practice requirements, what elements of an assessment practice model should any SEL continuous improvement system incorporate? This may differ somewhat by what is being assessed. Ideally, implementation, for example, will be assessed frequently enough to guide resources to support consistent and high-quality SEL programs. Too long an interval between assessments allows variation in consistency and quality across classrooms to persist. Too short an interval taxes the system. Assessment of outcomes might be done in the fall and again after a period of instruction. Armed with assessment data on student competence, educators can decide what social and emotional competencies to emphasize; with assessment data on climate, educators can decide what adult practices they might deploy to improve upon the conditions of learning. Initial assessment therefore serves a formative purpose, guiding resources and instruction to build on strengths and address needs. Assessing competence and climate after a period of instruction provides summative information about student progress in response to instruction. Interim assessments may serve as a mid-point check to see if things are moving in the desired direction and to make adjustments as needed based on assessment findings.

Program-Agnostic or Program-Specific?

One of the questions raised earlier in this chapter concerned the extent to which a single set of SEL assessments can provide equally useful and relevant data regardless of the specific SEL program under consideration. Some might argue that each program is sufficiently unique that the way implementation is measured should be tailored to each program. Similarly, the intended student outcome or dimension of school climate might vary some from one SEL program to another, and so the outcome measures need to be specific to each program. The unfortunate consequence of this line of reasoning is that it would require a vast array of assessment tools that vary slightly in emphasis. Developing technically sound assessments is a costly proposition. As a result, creating separate assessments for each program will mean that inadequate resources may be invested in each, resulting in variable quality at best. Even if quality were not an issue, separate assessments for each program will result in difficulty comparing implementation quality and outcomes from one program to another. Furthermore, SEL program developers generally do not offer assessments along with their curricular or programmatic resources. Indeed, they may have a perverse incentive not to do so, as assessment might demonstrate that their program is not effective, placing them at a competitive disadvantage. As a result, it seems highly unlikely that program developers will be in a position to develop the kinds of high-quality assessments the field requires.

For many reasons, then, it seems desirable that the field develop a flexible suite of program-agnostic SEL assessments akin to those integrated into PBIS. Such a system would offer usable and feasible assessments focused on implementation, climate, and competence that can be used in conjunction with any SEL program. Ideally, such a system would offer flexibility within structure, so that district decision makers might customize, to a degree, how and what they assess, while maintaining core assessment elements in every setting. Many forces would have to converge to realize such a vision. Nevertheless, were the policy context to support this general proposition, and sufficient funding available to support its development and implementation, this is an achievable vision. In fact, it would not require a whole-cloth invention of assessments, but could conceivably involve integrating or adapting the best available assessment tools into a single delivery system optimized for usability and feasibility.

Data Use Practices

Assessment tools themselves cannot benefit instruction or student outcomes unless educators review and reflect on assessment results, and make decisions about resources and instruction based on what they learn. In other words, data use practices are an essential element of assessment to support SEL program use. It is beyond the scope of this chapter to describe effective data use practices in depth. However, key elements include (1) leadership support for data use, (2) a shared understanding of what decisions will be made based on the assessment results, (3) a shared understanding of the meaning of assessment scores and reports, (4) access by decision makers to the assessment data, (5) opportunities to reflect on the meaning of the data independently, (6) regular time to meet for data review, and (7) structured group discussion of assessment results that includes reviewing the facts, interpreting their meaning, and developing a plan of action (McKown, 2019a). Data use in schools varies tremendously from district to district and depends on a number of factors, including access to data, leadership, norms, routines, and time (Coburn & Turner, 2011; McKown, 2019b). To the extent that integrated SEL assessment systems can also provide guidance for data use, much in the way PBIS does, this will lower barriers to effective data use.

• Pipe Dream or Possible?

One might reasonably ask whether the vision of an SEL assessment system designed to support ongoing SEL programs and impact is attainable. After all, assessment development is costly, and adding yet another administrative and assessment burden to school systems that are already brimming with regulatory obligations seems like a hard sell. The easiest path—in fact, the default position of the field—is that we should focus on programs, and that assessment is a luxury item to be used as time, interest, and resources permit. In short, the default position is to skip assessment altogether and operate under the assumption that if a program is evidence-based, it will continue to produce positive outcomes at scale.

The default position is risky. If educators do not assess the use of programs, and the outcomes they are intended to produce, the field will be susceptible to the "fidget spinner effect" described earlier in the chapter— all manner of ineffective activities will be ready to co-opt the label "SEL" while it is a hot topic and word will eventually spread (incorrectly) that SEL includes weak and faddish programs and/or the little evidence that is collected will demonstrate that it does not work. And that will mark the beginning of the end of the field of SEL. So the question ought not to be, can we afford to develop and integrate SEL assessment with SEL programs? It ought to be, can we afford not to do so? I believe the answer is that in the short run, we can; but soon, the field will pay a heavy price and be overrun by some new educational fad.

It is heartening that there are examples of educators integrating SEL assessment in programming to support consistent and high-quality program use (see McKown & Herman, 2020). The Wisconsin Department of Public Instruction, for example, has adopted social and emotional standards and is providing districts with resources to identify programs *and* competence assessments targeting the competencies in its standards. The CORE districts in California use social and emotional assessments—in this case self-reported student competence—as part of ongoing school improvement efforts. And forward-thinking school districts are using our direct assessment of student competencies, often in conjunction with implementation and climate assessment, to shine a light on the use of SEL programs, and the outcomes those programs are intended to produce. In those districts, educators benchmark competence and climate early to guide practice; they then monitor implementation and provide support as needed; and they then reassess competence and climate to measure change.

There are important questions about the level at which SEL assessment should be adopted and used to guide practice. At one extreme, although it is unlikely, one could imagine a national SEL assessment program. At another, one could imagine teachers deciding whether and how to assess SEL. It is difficult to imagine a national SEL assessment program that would be sensitive to local district needs. At the other extreme, it is difficult to imagine assessment data would be broadly useful if selected by individual teachers. States may play a role in guiding districts by, for example, providing guidance on what to assess and a range of options for how to assess those things. In our work, we have found that districts vary in their needs and their readiness to adopt SEL programs and SEL assessment to support program use. It therefore seems sensible to focus on statewide guidance for local decision making about SEL assessments and their uses (McKown & Herman, 2020). Ultimately, this is an important issue for the field and for policymakers to take up.

The assessment practice examples cited above speak to an appetite for assessment, and a broadly shared instinct that SEL assessment can support program use. However, there are some natural limits on what is possible in the current context. First, the field of SEL assessment, like the field of SEL programs, is a loose confederation of organizations each offering somewhat different assessment systems, each suited to achieving somewhat distinct assessment goals. Second, some assessment providers focus on student competence and some focus on climate, but very few focus on both, and very few also offer measures of implementation. Third, and perhaps obviously from the foregoing, few assessment systems measure program implementation, student competence, and climate in the ways that are needed to support consistently high-quality SEL programs at scale.

If there is broad agreement that high-quality assessment data are important for the field's health, longevity, and impact, the big question is, what would need to change to facilitate the integration of usable, feasible, program-agnostic assessments that measure implementation and outcomes? McKown and Herman (2020) described conditions that can support the use of SEL assessment to improve program use. Key among their recommendations were policies that incentivize the use of SEL assessment, that guide the manner of their use, and that support educators in using SEL assessment data to guide the consistent and high-quality execution of evidence-based programs. In answer to the question of whether the vision of integrating SEL assessment into programs in the way that PBIS has is a pipe dream or is possible, the answer depends, in this as in many things, on whether educators and policymakers can muster the will and foresight to invest in and support an unglamorous but foundational support for maintaining quality at scale. Perhaps visions of fidget spinners shimmering in classrooms across the heartland will motivate the field toward a commitment to systematic and ongoing assessment, so that hard-won evidence-based programs are not undermined by the encroachment of ineffective programs, be they fidget spinners or otherwise.

REFERENCES

Assessment Work Group. (2019). *Student social and emotional competence assessment: The current state of the field and a vision for its future.* Collaborative for Academic Social and Emotional Learning.

Atwell, M., & Bridgeland, J. (2019). *Ready to lead: A 2019 update of principals' perspectives on how social and emotional learning can prepare children and transform schools.* Civic Enterprises.

Barrett, S. B., Bradshaw, C. P., & Lewis-Palmer, T. (2008). Maryland statewide PBIS initiative: Systems, evaluation, and next steps. *Journal of Positive Behavior Interventions, 10,* 105–114.

Bradshaw, C. P., Koth, C. W., Bevans, K. B., Ialongo, N., & Leaf, P. J. (2008). The impact of school-wide positive behavioral interventions and supports (PBIS) on the organizational health of elementary schools. *School Psychology Quarterly, 23,* 462–473.

Bradshaw, C. P., Mitchell, M. M., & Leaf, P. J. (2010). Examining the effects of schoolwide positive behavioral interventions and supports on student outcomes: Results from a randomized controlled effectiveness trial in elementary schools. *Journal of Positive Behavior Interventions, 12,* 133–148.

Bryk, A. S., Gomez, L. M., Grunow, A., & LeMahieu, P. G. (2017). *Learning to improve: How America's schools can get better at getting better.* Harvard University Press.

Coburn, C. E., & Turner, E. O. (2011). Research on data use: A framework and analysis. *Measurement, 9,* 173–206.

Durlak, J. A., Weissberg, R. P., Dymnicki, A. B., Taylor, R. D., & Schellinger, K. B. (2011). The impact of enhancing students' social and emotional learning: A meta-analysis of school-based universal interventions. *Child Development, 82,* 405–432.

Dusenbury, L., Yoder, N., Dermody, C., & Weissberg, R. P. (March, 2020). *An examination of K–12 SEL learning competencies/standards in 18 states.* Collaborative for Academic Social and Emotional Learning. *https://casel.org/wp-content/uploads/2020/03/CSI-Frameworks.pdf.*

Fagan, A. A., Bumbarger, B. K., Barth, R. K., Bradshaw, C. P., Cooper, B. R., Supplee, L. H., & Walker, D. K. (2019). Scaling up evidence-based interventions in U.S. public systems to prevent behavioral health problems: Challenges and opportunities. *Prevention Science, 20,* 1147–1168.

Hamilton, L. S., Doss, C. J., & Steiner, E. D. (2019). *Teacher and principal perspectives on social and emotional learning in America's schools: Findings from the American educator panels.* RAND Corporation.

Hamre, B. K., & Pianta, R. C. (2001). Early teacher–child relationships and the trajectory of children's school outcomes through eighth grade. *Child Development, 72,* 625–638.

Jones, S., Bailey, R., Brush, K., & Kahn, J. (2017). *Kernels of practice for SEL: Low-cost, low-burden strategies.* Harvard University EASEL Lab.

Kane, M. T. (2013). Validating the interpretation and uses of test scores. *Journal of Educational Measurement, 50,* 1–73.

Mahoney, J. L., Durlak, J. R., & Weissberg, R. P. (2019). An update on social and emotional learning outcome research. *Kappan, 100,* 18–23.

McKown, C. (2017). Social-emotional assessment, performance, and standards. *The Future of Children, 27,* 157–178.

McKown, C. (2019a). *Assessing students' social and emotional learning: A guide to meaningful measurement.* Norton.

McKown, C. (2019b). Challenges and opportunities in the applied assessment of student social and emotional learning. *Educational Psychologist, 54,* 205–221.

McKown, C., Allen, A. A., Russo-Ponsaran, N. M., & Johnson, J. K. (2013). Direct assessment of children's social-emotional comprehension. *Psychological Assessment, 25,* 1154–1166.

McKown, C., & Herman, B. A. (2020). *SEL assessment to support positive social and emotional development.* The Pennsylvania State University.

National Practitioner Advisory Group. (2019). *Making SEL assessment work: Ten practitioner beliefs.* Collaborative for Academic Social and Emotional Learning. Available at *https://measuringsel.casel.org/wp-content/uploads/2019/09/NPAG.pdf.*

Thapa, A., Cohen, J., Guffey, S., & Higgins-D'Alessandro, A. (2013). A review of school climate research. *Review of Educational Research, 83,* 357–385.

CHAPTER 3

Defining and Measuring Young Children's Social–Emotional Development in Global Contexts

Dana Charles McCoy

Around the world, there is growing emphasis on supporting young children's social–emotional well-being. Global initiatives such as the United Nations' newly ratified Sustainable Development Goals (SDGs) are increasingly moving beyond traditional metrics of survival, physical health, and academic achievement to consider more holistic representations of "developmental potential" during the early childhood period (Black et al., 2017; Izutsu et al., 2015). Indeed, SDG Target 4.2 sets the explicit goal of ensuring that "all girls and boys have access to quality early childhood development," as measured by the proportion of young children who are "developmentally on track" not only in health and learning, but also in psychosocial well-being (United Nations, 2018). Reflecting this political momentum, a diverse range of stakeholders are increasingly prioritizing social and emotional learning (SEL) as part of their day-to-day practice. For example, a number of UN agencies and nongovernmental organizations (NGOs; e.g., Sesame Workshop) have developed explicit programming to encourage the social–emotional well-being of children around the world (Britto et al., 2017; Mares & Pan, 2013).

Despite enthusiasm for supporting young children's psychosocial well-being internationally, concrete guidance regarding how to define and measure social–emotional constructs during early childhood in different parts of the world remains lacking. This chapter introduces several approaches that can be used to conceptualize and measure young children's social–emotional development *within* and *across* diverse cultural contexts in an increasingly global society. The chapter begins with a brief review of key historical approaches and challenges to defining and measuring child development around the world. Next, it describes several core strategies for advancing global social–emotional research and practice into the 21st century. Specifically, this chapter emphasizes approaches necessary to (1) *deepen* understanding of social–emotional skills within as yet unstudied cultural settings, and (2) *widen* understanding of the universality of social–emotional development across diverse cultural contexts. In this chapter, *culture* is defined broadly as a force supporting the "organization of the developmental environment," or the ways in which children relate to their environments and the individuals within them (Super & Harkness, 2002). Although this chapter largely provides motivating examples from the early childhood years, the lessons provided here are intended to generalize to other developmental periods, as well.

● Historical Challenges to Defining and Measuring Developmental Processes Globally

Measuring young children's development has been a priority of researchers and practitioners for more than half a century. Assessments like the Bayley Scales of Infant and Toddler Development, the Ages & Stages Questionnaire, and the Denver Developmental Screening Test were developed in the United States as early as the 1960s to screen infants, toddlers, and preschoolers for early motor, cognitive, and language delays in pediatric settings. Starting in the 1980s, these one-on-one assessments were complemented by caregiver-reported instruments for understanding children's social–emotional and behavior challenges, including the Infant–Toddler Social and Emotional Assessment, the Child Behavior Checklist, and the Strengths and Difficulties Questionnaire. These tools are still used today, and typically focus on children's ability to complete tasks and demonstrate behaviors familiar in Western settings, such as stacking blocks or managing "negative" emotions (e.g., anger).

Despite their intended use as screening tools for Western children, the instruments listed above have been used extensively in international settings to measure normative child development in basic and applied research. Indeed, several recent meta-analyses indicate that the vast majority of early childhood development programs implemented in developing countries have been evaluated using screening tools originally created for high-income country populations (Engle et al., 2011; Nores & Barnett, 2010; Rao, Sun, Chen, & Ip, 2017). This approach is likely to be problematic for a number of reasons. In particular, measures developed and validated in so-called "WEIRD" (Western, Educated, Industrialized, Rich,

Democratic; Henrich, Heine, & Norenzayan, 2010) populations may not meet the criteria for adequacy outlined in the introductory chapter of this volume when they are implemented in different parts of the world or in diverse subgroups. For example, qualitative research has shown that the relevance of social–emotional measures may not be universal, with parents from different cultures reporting a lack of clarity with regard to both the purpose and the content of tools originating in WEIRD settings (Kersten, Dudley, et al., 2016). In turn, the psychometric properties of these assessments may also vary across settings and populations. In a study of the Strengths and Difficulties Questionnaire in low-income areas of Pakistan, for example, caregivers reported that certain concepts in the original measure (e.g., somatic symptoms in the absence of illness) were unfamiliar to them, whereas others (e.g., deviant behaviors like lying or cheating) were not developmentally salient for preschoolers in their communities. Perhaps unsurprisingly given this cultural mismatch, this same study also identified important differences in the validity and reliability of the Strengths and Difficulties Questionnaire in Pakistan relative to other contexts, calling into question the ability of this tool to generalize across settings (Finch, Yousafzai, Rasheed, & Obradović, 2018).

• Deepening Approaches to Consider Context-Specific Learning

The challenges highlighted above have stark implications for the field of SEL, both in terms of our understanding of what social–emotional skills look like and the actions we take to advance them in understudied environments (e.g., low- and middle-income countries, diverse communities in the United States). When engaging in research or practice in a new country, culture, or population, how can we better contextualize the approaches we use to understand and measure young children's social–emotional skills? How might we ensure that these approaches are sensitive to the unique values and priorities within a given setting?

Table 3.1 summarizes three tiered approaches for improving the cultural sensitivity or "contextualization" of social–emotional measurement in a given setting. This set of approaches reflects a growing recognition of the roles that societal norms, expectations, and practices play in informing all aspects of child well-being, ranging from the age at which basic motor milestones are achieved (Cintas, 1989; Hopkins & Westra, 1989; Onis, 2006) to the ways that emotions are socialized, understood, expressed, and regulated (Cole & Tamang, 1998; Cole & Tan, 2015; Garrett-Peters & Fox, 2007). In particular, it highlights the need to consider the role of culture not only in shaping the properties of the specific *measures* that we use, but also the broader *constructs* and *frameworks* that we target through

TABLE 3.1. Culturally Informed Approaches to High-Quality Social–Emotional Research and Practice

Area of consideration	Goal in culturally informed research	Example(s)
Framework	To ensure that the broader conceptual framework used to define social–emotional development is inclusive of all constructs that are valued within a given culture	• Including additional measures of constructs such as respect, religiosity, or community belonging
Construct	To ensure that a given construct of interest is defined according to local cultural perspectives	• Using measures that adhere to a social definition of intelligence, in place of a strictly cognitive one • Setting different expectations for the timing and order of skill acquisition
Measure	To ensure that a given measurement approach includes objects, language, and methods familiar within the culture	• Using an oral rather than written assessment format in cultures with low literacy levels • Using meaningful rather than literal translation of ideas like "temper tantrums" to ensure cultural relevance

this measurement. In other words, this approach to contextualization recognizes the need for work that restructures both our specific assessment tools and our broader way of thinking about and defining social–emotional skills in diverse settings. Below, each of these approaches is described in greater detail, followed by a section outlining the implications of this work and guidance on best practices.

• Contextualizing Frameworks, Constructs, and Measures of Social–Emotional Development

First, at the broadest level, stakeholders interested in understanding social–emotional development should begin by defining a conceptual *framework* for their work that is specific to their target cultural context. This framework should reflect a full list of the social–emotional constructs (skills, challenges, behaviors, etc.) that are considered to be relevant and important in this context. Very little attention has been paid to establishing such frameworks internationally. Rather, as noted above, when selecting social–emotional constructs to measure in research—and, by extension, to target through programming and policy—contemporary academics, practitioners, and other stakeholders (e.g., NGOs) have typically relied on the "transplantation" (Marfo, 2011) of conceptual frameworks from WEIRD settings, including frameworks from the Collaborative for Academic, Social, and Emotional Learning (CASEL) and the Organisation for Economic Co-operation and Development (OECD). Importantly, the cross-cultural validity of these frameworks has not been well established.

Furthermore, many of the existing frameworks for conceptualizing SEL have focused on school-age children, with less consideration for what social–emotional development might look like in the early childhood period. Indeed, the vast majority of the international literature on child development in the infant, toddler, and preschool periods has focused on children's motor, cognitive, and language development (e.g., Engle et al., 2011). In the rare instances where social–emotional constructs have been considered in frameworks of early childhood development, they have typically emphasized more negative behaviors that are commonly assessed in WEIRD contexts. The Child Behavior Checklist and Strengths and Difficulties Questionnaires, for example, are likely the two most commonly used social–emotional measures in international early childhood research, and both focus nearly exclusively on behavior problems related to aggression, inattention, anxiety, and withdrawal (Kersten, Czuba, et al., 2016; Ivanova et al., 2010). In contrast, few developmental frameworks in international settings have explicitly incorporated the more positive social, emotional, and behavioral skills that have been shown in focus groups to be valued by different societies, including young children's sense of belonging, respect for others, creativity, bravery, and independence (McCoy & Fink, 2016; Whiting, 1996). Furthermore, when these positive constructs are considered, they are often positioned exclusively as being relevant to subsequent cognitive or academic outcomes, rather than as also having value in their own right (Heckman & Kautz, 2012). This position is likely a direct product of policies that have been put in place regarding child development in international contexts, including SDG Target 4.2, which explicitly notes its goal of supporting preschool-age children's early health, learning, and psychosocial well-being "so that they are ready for primary education" (United Nations, 2018).

Second, and relatedly, stakeholders interested in measuring social–emotional development in early childhood should pay careful attention to how the particular social–emotional *constructs* in their frameworks are defined in their given setting. In particular, researchers and practitioners should take care to consider local definitions of their chosen constructs, rather than the definitions that have been used in prior research from different settings. Evidence suggests that cultural values help to shape not only what social–emotional behaviors are prioritized in a given setting, but also what these behaviors look like (e.g., Chen et al., 1998; Hopkins & Westra, 1989). Perhaps the most classic example of this issue has to do with how various cultures define "intelligence." In Western settings, intelligence is largely thought of as a cognitive construct and, as such, is typically measured using tasks of nonverbal reasoning (e.g., Raven's Progressive Matrices). However, in certain areas of sub-Saharan Africa, this construct is defined largely in terms of both cognitive alacrity and social responsibility (e.g., familial care) and could therefore also be considered as part of the social–emotional domain (Serpell, 2011). Relatedly, whereas children's regulation of attention, emotions, and behaviors is typically conceptualized as a progressively more independent skill in individualistic societies (i.e., "self-regulation"; Sameroff, 2010), emerging theory suggests that regulation may be better defined as a collective process in contexts that value interdependent decision making (Haslam, Mejia, Thomson, & Betancourt, 2019). Together, these findings highlight the importance of not just naming target constructs within frameworks (e.g., intelligence, regulation), but critically, also providing nuanced and contextualized definitions of these constructs.

Last, careful attention is needed to ensure that the *measures* used to quantify social–emotional development are aligned with the above-described constructs, their definitions, and frameworks, while also being culturally appropriate. One way to ensure this alignment is to develop a new measure for each specific construct and context of interest. Indeed, this "start from scratch" approach may be necessary when the goal of the measurement effort is to understand a construct that does not yet have an established method for assessment. The Acholi Psychosocial Assessment Instrument (APAI), for example, is a measure of northern Ugandan adolescents' psychosocial well-being that was developed to reflect locally generated frameworks and constructs of mental health (*two tam, par, kumu, ma lwor,* and *kwo maraca*; Betancourt et al., 2009). The framework, constructs, and items for the APAI were developed sequentially using in-depth qualitative interviews with adolescents and mental health experts in Uganda. The final tool was then validated using both traditional psychometric approaches (e.g., tests of inter-rater and test–retest reliability), as well as new approaches that are based on nomination of individuals within the community demonstrating symptoms of these mental health challenges (Bolton, 2001).

When attempting to measure more well-established constructs (e.g., aggressive behaviors, social problem solving) in a new context, however, it may be more pragmatic and efficient to "borrow" an existing measure and adapt it to meet the needs of a particular setting. This process of cultural adaptation of measures has been described extensively (e.g., Fernald, Prado, Kariger, & Raikes, 2017; Geisinger, 1994; Hui & Triandis, 1985;

Matafwali & Serpell, 2014). In particular, to ensure that the original inten-tion of the measure is preserved during this adaptation process, Peña (2007) highlighted the need to ensure the following:

1. *linguistic equivalence*, or that the words and language used in the translated measure mean the same thing as those used in the origi-nal version;
2. *functional equivalence*, or that the adapted instrument and its test-ing procedures yield similar results as those in the original version;
3. *cultural equivalence*, or that the measure is interpreted similarly and has similar salience across different cultures; and
4. *metric equivalence*, or that the difficulty of the measure is the same from the original to the adapted version.

There are numerous examples in the academic literature regarding how to adapt social–emotional measures to ensure these various forms of equivalence. For example, Cole and Tamang (1998) used several strate-gies to adapt the Challenging Situations Task—which includes a series of brief vignettes and accompanying line drawings that describe emotionally challenging situations—to help them to understand Nepali children's social problem-solving skills and emotional responses to conflict. To support the cultural equivalence of this task, the researchers updated the original vignettes to focus on situations and materials relevant to the Nepali con-text (e.g., dropping a vignette that focused on a birthday party, amending a vignette that referenced a television). Furthermore, to promote functional equivalence, they conducted formative research to ensure that the standard multiple-choice coding scheme—which forced responses into categories of prosocial, aggressive, manipulative, or avoidant strategies—was appropri-ate in the given setting, making adaptations as needed (Cole & Tamang, 1998).

Although adaptation is common in the social–emotional literature, only a small proportion of studies using adapted measures provide specific documentation of the adaptation process (i.e., what items were changed, how, and why) or the full item- and scale-level psychometric properties of the adapted tools (see the above-described 2018 study of the Strengths and Difficulties Questionnaire in Pakistan by Finch and colleagues for a help-ful exception). Providing such information is strongly recommended, as it allows readers to gauge the quality of the adaptation and its relevance for other settings. Indeed, in the absence of such information, it is impossible to know whether observed cross-contextual differences in social–emotional skills are "real," versus whether they may reflect differences (or flaws) in how the measures are being implemented or interpreted.

● Implications and Best Practices for Contextualization

In sum, to gain a better understanding of children's social and emotional development, stakeholders must move beyond the current practice of adapting *measures* to also consider the adaptation and local generation of larger *constructs* and *frameworks* of social–emotional well-being. Doing so will allow for a clearer and more accurate representation of the abilities and attributes of children living in diverse parts of the world (Miller-Jones, 1989). In particular, building measures that align with the values and priorities of local settings and diverse populations can help us to identify the social–emotional skills that children need to succeed *in their given context*, rather than holding them to a set of external expectations that are not consistent with their day-to-day realities. From a clinical perspective, this focus on context and culture is critical for making judgments regarding the "appropriateness" or "functionality" of children's social–emotional behaviors, and may lead to a more accurate identification and diagnosis of children's social–emotional needs (Canino & Alegría, 2008). Alignment and contextualization of measures, constructs, and frameworks can also support more optimal investments in education and learning. For example, the use of more contextualized approaches in the classroom can help teachers and other practitioners to devote precious time and financial resources toward the particular social and emotional capacities that are most relevant for well-being and learning for a given setting or population. Finally, from a program evaluation perspective, the use of culturally appropriate measures, constructs, and frameworks can support users' ability to precisely and reliably estimate the benefits (or harms) provided by interventions, programs, or policies. In particular, contextualized approaches are likely to be more sensitive to the impacts of locally informed programs whose benefits are meaningful but undetectable by typically used, WEIRD metrics, and may also help to avoid the scale-up of programs that are not benefiting—or potentially even harming—the specific social–emotional outcomes prioritized in local communities (Morelli et al., 2018).

On its own, measurement adaptation is a resource-intensive process, especially for stakeholders aiming to simultaneously accommodate a number of diverse cultures, languages, or subgroups (e.g., immigrants) within their samples. Redefining social–emotional constructs and generating new and more inclusive conceptual frameworks is even more difficult. Such work requires an intimate knowledge of how children develop within a given setting, as well as the practical resources necessary to gather, analyze, and interpret relevant data for decision making. Fernald and colleagues (2017) provided a helpful summary of the multistep (and often iterative) process necessary to contextualize measures for a particular cultural setting, including:

1. *preparatory work* to gather feedback from local experts (e.g., academics, parents, teachers, social workers, policymakers) regarding the developmental norms, expectations, and priorities in the given context, as well as potential candidate measures for exploring targeted constructs;
2. *translation* and back-translation of candidate measures to ensure linguistic and functional equivalence in the local context;
3. *in-depth review* of the content, procedures, and materials used in the measure by local experts to ensure functional, cultural, and metric equivalence;
4. *pilot testing* in local samples of children to examine the measure's psychometric properties (e.g., reliability, validity) in the given context; and
5. *documenting changes* to summarize what adaptations were made and why.

It is important to note that the above best practices are predominantly focused on the process of contextualizing measurement tools themselves. Although Fernald and colleagues acknowledge that a preparatory step should consider input from local experts, specific guidance on how to develop social–emotional frameworks and construct definitions that reflect local norms, expectations, and priorities is lacking. Future work clarifying best practices in this area is particularly needed.

Overall, it is clear that the processes to develop and test social–emotional frameworks, constructs, and measures require extensive financial and time-related investments on the parts of numerous stakeholders. Nevertheless, research suggests that this work is possible, even in the absence of ample resources. The Zambian Child Assessment Test (ZamCAT), for example, is an early childhood development "toolkit" that was adopted in Zambia for use in a national survey. The ZamCAT draws from measures originally developed in the West, but that went through an extensive selection, review, adaptation, and piloting process by local child development experts to ensure their cultural relevance (Fink, Matafwali, Moucheraud, & Zuilkowski, 2012; Matafwali & Serpell, 2014). The resulting tool captures a diversity of social–emotional skills relevant to both the existing child development literature and the Zambian cultural context, including executive function, prosocial, and task orientation skills. This effort— along with a number of others not mentioned here—suggests that locally informed approaches to measuring social–emotional skills are feasible, and may help to both deepen the field's understanding of local imperatives and generate tools that are most likely to detect culturally relevant changes in well-being over time.

● Widening Approaches to Clarify Social–Emotional "Universals"

The above-described process of ensuring cultural specificity of social–emotional frameworks, constructs, and measures can support additional "depth" in our understanding of what social–emotional development looks like *within* a given cultural setting. In the present section I argue the need to complement this work by comparing social–emotional processes *across* a wide range of contexts. The intention of such an approach is to develop a clearer picture regarding the degree to which the social–emotional frameworks and constructs generated in any given setting may be *universal* (i.e., manifest in similar ways around the world), *context-specific*, or somewhere in between.

At present, there is little consensus regarding questions of universality in children's social–emotional skills (Berry, 2002). Some models of child development—particularly those coming from the global health literature—posit that children reach basic social and emotional milestones on relatively similar timelines across cultures and contexts. Although little empirical evidence exists to back this claim, one recent study published in *Nature Communications* found relative consistency in the positive behaviors and affect of more than one thousand "healthy" 2-year-olds from relatively well-off families living across five different countries, concluding that these and other skills were likely "innate and universal, as long as nutritional and health needs are met" (Villar et al., 2019).

Contrasting these models of universality, several decades' worth of literature from cross-cultural psychology has demonstrated that both the timing and frequency of specific developmental behaviors—especially those in the social and emotional domain—are likely to vary meaningfully across cultures. For example, when interviewing children from two different Nepalese cultures (Brahman and Tamang) and the United States, Cole, Bruschi, and Tamang (2002) identified both age- and culturally related differences in the ways that children endorsed and expressed negative emotions such as shame and anger. In general, however, this sort of cross-cultural evidence is limited in several ways. In particular, many of the conclusions about global variability in social–emotional skills has been based on research from small samples that examines relatively extreme comparisons (e.g., contrasting urban, high-income contexts against more isolated, rural, low-income contexts), which may lead researchers to overstate cross-cultural differentiation. Relatedly, as globalization supports the interconnectedness of previously isolated communities and cultures, it is also unclear whether the research that uncovered developmental differences decades ago may still be relevant in modern society.

Collectively, this competing evidence suggests a need for further exploration of children's social–emotional skills across diverse parts of the world.

Doing so can help us to understand which—if any—of these skills may be universal and, in turn, the extent to which we may be able to borrow measures, interventions, and practices across contexts. Historically, a major barrier to this type of exploration has been a lack of available measures for drawing cross-cultural comparisons. Within the past few years, however, new measures have been designed to facilitate comparative research and global monitoring, with a particular eye to SDG Target 4.2 (Gove & Black, 2016; McCoy, Black, Daelmans, & Dua, 2016; Richter et al., 2019). Several of these tools include specific subscales for social–emotional development, including the Inter-American Development Bank's Regional Project on Child Development Indicators (PRIDI), Save the Children's International Development and Early Learning Assessment (IDELA), and the Measuring Early Learning Quality and Outcomes (MELQO) initiative (see Raikes, Chapter 9, this volume) for preschoolers, and the Caregiver-Reported Early Development Instruments (CREDI) and WHO's Infant and Young Children Development (IYCD) indicators for infants and toddlers. Instead of providing a "depth" of knowledge gained by locally derived or contextualized instruments, these tools aim to identify items, constructs, and frameworks of development that are comparable across—and potentially common to—many cultures around the world. They also aim to be relatively inexpensive and easy to implement as a means of facilitating large-scale data collection.

The CREDI, as an illustration of some of the processes described in this chapter, was developed using a multistep process that included expert consultation, an extensive literature review, qualitative interviews with caregivers in six sites, and multiple rounds of pilot testing in more than 15 countries (McCoy, Waldman, Team, & Fink, 2018). In addition to questions targeting children's motor, cognitive, and language skills, the CREDI's Long Form includes a set of 23 items (i.e., questions) related to children's social and emotional skills during the first 3 years of life (Waldman, McCoy, CREDI Field Team, & Fink, 2021). These items are reported by children's caregivers using a simple yes/no/don't know response scale, and are ordered in terms of developmental difficulty (e.g., whereby basic expressions of emotions come before more complex skills like emotion regulation). They cover a diverse range of children's social–emotional behaviors, including involvement in social play, sharing, demonstrations of sympathy, use of greetings, impulsivity, and attention control.

Data from the CREDI and the other instruments listed above offer promise for gaining insight into basic patterns of social–emotional development worldwide. For example, Figures 3.1–3.3 show developmental "trajectories" (i.e., patterns of growth across age) for three social–emotional items that were considered for inclusion in the CREDI based on piloting conducted in Chile, Ghana, and the Philippines. Although for the most part

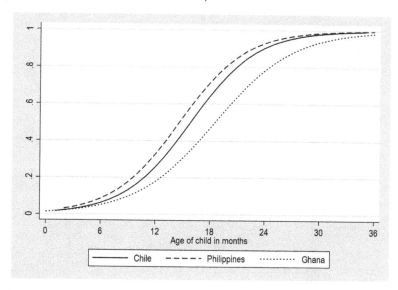

FIGURE 3.1. Proportion of children in the CREDI dataset who were kind to younger children, by age and site.

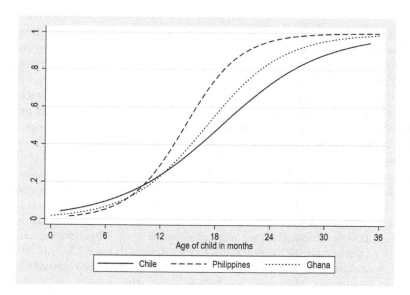

FIGURE 3.2. Proportion of children in the CREDI dataset who followed rules and obeyed adults, by age and site.

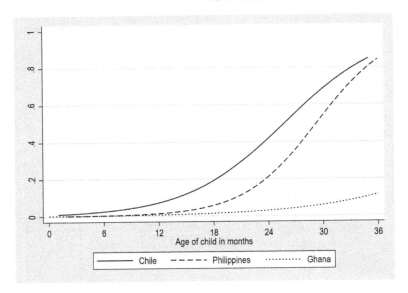

FIGURE 3.3. Proportion of children in the CREDI dataset who could identify how they were feeling emotionally, by age and site.

these trajectories follow the same patterns—with social–emotional skills developing progressively with age—the differences between the trajectories across items and countries are striking. First, in keeping with the cross-cultural literature, the average age of skill attainment for each item differed substantially across sites. Importantly, the setting with the lowest and highest median (average) age differed by item, suggesting that local processes likely inform the timing and order of social–emotional development. In Chile, for example, children followed rules and obeyed adults relatively late (about 2–5 months, on average, after children from Ghana and the Philippines), but identified emotions relatively early (at least 3 months before children from other countries). Second, the rates at which social–emotional skills were attained also varied across sites. In particular, for some sites all children developed particular skills within a relatively short time frame (e.g., a couple of months), whereas in other settings, there was greater variability in when the skills emerged. Compared with their Chilean peers, for example, children in the Filipino sample were initially relatively slow to begin to identify emotions, but by age three, the rates of emotional identification were similar across both countries. Third, the results presented in Figure 3.3 suggest that some milestones may simply be more salient in some settings than in others. Whereas approximately 4 out of 5 children in Chile and the Philippines talked about their emotions by age three, this was true of only about 1 in 10 Ghanaian children. This suggests that children in Chile and the Philippines may be encouraged to recognize and discuss their emotions at an earlier age relative to their peers from Ghana, where emotion socialization practices may differ. (For additional comparisons of social—emotional skills across 10 CREDI country sites, see McCoy, Cuartas, Waldman, & Fink, 2019.)

Collectively, these findings from the CREDI reinforce a theory of social—emotional development that is "universal" without being "uniform" (Mesman et al., 2018). It is clear from these data that the selected social—emotional skills grew predictably with age across all three settings, meaning that their development was somewhat universal. Nevertheless, when and in what order these skills develop appears to vary in different parts of the world. Alone, these curves cannot tell us *why* these social—emotional differences were occurring. Instead, they simply describe the degree to which particular skills may be more universal versus more culturally dependent, generating hypotheses about human development that can be confirmed through further research.

Cross-cultural data examining social—emotional universality are also useful outside of formal research and theory building. For example, when looking to implement a measure or program in a new setting, it may be useful to prioritize evidence-based approaches from contexts that share a similar "developmental profile," rather than attempting to integrate tools or interventions from a setting in which children's patterns of social—emotional development appear to be quite different. Based on the findings from the CREDI highlighted in Figure 3.3, for example, practitioners interested in supporting children's emotion identification skills in the Philippines may want to first see what types of approaches or programs worked in Chile (where patterns of emotion identification look quite similar), rather than what has been used in Ghana (where patterns are quite different).

Several ongoing initiatives are increasingly making large-scale data on children's social—emotional skills publicly available for analysis and comparison across cultures. Cross-national household surveys such as UNICEF's Multiple Indicator Cluster Surveys (MICS) and the Demographic and Household Surveys (DHS), for example, are increasingly incorporating measures of young children's social—emotional skills. In particular, the newly updated Early Childhood Development Index (ECDI2030)—one of the planned indicators to monitor SDG Target 4.2—will be incorporated into most MICS surveys moving forward, and includes a set of five "psychosocial" items reflecting basic emotional and social skills, as well as internalizing and externalizing behaviors. Consistent with increasing trends toward open science, the researchers and organizations responsible for developing tools like the CREDI and the IDELA are also taking steps toward sharing their data with others. Save the Children recently developed an "IDELA Data Explorer" (*data.idela-network.org*), which provides users with easy-to-navigate data summaries from more than 100 IDELA datasets around the world. Such resources can help a variety of stakeholders—including those with limited resources to conduct their own independent data collection—to begin to get a sense of basic patterns of social–emotional development in their own contexts, as well as how these patterns compare with those in other settings.

• Integrating the "Deep" and the "Wide"

Collectively, the above discussion implies a great need in the field of SEL for approaches that *deepen* knowledge regarding the measures, constructs, and frameworks that are most relevant within a given culture, as well as approaches that *widen* understanding of their universality. Such goals do not have to be in competition with one another. As stated by Marfo (2011), a "truly global discipline" is one "in which pursuit of uniquely culture-specific understandings is not antithetical to pursuit of understandings with cross-cultural generality." In particular, measures, constructs, and frameworks developed in one setting can be tested at a global level to determine whether they may be broadly applicable. As noted above, such work is particularly needed in aspects of social–emotional development that are often underemphasized in the traditional (WEIRD) psychological literature, including such concepts as creativity, respect, and social responsibility. In turn, patterns of development identified in large-scale quantitative data collection efforts can generate new hypotheses that can be later confirmed or better understood through more nuanced, "deep" approaches probing how and why social–emotional differences emerge in particular places. Collectively, this complementary set of approaches can support the generation of more contextualized and globalized theories of human development, as well as more targeted and scalable interventions.

• Conclusion

The past decade has seen tremendous advances in social–emotional research, practice, and policy around the world. The ratification of the SDGs and the expansion of programs to support children's holistic development have opened a window of opportunity for stakeholders interested in psychosocial well-being to make a marked difference in the lives of young children (Richter et al., 2017). Nevertheless, despite the fact that 90% of the world's 1.9 billion children live in low- and middle-income countries, less than 7% of the published psychological literature focuses on these contexts (Nielsen, Haun, Kärtner, & Legare, 2017; World Bank, 2019). Furthermore, the metrics typically used in evaluations of global interventions tend to be both outdated and situationally inappropriate. To optimize the evidence base on which critical decisions are made regarding when, where, and how social–emotional development should be prioritized, greater attention is needed toward (1) embedding the measures, constructs, and frameworks used to define and measure social–emotional well-being within specific cultural contexts, and (2) applying these frameworks across diverse settings to understand their flexibility and universality. Doing so in an iterative manner will provide researchers and practitioners with a deeper and broader understanding of the nature of young children's social–emotional development, the specific skills and behaviors to be emphasized within and across settings, and potential strategies for practice and intervention.

REFERENCES

Berry, J. W. (2002). *Cross-cultural psychology: Research and applications.* Cambridge University Press.

Betancourt, T. S., Bass, J., Borisova, I., Neugebauer, R., Speelman, L., Onyango, G., & Bolton, P. (2009). Assessing local instrument reliability and validity: A field-based example from northern Uganda. *Social Psychiatry and Psychiatric Epidemiology, 44*(8), 685–692.

Black, M. M., Walker, S. P., Fernald, L. C., Andersen, C. T., DiGirolamo, A. M., Lu, C., . . . Devercelli, A. E. (2017). Early childhood development coming of age: Science through the life course. *The Lancet, 389*(10064), 77–90.

Bolton, P. (2001). Cross-cultural validity and reliability testing of a standard psychiatric assessment instrument without a gold standard. *The Journal of Nervous and Mental Disease, 189*(4), 238–242.

Britto, P. R., Lye, S. J., Proulx, K., Yousafzai, A. K., Matthews, S. G., Vaivada, T., . . . MacMillan, H. (2017). Nurturing care: Promoting early childhood development. *The Lancet, 389*(10064), 91–102.

Canino, G., & Alegría, M. (2008). Psychiatric diagnosis—Is it universal or relative to culture? *Journal of Child Psychology and Psychiatry, 49*(3), 237–250.

Chen, X., Hastings, P. D., Rubin, K. H., Chen, H., Cen, G., & Stewart, S. L. (1998). Child-rearing attitudes and behavioral inhibition in Chinese and Canadian toddlers: A cross-cultural study. *Developmental Psychology, 34*(4), 677.

Cintas, H. M. (1989). Cross-cultural variation in infant motor development. *Physical & Occupational Therapy in Pediatrics, 8*(4), 1–20.

Cole, P. M., & Tamang, B. L. (1998). Nepali children's ideas about emotional displays in hypothetical challenges. *Developmental Psychology, 34*(4), 640.

Cole, P. M., & Tan, P. Z. (2015). Emotion socialization from a cultural perspective. In J. E. Grusec & P. D. Hastings (Eds.), *Handbook of socialization: Theory and research* (pp. 499–519). Guilford Press.

Cole, P. M., Bruschi, C. J., & Tamang, B. L. (2002). Cultural differences in children's emotional reactions to difficult situations. *Child Development, 73*(3), 983–996.

Engle, P. L., Fernald, L. C., Alderman, H., Behrman, J., O'Gara, C., Yousafzai, A., . . . Iltus, S. (2011). Strategies for reducing inequalities and improving developmental outcomes for young children in low-income and middle-income countries. *The Lancet, 378*(9799), 1339–1353.

Fernald, L. C., Prado, E., Kariger, P., & Raikes, A. (2017). *A toolkit for measuring early childhood development in low and middle-income countries.* World Bank.

Finch, J. E., Yousafzai, A. K., Rasheed, M., & Obradović, J. (2018). Measuring and understanding social-emotional behaviors in preschoolers from rural Pakistan. *PLOS ONE, 13*(11), e0207807.

Fink, G., Matafwali, B., Moucheraud, C., & Zuilkowski, S. S. (2012). *The Zambian Early Childhood Development Project: 2010 Assessment Final Report.* Harvard University.

Garrett-Peters, P. T., & Fox, N. A. (2007). Cross-cultural differences in children's emotional reactions to a disappointing situation. *International Journal of Behavioral Development, 31*(2), 161–169.

Geisinger, K. F. (1994). Cross-cultural normative assessment: Translation and adaptation issues influencing the normative interpretation of assessment instruments. *Psychological Assessment, 6*(4), 304.

Gove, A., & Black, M. M. (2016). Measurement of early childhood development and learning under the Sustainable Development Goals. *Journal of Human Development and Capabilities, 17*(4), 599–605.

Haslam, D., Mejia, A., Thomson, D., & Betancourt, T. (2019). Self-regulation in low-and middle-income countries: Challenges and future directions. *Clinical Child and Family Psychology Review, 22*(1), 104–117.

Heckman, J. J., & Kautz, T. (2012). Hard evidence on soft skills. *Labour Economics, 19*(4), 451–464.

Henrich, J., Heine, S. J., & Norenzayan, A. (2010). The weirdest people in the world? *Behavioral and Brain Sciences, 33*(2–3), 61–83.

Hopkins, B., & Westra, T. (1989). Maternal expectations of their infants' development: Some cultural differences. *Developmental Medicine & Child Neurology, 31*(3), 384–390.

Hui, C. H., & Triandis, H. C. (1985). Measurement in cross-cultural psychology: A review and comparison of strategies. *Journal of Cross-cultural Psychology, 16*(2), 131–152.

Ivanova, M. Y., Achenbach, T. M., Rescorla, L. A., Harder, V. S., Ang, R. P., Bilenberg, N., . . . Verhulst, F. C. (2010). Preschool psychopathology reported by parents in 23 societies: Testing the seven-syndrome model of the child behavior checklist for ages 1.5–5. *Journal of the American Academy of Child & Adolescent Psychiatry, 49*(12), 1215–1224.

Izutsu, T., Tsutsumi, A., Minas, H., Thornicroft, G., Patel, V., & Ito, A. (2015). Mental health and wellbeing in the Sustainable Development Goals. *The Lancet Psychiatry, 2*(12), 1052–1054.

Kersten, P., Czuba, K., McPherson, K., Dudley, M., Elder, H., Tauroa, R., & Vandal, A. (2016). A systematic review of evidence for the psychometric properties of the Strengths and Difficulties Questionnaire. *International Journal of Behavioral Development, 40*(1), 64–75.

Kersten, P., Dudley, M., Nayar, S., Elder, H., Robertson, H., Tauroa, R., & McPherson, K. M. (2016). Cross-cultural acceptability and utility of the strengths and difficulties questionnaire: Views of families. *BMC Psychiatry, 16*(1), 1–9.

Mares, M. L., & Pan, Z. (2013). Effects of *Sesame Street*: A meta-analysis of children's learning in 15 countries. *Journal of Applied Developmental Psychology, 34*(3), 140–151.

Marfo, K. (2011). Envisioning an African child development field. *Child Development Perspectives, 5*(2), 140–147.

Matafwali, B., & Serpell, R. (2014). Design and validation of assessment tests for young children in Zambia. *New Directions for Child and Adolescent Development, 2014*(146), 77–96.

McCoy, D. C., Black, M. M., Daelmans, B., & Dua, T. (2016). Measuring development in children from birth to age 3 at the population level. *Early Childhood Matters, 2016*, 34–39.

McCoy, D. C., Cuartas, J., Waldman, M., & Fink, G. (2019). Contextual variation in young children's acquisition of social-emotional skills. *PLOS ONE, 14*(11).

McCoy, D. C., & Fink, G. (2016). *Qualitative interview results from the Caregiver-Reported Early Development Instruments.* Unpublished raw data.

McCoy, D. C., Waldman, M., Team, C. F., & Fink, G. (2018). Measuring early childhood development at a global scale: Evidence from the Caregiver-Reported Early Development Instruments. *Early Childhood Research Quarterly, 45*, 58–68.

Mesman, J., Minter, T., Angnged, A., Cissé, I. A., Salali, G. D., & Migliano, A. B. (2018). Universality without uniformity: A culturally inclusive approach to sensitive responsiveness in infant caregiving. *Child Development, 89*(3), 837–850.

Miller-Jones, D. (1989). Culture and testing. *American Psychologist, 44*(2), 360–366.

Morelli, G., Bard, K., Chaudhary, N., Gottlieb, A., Keller, H., Murray, M., . . . Vicedo, M. (2018). Bringing the real world into developmental science: A commentary on Weber, Fernald, & Diop (2017). *Child Development, 89*(6), e594–e603.

Nielsen, M., Haun, D., Kärtner, J., & Legare, C. H. (2017). The persistent sampling bias in developmental psychology: A call to action. *Journal of Experimental Child Psychology, 162*, 31–38.

Nores, M., & Barnett, W. S. (2010). Benefits of early childhood interventions across the world: (Under) Investing in the very young. *Economics of Education Review, 29*(2), 271–282.

Onis, M. (2006). Assessment of sex differences and heterogeneity in motor milestone attainment among populations in the WHO Multicentre Growth Reference Study. *Acta Paediatrica, 95*(S450), 66–75.

Peña, E. D. (2007). Lost in translation: Methodological considerations in cross-cultural research. *Child Development, 78*(4), 1255–1264.

Rao, N., Sun, J., Chen, E. E., & Ip, P. (2017). Effectiveness of early childhood interventions in promoting cognitive development in developing countries: A systematic review and meta-analysis. *Hong Kong Journal of Pediatrics (New Series), 22*(1), 14–25.

Richter, L., Black, M., Britto, P., Daelmans, B., Desmond, C., Devercelli, A., . . . Vargas-Barón, E. (2019). Early childhood development: An imperative for action and measurement at scale. *BMJ Global Health, 4*(Suppl. 4), e001302.

Richter, L. M., Daelmans, B., Lombardi, J., Heymann, J., Boo, F. L., Behrman, J. R., . . . Bhutta, Z. A. (2017). Investing in the foundation of sustainable development: Pathways to scale up for early childhood development. *The Lancet, 389*(10064), 103–118.

Sameroff, A. (2010). A unified theory of development: A dialectic integration of nature and nurture. *Child Development, 81*(1), 6–22.

Serpell, R. (2011). Social responsibility as a dimension of intelligence, and as an educational goal: Insights from programmatic research in an African society. *Child Development Perspectives, 5*(2), 126–133.

Super, C. M., & Harkness, S. (2002). Culture structures the environment for development. *Human Development, 45*(4), 270–274.

United Nations. (2018). *Sustainable Development Goal Indicators*. United Nations.

Villar, J., Fernandes, M., Purwar, M., Staines-Urias, E., Di Nicola, P., Ismail, L. C., . . . Kunnawar, N. (2019). Neurodevelopmental milestones and associated behaviours are similar among healthy children across diverse geographical locations. *Nature Communications, 10*(1), 1–10.

Waldman, M., McCoy, D. C., CREDI Field Team, & Fink, G. (2021). Validation of motor, cognitive, language, and socio-emotional subscales using the Caregiver Reported Early Development Instruments: An application of multidimensional item factor analysis. *International Journal of Behavioral Development.*

Whiting, B. B. (1996). The effect of social change on concepts of the good child and good mothering: A study of families in Kenya. *Ethos, 24*(1), 3–35.

World Bank. (2019). *Total population between the ages 0 to 14*. World Bank.

CHAPTER 4

Stress Physiology in Context

On the Measurement and Meaning of Autonomic Nervous System and Hypothalamic–Pituitary–Adrenal Axis Functioning

Keira B. Leneman and Daniel Berry

When observing students in a classroom, there is much more than meets the eye. Their thoughts, emotions, and behaviors are supported by the complex, real-time coordination of multiple physiological systems—operating below the surface to support them as they navigate their ever-changing worlds. Given that these same systems play a crucial role in our abilities to respond to threats in the environment, they're sometimes referred to as physiological "stress" systems. However, managing acute stressors is just one of the many duties that these systems serve. In addition to preparing the brain and body to negotiate an approaching bully or speak publicly in front of a crowd, these systems coordinate neurochemical cascades that facilitate the way we interact with our environment (e.g., teachers and peers), how we attend to these experiences, and the way that we encode and consolidate these experiences for long-term use—in short, how we learn. As such, clarifying normative patterns and individual differences in children's physiological stress-system activity (PSA) provides an important window into the way children adapt to and learn from their experiences at home and school.

In this chapter, we introduce two core physiological stress systems—the autonomic nervous system (ANS), comprised of the sympathetic (SNS) and parasympathetic (PNS) nervous systems, and the hypothalamic–pituitary–adrenal (HPA) axis, along with some of the most common strategies for measuring them. We highlight, in particular, the role of PSA in children's growing capacity to regulate their thoughts, attention, and emotions, as well as the ways these processes are shaped by children's environments and social interactions.

• An Introduction to Primary Physiological Stress Systems

The concept of stress has taken on many definitions over the years. It has been used to refer to many distinct phenomena, including mechanical strain (e.g., from carrying something heavy), psychological distress (e.g., feelings of worry or anxiety), or the activation of our biological stress response systems (e.g., increases in heart rate). In psychology, the word *stressor* is commonly used as a catch-all term for experiences that can be deemed as threatening or challenging. Another way to think about this is as an imbalance between the contextual demands of a situation and our best prediction about our capacity to negotiate those demands (e.g., Blascovich, 1992). For example, consider what a student might be experiencing as she works through a challenging math or comprehension problem in class. Certain factors—for instance, having a good working knowledge of the content, or comfort with the testing format, or even having slept well the night prior—would likely support her inference that the immediate challenge is surmountable (perhaps, even fun!). Yet on a different day—perhaps one in which she forgot to study or had just experienced some peer drama in the hallway—the same level of challenge might lead her to experience the challenge as an overwhelming psychological stressor.

This process is often automatic and unconscious, though it can also be quite volitional. It draws from (1) perceptual information about changes in the external and internal environment (e.g., "We've started an exam; my heart just started pounding; am I excited, scared, both?"); (2) a search of the environment to make meaning of that perceptual information (e.g., "Everyone in class looks anxious, so maybe I'm nervous"); (3) an overall inventory of the individual's resources to manage those perceived demands (e.g., "I know this stuff cold; I don't love failing, but I usually learn from my mistakes; I am dead meat with my parents if I fail"); and (4) an iterative, updating process by which the demands-versus-resources weighting is refined. All of these "data points" are rapidly processed in the brain on a moment-by-moment basis. As the balance tips in favor of resources over demands, one's psychological experiences will tend toward a feeling of appropriate *arousal or engagement*—surmountable challenge. This, in turn, is supported by physiological changes that are roughly commensurate with those required by the change in the environment. In contrast, as the balance tips to favor demands over resources, one's psychological experiences will often tend toward a feeling of overarousal or *stress*—insurmountable challenge or threat—which, in turn, supports a physiological cascade that is aligned with this perceived heightened demand.

While the psychology of stress focuses on the cognitive and emotional experiences of feeling overwhelmed by situational demands, biological perspectives on stress tend to focus on the internal changes in the brain and body that tend to occur in these instances. In particular, biologically focused definitions of stress often center on concepts of *homeostasis* (Cannon, 1929) and *allostasis* (Seeman, McEwen, Rowe, & Singer, 2001). Homeostasis refers to the body's ability to come back to a set baseline level after reacting to challenges or stressors. The idea of allostasis was introduced to highlight the malleable properties of physiological systems—the ability to learn, predict, and reorganize based on our experiences—leading to a more adjustable baseline level, based on experiences and context. A common definition of *allostasis* is "stability through change" (Sterling & Eyer, 1988). The concept of allostasis also shifts the focus from physiological stress as a "bad guy"—something that we turn on to deal with threat and to be otherwise avoided—to an important tool in adjusting to changes in the environment. That is, on the one hand, it is true that our physiological stress systems support our abilities to escape and recover from acute threats (e.g., being chased by a lion) and facilitate the types of memories that keep us awake at night. On the other hand, these same physiological systems are what get us up in the morning and help to organize our attention, motivation, and learning toward particular goals.

The key to understanding the turning point between helpful and unhelpful stress seems to lie in the inverted-U-shaped curve—sometimes called the Yerkes–Dodson principle (see Figure 4.1; Hebb, 1955; Yerkes & Dodson, 1908). This model, also referred to as the "Goldilocks principle," proposes that optimal functioning often occurs at moderate levels of "stress," where physiological responses support the type of alertness and

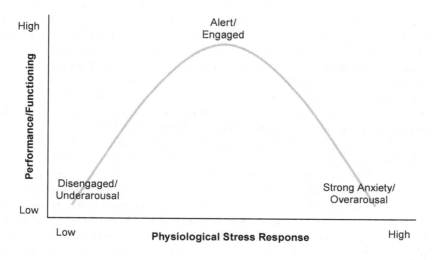

FIGURE 4.1. Hebbian version of the Yerkes–Dodson inverted-U-shaped curve.

engagement required for successful outcomes and performance. In contrast, too little or too much physiological reactivity is thought to undermine performance. This pattern of associations has been demonstrated across many different outcomes, including attention, memory, and cognitive flexibility, with long-term implications for psychopathology (e.g., anxiety and depression). Across this work, a moderate release of primary stress hormones (e.g., cortisol) has been related to enhanced performance, but a very low or very high response has been related to worse functioning (McEwen & Sapolsky, 1995; Salehi, Cordero, & Sandi, 2010; Sapolsky, 2015).

In addition to acute or "real-time" physiological stress activity (PSA), theoretical models of allostasis highlight the importance of considering multiple time scales. Whereas short-lived physiological activation supports real-time adaptive functioning, on longer time scales, allostasis involves our ability to systematically reorganize our psychological and physiological responses in accordance with repeated, systematic changes in environmental demands. When events in one's environment trigger substantial physiological activation repeatedly and chronically over time, it is posited to cause "wear and tear" that increasingly undermine these systems' real-time flexibility. This is called *allostatic (over)load* (Seeman et al., 2001). Indeed, allostatic load has been implicated as one of the key mechanisms through which the chronic exposure to economic adversity (e.g., poverty) and/or psychosocial threat (e.g., abuse), impact children's long-term risk for psychopathology and ill health (see Blair et al., 2011; Cicchetti, 2011; Evans, 2003). By analogy, one might think of allostasis as being like having well-tuned shocks on a car. While driving over a bumpy road, the shocks for each of the car's wheels work together (though often in complex, nonlinear ways) to maintain the overall stability of the car over rough terrain. This minimizes the bumps felt by the driver, as well as wear and tear that these bumps would have otherwise had on the car's body and engine. However, if one drives exclusively on very bumpy roads for extended periods of time, the shocks will eventually lose their cushioning. The driver will feel more of the bumps, and the friction among parts of the car's body and engine will begin to cause physical damage. As the damage increases and spreads, the overall functioning of the vehicle breaks down—allostatic load.

This analogy highlights an important element of allostatic load theories. Enduring bumpy roads for an extended period of time can be thought of as similar to experiencing chronic stress early in life (e.g., poverty, abuse). In the short term, adjustments are made to adapt to these repeated stressors. Like the shocks on a car, physiological systems adjust to meet the demands of the environment. One example of this is the heightened sensitivity to threat cues (Pine et al., 2005). For example, a child that experiences physical abuse hides in a corner after seeing an angry facial expression. This is adaptive in that it allows the child to react more quickly to threats in the environment and more quickly find safety. However, there may be short- and long-term consequences as well. For one, the child may react particularly strongly to something perceived as threatening—for example, another child being mean to him or her—which may escalate problems. Another consequence, aligned with the concept of allostatic load, is that later in life that child may not only develop anxiety or depression, but may also experience physical health consequences of heightened chronic physiological activity, such as cardiovascular disease (Taylor, Way, & Seeman, 2011).

• The ANS and HPA Axis: A Brief Overview

The most commonly referred to and measured physiological stress systems are the ANS and the HPA axis. The ANS is part of the peripheral nervous system and provides the most immediate response to a stressor. It comprises two branches—the PNS and the SNS—which function together to coordinate arousal and regulatory functions (see Figure 4.2).

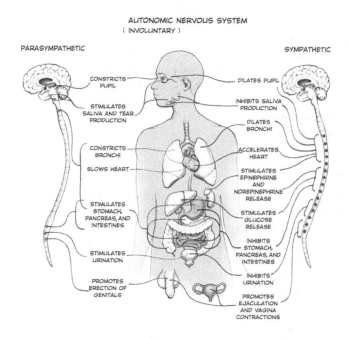

FIGURE 4.2. Parasympathetic (PNS) and sympathetic (SNS) branches of the autonomic nervous system (ANS) work in coordination to maintain allostasis. Image reprinted with permission from Backyard Brains, Inc. (*https://backyardbrains. com/experiments/Sympathetic_Nervous_System*).

The PNS and SNS

True to its nickname as the "rest and digest" system, the PNS supports a range of bodily activities that aid in maintenance and restoration of everyday functioning (see Berntson, Cacioppo, Quigley, & Fabro, 1994; Porges, 1995a). This includes slowing the heart, increasing sexual arousal, digestion, urination, and defecation and the inhibition of glucose (i.e., energy use) and norepinephrine (i.e., a hormone of the SNS). One key component of the PNS is the vagus nerve, also named the "wandering" nerve as it connects to so many parts of the body. The vagus has been referred to as a sort of physiological "brake"—working to slow activation of the SNS. In times of calm, greater vagal activity (sometimes referred to as vagal tone) is posited to promote social approach and attentional engagement. It is the activity of the PNS that is particularly supportive of children paying attention and interacting with other children and the teacher in class. When challenges arise, "withdrawal" of the vagal brake supports the engagement of other physiological systems, including sympathetic "fight or flight" activity if needed.

Although the PNS supports some actions of everyday life (e.g., social engagement), more substantial challenges/threats may require the full "fight-or-flight" response of the SNS. When a threat is detected, chemical messengers originating in the brain have far-reaching impacts that prepare the body to engage. In situations like higher-pressure exams or interpersonal conflict, activity of the SNS supports the associated bodily changes like increased heart rate and blood flow. The SNS–brain connection is slightly more complicated—involving the locus coeruleus–norepinephrine (LC-NE) system. However, for the sake of this chapter, we will stay focused on the SNS and its indicators.

The HPA Axis

Whereas the ANS is involved in stress reactivity to smaller, daily challenges requiring allostatic adjustment, HPA axis activation is typically reserved for larger, more threatening events (Del Giudice, Ellis, & Shirtcliff, 2011; Sapolsky, Romero, & Munck, 2000). For a young child, this includes experiences like physical pain and the extended absence of a caregiver; for older children, adolescents, and adults, this includes experiences where one feels socially evaluated, a lack of control, or in danger (e.g., public speaking, peer appraisal, bullying; Dickerson & Kemeny, 2004). When humans are exposed to a substantial social or physical stressor, it triggers a physiological cascade, resulting in the release of the hormone cortisol into the bloodstream for broad circulation to the body and brain (see Figure 4.3; Tarullo & Gunnar, 2006). Cortisol readily enters the brain to impact neural functioning, especially in regions important for learning and memory

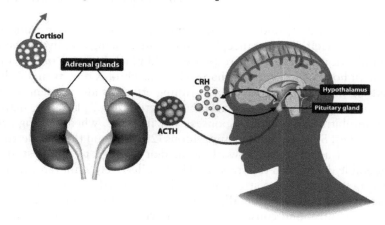

FIGURE 4.3. HPA axis and process to release cortisol. CRH, corticotropin-releasing hormone; ACTH, adrenocorticotropic hormone. Image reprinted with permission from the Biology Dictionary (*https://biologydictionary.net/hpa-axis*).

(hippocampus), emotions (amygdala), and self-regulation and reasoning (prefrontal cortex) (Gunnar & Vazquez, 2006; McEwen & Sapolsky, 1995).

In addition to its role in the acute stress response, the HPA axis produces a diurnal pattern of weaker, ongoing bursts of cortisol throughout the day to support normative metabolic and cognitive processes. For those keeping a typical 24-hour sleep-wake cycle, diurnal cortisol levels tend to peak shortly after waking and trough shortly after the onset of sleep (Adam et al., 2017). The diurnal cortisol rhythm plays an important role in maintaining HPA axis functioning, including influences on the magnitude of acute HPA axis stress responses (Adam, Hawkley, Kudielka, & Cacioppo, 2006; Gunnar & Quevedo, 2007). Due to this fluctuation across the day, the timing of stressful or challenging experiences can make a big difference on performance—either lifting the individual up to the optimal level of activity at the apex of the inverted-U-shaped curve, or pushing the individual beyond the optimal peak and undermining performance. Het, Ramlow, and Wolf (2005) provided some support for this idea in their meta-analysis of a number of studies testing the relation between cortisol and memory. Specifically, these authors found that after pharmacologically manipulating adult participants' cortisol levels, the direction of the effect on memory varied as function of time of day. When administered in the morning—when cortisol is at its diurnal peak—cortisol undermined memory performance. In contrast, when administered in the afternoon, cortisol supported memory functioning.

Furthermore, unlike the rapid response from the ANS, an acute HPA axis stress response initiates bodily changes that can last up to hours or even days, potentially undermining learning processes occurring long after the response itself. For instance, imagine a child facing a bully on the way to school. An acute HPA axis response could block learning of new information an hour or so later—perhaps when the child is now trying to learn something new in class. This idea of timing effects is also evident in other aspects of cognition, such as executive function (e.g., planning, manipulating, inhibiting automatic responses). For instance, when looking across many studies, Shields, Bonner, and Moons (2015) found that the detrimental effects of acute stress on working memory tended to manifest after a considerable delay from the stressor. Thus, collectively, children can arrive in classrooms long after a stressful event has occurred with the residue of a stress response that quite literally makes it more difficult for their brains to encode, organize, and consolidate new information (i.e., learn). This may be especially true for children experiencing stress in their home environment in the time between school hours—a context that can also disrupt diurnal cortisol patterns important for supporting learning and memory (Suor, Sturge-Apple, Davies, Cicchetti, & Manning, 2015).

Normative Growth in Children's Physiological Stress Systems

Although establishment of the PNS begins prenatally, the system develops rapidly over the first years of life (Porges & Furman, 2011). This is reflected in normative increases in children's "resting" vagal tone across infancy and early childhood (Alkon, Boyce, Davis, & Eskenazi, 2011; Berry, Blair, Willoughby, & Granger, 2012; Bornstein & Suess, 2000). Longitudinal studies of SNS markers during rest (Alkon et al., 2011; Berry et al., 2012) show similar positive growth over this span. In contrast, children's resting cortisol levels tend to decline across infancy and early childhood (Berry et al., 2012), with some indication of an uptick into middle childhood and adolescence (Gunnar, Brodersen, Krueger, & Rigatuso, 1996; Lupien, King, Meaney, & McEwen, 2001).

Given the variety of stressors (e.g., cognitively challenging tasks, social stress, physical stress) and methods for assessing reactivity (e.g., simple differences from baseline, growth rates), normative developmental patterns for the reactivity and recovery of these systems are less clear. Some work has suggested that vagal reactivity to modest cognitive (Alkon et al., 2011; Berry et al., 2018; Bornstein & Suess, 2000) or social (El-Sheikh, 2005) challenges declines across infancy to early childhood. Taken with the well-replicated finding that both children and adults tend to show vagal withdrawal in the context of more substantial challenges, this suggests that the threshold for PNS reactivity grows as children mature. Changes in the reactivity of the SNS and HPA axis are also complex and somewhat less clear. The limited available longitudinal (e.g., Alkon et al., 2014; Stephens, Bush,

Weiss, & Alkon, 2020) and cross-sectional (Buss, Davidson, Kalin, & Goldsmith, 2004; Quigley & Stifter, 2006) data suggest rather limited SNS reactivity to cognitive and emotional challenges across infancy and early childhood, yet increased reactivity into middle childhood and adolescence (Allen & Mathews, 1997; Matthews, Salomon, Kenyon, & Allen, 2002). In contrast, developmental findings concerning HPA axis reactivity suggest a potential curvilinear function. Specifically, some work suggests that while young infants tend to show pronounced acute HPA axis responses to physical (e.g., inoculation) and social (e.g., caregiver separation) and even mild (e.g., removal from bath) stressors, these responses tend to diminish into toddlerhood and early childhood, reappearing during later childhood (Gunnar, Talge, & Herrera, 2009; Seddon et al., 2020).

Thus, collectively, we see considerable normative developmental changes in children's physiological stress systems across infancy and childhood. This growth parallels the massive increases we see in children's capacities to manage their thoughts, behavior, and emotions across this span, likely driven by development in key brain regions like the hippocampus (memory), amygdala (emotions), and prefrontal cortex (attention, planning, goal-setting) (e.g., Garon, Bryson, & Smith, 2008). Although the complex dynamics of these systems over time remains unclear, changes in individual systems suggest a trend by which activity in both branches of the ANS increases across infancy and early childhood, whereas both the resting and the stress-reactive HPA axis activity tend to decline across this same period, then increase across adolescence. Of course, it is important to keep in mind that developmental changes also impact what is perceived as stressful and therefore which physiological systems require activation and when. This is a point we will return to later in the chapter.

• Measuring the ANS and HPA Axis

Measuring the PNS

Research on parasympathetic stress reactivity in children has focused largely on a specific component of heart activity: respiratory sinus arrhythmia (RSA). Unlike the constant beat of a metronome, healthy heart rates tend to vary—speeding up and slowing down. This is aptly referred to as heart rate variability (HRV; Beauchaine & Thayer, 2015; Cacioppo et al., 1994; Shader et al., 2018). Vagal (parasympathetic) influences on HRV are thought to be captured within a particular high-frequency band that occurs at the frequency of spontaneous breathing (respiration), and is therefore termed respiratory sinus arrhythmia (RSA). You can get a first-hand sense of RSA by taking your pulse. You'll find that your heart rate increases slightly during an inhale and slows down slightly during an exhale. Because of this, the quality of one's RSA estimates hinge on accurately characterizing respiration (see Shader et al., 2018). Some methods require direct physical measurement of respiration (e.g., a sensor worn around the chest), while other more indirect approaches use mathematical algorithms to estimate and control for respiration (see Malik et al., 1996; Shaffer & Ginsberg, 2017).

Respiration should also be considered carefully in one's study design. For instance, many studies collect HRV data during a "resting baseline" task, where participants are asked to sit quietly for several minutes before moving on to some sort of active challenge task. Here, differences between resting and challenge task RSA are commonly interpreted as "vagal reactivity" to the task. However, if the challenge task also elicited changes in respiration (e.g., talking, physical activity, posture), this could readily lead to RSA changes that are not related to vagal control, thereby leading to inaccurate reactivity data. The how, whether, and when of addressing respiration confounds has been debated extensively (Berntson, Cacioppo, & Grossman, 2007; Denver, Reed, & Porges, 2007). Although much disagreement remains, careful consideration in the design stage is a critical first step.

Cardiac data used to calculate HRV or RSA can be collected rather noninvasively using electrocardiography (ECG) or more basic ambulatory heartbeat detectors. Typically this includes applying electrodes to the torso and connecting to a bioamplifier to detect subtle changes in the electrical signals of the heart as it beats. Aside from ECG, there are a number of reliable ambulatory heart rate detectors that only provide heart rate data (i.e., amount of time between beats), as opposed to the full wave form (e.g., First Beat BodyGuard2; Actiheart). Although they lack some of the bells and whistles found with lab-based ECG, these devices can provide reliable heart rate information in a very nonintrusive and comparatively inexpensive way (Palmer, Distefano, Leneman, & Berry, 2021). Basic heart rate can also be measured using photoplethysmography (PPG), which is the software used in wrist-worn personal fitness trackers, like Apple Watch and FitBit. PPG measures volumetric changes in the heart by measuring how changes in arterial pulse pressure impacts light waves sent into the skin. These can be fine for personal use and rough indices of cardiac function. However, we recommend against using these types of monitors for research purposes, as we have yet to find one that can produce research-quality data. Once one has collected the raw heart rate data, it requires careful cleaning. Movement artifacts, missed, and misread individual heart beats are common, even with careful data collection. These need to be located and corrected before applying any HRV or RSA calculation approaches. For a more detailed description of collection and processing of RSA data, we refer readers to Malik et al. (1996), Shader et al. (2018), and Shaffer and Ginsberg (2017).

Measuring the SNS

There are variety of ways to measure SNS activity, including cardiac indices, like pre-ejection period (PEP); salivary surrogate markers, like alpha-amylase (sAA); electrodermal activity (EDA; i.e., sweat); and eye-tracking approaches, like pupillometry. We concentrate on PEP and sAA, given that they are the most common and most easily implemented with children, inside and outside of the lab. For more information on EDA, see Shields, MacDowell, Fairchild, and Campbell (1987); for pupillometry, see Loewenfeld (1993).

Pre-Ejection Period

PEP measures the time between when the heart's left ventricle is just about to contract to send blood to the aorta and just before the aortic valve opens to receive that blood (Newlin & Levenson, 1979). In simple terms, one can think of it as the span occurring just after the "lub" sound and just before the "dub" sound of the heart. The speed at which this transfer of blood occurs is under SNS control, such that shorter PEP times indicate greater activation of the SNS. Measuring PEP is somewhat more involved than RSA because it requires collecting nuanced timing information about specific elements of heart activity, typically requiring a signal of both electrical activity in the heart and blood flow. In this way PEP is more nuanced than heart rate alone, capturing the way the SNS cues the heart to increase its overall cardiac output to align with a fight-or-flight response.

Collection of the cardiac signals needed to calculate PEP can be set up with multiple different arrangements of electrodes on the chest and body. Broadly, though, collection is more involved than that for RSA or HRV— more electrodes, more wire leads, and more time to set up. Depending on the age and mood of the child, it can be tricky to collect PEP with children. Our research group has found that distractors can go a long way in helping our young participants manage the setup process; for example, bubble-blowing toys have been perennial winners. The nuanced data required for PEP are also typically much messier than for RSA, including being particularly susceptible to movement. Cleaning these data is a nontrivial undertaking and requires a good amount of training and practice to become reliable. Finally, like RSA, PEP is also influenced by respiration and posture (see Cacioppo et al., 1994). Thus, care must be taken to minimize the impact of these potential confounds.

Salivary Alpha-Amylase

sAA is a protein found in saliva that increases in the context of high levels of norepinephrine—a key chemical messenger of the SNS (see Nater &

Rohleder, 2009). sAA can be assayed in the lab from saliva samples collected via "passive drool" (i.e., spitting into vial) or salivettes (i.e., swabs made of synthetic cotton). These samples can be reliably collected from even young infants, and many commercial salivary testing labs provide sAA analyses, making collection and analysis fairly simple and noninvasive. One limitation is that lab analyses can be quite costly (around $5.00 per sample, as of the year 2020). Experiments show that acute psychosocial stress leads to sAA increases that tend to peak around 10 minutes after stress induction (e.g., Nater & Rohleder, 2009). This delay means that at any given time saliva is collected for later sAA extraction, this reflects SNS activity from 10 minutes prior; therefore this timing must be considered when collecting saliva for sAA data.

Measuring the HPA Axis

One of the reasons that cortisol has featured so prominently in stress research is likely due to its ease of collection. Although cortisol can be measured more directly from blood plasma and extracted from urine, it can also be reliably assayed from saliva—typically collected by passive drool or salivettes (Kirschbaum & Hellhammer, 1989). The latter are particularly common with infants and young children, given the motor coordination required for spitting into a vial. Like sAA, cortisol can be assayed (extracted/analyzed) by many commercial labs.

Also like sAA, a number of methodological issues should be considered to ensure valid interpretations. To start, unlike with plasma, changes in cortisol output from the HPA axis take approximately 20 minutes to be reflected in saliva (Kirschbaum & Hellhammer, 1989). Therefore, collection times must be appropriately delayed from target events. Acute cortisol responses are also impacted by the daily diurnal cycle. Reactivity tends to be weaker in the morning, when diurnal cortisol levels are near their daily peak, and stronger in the afternoon, when diurnal levels are lower (Kudielka, Schommer, Hellhammer, & Kirschbaum, 2004). Other factors that require consideration include: gender (differences typically emerging after puberty), menstrual cycle (if the child is older), how recently a meal or caffeine were consumed or a nap was taken, medications (especially steroidal or antianxiety medications), and contamination (e.g., blood, dairy products) (see Clements, 2013, for overview).

For those interested in longer-term changes in HPA axis functioning, as opposed to acute reactivity, hair-based cortisol (HCC) has garnered increasing interest (e.g., Russell, Koren, Rieder, & Van Uum, 2012). Although the biological mechanisms remain somewhat unclear, research with both human and nonhuman animals indicate that long-term stress levels can be captured by cortisol levels found in hair follicles. Hair samples are typically cut from close to the scalp to recover a retrospective account of overall HPA axis activity for the individual, as reflected in his or her most recent hair growth. For example, Groeneveld and colleagues (2013) showed that the novel transition to formal schooling was associated with nontrivial increases in children's HCC, with other studies finding similar relations for broad markers of environmental risk (e.g., family income; Vaghri et al., 2013). However, a good deal needs to be clarified to fully establish the validity of this marker.

Age-Based Considerations in PSA Assessment and Measurement

Age of the child is an important consideration when assessing and interpreting PSA. For one, general developmental trends are important to consider, like those outlined in the earlier section on developmental norms. There are also important social and cognitive changes that will affect reactivity depending on a child's age. For example, in infancy, when caregivers are the primary source of safety and comfort, a parent leaving the room for an extended period of time can stimulate a cortisol response, whereas by middle childhood that same context would not (Gunnar et al., 2009). For adolescents, but not younger children, social evaluation produces a reliable cortisol response (Dickerson & Kemeny, 2004). This has led to the widespread use of the Trier Social Stress Test (TSST), a combination of public speaking and arithmetic in front of a panel of nonfriendly judges (e.g., Seddon et al., 2020). This research paradigm reliably elicits a sympathetic and HPA axis response from older adolescents and adults. While the TSST, or any lab-based experiment for that matter, may not be easily comparable to a real-world context, it remains a useful research tool for evaluating physiological stress responses.

Eliciting cortisol reactivity with the TSST has been far less reliable in younger children, perhaps due to cognitive differences in perceptions of social evaluation. In response to this, some research groups have designed alternate social stress tests for children. One version involves the child devising and delivering the ending for a developmentally appropriate story stem rather than applying for a job (TSST-C; Buske-Kirschbaum et al., 1997). Another version involves the child getting negative feedback on his or her performance while engaging in various age-appropriate tasks, like making animal sounds and building a tower out of cans (de Weerth, Zijlmans, Mack, & Beijers, 2013). With even younger children, where social evaluation may not be on the cognitive radar, extremely frustrating performance tasks (e.g., being asked to complete a puzzle with not enough time) or scary tasks (e.g., having a stranger put on a scary mask and interacting with him or her) seem to elicit cortisol reactivity (Kryski, Smith, Sheikh, Singh, & Hayden, 2011).

ANS/HPA Axis Function and Measurement Summary

The ANS and HPA axis systems function in different ways and on different time scales. Yet, they coordinate with each other and the brain in complex ways to support real-time responses to our ever-changing environments—also called allostasis. This flexible coordination is central to physical and psychological health. Notably, in the context of chronic activation—such as when one's environment is perpetually threatening or unpredictable—this allostasis can begin to break down, leading to allostatic load and long-term negative impacts on health.

There are a number of ways to collect biological indicators of ANS and HPA axis functioning—some trickier than others. We outline these in Table 4.1. Briefly, parasympathetic (RSA) and sympathetic (PEP) responses are typically measured via cardiac activity. Historically, both approaches have required lab-based equipment (e.g., ECG). However, the advent of commercially available, research-grade ambulatory heart rate monitors has created new opportunities for increasingly ecologically valid measurement of RSA in the field. For instance, in our collaborations with Ann Masten's lab at the University of Minnesota Institute of Child Development, we have been collecting cardiac data with homeless and highly mobile families living in a local emergency shelter. Also, as described by Wilder and Palumbo (Chapter 5, this volume), similar cardiac data are being integrated into classroom physiological measurement. Given the complexity of the cardiac waveforms required to estimate PEP, we are unaware of ambulatory measures that are up to the task. However, we suspect that it is only a matter of time before they are. All of these data require careful scrutiny with respect to data cleaning and designs that minimize measurement artifacts and confounding (e.g., respiration, posture). Other biomarkers, such as sAA and cortisol, can be collected noninvasively from saliva. However, understanding the lagged timing of these indicators are crucial to their ultimate utility.

Developmental changes will also impact measurement and interpretation of physiological stress responses. Some of these changes are based in biological system functioning. For example, while the ANS is well established by the end of the first year of life, the HPA axis demonstrates protracted development—expressing reactivity in infancy, dipping in early childhood, and then steadily increasing again across later childhood and adolescence. These systems also interact with rapidly developing brain regions important for learning, memory, emotions, and more. Importantly, these trends are based on average patterns across development; however, there is significant variability in this when considering an individual child's changes across time. This individual variability has been shown across indicators of children's parasympathetic (Berry et al., 2018; Bornstein &

TABLE 4.1. Summary of Reviewed Methods for Collecting PNS, SNS, and HPA Axis Activity Data

System	Output	General measurement	Specific measurement	Benefits	Considerations	Collection/ cleaning ease
PNS	RSA (from HRV)	Cardiac electro physiology	ECG	Can be wireless, can verify R-peaks and data quality, can collect with all ages	Have to connect to a bioamplifier, need to measure or estimate respiration, appropriate baseline task, training required for cleaning	Moderate/ easy
			Heart beat (R-peaks)	Can be self-contained (can collect outside of a lab setting), can collect with all ages	Careful of "watch" monitors (reliability), need to measure or estimate respiration, appropriate baseline task, some training required for cleaning	Easy/easy
SNS	PEP	Cardiac electro physiology	ECG and ICG (impedance cardiography)	Same general time scale and organ measured for RSA, reliable SNS indicator, can be wireless	Have to connect to a bioamplifier, many more electrodes, difficult to collect with infants, sensitive signal (messy), lots of training required for cleaning	Difficult/very difficult
	sAA	Saliva	Assay (lab)	Easy to collect with all ages, no internal data cleaning	Adjust for flow rate, appropriate timing delay relevant to task	Easy/easy (expensive)
	EDA	Sweat	—	(not covered)	(not covered)	
	—	Pupillometry	—	(not covered)	(not covered)	
Nonspecific ANS	HR	Cardiac electro physiology	ECG or Heart beat (R-peaks)	Easy to collect	Cleaning required	Easy/easy
	HRV	Cardiac electro physiology	ECG or Heart beat (R-peaks)	Easy to collect	Cleaning required	Easy/easy
HPA Axis	Cortisol	Saliva	Assay (lab)	Easy to collect with all ages, no internal data cleaning	Time of day; age of child; appropriate timing delay relevant to task, recent food/drink intake or sleep; gender; threat perception; task/stressor type; BMI	Easy/easy (expensive)
		Hair	Assay (lab)	More general indicator of accumulated stress	Can be difficult to collect, hair growth rate, difficult for infants and others with little hair	Very difficult/ difficult
		Plasma	—	(not covered)	(not covered)	
		Urine	—	(not covered)	(not covered)	

Suess, 2000), sympathetic (e.g., Alkon et al., 2006; Berry et al., 2012), and HPA axis functioning (e.g., Berry et al., 2012). As stress is influenced by a child's perception of the contextual demands and his or her ability to handle it, psychological developments also shape physiological reactivity. What is perceived as stressful early in life (e.g., lack of a caregiver in a novel setting) is starkly different later in life (e.g., negative peer evaluation). Interestingly, measures of physiological stress reactivity regularly do not line up with self-reports of stress levels, so physiological indicators appear to be measuring something related but unique from perceptions of stress (e.g., Kiecolt-Glaser, Renna, Shrout, & Madison, 2020).

• Stress Physiology and Self-Regulation in Social Context

It is widely held that, in coordination with the brain, the development of children's physiological stress systems play a critical role in their increasing abilities to manage their thoughts, emotions, and behavior—broadly termed *self-regulation* (e.g., Beauchaine, 2015; Feldman, 2009). For example, even with very young infants (e.g., 5–12 weeks), those with higher levels of resting RSA (i.e., vagal tone) and/or greater reductions in RSA during social and cognitive challenges (i.e., vagal withdrawal) tend to show more positive social engagement and greater regulatory capacity than their low-resting and low-withdrawal peers (Huffman et al., 1998). Some work with young infants has shown that high resting RSA is associated with both positive and negative emotion (Porges, Doussard-Roosevelt, Lourdes Portales, & Suess, 1994; Stifter & Fox, 1990), raising the possibility that high resting RSA in infancy may be a broader marker of emotional engagement, as opposed to positive emotion alone.

From toddlerhood into childhood, a number of studies have similarly shown that children with higher resting RSA and greater vagal withdrawal tend to regulate their emotions more effectively (e.g., Calkins, 1997). This is also true for broader behavioral indicators of dysregulation. Meta-analytic studies, comprising evidence across many separate studies, indicate robust—albeit, modest—relations between sluggish RSA withdrawal and heightened behavioral problems (Graziano & Derefinko, 2013). Indeed, some have proposed that dysregulated vagal processes may be a key transdiagnostic risk factor underlying developmental psychopathology (Beauchaine, 2015; Beauchaine & Thayer, 2015).

Social Engagement and Dyadic Shaping of Stress Systems

In addition to influences of normative developmental trends, interactions with social others play a key role in shaping physiological system functioning. One theory has connected activity in the parasympathetic system to socioregulatory functioning, mostly due to the unique connections of the vagus nerve to muscles in the head, face, and neck that are central to effective social communication (e.g., smiling/frowning, visual shifting, sound production, and perception) (Porges, 1995b). This theory has been supported by research assessing RSA during social interactions. For example, a common paradigm for inducing temporary social stress with young infants—the Still-Face paradigm (Tronick, Adamson, Wise, & Brazelton, 1978)—involves the caregiver's abrupt transition from active infant play to displaying a still, expressionless face to the baby. This break in social coordination tends to elicit pronounced behavioral distress and decreases in infants' RSA levels (i.e., vagal withdrawal), suggesting parasympathetic regulation during this stressor (see Jones-Mason, Alkon, Coccia, & Bush, 2018). Notably, even subtle caregiver supports during a Still-Face episode—such as physical touch—can mitigate this parasympathetic response, highlighting the regulatory role of meaningful others (Feldman, Singer, & Zagoory, 2010; Pratt, Singer, Kanat-Maymon, & Feldman, 2015).

Similar findings are evident with somewhat older infants undergoing the Strange Situation (Salter Ainsworth, Blehar, Waters, & Hall, 1978)—a procedure developed to measure attachment security (quality of infant-caregiver relationship), in which the infant is left alone or with a stranger in an unfamiliar room. Irrespective of the infants' attachment quality (i.e., secure, insecure), infants tend to show dramatic decreases in RSA (Hill-Soderlund et al., 2008; Smith, Woodhouse, Clark, & Skowron, 2016). However, consistent with the regulatory role of caregivers, infants with secure attachments tend to show more effective physiological recovery upon reunion with their caregivers, compared with the recovery of their insecurely attached peers. Related findings have been noted for SNS and HPA axis functioning in the Strange Situation (see Hostinar, Sullivan, & Gunnar, 2014). Infants with secure attachments tend to show comparatively weaker sympathetic and HPA axis responses than their insecurely attached peers do when faced with caregiver separations (Hertsgaard, Gunnar, Erickson, & Nachmias, 1995; Spangler & Grossman, 1993).

Beyond top-down supports provided by caregivers to children, contemporary theoretical models highlight the dynamic nature of caregiver–child interactions at both the behavioral and physiological levels (Beauchaine, Gatzke-Kopp, & Mead, 2007; Feldman, 2007; Masten & Cicchetti, 2010). Our physiological stress systems are powerful conduits of the neural processes underlying emotion, attention, and social engagement. When interacting with others, it is proposed that stress-system functioning is aligned at the dyadic level—coordinating each partner's attention, social cognition, behavior, and physiological feedback with the other's (Feldman, Magori-Cohen, Galili, Singer, & Louzoun, 2011; Porges, 1995b). As such, physiological coordination is theorized to facilitate emotional and behavioral coordination between individuals.

There is growing empirical support for the importance of physiological coordination in developing positive outcomes. For example, Feldman and colleagues (2011) showed that the cardiac rhythms of mothers and their infants tended to synchronize in the context of mother–infant play and that this physiological coordination was particularly pronounced when the dyad showed behavioral alignment in their affect, vocal prosody (rhythm and intonation), and gaze (Feldman et al., 2011). Similar relations are also evident with older children. For instance, Lunkenheimer and colleagues (2015) found that RSA in both mothers and their preschoolers tended to positively coordinate in real time, as they engaged in a series of dyadic tasks. Importantly, they also noted meaningful differences in the degree of RSA coordination between dyads, such that children in physiologically uncoordinated dyads tended to be rated by their teachers as showing more externalizing behaviors (e.g., aggression, acting out). Again, this implies that dyadic physiological coordination may play a foundational role in children's emerging self-regulatory capacities.

The importance of meaningful others in these processes extends to caregivers outside of the home as well. Meta-analytic findings across a number of studies provide reliable evidence that attending child care shifts HPA axis functioning. Unlike typical diurnal declines at home, children tend to either maintain their morning cortisol peaks or show increases in their cortisol levels over the course of the day, on days when they attend child care (Vermeer & van IJzendoorn, 2006). One inference from these data is that the typical demands of child care, such as having to negotiate noise, more densely populated physical spaces, and unpredictable peer behavior, prompt ongoing activation of the HPA axis. Critically, though, the data also indicate that child care effects can be mitigated in the context of high-quality care, marked by responsive child care provider–child interactions (e.g., Badanes, Dmitrieva, & Watamura, 2012; Hatfield, Hestenes, Kintner-Duffy, & O'Brien, 2013). Indeed, the results from a recent randomized intervention indicated that improving teacher–child relationship quality can both improve preschooler behavior and normalize preschoolers' diurnal cortisol levels (i.e., declines across the day; Hatfield & Williford, 2017). Although far less research has been done with older children, the extant findings suggest similar relations in the early elementary school years (Ahnert, Harwardt-Heinecke, Kappler, Eckstein-Madry, & Milatz, 2012; Lisonbee, Mize, Payne, & Granger, 2008).

Taken together, developmental differences are explained, in part, by children's social interactions with meaningful adults. Although the majority of this work has concentrated on young children in the context of their primary caregivers (largely, mothers), a growing body of work indicates that these processes extend beyond early childhood and to caregivers outside of the home.

• Conclusions and Remaining Questions

Our physiological stress systems support our ability to navigate the ups and downs of daily life, as well as our capacity to negotiate pronounced threats to life and well-being. These systems are highly dynamic and flexibly organize in real time to support adaptive neurocognitive and bodily responses to the environment. Given the highly social nature of our species, it is likely unsurprising that children's social interactions with caregivers—both inside and outside of the home—serve as key catalysts for developmental change in these systems and, in turn, children's capacity to regulate thoughts, behavior, and emotions.

Many of these physiological systems can be measured nonintrusively in both the lab and in daily life. To date, research-grade ambulatory measures of cardiac activity—for heart rate and RSA (e.g., FirstBeat)—and saliva collection—for sAA and cortisol—have proven to be the most reliable and easy to collect. However, each method involves a number of specific, nontrivial concerns in order to maximize the integrity of the collected data (e.g., developmental differences in stimuli; timing/sampling rate of collection; participant compliance; methodical confounding; data preprocessing/cleaning; modeling meaningful change). Additionally, cost is an important consideration, especially for saliva assays.

Technological advances have made it increasingly possible to collect some of these physiological markers outside of the lab (e.g., RSA, sAA, cortisol). Given that research laboratories can be quite different than children's typical "free range" environments, this is a critically important innovation because it provides a window into how these processes unfold in real life. Of course, it comes with trade-offs. Data collected in the field can be considerably messier in terms of the actual data itself as well as the alignment with the overall study design (e.g., precise measures of time and behavior; reliable implementation of a research protocol). Potential measurement confounds that can be adjusted in the lab (e.g., respiration, speaking, posture), are often difficult to manage in the field. Some measures, like PEP, are likely too impractical to be implemented outside of the lab.

Despite noteworthy progress in our understanding of children's physiological stress-system functioning, many pressing issues remain. For example, although there is some methodological standardization in the way that different research groups elicit and measure acute stress responses, there is also substantial variability. This can make it difficult to aggregate findings across studies, as it is nearly impossible to distinguish true differences from differences in methods. Additionally, because children are developing, what evokes a stress response at one point in development may not function the same way in a subsequent period. For instance, a two-minute separation from a caregiver tends to elicit a strong physiological response for infants, yet doesn't move the needle for adolescents. This developmental discrepancy creates fundamental differences in the meaning of a stressor and interpretation of a stress response—a factor that must be considered in any measure of developmental change, because change across time is inherently confounded with changes in the measure.

Additionally, drawing largely from studies of nonhuman animals, it is well accepted that our core physiological stress systems coordinate in complex and dynamic ways, and across multiple developmental time scales (i.e., seconds to decades), to support adaptation. The brain, PNS, SNS, and HPA axis all work together to support every activity of daily life. Unfortunately, practical and methodological limitations have made it difficult to unpack these complex cross-system processes within humans. This is an exciting and active area of research that will benefit from ongoing advances in the way we both measure and model these highly dimensional physiological processes.

Despite these challenges, the integration of physiological measures of children's stress systems into studies of development has produced important insights into the complex processes underlying the ways experience "gets under the skin" to support contextually adaptive functioning. Given both the remarkable growth in physiologically informed models of stress and development and the rates of methodological and technical advancement in this area, this work is poised for continued innovation and application in children's lives.

REFERENCES

Adam, E. K., Hawkley, L. C., Kudielka, B. M., & Cacioppo, J. T. (2006). Day-to-day dynamics of experience-cortisol associations in a population-based sample of older adults. *Proceedings of the National Academy of Sciences of the United States of America, 103*(45), 17058–17063.

Adam, E. K., Quinn, M. E., Tavernier, R., McQuillan, M. T., Dahlke, K. A., & Gilbert, K. E. (2017). Diurnal cortisol slopes and mental and physical health outcomes: A systematic review and meta-analysis. *Psychoneuroendocrinology, 83*, 25–41.

Ahnert, L., Harwardt-Heinecke, E., Kappler, G., Eckstein-Madry, T., & Milatz, A. (2012). Student–teacher relationships and classroom climate in first grade: How do they relate to students' stress regulation? *Attachment & Human Development, 14*(3), 249–263.

Alkon, A., Boyce, W. T., Davis, N. V., & Eskenazi, B. (2011). Developmental changes in autonomic nervous system resting and reactivity measures in Latino children from 6 to 60 months of age. *Journal of Developmental & Behavioral Pediatrics, 32*(9).

Alkon, A., Boyce, W. T., Tran, L., Harley, K. G., Neuhaus, J., & Eskenazi, B. (2014). Prenatal adversities and Latino children's autonomic nervous system reactivity trajectories from 6 months to 5 years of age. *PLOS ONE, 9*(1), e86283.

Alkon, A., Lippert, S., Vujan, N., Rodriquez, M. E., Boyce, W. T., & Eskenazi, B. (2006). The ontogeny of autonomic measures in 6- and 12-month-old infants. *Developmental Psychobiology, 48*(3), 197–208.

Allen, M. T., & Matthews, K. A. (1997). Hemodynamic responses to laboratory stressors in children and adolescents: The influences of age, race, and gender. *Psychophysiology, 34*(3), 329–339.

Badanes, L. S., Dmitrieva, J., & Watamura, S. E. (2012). Understanding cortisol reactivity across the day at child care: The potential buffering role of secure attachments to caregivers. *Early Childhood Research Quarterly, 27*(1), 156–165.

Beauchaine, T. P. (2015). Respiratory sinus arrhythmia: A transdiagnostic biomarker of emotion dysregulation and psychopathology. *Current Opinion in Psychology, 3*, 43–47.

Beauchaine, T. P., Gatzke-Kopp, L., & Mead, H. K. (2007). Polyvagal theory and developmental psychopathology: Emotion dysregulation and conduct problems from preschool to adolescence. *Biological Psychology, 74*(2), 174–184.

Beauchaine, T. P., & Thayer, J. F. (2015). Heart rate variability as a transdiagnostic biomarker of psychopathology. *International Journal of Psychophysiology, 98*(2), 338–350.

Berntson, G. G., Cacioppo, J. T., & Grossman, P. (2007). Whither vagal tone. *Biological Psychology, 74*(2), 295–300.

Berntson, G. G., Cacioppo, J. T., Quigley, K. S., & Fabro, V. T. (1994). Autonomic space and psychophysiological response. *Psychophysiology, 31*(1), 44–61.

Berry, D., Blair, C., Willoughby, M., & Granger, D. A. (2012). Salivary alpha-amylase and cortisol in infancy and toddlerhood: Direct and indirect relations with executive functioning and academic ability in childhood. *Psychoneuroendocrinology, 37*(10), 1700–1711.

Berry, D., Vernon-Feagans, L., Mills-Koonce, W. R., Blair, C., Cox, M., Burchinal, P., . . . Willoughby, M. (2018). Otitis media and respiratory sinus arrhythmia across infancy and early childhood: Polyvagal processes? *Developmental Psychology, 54*(9), 1709–1722.

Blair, C., Raver, C., Granger, D., Mills-Koonce, R., Hibel, L., & Investigators, F. L. P. K. (2011). Allostasis and allostatic load in the context of poverty in early childhood. *Development and Psychopathology, 23*(3), 845.

Blascovich, J. (1992). A biopsychosocial approach to arousal regulation. *Journal of Social and Clinical Psychology, 11*(3), 213–237.

Bornstein, M. H., & Suess, P. E. (2000). Child and mother cardiac vagal tone: Continuity, stability, and concordance across the first 5 years. *Developmental Psychology, 36*(1), 54–65.

Buske-Kirschbaum, A., Jobst, S., Wustmans, A., Kirschbaum, C., Rauh, W., & Hellhammer, D. (1997). Attenuated free cortisol response to psychosocial stress in children with atopic dermatitis. *Psychosomatic Medicine, 59*(4), 419–426.

Buss, K. A., Davidson, R. J., Kalin, N. H., & Goldsmith, H. H. (2004). Context-specific freezing and associated physiological reactivity as a dysregulated fear response. *Developmental Psychology, 40*(4), 583–594.

Cacioppo, J. T., Berntson, G. G., Binkley, P. F., Quigley, K. S., Uchino, B. N., & Fieldstone, A. (1994). Autonomic cardiac control. II. Noninvasive indices and basal response as revealed by autonomic blockades. *Psychophysiology, 31*(6), 586–598.

Calkins, S. D. (1997). Cardiac vagal tone indices of temperamental reactivity and behavioral regulation in young children. *Developmental Psychobiology, 31*(2), 125–135.

Cannon, W. B. (1929). Organization for physiological homeostasis. *Physiological Reviews, 9*(3), 399–431.

Cicchetti, D. (2011). Allostatic load. *Development and Psychopathology, 23*(3), 723–724.

Clements, A. D. (2013). Salivary cortisol measurement in developmental research: Where do we go from here? *Developmental Psychobiology, 55*(3), 205–220.

de Weerth, C., Zijlmans, M. A., Mack, S., & Beijers, R. (2013). Cortisol reactions to a social evaluative paradigm in 5- and 6-year-old children. *Stress, 16*(1), 65–72.

Del Giudice, M., Ellis, B. J., & Shirtcliff, E. A. (2011). The adaptive calibration model of stress responsivity. *Neuroscience and Biobehavioral Reviews, 35*(7), 1562–1592.

Denver, J. W., Reed, S. F., & Porges, S. W. (2007). Methodological issues in the quantification of respiratory sinus arrhythmia. *Biological Psychology, 74*(2), 286–294.

Dickerson, S. S., & Kemeny, M. E. (2004). Acute stressors and cortisol responses: A theoretical integration and synthesis of laboratory research. *Psychological Bulletin, 130*(3), 355–391.

El-Sheikh, M. (2005). Stability of respiratory sinus arrhythmia in children and young adolescents: A longitudinal examination. *Developmental Psychobiology, 46*(1), 66–74.

Evans, G. W. (2003). A multimethodological analysis of cumulative risk and allostatic load among rural children. *Developmental Psychology, 39*(5), 924.

Feldman, R. (2007). Parent-infant synchrony: Biological foundations synchrony and developmental outcomes. *Current Directions in Psychological Sciences, 16*(6), 340–345.

Feldman, R. (2009). The development of regulatory functions from birth to 5 years: Insights from premature infants. *Child Development, 80*(2), 544–561.

Feldman, R., Magori-Cohen, R., Galili, G., Singer, M., & Louzoun, Y. (2011). Mother and infant coordinate heart rhythms through episodes of interaction synchrony. *Infant Behavior and Development, 34*(4), 569–577.

Feldman, R., Singer, M., & Zagoory, O. (2010). Touch attenuates infants' physiological reactivity to stress. *Developmental Science, 13*(2), 271–278.

Garon, N., Bryson, S. E., & Smith, I. M. (2008). Executive function in preschoolers: A review using an integrative framework. *Psychological Bulletin, 134*(1), 31–60.

Graziano, P., & Derefinko, K. (2013). Cardiac vagal control and children's adaptive functioning: A meta-analysis. *Biological Psychology, 94*(1), 22–37.

Groeneveld, M. G., Vermeer, H. J., Linting, M., Noppe, G., van Rossum, E. F. C.,

& van IJzendoorn, M. H. (2013). Children's hair cortisol as a biomarker of stress at school entry. *Stress, 16*(6), 711–715.

Gunnar, M. R., Brodersen, L., Krueger, K., & Rigatuso, J. (1996). Dampening of adrenocortical responses during infancy: Normative changes and individual differences. *Child Development, 67*(3), 877–889.

Gunnar, M. R., & Quevedo, K. (2007). The neurobiology of stress and development. *Annual Review of Psychology, 58,* 145–173.

Gunnar, M. R., Talge, N. M., & Herrera, A. (2009). Stressor paradigms in developmental studies: What does and does not work to produce mean increases in salivary cortisol. *Psychoneuroendocrinology, 34,* 953–967.

Gunnar, M. R., & Vazquez, D. (2006). Stress neurobiology and developmental psychopathology. In D. Cicchetti (Ed.), *Developmental psychopathology: Developmental neuroscience* (Vol. 2, 2nd ed., pp. 533–577). Wiley.

Hatfield, B. E., Hestenes, L. L., Kintner-Duffy, V. L., & O'Brien, M. (2013). Classroom emotional support predicts differences in preschool children's cortisol and alpha-amylase levels. *Early Childhood Research Quarterly, 28*(2), 347–356.

Hatfield, B. E., & Williford, A. P. (2017). Cortisol patterns for young children displaying disruptive behavior: Links to a teacher–child, relationship-focused intervention. *Prevention Science, 18*(1), 40–49.

Hebb, D. O. (1955). Drives and the C. N. S. (conceptual nervous system). *Psychological Review, 62*(4), 243–254.

Hertsgaard, L., Gunnar, M., Erickson, M. F., & Nachmias, M. (1995). Adrenocortical responses to the Strange Situation in infants with disorganized/disoriented attachment relationships. *Child Development, 66*(4), 1100–1106.

Het, S., Ramlow, G., & Wolf, O. T. (2005). A meta-analytic review of the effects of acute cortisol administration on human memory. *Psychoneuroendocrinology, 30*(8), 771–784.

Hill-Soderlund, A. L., Mills-Koonce, W. R., Propper, C., Calkins, S. D., Granger, D. A., Moore, G. A., . . . Cox, M. J. (2008). Parasympathetic and sympathetic responses to the strange situation in infants and mothers from avoidant and securely attached dyads. *Developmental Psychobiology, 50*(4), 361–376.

Hostinar, C. E., Sullivan, R. M., & Gunnar, M. R. (2014). Psychobiological mechanisms underlying the social buffering of the hypothalamic–pituitary–adrenocortical axis: A review of animal models and human studies across development. *Psychological Bulletin, 140*(1), 256–282.

Huffman, L. C., Bryan, Y. E., del Carmen, R., Pedersen, F. A., Doussard-Roosevelt, J. A., & Forges, S. W. (1998). Infant temperament and cardiac vagal tone: Assessments at twelve weeks of age. *Child Development, 69*(3), 624–635.

Jones-Mason, K., Alkon, A., Coccia, M., & Bush, N. R. (2018). Autonomic nervous system functioning assessed during the still-face paradigm: A meta-analysis and systematic review of methods, approach and findings. *Developmental Review, 50*(May), 113–139.

Kiecolt-Glaser, J. K., Renna, M. E., Shrout, M. R., & Madison, A. A. (2020). Stress reactivity: What pushes us higher, faster, and longer—and why it matters. *Current Directions in Psychological Science, 29*(5), 492–498.

Kirschbaum, C., & Hellhammer, D. H. (1989). Salivary cortisol in psychobiological research: An overview. *Neuropsychobiology, 22*(3), 150–169.

Kryski, K. R., Smith, H. J., Sheikh, H. I., Singh, S. M., & Hayden, E. P. (2011). Assessing stress reactivity indexed via salivary cortisol in preschool-aged children. *Psychoneuroendocrinology, 36*(8), 1127–1136.

Kudielka, B. M., Schommer, N. C., Hellhammer, D. H., & Kirschbaum, C. (2004). Acute HPA axis responses, heart rate, and mood changes to psychosocial stress (TSST) in humans at different times of day. *Psychoneuroendocrinology, 29*(8), 983–992.

Lisonbee, J. A., Mize, J., Payne, A. L., & Granger, D. A. (2008). Children's cortisol and the quality of teacher–child relationships in child care. *Child Development, 79*(6), 1818–1832.

Loewenfeld, I. E. (1993). *The pupil: Anatomy, physiology, and clinical applications* (Vol. 2). Iowa State University Press.

Lunkenheimer, E., Tiberio, S. S., Buss, K. A., Lucas-Thompson, R. G., Boker, S. M., & Timpe, Z. C. (2015). Coregulation of respiratory sinus arrhythmia between parents and preschoolers: differences by children's externalizing problems. *Developmental Psychobiology, 57*(8), 994–1003.

Lupien, S. J., King, S., Meaney, M. J., & McEwen, B. S. (2001). Can poverty get under your skin? Basal cortisol levels and cognitive function in children from low and high socioeconomic status. *Development and Psychopathology, 13*(3), 653–676.

Malik, M., Bigger, J. T., Camm, A. J., Kleiger, R. E., Malliani, A., Moss, A. J., & Schwartz, P. J. (1996). Heart rate variability: Standards of measurement, physiological interpretation, and clinical use. *European Heart Journal, 17*(3), 354–381.

Masten, A. S., & Cicchetti, D. (2010). Developmental cascades. *Development and Psychopathology, 22*, 491–495.

Matthews, K. A., Salomon, K., Kenyon, K., & Allen, M. T. (2002). Stability of children's and adolescents' hemodynamic responses to psychological challenge: A three-year longitudinal study of a multiethnic cohort of boys and girls. *Psychophysiology, 39*(6), 826–834.

McEwen, B. S., & Sapolsky, R. M. (1995). Stress and cognitive function. *Current Opinion in Neurobiology, 5*, 205–216.

Nater, U. M., & Rohleder, N. (2009). Salivary alpha-amylase as a non-invasive biomarker for the sympathetic nervous system: Current state of research. *Psychoneuroendocrinology, 34*(4), 486–496.

Newlin, D. B., & Levenson, R. W. (1979). Pre-ejection period: Measuring beta-adrenergic influences upon the heart. psychophysiology. *Psychophysiology, 16*(6), 546–553.

Palmer, A. R., Distefano, R., Leneman, K. B., & Berry, D. (2021). Reliability of the BodyGuard2 (FirstBeat) in the detection of heart rate variability. *Applied Psychophysiology and Biofeedback, 46*(3), 251–258.

Pine, D. S., Mogg, K., Bradley, B. P., Montgomery, L. A., Monk, C. S., McClure, E., . . . Kaufman, J. (2005). Attention bias to threat in maltreated children: Implications for vulnerability to stress-related psychopathology. *American Journal of Psychiatry, 162*(2), 291–296.

Porges, S. W. (1995a). Cardiac vagal tone: A physiological index of stress. *Neuro-science & Biobehavioral Reviews, 19*(2), 225–233.

Porges, S. W. (1995b). Orienting in a defensive world: Mammalian modifications of our evolutionary heritage. A polyvagal theory. *Psychophysiology, 32*(4), 301–318.

Porges, S. W., Doussard-Roosevelt, J. A., Lourdes Portales, A., & Suess, P. E. (1994). Cardiac vagal tone: Stability and relation to difficultness in infants and 3-year-olds. *Developmental Psychobiology, 27*(5), 289–300.

Porges, S. W., & Furman, S. A. (2011). The early development of the autonomic nervous system provides a neural platform for social behavior: A polyvagal perspective. *Infant and Child Development, 20*(1), 106–118.

Pratt, M., Singer, M., Kanat-Maymon, Y., & Feldman, R. (2015). Infant negative reactivity defines the effects of parent–child synchrony on physiological and behavioral regulation of social stress. *Development and Psychopathology, 27*(4), 1191–1204.

Quigley, K. S., & Stifter, C. A. (2006). A comparative validation of sympathetic reactivity in children and adults. *Psychophysiology, 43*, 357–365.

Russell, E., Koren, G., Rieder, M., & Van Uum, S. (2012). Hair cortisol as a biological marker of chronic stress: Current status, future directions and unanswered questions. *Psychoneuroendocrinology, 37*(5), 589–601.

Salehi, B., Cordero, M. I., & Sandi, C. (2010). Learning under stress: The inverted-U-shape function revisited. *Learning and Memory, 17*(10), 522–530.

Salter Ainsworth, M. D., Blehar, M. C., Waters, E., & Hall, S. (1978). *Patterns of attachment: A psychological study of the strange situation*. Erlbaum.

Sapolsky, R. M. (2015). Stress and the brain: Individual variability and the inverted-U. *Nature Neuroscience, 18*(10), 1344–1346.

Sapolsky, R. M., Romero, L. M., & Munck, A. U. (2000). How do glucocorticoids influence stress responses? Integrating permissive, suppressive, stimulatory, and preparative actions. *Endocrine Reviews, 21*(1), 55–89.

Seddon, J. A., Rodriguez, V. J., Provencher, Y., Raftery-Helmer, J., Hersh, J., Labelle, P. R., & Thomassin, K. (2020). Meta-analysis of the effectiveness of the Trier Social Stress Test in eliciting physiological stress responses in children and adolescents. *Psychoneuroendocrinology, 116*, 104582.

Seeman, T. E., McEwen, B. S., Rowe, J. W., & Singer, B. H. (2001). Allostatic load as a marker of cumulative biological risk: MacArthur studies of successful aging. *Proceedings of the National Academy of Sciences, 98*(8), 4770–4775.

Shader, T. M., Gatzke-Kopp, L. M., Crowell, S. E., Jamila Reid, M., Thayer, J. F., Vasey, M. W., & Beauchaine, T. P. (2018). Quantifying respiratory sinus arrhythmia: Effects of misspecifying breathing frequencies across development. *Development and Psychopathology, 30*(1), 351–366.

Shaffer, F., & Ginsberg, J. P. (2017). An overview of heart rate variability metrics and norms. *Frontiers in Public Health, 5*, 258.

Shields, G. S., Bonner, J. C., & Moons, W. G. (2015). Does cortisol influence core executive functions? A meta-analysis of acute cortisol administration effects on working memory, inhibition, and set-shifting. *Psychoneuroendocrinology, 58*, 91–103.

Shields, S. A., MacDowell, K. A., Fairchild, S. B., & Campbell, M. L. (1987). Is mediation of sweating cholinergic, adrenergic, or both? A comment on the literature. *Psychophysiology, 24*(3), 312–319.

Smith, J. D., Woodhouse, S. S., Clark, C. A. C., & Skowron, E. A. (2016). Attachment status and mother-preschooler parasympathetic response to the Strange Situation procedure. *Biological Psychology, 114,* 39–48.

Spangler, G., & Grossman, K. E. (1993). Biobehavioral organization in securely and insecurely attached infants. *Child Development, 64*(5), 1439–1450.

Stephens, M., Bush, N., Weiss, S., & Alkon, A. (2020). Distribution, stability, and continuity of autonomic nervous system responsivity at 18- and 36-months of age. *Biological Research for Nursing,* 1099800420943957.

Sterling, P., & Eyer, J. (1988). Allostasis: A new paradigm to explain arousal pathology. In S. Fisher & J. Reason (Eds.), *Handbook of life stress, cognition and health* (pp. 629–649). Wiley.

Stifter, C. A., & Fox, N. A. (1990). Infant reactivity: Physiological correlates of newborn and 5-month temperament. *Developmental Psychology, 26*(4), 582–588.

Suor, J. H., Sturge-Apple, M. L., Davies, P. T., Cicchetti, D., & Manning, L. G. (2015). Tracing differential pathways of risk: Associations among family adversity, cortisol, and cognitive functioning in childhood. *Child Development, 86*(4), 1142–1158.

Tarullo, A. R., & Gunnar, M. R. (2006). Child maltreatment and the developing HPA axis. *Hormones and Behavior, 50*(4), 632–639.

Taylor, S. E., Way, B. M., & Seeman, T. E. (2011). Early adversity and adult health outcomes. *Development and Psychopathology, 23*(3), 939–954.

Tronick, E., Als, H., Adamson, L., Wise, S., & Brazelton, T. B. (1978). The infant's response to entrapment between contradictory messages in face-to-face interaction. *Journal of the American Academy of Child Psychiatry, 17*(1), 1–13.

Vaghri, Z., Guhn, M., Weinberg, J., Grunau, R. E., Yu, W., & Hertzman, C. (2013). Hair cortisol reflects socio-economic factors and hair zinc in preschoolers. *Psychoneuroendocrinology, 38*(3), 331–340.

Vermeer, H. J., & van IJzendoorn, M. H. (2006). Children's elevated cortisol levels at daycare: A review and meta-analysis. *Early Childhood Research Quarterly, 21*(3), 390–401.

Yerkes, R. M., & Dodson, J. D. (1908). The relation of strength of stimulus to rapidity of habit-formation. *Punishment: Issues and Experiments,* 27–41.

CHAPTER 5

Measuring Noncognitive Skills
Using Ambulatory Psychophysiology

Oliver Saunders Wilder and Richard Palumbo

It has been well established that identifiable patterns of physiological activity underlie many psychological processes, including cognition, emotion, and behavior (Cacioppo, Tassinary, & Berntson, 2007). A growing body of research has also established that identifiable patterns of physiological activities underlie many social processes (Haataja, Malmberg, & Järvelä, 2018), including leadership, engagement, and collaborative learning (Järvelä, Malmberg, Haataja, Sobocinski, & Kirschner, 2019). Though few studies have used measures of physiology in educational settings (Malmberg, Haataja, Seppänen, & Järvelä, 2019), recent technological advances enable their use in a scholastic environment (Malmberg et al., 2019). These advances offer compelling opportunities to further the research and practice of education. To review these possibilities and challenges, this chapter is structured in the following way: First we review relevant psychophysiological, social, and affective theory; second we discuss practical considerations when measuring psychophysiology in real-world educational settings; and finally we discuss two recent research studies in which we applied ambulatory psychophysiology to the measurement of noncognitive skills in young children.

● Physiology and Emotion

In education contexts, key questions often relate to emotion. Is a student currently stressed? How well can they[1] self-regulate (e.g., calm him- or

---

[1] We use "they" as a generic, singular, third-person pronoun, as recommended in the 7th edition of the *Publication Manual of the American Psychological Association*.

herself)? Is the child engaged with the class? Such important and relevant questions have, at their core, a measurable physiological component. To understand the utility of physiological measures in this context, it is important to first consider the relationship between physiology and emotion. This relationship is helpfully defined by the circumplex model of emotion (Figure 5.1).

In this model, emotion is considered a combination of two constructs: valence (e.g., mood; affect) and arousal (cf. Russell, 1980; Russell & Barrett, 1999). Valence refers to an individual's appraisal of his or her experience, ranging from positive to negative. This schema places positive emotions such as happy and joyful at one end of the spectrum, and negative experiences such as fear and frustration at the other. Emotional valence can be assessed through numerous methods, including self-reports, observations, and increasingly, automated analyses of facial expressions.

The second construct, arousal, refers to physiological activation associated with a given emotion. Low arousal levels indicate low levels of physiological activation (e.g., lower heart rate), whereas high arousal states indicate high levels of physiological activation (e.g., higher heart rate). This simply means arousal is a measure of how energetic someone is. Higher

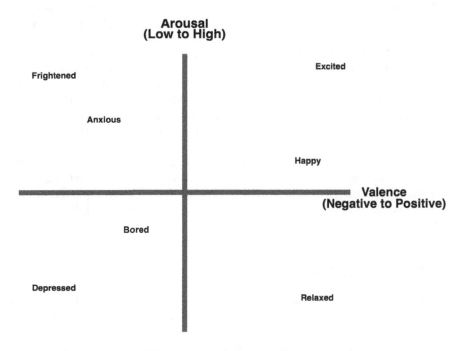

FIGURE 5.1. Circumplex model of emotion.

physiological arousal means someone is physiologically more energetic and activated, and tends to include positive experiences like feeling enthusiastic and happy, as well as negative ones, like being frustrated and anxious. Lower physiological arousal tends to coincide with times people feel less energetic and more inactive, like feeling calm and peaceful, or bored and tired.

Arousal data can be useful in a variety of contexts, such as investigations of stress, reactivity, and regulation, but has interpretive limitations. A primary consideration is that the same physiological activity can occur across a variety of emotions. This means physiological activity during high-arousal negative emotions such as frustration (e.g., heightened heart rate) is currently indistinguishable from physiological activity during high-arousal positive emotions, such as excitement. To differentiate these experiences, we need supporting data to determine valence, such as self-reports or behavioral observations. Another consideration is that arousal is not always observable through behavior. For instance, someone feeling worried may try to hide his or her internal experience and behave as if he or she is relaxed and comfortable. Further, individuals are not always aware of their own internal state, such as someone who does not realize how anxious and stressed he or she really is. This means people may not be consciously aware of or feel connected to measures displaying their own physiology.

Together, valence and arousal encompass the full range of emotions, from low-arousal positive states such as calm and peaceful, to high-arousal negative states such as anger and anxiety. As this chapter is focused on physiology, we primarily address the measurement and interpretation of emotional arousal.

Measuring Physiology

Physiology is a general term encompassing all biological processes, but due to current measurement and interpretative factors, only a few are viable options for classroom use. For instance, students' neural activity during classroom activities could provide interesting information, such as brain areas activated during different learning activities. However, devices needed to collect neural data are prohibitively cumbersome, and resulting data may not be useful for students or teachers. Fortunately, versatile sensors that measure *autonomic nervous system activity* are increasingly accessible, and autonomic data can be used in a variety of important ways, and for our purposes can offer a way to measure the *arousal* dimension of children's affective experience.

To briefly review, the autonomic nervous system is primarily composed of the sympathetic nervous system (SNS) and parasympathetic nervous system (PNS). The SNS is largely a catabolic system (i.e., using energy) associated with physiological activation. Increased SNS activity indicates increased *arousal,* and peaks with a "fight-or-flight" response. The SNS is always active to some degree, so SNS activity can be measured continuously to track changes in an individual's physiological arousal. The PNS is an anabolic system (i.e., storing/processing energy) associated with restoration and repair. Increased PNS activity is indicative of decreased physiological arousal, toward a state of "rest and digest." The dynamic activity of these two systems helps regulate internal processes, constantly adjusting toward an affective state that balances autonomic function with actual demands (Fox, 1996). In this chapter, we will focus on two measures of SNS activity, both of which are commonly used in psychophysiology research as a proxy for arousal and are common measures of cardiac physiology—electrodermal activity (EDA), an indirect measure of eccrine sweat glands and heart rate, and heart rate variability (Boucsein, 1992; Berntson et al., 2017).

Interpersonal Physiology

In addition to telling us about the affective experience of a single individual, a growing body of work indicates that when we look at physiological signals across multiple individuals they also reflect social dynamics. Findings show that interdependencies between peoples' nervous system activity can emerge during social interactions, often described as "physiological synchrony" (Palumbo et al., 2017). The presence of such physiological synchrony has been considered a component of numerous psychosocial constructs, including empathy (Adler, 2002, 2007), attachment (Diamond, 2008), conflict (e.g., Levenson & Gottman, 1983), and emotional coregulation (Field, 2012; Sbarra & Hazan, 2008). At its core, physiological synchrony reflects a simple fact we know well—that groups of people often have shared experiences. Whether a group is laughing together, arguing, or quiet and calm, group patterns are often visible in physiology. Though interactions are sometimes clear through behavior, social dynamics are often too subtle to detect, and can involve complex exchanges that are difficult to measure. For instance, if a student is struggling with an assignment and a peer approaches to help, it may not be apparent whether this support made an impact. However, data may be explored for evidence of reduced arousal in the struggling student, which could indicate lowered anxiety. In addition, if physiological synchrony developed between the students, it would indicate they shared similar internal states, which can be a sign of an empathic interaction. Though procedures are still being developed, it is clear that a component of social constructs can be assessed through our physiology. This brings the potential to continuously and objectively measure abstract social constructs, including leadership, engagement, and collaboration.

While these procedures are just beginning to be used in education research, studies have already identified physiological synchrony between students and found these periods are related to components of learning, including student engagement (Gao, Shao, Rahaman, & Salim, 2020), collaboration (Haataja et al., 2018), and decision making (Thorson, Dumitru, Mendes, & West, 2019). For instance, recent work found when students' mental efforts were matched, group members' SNS activity was synchronized (Dindar, Järvelä, & Haataja, 2020). Pijeira-Díaz, Drachsler, Järvelä, and Kirschner (2019) also identified interactions in arousal states of collaborating students at the dyad level, as well as relationships between physiological synchrony among collaborating students, and those students' learning (Pijeira-Díaz, Drachsler, Järvelä, & Kirschner, 2016). Findings of physiological synchrony between students indicate that at times, their nervous system activities change together (e.g., students' heart rates will increase and decrease in unison). At times, students may function more like a single entity (e.g., a team or cohesive class) than a collection of independent individuals. In turn, these shared states co-occur with similarities in student learning. This simply means that at times, the same descriptions of student behavior (e.g., attentive) and learning (e.g., engaged) will simultaneously apply to every student.

Physiological Regulation

Physiological measurement is also well matched to explore regulatory processes, often considered critical to learning. Regulatory processes include self-regulation (regulating oneself), coregulation (directly supporting each other), and socially shared regulation (regulating together; Järvelä et al., 2019). Self-regulation occurs when an individual chooses to change his or her arousal level, such as a student calming him- or herself down after a stressful class presentation. Because changes in arousal are physiological, they are reflected in measures such as heart rate. Though definitions of self-regulation emphasize an individual's control over his or her own arousal, it is also influenced by social interactions. For instance, if a class as a whole is having difficulty settling down after recess, each individual may have a more difficult time regulating him- or herself. In coregulation, when social factors help someone regulate, self-regulation can become an interpersonal process. This occurs when someone regulates him- or herself with the intent of having a regulatory impact on another person. For example, as part of an effort to help an anxious student, a teacher may slow his or her breathing to become calm as they talk with the student. If successful, the student's arousal will decrease as he or she relaxes. Further, in instances of physiological synchrony, the student's breathing may mirror the teacher's, and they both can relax at the same pace. Socially shared regulation occurs when a group chooses to regulate together for a shared purpose, such as all individuals in a study group working together to remain engaged with a task. This can be thought of as a combination of self- and coregulation, where individuals aim to keep their own and others arousal within the same boundaries. These dynamics may be most recognizable in teamwork, where the individuals conform to the activity of the group.

These regulatory processes can impact motivation, emotion, cognition, and behavior of individuals and groups (Järvenoja et al., 2018). For example, Dindar, Alikhani, Malmberg, Järvelä, and Seppänen (2019) studied self-regulation and physiological synchrony among high school students during collaborative learning tasks and found relationships between physiological synchrony and cognitive regulation. A common situation this may reflect occurs when a group of students is excited and off task—too silly and energetic to focus on and process the lesson being presented, then calming down (regulating) together such that they are able to focus on their schoolwork.

Interpreting Interpersonal Physiological Patterns

To better understand some of the dynamics being addressed in physiological synchrony research, it may be helpful to consider a few key interpersonal physiological patterns that have been defined to date. These are magnitude, direction and lag, and timing (Palumbo et al., 2017). Magnitude refers to the strength of synchrony (e.g., effect size), with higher magnitudes indicating greater interdependence or association between individuals' physiological patterns. At high magnitudes, there can be remarkable levels of synchrony between individuals—times when students may be laughing together or deeply engaged in conversation with one another. At lower magnitudes, individuals are not sharing the same states. Whereas high magnitudes of synchrony can reflect positive social contexts such as shared attention, they can also reflect negative contexts, such as shared frustration. Similarly, low magnitudes of synchrony can be problematic, such as a hyperactive student in an otherwise calm class, but can also be useful, such as a student who remains uninfluenced by distractingly energetic peers. Direction refers to the predictability of one person's physiology from another's. For instance, one person's physiology is sometimes predicted by another's, but not vice versa. A similar pattern can be found through lag, which refers to statistical results showing a pattern in one person is followed by a similar pattern in another person. These patterns have potential to be indicators of influence. For instance, if a student's physiology tracks the teacher's, but not vice versa, it could indicate that the student is responding to the teacher, but the teacher is not responding to that student (perhaps because the teacher's focus is on a different student). This pattern has been described as a metric of leadership, as it can indicate whether changes in one person lead to similar changes in others. Finally, timing refers to the length of time that a given interaction is assessed or observed. Multiple interpersonal physiological processes have been found to operate at different time scales simultaneously, meaning synchrony measured in short time scales (e.g., minutes or hours) can reveal patterns related to momentary interactions, whereas long-term measures (e.g., days or months) can reveal interactions that take longer to develop. For example, a single brief interaction between a student and teacher may be of interest, enabling assessment of behaviors such as self- and coregulation. However, it may also be useful to track their relationship over the course of the school year to observe how each individual and their relationship changes over time. Both time scales are equally valid, but results reflect different processes.

• Measuring Psychophysiology in Real-World Educational Settings

Now that we have learned about what psychophysiological signals can tell us, we look practically at how we can measure psychophysiological signals in real-world environments. While most research with psychophysiology has been done in tightly controlled laboratory environments, the last decade has seen significant advances in the field of *ambulatory psychophysiology*. Modern wearable sensing technology means it is now possible to capture high-quality psychophysiology data in a variety of contexts without the use of traditional wired sensors. We believe this is particularly important, because laboratory environments offer poor *ecological validity*—that is to say, they are not very good at re-creating a real-world classroom environment with its many environmental distractions, complex interpersonal classroom dynamics, and day-to-day variability.

What Can We Sense Noninvasively?

The majority of modern wearable psychophysiology devices measure either EDA, cardiac physiology, or both and are typically worn on the wrist to minimize interference with everyday activities (see Figure 5.2 for considerations in selecting a device). Both measures may be suitable for psychophysiological measurement, and indeed an increasing number of devices provide sensors for both EDA and cardiac physiology, but each has some unique considerations.

Selecting a Wearable Sensing Device for Ambulatory Psychophysiology

The proliferation of personal-fitness wearables in recent years has helped to spur significant innovation in physiological sensing technology, but not all devices on the market today are appropriate for ambulatory psychophysiology and there are several important considerations when selecting a wearable sensor.

1. **Sample rate: How frequently are measurements taken?** In order to maximize battery life, many non-research-grade consumer devices are designed to sample physiological parameters infrequently, often once every few seconds. While this may be sufficient for fitness-related applications that are mostly concerned with estimating an individual's activity level, it does not provide sufficient detail for psychophysiological measurement. We recommend only using devices that collect at least four samples per second (for EDA) or that report instantaneous estimated heart rate values with a temporal resolution of at least 1 second.

2. **Access to raw time-series data: Can you access all the data?** Many consumer devices only provide periodic averages of physiological parameters (for example, average heart rate every 10 minutes); this is typically not suitable for psychophysiological analysis.

3. **Avoid (excessive) built-in data postprocessing:** Some wearable devices will attempt to "fix" questionable data readings either via interpolation (for example, filling in heart rate measurements that were compromised due to movement artifacts with an average heart rate) or by heavily smoothing outputs. This can be problematic as it often masks problems with the underlying data and can heavily skew measures of variability; such devices should be avoided for purposes of ambulatory psychophysiology.

FIGURE 5.2. Considerations in selecting a wearable psychophysiology device.

Electrodermal Activity

EDA sensors work by passing a small voltage across two points on the skin and measuring the resulting electrical current, providing a measure that covaries with the sweat content in the upper layers of the skin. Because EDA is a measure of electrical conductance, it requires a set of two electrodes that must be physically and electrically connected with the skin at all times. Figure 5.3 shows some example EDA data.

Practical Consideration: Electrode Type

These may be either "dry electrodes," usually made of a surgical steel or steel plated with silver, or disposable "wet electrodes," which are coated with a conductive gel to enhance the connection with the skin and often include a gentle adhesive pad to keep them in place. Some devices, such as

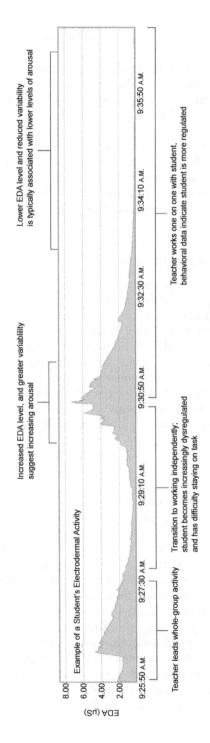

FIGURE 5.3. Example of a student's EDA.

115

the Empatica E4 offer both types of electrodes, whereas others are compatible with only one or the other. The choice of electrode type, like many considerations with ambulatory psychophysiology, is a question of balancing wearer comfort and measurement quality: Pregelled wet electrodes will almost always provide better, more consistent data but may be unsuitable to wear for very long periods and typically need to be replaced each time the device is removed; dry electrodes are more comfortable for the wearer, but may reduce sensitivity of the EDA measurement. For our research in classroom settings with young children, we have found that the benefits of pregelled electrodes outweigh potential downsides and are typically well tolerated by children.

Practical Consideration: Electrode Placement

In addition to electrode type, it is very important to consider electrode placement when using a wearable EDA sensor, as sensitivity depends significantly upon the density of eccrine sweat glands in the area of skin where the electrodes are located, and as a result only certain areas of the body will yield good-quality signal. The highest density of eccrine sweat glands occurs on the fingertips, palms, and soles of our feet, and density decreases as you move away from the extremities. In our work, we've found that placing electrodes on the underside of the wrist, within about 1 inch of the wrist joint, provides a good compromise between signal quality and wearer comfort. Although less common, it is also possible to measure EDA on the foot and ankle.

Cardiac Physiology

An alternative measure of autonomic nervous system activity is cardiac physiology. Like EDA, cardiac physiology can be used to measure arousal, but because our heart is involved in regulating many systems (such as our blood pressure) its interpretation is a bit more complex than EDA (see Table 5.1). However, heart rate monitors are among the most common physiological sensors built into consumer devices and, as the quality of these devices improve and their cost decreases, they become an increasingly attractive choice for use in classroom settings.

Wearable cardiac physiology is most commonly measured using a method known as *photoplethysmography*—essentially an infrared light is shined on the skin, and the amount of reflected light is measured, which varies as the heart pumps blood through your veins. The resulting measure is known as blood volume pulse, or BVP. More recently, some wearable devices also include *electrocardiogram* (ECG) sensors, which measure electrical signals from the heart. The raw values of both measures are complex

TABLE 5.1. EDA Compared to Cardiac Physiology

EDA		Cardiac physiology	
Measure	Description	Measure	Description
Skin conductance level (SCL)	The average EDA over several minutes: Higher SCL is generally associated with increased arousal, but specific values may vary across individuals.	Beats per minute	The number of heartbeats per minute. This may be estimated for periods less than 60 seconds by extrapolation from the time between beats.
Skin conductance response (SCR)	A brief "peak" in EDA in response to a particular stimulus (such as a loud sound)	Interbeat interval (IBI)	The time in milliseconds between successive heartbeats
SCRs per minute	A measure of how many SCRs occur in a 60-second window: More SCRs per minute is typically associated with increased arousal, and this measure is typically more consistent across individuals than SCL.	Heart rate variability (HRV)	Because many nonpsychological factors, such as breathing, influence heart rate, measures of variability (such as the standard deviation of IBI values in a time window) are better predictors of psychophysiological arousal. Decreased variability is typically associated with increased arousal.

Note. For a great introduction to EDA, we highly recommend Dawson, Schell, and Filion (2017), and for cardiac physiology, Berntson, Quigley, Norman, and Lozano (2017).

to interpret, so most vendors offer an automated means of calculating the commonly used metrics of heart rate (measured in beats per minute; see example in Figure 5.4) or interbeat interval (IBI) a time series consisting of the time in milliseconds between subsequent heart beats. We will address the interpretation of these metrics below.

Practical Consideration: Motion Artifacts

Because cardiac measures rely on resolving relatively weak optical and electrical signals, ambulatory cardiac measures are particularly sensitive to *motion artifacts,* changes in the raw signal caused by movement of the device on the wearer (e.g., the sensor device slipping back and forth on a person's wrist). This makes fit especially important, as a loose sensor will likely yield little usable data, and makes cardiac sensors most appropriate for situations in which participants are relatively stationary. As such,

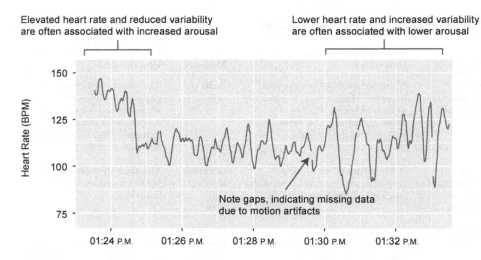

FIGURE 5.4. Example of heart rate variability measured in beats per minute (BPM).

cardiac measures are not commonly used with very young children, but could be a good fit for measurement in classroom settings in which children spend more time seated.

Interpreting Ambulatory Psychophysiology Data

Always Reference Within-Person

Unlike many traditional psychometric measures, for which norms exist against which an individual's data may be compared, ambulatory psychophysiological measures should typically be interpreted within-person as absolute values in the context of the range of variation in a given individual. For example, an average EDA of 4.2 μS or a resting heart rate of 100 beats per minute could indicate high arousal (e.g., intense anxiety, or excitement) for one individual, but might be associated with average arousal for another individual due to each person's unique physiology. Instead of focusing on such absolute numbers, it's best to look at changes in psychophysiological measures across *time* and *context* (e.g., the situation or environment) for each individual, and then if desired to analyze these within-person changes at a group level.

This has important implications for study design—it is best to include some sort of baseline activity against which physiology data collected during other activities can be compared. This can often be quite simple: For example, in one study in which we were examining emotional reactivity in young children using EDA, we began with a 5-minute rest period in which children sat on a parent's lap while the parent read aloud a book. We used this baseline data to compare with each child's data during a subsequent task designed to induce mild frustration, allowing us to interpret changes in each child's physiology during frustration relative to his or her physiology during rest. In another more naturalistic study in a classroom setting, we simply identified a 5 minute period of relatively low-key activity for each child and used this as a baseline.

The Importance of the Social and Behavioral Context

Regardless of which type of physiological data are used, it is important to consider how you will capture the social and behavioral context when recording physiological data. Psychophysiology data are rarely interpretable in the absence of information about the situation in which it was collected, and this is particularly true when we consider using these data to make inference about noncognitive skills. Any affective or regulatory response represents a transaction between the individual and his or her environment (including the other individuals with whom he or she may be interacting), so capturing this environment is vital to interpreting an individual's psychophysiology data (Bronfenbrenner, 1992). In our work, we have frequently found time-stamped video recording to be an extremely valuable means of collecting context data, but any number of other approaches may be effective depending upon the circumstances. Video data have qualitative value in interpreting observed physiological dynamics, but can also offer quantitative data because it can be *coded* after the fact by viewers blind to the physiology data, providing complementary measures of children's behavior, affect, or environment that can be analyzed together with physiology data (see Example 2 later in this chapter).

Paying close attention to this contextual information will also help to protect against our natural tendency to ascribe intrinsic value to a particular physiological state, for example assuming that high arousal is "problematic" or "dysregulated." Arousal should always be considered as a *transaction* between an individual and the environment, so the adaptiveness of a given arousal level needs to be considered in terms of the environmental context in which it occurs. For example, persistent elevated physiological arousal (e.g., elevated heart rate or EDA) may be maladaptive at bedtime, but is perfectly adaptive if the individual is currently taking a timed test. Likewise, highly variable arousal could be indicative of poor regulation in one context, but might be perfectly appropriate in a situation in which the cognitive or attentional demands are rapidly changing.

● Real-World Applications of Ambulatory Physiology to Measure Noncognitive Skills

Now that we have explored some of the theoretical and practical considerations of using ambulatory psychophysiology to measure noncognitive skills, we want to share two recent examples of real-world research in naturalistic settings. The first example focuses on using ambulatory psychophysiology to quantify social reciprocity ability in preschool-aged children; the second focuses on research into intrapersonal regulation as part of a larger study conducted in early childhood classrooms in a public school setting. We hope that these examples highlight what is possible using existing technology, and inspire others to leverage ambulatory psychophysiology tools to gain new insight in their own work.

Example 1: Using Ambulatory Psychophysiology to Measure Social Development

A key challenge to studying the development of social reciprocity in young children is that social interactions are fundamentally transactional, taking place within a system rather than in isolation, and that people affect and are affected by their interactions with others. As such, it is important to consider the child, the caretaker, and their dyadic interaction as three separate but complementary lines of inquiry when exploring social cognition and social reciprocity in the developing brain. In this study we aimed to see if dyadic ambulatory psychophysiology data correlated with standard informant-report scores of social reciprocity development, theorizing that the ability to "sync up" affect (and by extension arousal measured by EDA) would be related to a child's social development.

To investigate this, we collected dyadic ambulatory EDA data on 22 typically developing children, and had each child's caregiver complete a standard informant-report measure (the Social Responsiveness Scale 2nd Ed., or SRS-2; Bruni, 2014) assessing various aspects of each child's social development relative to other children the child's age. With the caregiver present, each child interacted for approximately 10 minutes with an unfamiliar adult (researcher) who attempted to engage him or her in a series of age-appropriate social interaction and affective regulation tasks adapted from the Autism Diagnostic and Observation Scale (ADOS-2). We collected time-stamped EDA data at a rate of 32 samples per second simultaneously from both the child and unfamiliar adult researcher, and subsequently analyzed these data to examine how dyadic physiological dynamics related to the informant-report measures of social development.

In order to quantify the degree of mutual influence between the two EDA time series for each adult-child dyad, we utilized *time-varying dynamical systems modeling,* a statistical method we developed that provides a statistic called I^2 that quantifies the magnitude of interdependence between two time series as a number between 0 and 1.0, representing the degree of interconnection or "synchrony" in a dyad. After calculating the average I^2 statistic for each dyad, we correlated these with the SRS-2 measure. The Social Awareness *t*-score of the SRS-2 was significantly negatively correlated with the I^2, $r(19) = -0.45$, $p < .05$, indicating that higher levels of physiological interdependence between child and researcher during the study was associated with lower levels of social impairment (e.g., improved social awareness) relative to other children of the same age (Saunders Wilder, 2017). These findings are consistent with theory that physiological dynamics may underlie our experience of social connection and social reciprocity, and suggest that ambulatory psychophysiology could offer a valuable, sensitive, and complimentary means of measuring social emotional development.

Example 2: Measuring Intra- and Interpersonal Psychophysiological Regulation in a Classroom Setting

One of the particularly exciting aspects of ambulatory psychophysiology is that it can allow for measurement with participants who would not tolerate traditional bulky wired psychophysiology equipment. In the case of this pilot study, we were interested in examining the relationship between psychophysiological signals and observational measures of behavioral regulation in a typical early childhood classroom setting, so it was vital that the sensing equipment be both unobtrusive and wireless.

Method and Data Collection

Because the participants would be kindergarten-age children, and were therefore unlikely to be stationary, we chose to use EDA as our primary measure since it is more robust to motion artifacts than cardiac measures. We selected the Empatica E4 sensor for use in this study because it was relatively small, worn on the wrist, robust to wear-and-tear, and allowed us the option of either pregelled adhesive electrodes or dry electrodes. For this study, we opted to go with the pregelled adhesive electrodes in order to maximize our signal sensitivity and to ensure that impact of physical motion on signal quality was minimized. To help prevent children in the study from playing with the sensor, we covered each sensor with a colored sweatband after placing it on the child.

At the beginning of each day of data collection children would come over individually to be fitted with a E4 sensor, a process that took approximately 2 minutes per child. We also recorded EDA data from the classroom teacher, to allow us to examine how changes in the teacher's physiology related to children's physiology and behavior. We were pleased to find that nearly all children in the study tolerated wearing the E4 without issue. In order to capture context data, time-stamped video and audio recording was also collected each day during the study period. This video was later coded for regulation-related behaviors using the Regulation-Related Skills Measure (*https://projects.iq.harvard.edu/rrsm/what-rrsm*), and this coding was analyzed together with the data.

Analysis

The first step in analyzing any psychophysiology dataset is to screen data for data quality. In this study, we performed this screening manually but there are a number of open-source tools that can also be utilized for this purpose (e.g., *https://github.com/iankleckner/EDAQA*). Using video data, we identified periods of time of particular interest—such as transitions between free-play and teacher-directed activities, which required children to exercise self-regulation. EDA data for each of these time periods was then analyzed and compared to behavioral ratings from the video. In order to look at *regulation* we used measures of variance (e.g., standard deviation) and slope (the degree to which physiology was increasing or decreasing over time) to quantify how arousal changed during these time periods. By looking at these measures, in connection with behavioral measures of regulation coded independently based on the video data, we were able to explore potential connections between behavioral and psychophysiological regulation. Ultimately, such measures may offer a powerful quantitative means of assessing development related to self-regulation and executive functions, as well as offering qualitative insights into the relationship between classroom practices, children's behavior, and their internal state. Collecting such data at the classroom level can offer many opportunities to look for patterns across multiple children and over time. Figure 5.5 shows some example data and interpretation.

● Conclusion

Recent advances in wearable sensing technology make ambulatory psychophysiology a powerful and accessible means of measuring noncognitive skills in a variety of settings. Using relatively unobtrusive wearable physiology sensors, it is possible to quantify both intra- and interpersonal psychophysiological dynamics, and these measures provide a valuable complement to qualitative and self-report measures when examining socioaffective dynamics. We believe these measures offer a unique opportunity to

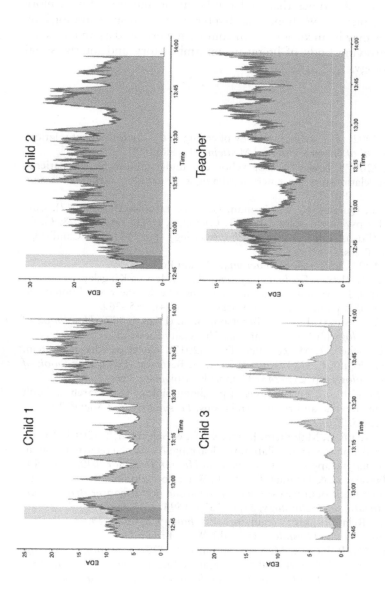

FIGURE 5.5. EDA for three students and a teacher in a classroom setting. The shaded region represents the "baseline" for each participant, a "calm" period of time we selected based on video. Note the different regulation profiles shown by each student: Child 2's EDA exhibited significant high-frequency variability and elevated skin conductance level (SCL) relative to baseline for nearly the entire session, suggesting persistent elevated arousal, whereas Child 3's EDA exhibited three discrete periods of increased SCL and variability each followed by a rapid recovery to baseline. All three children and the teacher showed a trend toward increased variability and higher SCL relative to baseline after 13:30, which is likely a reflection of the demands of the classroom activity during that period of time.

look beyond children's behavior and self-report, providing insight into the social–emotional dynamics that underlie behavior and providing a more comprehensive picture. We hope this chapter serves as inspiration for how such measures may be incorporated in your own work, and as an introduction to the growing body of literature on ambulatory and interpersonal psychophysiology.

REFERENCES

Adler, H. M. (2002). The sociophysiology of caring in the doctor patient relationship. *Journal of General Internal Medicine, 17*, 883–890.

Adler, H. M. (2007). Toward a biopsychosocial understanding of the patient–physician relationship: An emerging dialogue. *Journal of General Internal Medicine, 22*, 280–285.

Berntson, G. G., Quigley, K. S., Norman, G. J., & Lozano, D. L. (2017). Cardiovascular psychophysiology. In J. T. Cacioppo, L. G. Tassinary, & G. G. Berntson (Eds.), *Handbook of psychophysiology* (pp. 183–216). Cambridge University Press.

Boucsein, W. (1992). *Electrodermal activity.* Plenum Press.

Bronfenbrenner, U. (1992). *Ecological systems theory.* Jessica Kingsley.

Bruni, T. P. (2014). Test review: Social Responsiveness Scale—Second edition (SRS-2). *Journal of Psychoeducational Assessment, 32*(4), 365–369.

Cacioppo, J. T., Tassinary, L. G., & Berntson, G. G. (Eds.). (2007). *Handbook of psychophysiology* (3rd ed.). Cambridge University Press.

Dawson, M. E., Schell, A. M., & Filion, D. L. (2017). The electrodermal system. In J. T. Cacioppo, L. G. Tassinary, & G. G. Berntson (Eds.), *Handbook of psychophysiology* (pp. 217–243). Cambridge University Press.

Diamond, L. M. (2008). Contributions of psychophysiology to research on adult attachment: Review and recommendations. *Personality and Social Psychology Review, 5*, 276–295.

Dindar, M., Alikhani, I., Malmberg, J., Järvelä, S., & Seppänen, T. (2019). Examining shared monitoring in collaborative learning: A case of a recurrence quantification analysis approach. *Computers in Human Behavior, 100*, 335–344.

Dindar, M., Järvelä, S., & Haataja, E. (2020). What does physiological synchrony reveal about metacognitive experiences and group performance? *British Journal of Educational Technology, 51*(5), 1577–1596.

Field, T. (2012). Relationships as regulators. *Psychology, 3*, 467–479.

Fox, S. I. (1996). *Human physiology* (5th ed.). W. C. Brown.

Gao, N., Shao, W., Rahaman, M. S., & Salim, F. D. (2020). n-Gage: Predicting in-class Emotional, Behavioural and Cognitive Engagement in the Wild. *Proceedings of the ACM on Interactive, Mobile, Wearable and Ubiquitous Technologies, 4*(3), 1–26.

Haataja, E., Malmberg, J., & Järvelä, S. (2018). Monitoring in collaborative learning: Co-occurrence of observed behavior and physiological synchrony explored. *Computers in Human Behavior, 87*, 337–347.

Järvelä, S., Malmberg, J., Haataja, E., Sobocinski, M., & Kirschner, P. A. (2019). What multimodal data can tell us about the students' regulation of their learning process. *Learning and Instruction, 101203.*

Järvenoja, H., Järvelä, S., Törmänen, T., Näykki, P., Malmberg, J., Kurki, K., . . . Isohätälä, J. (2018). Capturing motivation and emotion regulation during a learning process. *Frontline Learning Research, 6*(3), 85–104.

Levenson, R. W., & Gottman, J. M. (1983). Marital interaction: Physiological linkage and affective exchange. *Journal of Personality and Social Psychology, 45,* 587–597.

Malmberg, J., Haataja, E., Seppänen, T., & Järvelä, S. (2019). Are we together or not? The temporal interplay of monitoring, physiological arousal and physiological synchrony during a collaborative exam. *International Journal of Computer-Supported Collaborative Learning, 14*(4), 467–490.

Pijeira-Díaz, H. J., Drachsler, H., Järvelä, S., & Kirschner, P. A. (2016, April). Investigating collaborative learning success with physiological coupling indices based on electrodermal activity. In *Proceedings of the sixth international conference on learning analytics & knowledge* (pp. 64–73).

Pijeira-Díaz, H. J., Drachsler, H., Järvelä, S., & Kirschner, P. A. (2019). Sympathetic arousal commonalities and arousal contagion during collaborative learning: How attuned are triad members? *Computers in Human Behavior, 92,* 188–197.

Palumbo, R. V., Marraccini, M. E., Weyandt, L. L., Wilder-Smith, O., McGee, H. A., Liu, S., & Goodwin, M. S. (2017). Interpersonal autonomic physiology: A systematic review of the literature. *Personality and Social Psychology Review, 21*(2), 99–141.

Russell, J. A. (1980). A circumplex model of affect. *Journal of Personality and Social Psychology, 39,* 1161–1178.

Russell, J. A., & Barrett, L. F. (1999). Core affect, prototypical emotional episodes, and other things called emotion: Dissecting the elephant. *Journal of Personality and Social Psychology, 76,* 805–819.

Saunders Wilder, O. (2017). *Quantitative assessment of socio-affective dynamics in autism using interpersonal physiology.* Northeastern University.

Sbarra, D. A., & Hazan, C. (2008). Coregulation, dysregulation, self-regulation: An integrative analysis and empirical agenda for understanding adult attachment, separation, loss, and recovery. *Personality and Social Psychology Review, 12,* 141–167.

Thorson, K. R., Dumitru, O. D., Mendes, W. B., & West, T. V. (2021). Influencing the physiology and decisions of groups: Physiological linkage during group decision-making. *Group Processes & Intergroup Relations, 24*(1), 145–159.

CHAPTER 6

Conceptualizing and Measuring Character Virtues and Related Attributes Using the Bornstein Specificity Principle

A Relational Developmental Systems-Based Perspective

Paul A. Chase, Dian Yu, Jonathan M. Tirrell, Mary H. Buckingham, Patricia Gansert, Yerin Park, Carolina Goncalves, and Richard M. Lerner

Jones, Lesaux, and Barnes (see Introduction, this volume) have explained that measurement of noncognitive attributes should integrate good science, psychometric rigor, and practical utility. We agree. Theory-predicated and methodologically rigorous science—that establishes validity, reliability, and invariance across individuals, contexts, and time—must be the basis of measures used to describe, explain, or optimize whole-child development, learning, and thriving for diverse youth (Cantor, Lerner, Pittman, Chase, & Gomperts, 2021).

At this writing, the scientific work within which measurement is undertaken is embedded in a controversy that is akin to the paradigm shifts discussed by Kuhn (1962, 1970). As we shall explain, this controversy involves what should be measured when measuring noncognitive attributes, for example, character attributes. Should measurement be focused on attempting to learn about the nature of a character variable (e.g., gratitude) as it is manifested among groups of individuals? Here, measures of average scores for, say, gratitude, might be computed for groups varying in age, and a researcher could then report whether gratitude, on average, is a character attribute that varies across age groups. Alternatively, should measurement be focused on a character variable (e.g., gratitude) as it is manifested within a specific individual? Here, measures of a specific individual's scores on a measure of gratitude might be assessed across time, and a researcher could report whether gratitude increased, decreased, or was unchanged across time for this specific person. The former type of measurement is termed *variable-focused assessment;* the latter type of measurement is termed *person-specific assessment.*

Our contention in this chapter is that, *if* researchers or practitioners want to understand if noncognitive attributes such as character-related ones change in relation to specific experiences (e.g., character education programs; Berkowitz, Bier, & McCauley, 2017) or in the course of a child's or an adolescent's development (Lerner, 2018a, 2018b, 2018c), *then* the focus of measurement must be placed on *people,* and not on variables. In computing a group score, such as an average, it is not likely that each individual in the group will have the same score. In other words, an assessment of whether an average score for an attribute of character for a particular group of people varies across time is not equivalent to an assessment of whether a score for the character attribute varies for a specific individual within the same group (Lerner, 2018a, 2018b, 2018c; Rose, 2016). Simply, focusing on variables is not the same as focusing on an individual. Learning about if average scores for a variable change across time or in different settings (contexts, places) is not the same as learning about if a specific individual has differences in scores for a variable across time or place.

The purpose of this chapter, therefore, is to present the conceptual and methodological bases of person-specific measurement of character (i.e., measurement focused on individual change). Person-specific change is also termed *idiographic* (Allport, 1937, 1968; Rose, 2016). We argue that a focus on such specificity is a necessary starting point for *developmental* measurement, research design, and data analyses (Bornstein, 2017; Molenaar & Nesselroade, 2015; Rose, 2016), especially when research is framed by ideas associated with the relational developmental systems (RDS) metatheory of human development, which focuses on the holistic functions of a living, open, self-constructing, and integrated system (Overton, 2015).

Our focus is based on the long-understood fact that in some respects, each person is like all other people (e.g., all people have respiratory, digestive, circulatory, and nervous systems), in some respects each person is like only some other people (e.g., people in one culture may have customs, mores, and institutional systems unlike those of people from another culture; Raeff, 2016), and each person is like no other person (Allport, 1937, 1968; Kluckhohn & Murray, 1948). For instance, no two people in the world have the same complement of DNA; for instance, whereas monozygotic twins have the same nuclear DNA, the DNA in the mitochondria of their cells are different (e.g., Richardson, 2017); and, because all people have different histories of relations with their context across their lives, their epigenetics will also be different (Slavich, 2020; Slavich & Cole, 2013). As we shall explain in this chapter, Bornstein (2017, 2019) has presented a specificity principle to depict the dimensions of biological and contextual individuality that must be understood if researchers are to provide a thorough account of human development and, as well, if practitioners are to maximize the chances that their approaches and the programs they implement promote positive outcomes for every program participant.

Accordingly, we believe that a deeper understanding of an individual's specific journey across life is critical to the practices of policymakers, administrators, and practitioners. That is, we will argue that the work of these groups would be enhanced by a specificity focus instead of a focus on average scores for a group of individuals. Arriving at group averages is the measurement target when variables are of focal interest, but knowing about how a group fares in response to a character education program would not help a practitioner understand why some participants gained more than others from their program (Shonkoff & Center on the Developing Child, 2017). That is, policymakers, administrators, and practitioners must understand how an individual's characteristics emerge in relation to the mutual influences (also termed *dynamic coactions;* Lerner, 2018a, 2018b, 2018c; Mascolo & Fischer, 2015) of the important contexts of their lives—for example, families, peer groups, and in-school or out-of-school-time (OST) programs.

To support our contentions, we begin with reviewing our conceptualization of character, followed by a discussion of the specificity principle from the perspective of RDS metatheory. We then discuss implications for the design and implementation of developmental research pertinent to attributes of character and related constructs. We illustrate these implications by reference to findings from the Measures and Methods across the Developmental Continuum (MMDC) project (e.g., Yu et al., 2020, 2021, in preparation).

• Character and Related Attributes

The study of character and attributes related to it—for example, constructs studied under the heading of social and emotional learning (SEL) (e.g., Jones et al., 2017; Jones & Kahn, 2017) or positive youth development (PYD) (e.g., Lerner, Lerner, Bowers, & Geldhof, 2015; Lerner et al., 2021a)—have contributed to theory, research, and design principles to guide creating programs or policies to enhance the positive behavior and development of diverse youth. Figure 6.1 presents a Venn diagram representing the possible overlap among the attributes studied under the labels of SEL, PYD, and character virtues (see Lerner et al., 2021a, for further discussion).

The portion of the Venn diagram representing the attributes of a thriving young person that are specific to character virtues pertains to morally based actions that enable individuals and the people and institutions comprising their social worlds to thrive across time and place (Berkowitz, 2012;

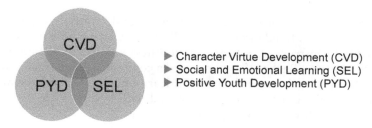

▶ Character Virtue Development (CVD)
▶ Social and Emotional Learning (SEL)
▶ Positive Youth Development (PYD)

FIGURE 6.1. The study of character virtue development (CVD), social and emotional learning (SEL), and positive youth development (PYD) involves overlapping constructs.

Nucci, 2017). For example, Berkowitz et al. (2017) defined character as "the set of psychological characteristics that motivate and enable one to function as a moral agent, to perform optimally, to effectively pursue knowledge and intellectual flourishing, and to be an effective member of society" (p. 34). If this definition is deconstructed, we believe that Berkowitz et al. (2017) are pointing to an understanding of character virtues as complex (having multiple components), as composed of moral motivation and moral actions (involving an individual feeling impelled to act to "do the right thing"), and of the individual acting as a competent moral agent (i.e., having the agency to act on the context that is acting on him or her so that the correct actions are enacted at specific times and in specific places) (e.g., Callina & Lerner, 2017; Lerner, 2018b; Lerner & Callina, 2014; Nucci, 2017).

Similarly, Narvaez (2008) has noted that character involves individual agency in producing a life that is good for one to live within one's community. In turn, Nucci (2001) pointed out that character involves human welfare, justice, and rights that function as core components of interpersonal relations. As well, Berkowitz (2012) noted that character virtues involve "a *public system* of universal concerns about human welfare, justice, and rights that all rational people would want others to adhere to" (p. 249).

Although most models of character virtues emphasize that a moral component must be associated with actions that reflect positive instances of character (Berkowitz, 2012; Nucci, 2017), several other domains of character have been suggested. For example, Lickona and Davidson (2005) noted that, in addition to moral character, another instantiation of virtues involved performance character, conceptualized as "the qualities such as effort, diligence, perseverance, a strong work ethic, a positive attitude, ingenuity, and self-discipline needed to realize one's potential for excellence in academics, co-curricular activities, the workplace, or any other area of endeavor" (p. 18). In turn, Seider (2012) suggested that another possible component of character consists of attributes that constitute contributions to civil society; that is, civic character is comprised of the knowledge, skills, and commitments involved in being an active and positively engaged citizen (Seider, 2012). In addition, Seider, Tamerat, Clark, and Soutter (2017) included the construct of critical consciousness within this notion of civic character. In turn, Baehr (2017) proposed a component of character involving intellectual attributes such as love of learning, seeking truth, creativity, and other attributes of cognition associated with leading a life devoted to "the pursuit of distinctively epistemic goods" (p. 1).

These ideas about the composition of character virtues have been embedded in conceptions of programs that seek to promote specific instances of character, for instance, purpose (e.g., Bundick, Yeager, King, & Damon, 2010) or spirituality (e.g., King, Carr, & Boitor, 2011) or, in turn, character virtues in general (e.g., Berkowitz, 2021; Berkowitz et al., 2017). For instance, the Berkowitz et al. model is targeted for use within schools and in OST settings. Berkowitz (2021; Berkowitz et al., 2017) noted that effective character education programs are consistent with their PRIMED model (i.e., involving the Prioritization of character education, Relationships that build character, Intrinsic motivation to manifest character, Modeling of character virtues, Empowering youth, and Developmental pedagogy). Moreover, and illustrative of the Venn diagram in Figure 6.1, Berkowitz et al. noted that their PRIMED approach to character virtue development (CVD) aligns with the SEL programs promoted by the Collaborative for Academic, Social, and Emotional Learning (CASEL), and, in fact, scholars working across the areas of both CVD and SEL agree that such alignment exists (e.g., Durlak, 2017; Elias, Ferrito, & Morceri, 2015; Moroney & Devaney, 2017).

In sum, character virtues function in the actual ecology of human development to align the individual and context in manners that reflect, support, maintain, and further moral actions and ideology that support just, equitable, and democratic principles and practices. This conception of character virtues links a thriving individual to community contexts having such principles and practices. Therefore, the focus of developmental theory and methodology must be on describing, explaining, and optimizing the bases of the evolving relations between a specific individual and a specific context, at a specific time that contribute positively to the betterment of the world that is contributing to an individual's betterment (Bornstein, 2019; Lerner & Callina, 2014).

For example, imagine that two groups of fifth graders participated in a well-designed study of a character education program intended to increase the character virtue of gratitude. Both the participants receiving the educational program and a carefully matched comparison group of students who did not take part in the program were studied over the course a semester. At the beginning of the study, both groups had comparable average scores on a measure of gratitude but, at the end of the semester the average score for the treatment group was 30% higher than the average scores for the comparison youth (whose average score did not change). This difference would be statistically significant.

Would these results show that the gratitude education program was useful? Yes. However, an average increase of 30% means that some participants showed a greater increase and other participants showed less of an increase. In addition, if the program evaluator inspected the initial and final scores for each student in the treatment group, it might also be the case that some fifth graders showed no change in scores and, perhaps as well, that some students actually showed decreases in gratitude.

The point is that demonstrating a 30% improvement for the group does not demonstrate anything about the specific changes, or lack thereof, of any specific member of the group. To go beyond just describing what specific scores were shown across time for which specific students, a program evaluator using the approach to describing, explaining, and optimizing the CVD that we are recommending would need to try to ascertain the specific relations between each student and the specific experiences in the specific contexts of their lives that were associated with their scores for gratitude. In other words, the evaluator would want to identify the specific events or relationships that were associated with specific changes for specific youth. With such knowledge from program evaluations of this sort, practitioners could then have information potentially useful for creating new youth–context relations that might better promote the development of gratitude.

However, such a focus, on mutually influential and beneficial relations between a specific individual and a specific context, involves innovations in theory and theory-predicated methodology. This point will return us to the specificity principle (Bornstein, 2017, 2019) and the ideas from RDS metatheory (Overton, 2015) that frame it.

• Innovations in Developmental Theory

A foundational idea of RDS metatheory is that the basic process of human development is a *dynamic* (mutually influential) relation between a specific individual and the specific features of the individual's context (Overton, 2015). These dynamic relations may be represented as individual⇔context relations, and when these relations are *mutually beneficial* to both the individual and the context, healthy and positive development will emerge (Lerner, 2018c). For example, a civically engaged citizen might contribute positively to their community, and might benefit personally from a sense of purpose, and an increase in social capital in their community. The development of character virtues, then (and of the other sets of constructs pointed to in Figure 6.1), involves specific, mutually beneficial individual⇔context relations between a specific individual and specific contexts across specific ages and historical time points.

Clearly, such specificity means that average scores for a group of program participants or summarizing how, on average, a variable has changed across the course of the administration of a character development program, will not suffice to provide practitioners or program evaluations with the information needed to know how any particular program participants fared as a consequence of the program. The complexity of character development certainly represents a challenge for researchers to study (Lerner & Callina, 2014). As well, this complexity presents formidable issues of program design and evaluation for practitioners who, in recognition of the specificity of each of the participants in their programs, have to accommodate to the fact that interventions will not work in the same way for all participants. As Shonkoff and colleagues (2017) have explained:

> The conventional definition of an "evidence-based" program is met by a statistically significant difference on average between a measured outcome in a group that received an intervention (which typically includes multiple components that are not defined precisely) and that same outcome assessed in a control or comparison group. We believe that assessing program effects on average misses what may work exceptionally well for some and poorly (or not at all) for others. Moreover, attempting to create a single "did it work?" test for a multi-faceted intervention obscures its active ingredients, leaving only a "black box" that must be adopted in its entirety. (p. 4)

Rose (2016) complemented the points of Shonkoff et al. (2017) by explaining why practitioner attention to participant specificity (e.g., educator attention to differences among their students) is vital in programs seeking to promote comparable positive outcomes among all participants; examples are programs that seek to develop such character virtues as gratitude (Froh & Bono, 2014), forgiveness (Enright, 2001; Lin, Enright, & Klatt, 2011), or positive (noble) purpose (Burrow, Agans, & Rainone, 2018; Damon, 2008). In his book *The End of Average,* Rose (2016) discussed three concepts that, together, explain why a focus on the specificity of developmental change, and not an exclusive focus on averages, should become the initial focus in developmental analysis:

1. *Jaggedness:* At any point in time each person has a specific and unique constellation of attributes (e.g., academic, moral, civic, social, and leadership);
2. *Context:* The attributes manifested by an individual at any point in time are moderated by the specific context of development; and
3. *Pathways:* All individuals walk the road less traveled, in that each person will have their own specific history of development across time and place.

Together, the ideas of Shonkoff et al. (2017) and Rose (2016) lead to the conclusion that theories or models of character development (and of the development of related attributes) that account for the specificity of development that arises from each individual's specific history of individual⇔context relations are needed to frame research and its applications to program design and evaluation. RDS metatheory is a useful frame for such models.

RDS-based theories of human development focus on the holistic functions of a living, open, self-constructing, and integrated system (e.g., Molenaar, 2014; Overton, 2015; Witherington, 2014, 2015). These models emphasize that each person's behavior and development is an integration of specific and mutually influential relations between a specific individual and their specific context (i.e., each person has a specific history of individual⇔context relations; Bornstein 2017, 2019; Rose, 2016). This individual⇔context coaction means that a person is always a physical, psychological/behavioral, and sociocultural entity (Overton, 2015; Raeff, 2016), although the specifics of the times and places of these coactions for each person creates fundamental, specific facets of each person's life course (Elder, 1998; Elder, Shanahan, & Jennings, 2015). Simply, in agreement with Rose (2016), each person has a unique journey through life.

Using these concepts, the Bornstein (2017) specificity principle promotes the idea that person-specific analyses must be the starting point of developmental analysis and of program design and evaluation. Bornstein (2017) noted that "the specificity principle advances a theory that is particularistic in nature" (p. 5). As such, a prototypic use of the specificity principle for research involves forwarding multipart questions such as "What specific attributes (e.g., of character virtues), of what specific individuals, develop in what specific places (contexts), through what specific experiences, occurring at what specific points in the life span, and within what specific periods of history?" This research question is readily translated into a question that practitioners and program evaluators may ask for each of the participants in a specific CVD (education) program. That is, "What specific character virtues may be promoted in what specific participants, through what specific program features, of what specific durations and intensities, in what specific communities, societies, and cultures, at what specific times in participants' lives?"

Taken together, the ideas of Shonkoff et al. (2017), Rose (2016), and Bornstein (2017, 2019) imply that a change in emphasis must be instituted by researchers and practitioners interested in studying and enhancing, respectively, CVD. That is, research and programs should focus first on the individual. Then, following points made by Kluckhohn and Murray (1948) and more recently by Molenaar and Nesselroade (e.g., 2015), Ram and Grimm (2015), Lerner (2018c), and Cantor et al. (2021), researchers and practitioners must assess if information about individual development—or changes in character virtues associated with program participation—can be aggregated to other individuals or an entire group (i.e., an entire sample of research participants or an entire cohort of program participants). Admittedly, the assess-then-aggregate approach is likely more time-consuming than the alternative of focusing first on average changes in character virtues over the course of a study or the duration of a program. However, the potential to better understand how to enhance the lives of each individual in a program is a decided advantage of embracing such complexity.

What, then, would be needed by researchers or practitioners who wanted to explore whether such enhanced understanding was feasible through what we have labeled as the assess-then-aggregate approach (which, more precisely is the "first assess individuals, and then ascertain if empirically justifiable aggregation is possible" approach)? We address this question in the next section and, for ease of communication, we shall label this approach as a person-specific one.

● What Is Needed to Adopt a Person-Specific Approach to Character Virtues Development Research and Programs?

A person-specific approach to research and programs pertinent to CVD rests on more than rejecting a focus on studying variables and placing primary emphasis on computing group averages. A person-specific approach involves replacing variable-centered approaches and emphases on averages with developing measures that are able to assess an individual's changes in character virtues if they, in fact, occur across time and place and/or in relation to program participation. A person-specific approach also requires using these measures with research or evaluation designs that have sufficient opportunity and statistical power to ascertain if meaningful individual pathways of CVD have occurred. Finally, a person-specific approach also requires that data analyses be used that can both assess the presence of meaningful individual pathways *and* whether aggregation is possible across individuals. Indeed, such analyses are critical for researchers and practitioners who wish to interrogate the differences in knowledge about CVD that occur through the specificity-principle-based person-specific approach we are advocating versus a variable-centered approach (Yu et al., 2021).

However, at this writing, the emphases in these domains of developmental methodology have been to use measures, designs, and analyses ill-equipped to identify meaningful individual change if it exists. In prior publications, we (e.g., Yu et al., 2020, 2021, in preparation) and others (e.g., Molenaar & Nesselroade, 2012, 2014, 2015; Ram et al., 2005; Rose, Rouhani, & Fischer, 2013; Rose, 2016) have explained some of the historical, mathematical, and statistical bases of this situation. However, in addition to these reasons for a focus on variables and averages and not on individuals, it is simply the case that it is hard to develop change-sensitive measures and then couple them with appropriate change-sensitive designs and data analyses.

To be change-sensitive, a measure must be able to detect changes (within an individual) if changes occur. Rather than being a measure intended to identify a score at one time and/or in one context, change-sensitive measures need to be able to detect change across divisions of the x-axis (time) and be able to be used in research or programs wherein different constructs (different character virtues) may develop at different rates and or with different tipping (change) points (Lerner, Schwartz, & Phelps, 2009).

To be a change-sensitive design, data must be collected in a manner that enables within-person change, if it occurs, to be identified. There are several examples of change-sensitive, person-specific research designs that are appropriate for using change-sensitive measures to index change. All designs are of course longitudinal (Collins, 2006), but they vary in regard to sampling x-axis points and, in addition to quantitative methods, they may involve use of, or triangulation with, qualitative assessments (e.g., Tolan & Deutsch, 2015; von Eye, Bergman, & Hsieh, 2015). These research designs include person-specific qualitative and mixed-method designs (Lerner et al., 2021b).

To be a change-sensitive data analysis method, the procedure must be able to identify meaningful person-specific change (e.g., Molenaar & Nesselroade, 2012, 2014, 2015). The analysis must be able to analyze the interconnections of changes across time (the dynamics of change) for each individual studied. There are a growing number of change-sensitive approaches to data analysis (e.g., Hamaker, Asparouhov, Brose, Schmiedek, & Muthén, 2018; Molenaar, Lerner, & Newell, 2014; Molenaar & Nesselroade, 2014, 2015; Ram & Grimm, 2015; von Eye et al., 2015).

Within developmental science, there are relatively few research programs using change-sensitive measures, designs, and analytic methods, perhaps especially during the first three decades of life (Lerner, 2018c). In particular, the study of character virtues and related constructs, such as those associated with the study of SEL and PYD (again, see Figure 6.1) is largely absent during these decades. As such, researchers and practitioners might rightly be skeptical about whether the person-specific approach for which we are advocating is feasible to implement among children and adolescents.

However, although admittedly still in its initial phases, we are conducting a person-specific study of the development of character virtues and related constructs among youth across the K–12 grade range. We will describe briefly some of the findings of this project and discuss implications for development and education, in both in-school and OST settings.

• Engaging Complexity: The Science of Learning and Development Alliance and the MMDC Project

The Science of Learning and Development (SoLD) Alliance is predicated on the study of person-specific pathways across life (Cantor, Osher, Berg, Steyer, & Rose, 2019; Cantor & Osher, 2021; Darling-Hammond, Flook, Cook-Harvey, Barron, & Osher, 2019; Osher, Cantor, Berg, Steyer, & Rose, 2020). The SoLD Alliance involves a collaboration involving universities, nongovernmental organizations, and practitioner groups. Drawing integratively from scientific disciplines ranging from biology through sociology, economics, policy/law, and history, SoLD pursues the idea that each individual has a developmental trajectory that, at least in part, involves systematic, personalized components.

As part of the research and development work of the scientists involved in SoLD, the MMDC project was launched in 2019 in order to understand whole-child development and thriving; the specific focus was on how children develop the full set of complex skills for learning, work, adaptation, and fulfillment in relation to their assets, vulnerabilities, and the specific contexts in which they live. The MMDC collaborators seek to promote healthy growth and development of every child, and especially children whose lives and families have, and have historically had, adverse experiences or, even more, trauma, associated with racism, poverty, and profound inequities.

Accordingly, the researchers involved in MMDC assessed about 100 youth from different parts of the United States who were students in either elementary, middle, or high schools. Participants were assessed across several weeks of the 2019–2020 academic year (until data collection in schools was halted because of school closures associated with the COVID-19 pandemic). The majority of the participants in the study were youth of color.

MMDC researchers seek to understand the cultural and historical contextual conditions that may mask—or, in turn, expand—the developmental range and human potential of each child. The goal of the research is to provide an evidence base for the creation of educational tools enabling schools and communities to identify and enhance each child's relations with the context that promote a pathway for each child's holistic thriving. The core assumption guiding this work is that, to address inequality and to achieve equity, developmental scientists must be able to account for the complexity and specificity of the developmental processes involved in human resilience and thriving; the assaults on development and health; children's capacities to heal, surmount, and grow; and the assets children have that are borne of their cultures and prior experiences (Cantor et al., 2021).

RDS-based concepts, such as dynamic individual⇔context relations and, centrally, the Bornstein specificity principle, frame research undertaken in the MMDC project. The research objectives of the MMDC project are to develop and use person-specific, change-sensitive measures of constructs included in the Building Blocks for Learning (BBFL) framework (Stafford-Brizard, 2016). The BBFL framework depicts the foundations of healthy development, school readiness, mindsets for self and school, perseverance, and independence and sustainability (Stafford-Brizard, 2016). The constructs included in the framework reflect several of the key contributors identified in the developmental science literature that contribute to thriving (see Figure 6.2).

In Phase 1 of the project, MMDC researchers focused on measuring attributes related to CVD. That is, the empathic-concern and perspective-taking components of empathy were assessed. These two facets of empathy were regarded as instances of the relationship skills involved in the mutually beneficial individual⇔context relations discussed by Berkowitz (2012) and others (e.g., Narvaez, 2008; Nucci, 2001) as foundational for enactment of moral virtues.

MMDC researchers also focused on measuring constructs related to the SEL and PYD areas of scholarship, which we have depicted in Figure 6.1 as covarying with CVD. We will illustrate this MMDC work by reporting

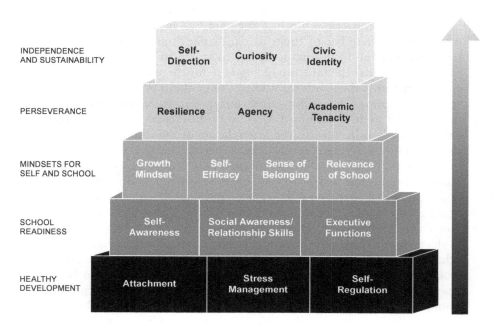

FIGURE 6.2. The Building Blocks for Learning (BBFL) framework (Stafford-Brizard, 2016). Reprinted with permission of Turnaround for Children.

findings about executive functioning (EF). EF describes complex cognitive functioning that enables reasoning, problem-solving, and goal-directed thinking and behaviors (Blair & Ursache, 2011; Miyake & Friedman, 2012; Miyake et al., 2000). EF provides a foundation for social–emotional development because it enables higher-level self-regulatory processes (e.g., emotional self-regulation) and is essential for youth to establish social relationships and mental well-being (Blair & Ursache, 2011; Cantor et al., 2019; Lantrip, Isquith, Koven, Welsh, & Roth, 2016; Osher et al., 2020; Stafford-Brizard, 2016). In MMDC we assessed three components of EF: cognitive flexibility, behavioral inhibition, and working memory.

Reflecting the use of the specificity principle, the initial phase of the MMDC project collected data aimed at providing answers to two questions of fundamental theoretical significance for legitimating a child-specific approach: (1) Are average scores of developmental pathways adequate representations of individual pathway scores?; and (2) If not, are person-specific trajectories meaningful? These questions were asked of both the empathy and the EF data collected as part of MMDC.

Turning first to the measurement of empathy, MMDC researchers collected data about the components of empathy that we assessed (empathic concern and perspective taking) from 35 adolescent participants across several weeks of the academic year (until the COVID-19 pandemic halted in-school data collection). Each participant was measured several times a week, and the number of times of data collection varied across participants from about 30 testing occasions to about 50 testing occasions. We examined whether the measure of empathy for these two components was equivalent across the youth we studied (Yu et al., in preparation). We used statistical methods (Jak & Jorgensen, 2017; Muthén & Asparouhov, 2018) that allowed us to ascertain if there were differences in the structure of empathy or, in other words, the interrelation of the components of empathy, when group averages versus person-specific changes were compared.

We found that the two components were present in analyses of both group averages and person-specific changes. Such a finding might lead a practitioner in a character education program to conclude that knowledge of the group average for this facet of character was equivalent to knowledge about how this facet of character functioned for each of the participants in the program. However, such a conclusion would be incorrect based on other results of our analyses. We compared some statistical scores that would need to be equivalent for information about the group to be interchangeable with information about each of the individuals in the group. We found that these scores were not the same across individuals. This finding indicates that information about the development of empathy derived from the measure we used was not comparable across individuals. Certainly, then, an averaging of scores for this attribute of character would mask the different course of development of empathy for each of the individuals we studied.

Simply, then, based on these MMDC analyses, a practitioner who relied on average scores to provide information about the effectiveness of a character education program would make erroneous conclusions about program effectiveness. Thus, comparing individuals based on the score from measurements that are not invariant across individuals can lead to invalid conclusions. Such an error in interpreting program evaluation data would not be surprising to Bornstein (2019), Rose (2016), or Shonkoff et al. (2017). However, it might be surprising to practitioners or program evaluators who base their work on variable-centered approaches. Proponents of variable-centered approaches rarely examine the equal applicability of findings across individual youth; yet, comparisons across individual youth are often made based on potentially meaningless scores aggregated across individuals.

Similar issues of problematic applications to practice and evaluation exist if the MMDC data about constructs related to character virtues are considered. Turning, then, to EF, we used data from 64 children and adolescents, which was also gathered across 30 to 50 measurement occasions. EF findings pertinent to the two research questions were commensurate with those pertinent to empathy.

First, we found that person-specific trajectories cannot be adequately represented by group-average trajectories (Yu et al., 2020, 2021). In analyses that assessed each individual across time, we found a wide range of intraindividual fluctuations. No one average path was able to represent all participants. Said another way, the average EF trajectory for the group was not sufficient to represent individual EF trajectories (Yu et al., 2020).

Moreover, the person-specific fluctuations did not reflect random change. That is, we found that person-specific EF trajectories were associated with individual characteristics. One example is age. Older children had lower levels of variation across time (Yu et al., 2021). In addition, we analyzed the changes in the relations among the three EF components that we assessed among the 64 youth involved in these analyses. We found that the relations among the three components of EF that were derived from computing group averages were not equivalent to the relationships found when person-specific changes were computed (Yu et al., 2020).

● Conclusions

The evidence from Phase 1 of MMDC project suggests that, insofar as our measures of empathy and EF are concerned, average pathways do not represent adequately the variability in the individual pathways that are aggregated to constitute the average. Moreover, we found that the individual pathways of youth, for both empathy and EF, reflected meaningful variation and not merely random changes around a group mean.

Focus on individual specificity, as framed by the Bornstein specificity principle (2017, 2019), provides researchers, practitioners, and program evaluators with a lens to understand and enhance the development of character virtues and related constructs that is of quite different value than a lens that focuses on averages. We agree with Rose and colleagues (2013) who noted:

> By analyzing statistical averages, not individuals, . . . models provide descriptions about global regularities in everything from cancer . . . to cognition. . . . Traditional models often assume that insights about the population automatically apply to all individuals. . . . This assumption is simple, it is understandable, and it is necessary to justify the use of averages to understand individuals. However, it is also wrong! (p. 152)

Understanding the ways in which specific individual⇔context coactions provide the foundation for specific pathways of CVD and/or of specific changes involved through participating in specific CVD programs can empower practitioners to seek ways to make their actions better attuned to the attributes of each participant in their charge. As well, program evaluations that use measures, designs, and analyses such as the ones involved in MMDC (e.g., Yu et al., 2020, 2021) will be able to enact evaluations with greater validity regarding specific program effects for specific individuals (Shonkoff et al., 2017). Their work will have greater precision in ascertaining how specific program features may impact specific participants in specific ways. Commitment to such precision will prevent practitioners and evaluators from making the error noted by Rose et al. (2013). In particular, and as emphasized by Cantor et al. (2021), a focus on specificity will eliminate the comparison of a specific individual to "norms" irrelevant to their racial, ethnic, or cultural groups. Therefore, a focus on specificity may reduce potential inequities in using inappropriately applied norms to understand individuals from marginalized groups (Cantor et al., 2021; Spencer, 2021).

If theory and methodology are focused on the relations between a specific individual coherently coacting with specific features of specific contexts that promote character virtues, there may be greater likelihood of the greater presence of mutually beneficial individual⇔context relations contributing to the public good (Berkowitz, 2012). Such an optimistic approach will benefit from using the specificity principle to frame character education assessments and thereby focus on indexing individual coherence in enacting virtues adaptively across contexts.

In sum, the idea that an average score for any group can adequately represent the meaningful, specific character virtues across time and place of any individual in the group does not contribute to either good developmental science, or to appropriate applications to education or to youth programming more generally. The 20th-century interpretation that deviations from average scores mean that some youth are in deficit and, therefore, in need of remediation, contributes mightily to bad science, bad education, and bad youth programming. We believe that a much better job can be done by describing, explaining, and enhancing the specific ways in which each young person can thrive across time and place.

ACKNOWLEDGMENTS

The preparation of this chapter was supported in part by the Chan Zuckerberg Initiative, the Bergstrom Family Foundation, the Templeton Religion Trust, the Templeton World Charity Foundation, Compassion International, and King Philanthropies.

REFERENCES

Allport, G. W. (1937). *Personality: A psychological interpretation.* Holt.
Allport, G. W. (1968). *The person in psychology: Selected essays.* Beacon Press.
Baehr, J. (2017). The varieties of character and some implications for character education. *Journal of Youth and Adolescence, 46*(6), 1153–1161.
Berkowitz, M. (2021). *PRIMED for character education: Six design principles for school improvement.* Routledge.
Berkowitz, M. W. (2012). Moral and character education. In K. R. Harris, S. Graham, & T. Urdan (Eds.), *APA educational psychology handbook: Vol. 2. Individual differences and contextual factors* (pp. 247–264). American Psychological Association.
Berkowitz, M. W., Bier, M. C., & McCauley, B. (2017). Towards a science of character education: Frameworks for identifying and implementing effective practices. *Journal of Character Education, 13*(1), 33–51.
Blair, C., & Ursache, A. (2011). A bidirectional model of executive functions and self-regulation. In R. F. Baumeister & K. D. Vohs (Eds.), *Handbook of self-regulation* (2nd ed., pp. 300–320). Guilford Press.
Bornstein, M. H. (2017). The specificity principle in acculturation science. *Perspectives in Psychological Science, 12*(1), 3–45.
Bornstein, M. H. (2019). Fostering optimal development and averting detrimental development: Prescriptions, proscriptions, and specificity. *Applied Developmental Science, 23*(4), 340–345.
Bundick, M. J., Yeager, D. S., King, P. A., & Damon, W. (2010). Thriving across the life span. In W. F. Overton (Ed.), *The handbook of life-span development: Vol. 1. Cognition, biology, and methods across the lifespan* (pp. 882–923). Wiley.

Burrow, A. L., Agans, J. P., & Rainone, N. (2018). Exploring purpose as a resource for promoting youth program engagement. *Journal of Youth Development, 13*(4), 164–178.

Callina, K. S., & Lerner, R. M. (2017). On the importance of coherence in the study of character development. *Journal of Character Education, 13*(1), 19–27.

Cantor, P., Lerner, R. M., Pittman, K., Chase, P. A., & Gomperts, N. (2021). *Whole-child development and thriving: A dynamic systems approach.* Cambridge University Press.

Cantor, P., & Osher, D. (Eds.). (2021). *The science of learning and development: Enhancing the lives of all young people.* Routledge.

Cantor, P., Osher, D., Berg, J., Steyer, L., & Rose, T. (2019). Malleability, plasticity, and individuality: How children learn and develop in context. *Applied Developmental Science, 23*(4), 307–337.

Collins, L. M. (2006). Analysis of longitudinal data: The integration of theoretical model, temporal design, and statistical model. *Annual Review of Psychology, 57,* 505–528.

Damon, W. (2008). *The path to purpose: Helping our children find their calling in life.* Simon and Schuster.

Darling-Hammond, L., Flook, L., Cook-Harvey, C., Barron, B., & Osher, D. (2019). Implications for educational practice of the science of learning and development. *Applied Developmental Science, 4*(2).

Durlak, J. A. (2017). The fundamental importance of effective program implementation for successful character development. *Journal of Character Education, 13*(2), 1–11.

Elder, G. H., Jr. (1998). The life course and human development. In W. Damon (Series Ed.) & R. M. Lerner (Vol. Ed.), *Handbook of child psychology: Vol. 1. Theoretical models of human development* (5th ed., pp. 939–991). Wiley.

Elder, G. H., Shanahan, M. J., & Jennings, J. A. (2015). Human development in time and place. In M. H. Bornstein and T. Leventhal (Eds.), *Handbook of child psychology and developmental science: Vol. 4. Ecological settings and processes in developmental systems* (7th ed., pp. 6–54). Wiley.

Elias, M. J., Ferrito, J. J., & Moceri, D. C. (2015). *The Other side of the report card: Assessing students' social, emotional, and character development.* Corwin Press.

Enright, R. D. (2001). *Forgiveness is a choice: A step-by-step process for resolving anger and restoring hope.* American Psychological Association.

Froh, J. J., & Bono, G. (2014). *Making grateful kids: A scientific approach to help youth thrive.* Templeton Press.

Hamaker, E. L., Asparouhov, T., Brose, A., Schmiedek, F., & Muthén, B. (2018). At the frontiers of modeling intensive longitudinal data: Dynamic structural equation models for the affective measurements from the COGITO study. *Multivariate Behavioral Research, 53,* 820–841.

Jak, S., & Jorgensen, T. D. (2017). Relating measurement invariance, cross-level invariance, and multilevel reliability. *Frontiers in Psychology, 8,* 1640.

Jones, S. M., Brush, K. E., Bailey, R., Brion-Meisels, G., McIntyre, J., Kahn, J., . . . Stickle, L. (2017). Navigating social and emotional learning from the inside out: Looking inside and across 25 leading SEL programs. Retrieved from *www.wallacefoundation.org/knowledge-center/Documents/Navigating-Social-and-Emotional-Learning-from-theInside-Out.pdf*.

Jones, S. M., & Kahn, J. (2017). *The evidence base for how we learn: Supporting students' social, emotional, and academic development*. National Commission on Social, Emotional, and Academic Development, Aspen Institute. Retrieved from *https://assets.aspeninstitute.org/content/uploads/2017/09/SEAD-Research-Brief-11.1.17.pdf*.

King, P. E., Carr, D., & Boitor, C. (2011). Religion, spirituality, positive youth development, and thriving. *Advances in Child Development and Behavior, 41*, 161–195.

Kluckhohn, C., & Murray, H. (1948). Personality formation: The determinants. In C. Kluckhohn & H. Murray (Eds.), *Personality in nature, society, and culture*. Knopf.

Kuhn, T. S. (1962). *The structure of scientific revolutions*. University of Chicago Press.

Kuhn, T. S. (1970*). The structure of scientific revolution* (2nd ed.). University of Chicago Press.

Lantrip, C., Isquith, P. K., Koven, N. S., Welsh, K., & Roth, R. M. (2016). Executive function and emotion regulation strategy use in adolescents. *Applied Neuropsychology: Child, 5*(1), 50–55.

Lerner, R. M. (2018a). Character development: Four facets of virtues. *Child Development Perspectives, 13*(2), 79–84.

Lerner, R. M. (2018b). Character development among youth: Linking lives in time and place. *International Journal of Behavioral Development, 42*(2), 267–277.

Lerner, R. M. (2018c). *Concepts and theories of human development* (4th ed.). Routledge.

Lerner, R. M., & Callina, K. S. (2014). The study of character development: Towards tests of a relational developmental systems model. *Human Development, 57*, 322–346.

Lerner, R. M., Lerner, J. V., Bowers, E., & Geldhof, G. J. (2015). Positive youth development and relational developmental systems. In W. F. Overton & P. C. Molenaar (Eds.), *Handbook of child psychology and developmental science: Vol. 1. Theory and method*. (7th ed., pp. 607–651). Wiley.

Lerner, R. M., Lerner, J. V., Murry, V. M., Smith, E. P., Bowers, E. P., Geldhof, G. J., & Buckingham, M. H. (2021a). Positive youth development in 2020: Theory, research, programs, and the promotion of social justice. *Journal of Research on Adolescence*.

Lerner, R. M., Schwartz, S. J., & Phelps, E. (2009). Problematics of time and timing in the longitudinal study of human development: Theoretical and methodological issues. *Human Development, 52*, 44–68.

Lerner, R. M., Tirrell, J. M., Gansert, P. K., Lerner, J. V., King, P. E., Geldhof, G. J., . . . Sim, A. T. R. (2021b). Longitudinal research about, and program evaluations of, positive youth development in low- and middle-income countries: Methodological issues and options. *Journal of Youth Development, 16*(2 & 3), 100–123.

Lickona, T., & Davidson, M. (2005). *Smart & good high schools: Integrating excellence and ethics for success in school, work, and beyond.* Character Education Partnership.

Lin, W. N., Enright, R., & Klatt, J. (2011). Forgiveness as character education for children and adolescents. *Journal of Moral Education, 40*(2), 237–253.

Mascolo, M. F., & Fischer, K. W. (2015). Dynamic development of thinking, feeling, and acting. In W. F. Overton & P. C. Molenaar (Eds.), *Theory and method. Volume 1 of the* Handbook of Child Psychology and Developmental Science (7th ed., pp. 113–161). Wiley.

Miyake, A., & Friedman, N. P. (2012). The nature and organization of individual differences in executive functions: Four general conclusions. *Current Directions in Psychological Science, 21*(1), 8–14.

Miyake, A., Friedman, N. P., Emerson, M. J., Witzki, A. H., Howerter, A., & Wager, T. D. (2000). The unity and diversity of executive functions and their contributions to complex "frontal lobe" tasks: A latent variable analysis. *Cognitive Psychology, 41*(1), 49–100.

Molenaar, P. C. M. (2014). Dynamic models of biological pattern formation have surprising implications for understanding the epigenetics of development. *Research in Human Development, 11,* 50–62.

Molenaar, P. C. M., Lerner, R. M., & Newell, K. (Eds.). (2014). *Handbook of developmental systems theory and methodology.* Guilford Press.

Molenaar, P. C. M., & Nesselroade, J. R. (2012). Merging the idiographic filter with dynamic factor analysis to model process. *Applied Developmental Science, 16,* 210–219.

Molenaar, P. C. M., & Nesselroade, J. R. (2014). New trends in the inductive use of relation developmental systems theory: Ergodicity, nonstationarity, and heterogeneity. In P. C. Molenaar, R. M. Lerner, & K. M. Newell (Eds.), *Handbook of developmental systems and methodology* (pp. 442–462). Guilford Press.

Molenaar, P. C. M., & Nesselroade, J. R. (2015). Systems methods for developmental research. In W. F. Overton & P. C. M. Molenaar (Eds.), *Handbook of child psychology and developmental science: Vol. 1. Theory and method* (7th ed., pp. 652–682). Wiley.

Moroney, D. A., & Devaney, E. (2017). Ready to implement? How the out-of-school time workforce can support character development through social and emotional learning: A review of the literature and future directions. *Journal of Character Education, 13*(1), 67–87.

Muthén, B., & Asparouhov, T. (2018). Recent methods for the study of measurement invariance with many groups: Alignment and random effects. *Sociological Methods & Research, 47*(4), 637–664.

Narvaez, D. (2008). Human flourishing and moral development: Cognitive and neurobiological perspectives of virtue development. In L. Nucci & D. Narvaez (Eds.), *Handbook of moral and character education* (pp. 310–327). Routledge.

Nucci, L. P. (2001). *Education in the moral domain.* Cambridge University Press.

Nucci, L. P. (2017). Character: A multi-faceted developmental system. *Journal of Character Education, 13*(1), 1–16.

Osher, D., Cantor, P., Berg, J., Steyer, L. & Rose, T. (2020). Drivers of human development: How relationships and context shape learning and development. *Applied Developmental Science, 24*(1), 3–36.

Overton, W. F. (2015). Process and relational developmental systems. In W. F. Overton & P. C. M. Molenaar (Eds.), *Handbook of child psychology and developmental science: Vol. 1. Theory and method* (7th ed., pp. 9–62). Wiley.

Raeff, C. (2016). *Exploring the dynamics of human development: An integrative approach.* Oxford University Press.

Ram, N., Chow, S. M., Bowles, R. P., Wang, L., Grimm, K., Fujita, F., & Nesselroade, J. R. (2005). Examining interindividual differences in cyclicity of pleasant and unpleasant affect using spectral analysis and item response modeling. *Psychometrika, 70,* 773–790.

Ram, N., & Grimm, K. J. (2015). Growth curve modeling and longitudinal factor analysis. In W. F. Overton & P. C. M. Molenaar (Eds.), *Handbook of child psychology and developmental science: Vol. 1. Theory and method* (7th ed., pp. 758–788). Wiley.

Richardson, K. (2017). *Genes, brains, and human potential: The science and ideology of human intelligence.* Columbia University Press.

Rose, L. T., Rouhani, P., & Fischer, K. W. (2013). The science of the individual. *Mind, Brain, and Education, 7*(3), 152–158.

Rose, T. (2016). *The end of average: How we succeed in a world that values sameness.* HarperCollins.

Seider, S. (2012). The influence of parental support on the community service learning experiences of American college students. *Education, Citizenship and Social Justice, 7*(3), 271–288.

Seider, S., Tamerat, J., Clark, S., & Soutter, M. (2017). Investigating adolescents' critical consciousness development through a character framework. *Journal of Youth and Adolescence, 46*(6), 1162–1178.

Shonkoff, J. P., & Center on the Developing Child. (2017). *Building a system for science-based R&D that achieves breakthrough outcomes at scale for young children facing adversity.* Center on the Developing Child, Harvard University.

Slavich, G. M. (2020). Social safety theory: A biologically based evolutionary perspective on life stress, health, and behavior. *Annual Review of Clinical Psychology, 16,* 256–295.

Slavich, G. M., & Cole, S. W. (2013). The emerging field of human social genomics. *Clinical Psychological Science, 1,* 331–348.

Spencer, M. B. (2021). Interrogating the developmental context of "We the People." In P. Cantor, R. M. Lerner, K. Pittman, P. A. Chase, & N. Gomperts (Eds.), *Whole-child development and thriving: A dynamic systems approach* (pp. 18–19). Cambridge University Press.

Stafford-Brizard, B. (2016). *Building blocks for learning: A framework for comprehensive student development.* Turnaround for Children.

Tolan, P. H., & Deutsch, N. L. (2015). Mixed methods in developmental science. In W. F. Overton & P. C. M. Molenaar (Eds.), *Handbook of child psychology and developmental science: Vol. 1. Theory and method.* (7th ed., pp. 713–757). Wiley.

von Eye, A., Bergman, L. R., & Hsieh, C. (2015). Person-oriented methodological approaches. In W. F. Overton & P. C. M. Molenaar (Eds.), *Handbook of child psychology and developmental science: Vol. 1. Theory and method* (7th ed., pp. 789–842). Wiley.

Witherington, D. C. (2014). Self-organization and explanatory pluralism: Avoiding the snares of reductionism in developmental science. *Research in Human Development, 11*(1), 22–36.

Witherington, D. C. (2015). Dynamic systems in developmental science. In W. F. Overton & P. C. Molenaar (Eds.), *Handbook of child psychology and developmental science: Vol. 1. Theory and method* (7th ed., pp. 63–112). Wiley.

Yu, D., Geldhof, G. J., Buckingham, M. H., Goncalves, C., Yang, P-J., Michaelson, L. E., . . . Lerner, R. M. (in preparation). *"Today, I cared about how a classmate felt:" Fluctuations in empathy are linked to daily mood in adolescence.*

Yu, D., Yang, P.-J., Geldhof, G. J., Tyler, C., Gansert, P. K. Chase, P. A., & Lerner, R. M. (2020). Exploring idiographic approaches to children's executive function performance: An intensive longitudinal study. *Person-Oriented Research, 6*(2), 73–87.

Yu, D., Yang, P.-J., Michaelson, L. E., Geldhof, G. J., Chase, P. A., Gansert, P. K., . . . Lerner, R. M. (2021). Understanding child executive functioning through use of the Bornstein Specificity Principle. *Journal of Applied Developmental Psychology, 73*(1), 101240.

PART II

IN THE CLASSROOM

Setting- and Behavior-Focused Approaches

CHAPTER 7

Behavior and Discipline

Direct Behavioral Indicators for Use in the Classroom

Sandra M. Chafouleas and Amy M. Briesch

As noted by Jones, Lesaux, and Barnes (Introduction, this volume), measurement is the foundation to advancements for both science and practice. We agree that data are critical to inform our understanding of what works, how it works, and for whom; data are used for both summative and formative purposes to make decisions regarding the effectiveness of strategies intended to facilitate positive outcomes. However, as noted, expanded definitions of success, which include key nonacademic indicators such as critical classroom behaviors, social skills, and emotional competencies, have been plagued by assessment gaps regarding consensus definitions, method options, and practical systems for efficient use. These assessment gaps have become even more prominent as schools embrace a broader mission that extends to whole-child well-being, striving to serve the needs of every child across domains of functioning (academic, social, emotional, behavioral, physical).

In this chapter, we tackle these issues from a classroom assessment perspective grounded in direct behavioral indicators. We focus on measurement associated with direct behavioral indicators that contribute to positive classroom environments. Positive classroom environments have been associated with both short-term (e.g., engaged participation) and long-term (e.g., educational attainment) academic outcomes, and refer to conditions that foster a climate conducive to learning, such as a sense of emotional and physical safety, social connectedness, engagement in activities, and positive disciplinary practices. A positive classroom environment is critically important not only because of its links to student outcomes, but also to the well-being and instructional practices of classroom teachers.

Classroom management has repeatedly been reported to be the top struggle among teachers, and challenges with student behavior have been noted to be central causes of both teacher burnout and teachers leaving the profession altogether (Hulac & Briesch, 2017). Further complicating this issue is the fact that high levels of teacher stress and a lack of self-efficacy to handle student behavior are contributors to use of exclusionary school discipline practices (Ducharme & Shecter, 2011). Disproportional use of exclusionary discipline has been repeatedly documented, with students from minoritized backgrounds and those receiving special education services more likely to receive punitive exclusionary disciplinary practices such as suspension or expulsion (Losen, Hodson, Keith, Morrison, & Belway, 2015). Taken together, there is critical need for assessment data to inform strategies that enable positive classroom environments for all students and staff members.

Assessment data are integral to the day-to-day problem solving that occurs in a classroom. Assessment data are collected across multiple methods, sources, and dimensions to understand the "what" and "why" regarding challenges in meeting academic and behavioral expectations. For example, a classroom teacher may use daily data generated from a student's behavior contract to monitor and adjust an intervention, whereas a school team may review monthly attendance and disciplinary referrals to identify schoolwide patterns that suggest a need for strengthened system support. Problem solving using assessment data should consider the following features: (1) instruction, (2) curriculum, (3) environment, and (4) learner (Wright, 2010; Ysseldyke & Christenson, 1987). Assessment with this problem-solving focus emphasizes that challenges do not exist solely within the child, but in fact a range of explanations exist for a gap between current and expected performance. In this chapter, we share our perspective on how direct behavioral indicators can play an important role in timely classroom decisions, leading to positive classroom outcomes for both the learner (student) and the environment. Although our focus is on direct behavioral indicators specific to the child (i.e., the learner), we acknowledge that interpretation must include consideration of contextual conditions in problem solving.

By direct behavioral indicators, we mean those markers of child performance that can be collected with greater objectivity, reducing inference in interpretation given two primary features. A first feature of a direct behavioral indicator is *a priori* identification of the targets to be measured. In his taxonomy of behavioral assessment, Cone (1978) suggested that behavioral targets can be physiological (e.g., heart rate, respiration), motor (e.g., hitting, talking, hand raising), or cognitive (e.g., thoughts, feelings). A second feature refers to data collection that reduces latency between observation and recording, given error is more likely to increase as time passes (Briesch, Chafouleas, & Riley-Tillman, 2016). Examples that meet both features might include observation or rating of active student engagement that occurs during a predetermined period such as morning seat work or science block. In Figure 7.1, we present a grid that shows how the instrumentation and procedures associated with different methods align with these features—noting that the shaded box represents those methods that can be considered direct behavioral indicators.

In this chapter, we specifically review Direct Behavior Rating (DBR) as a direct behavioral indicator relevant to social, emotional, and behavioral functioning. In the early 2000s, DBR emerged as the hybrid method that combines the features of systematic direct observation and rating scales. Born out of the Daily Behavior Report Card (DBRC) intervention, in which teachers provide students with regular behavioral feedback throughout the school day, DBR has been defined as "an evaluative rating that is generated at the time and place that behavior occurs by those persons who are naturally occurring in the context of interest" (Christ, Riley-Tillman, & Chafouleas, 2009, p. 205). Like behavior rating scales, DBR procedures ask individuals to rate *a priori* defined behavior(s) using a standard scale. For example, a teacher might be asked to rate the degree to which a student engaged in disruptive behavior during morning meeting using a 0–10 scale (0 = "not at all disruptive," 10 = "completely disruptive"). However, DBR is also akin to systematic direct observation in that targets of measurement are operationally defined in advance (e.g., examples and nonexamples of the target are provided), and procedures include rating in close proximity to when the behaviors actually occur. Given that raters are provided with specific, concrete examples of what should (and should not) be considered when rating a particular target, the potential for differences across raters is reduced. Furthermore, rating occurs following a short observation interval (e.g., end of an instructional block, end of morning instruction) to minimize

		Degree to Which Targets of Measurement Defined *A Priori*		
		Low	Medium	High
Latency between Occurrence and Recording	*Longer*	• Unstructured interviews	• Semistructured interviews	• Rating scales • Structured interviews
	Shorter	• Nonsystematic observation	• Office discipline referrals	• **Direct behavior rating** • **Systematic direct observation**

FIGURE 7.1. Behavioral assessment options by feature, with the shaded box representing those methods considered direct behavioral indicators.

latency between occurrence and recording, thus reducing degree of inference in interpretation. As we dive further into the instrumentation and procedures associated with DBR, we begin with a brief review of the evolution of direct behavioral indicators as an assessment option with potential widespread utility in informing teaching and learning environments.

• Origins of Direct Behavioral Indicators

The history of direct behavioral indicators lies within the field of applied behavior analysis, which grew as a field in the 1960s. Rooted in the principles of behaviorism, a foundation of applied behavior analysis is that the environment plays a prominent role in determining behavior, in contrast to a perspective that the causes of behavior lie within the individual. Classroom behaviors that are of most interest to educators (e.g., academic engagement, prosocial behavior) are often ones that are expected to fluctuate from one context to the next. For example, student engagement may vary both within and across days as a function of a number of variables including academic content (e.g., Language Arts vs. Science), and environmental context (e.g., sitting at the rear of the classroom next to a friend vs. in the front row next to the teacher). The emphasis of direct behavioral indicators is therefore centered on understanding what an individual does in a particular context (i.e., situation-specific behaviors or states) as opposed to trying to describe who an individual is in some absolute way (i.e., characteristics or traits). To do this, the focus of assessment is on obtaining individual samples of situation-specific behavior; it is expected that these states (i.e., observed behaviors) will vary over time and setting due to interactions between the individual and environment. For example, a child who comes into the classroom hungry or having had a negative peer interaction on the bus may have difficulty settling into expected learning activities. In this situation, direct behavioral indicators are used to identify that the child is not performing as typical or expected, which can drive an immediate problem-solving strategy that is directed toward changing contextual features (e.g., access to snack, mediation of conflict with peer) in the teaching and learning environment. Initially, the practical application of the principles of applied behavior analysis focused on clinical settings that tended to address severe behavioral challenges, and in which substantial data resources were available to collect observational data to drive intervention decisions.

The extension of this work to classroom environments gained momentum as inclusion practices increased, which meant students with a range of behavioral challenges were being served in the general education environment. Links between academic performance and student behavior became recognized and emphasized, supporting the need to expand educational practices to include teaching and reinforcing social, emotional, and behavioral skills (Lane, Menzies, Ennis, & Oakes, 2020). By social, emotional, and behavioral, we reference the noncognitive skills that facilitate positive relationships, feelings, and actions. Tiered prevention frameworks initiated in public health gained popularity in education (e.g., multi-tiered systems of support) as a way to organize service delivery for students with varied needs across multiple domains of functioning. Assessment within tiered prevention frameworks relies on early identification of risk (i.e., screening) and progress monitoring response to instruction and intervention strategies (Chafouleas, Johnson, Riley-Tillman, & Iovino, 2020). As such, the demand was established for direct behavioral indicators that could nimbly assist with these classroom assessment needs. Given that measures were scaled for use beyond highly controlled and specific intervention focused on individual response to use with entire-classroom and whole-school environments, however, a major lingering question related to what constituted relevant targets of measurement and associated psychometric adequacy.

The methodological controversies associated with expansion and integration of behavioral assessment techniques are carefully documented in Silva (1993). For example, traditional psychometric indices such as test–retest reliability (i.e., consistency of scores across testing occasions) used in assessments such as statewide achievement tests or comprehensive rating scales may not be relevant for direct behavioral indicators that measure situation-specific samples of behavior such as how actively engaged Amy is during sustained silent reading time. It is expected that scores will fluctuate (e.g., engagement with the book may be much lower at the end of the day on a Friday), and as such, capturing variability and sensitivity to change over time are important features of direct behavioral indicators. As noted by Jones, Lesaux, and Barnes (Introduction, this volume), the "what" to measure with regard to the social, emotional, and behavioral skills needed for success in the future workforce varies based on theoretical lens and specialty training—with debates extending to a larger field referred to as the noncognitive domain. Yet, many parallels in their key considerations of noncognitive measurement defined today—relevant, contextualized, actionable, developmentally salient, sensitive and nuanced, psychometrically sound—can be drawn to the body of literature on controversies surrounding integration of traditional and behavioral assessment techniques. For example, key considerations with high relevance to direct behavioral indicators—as mapped onto the recommendations presented by Jones and colleagues (Introduction, this volume)—include:

- *Flexibility*—capacity to adapt targets of measurement to fit the assessment context (i.e., classroom relevant, developmentally salient)
- *Repeatability*—ability to administer on multiple occasions so as to facilitate efficient monitoring of responsiveness to intervention over time (i.e., actionable)
- *Defensibility*—demonstrates evidence of technical adequacy beyond traditional options (e.g., test–retest reliability), such as sensitivity to change in response to intervention (i.e., psychometrically sound, sensitive and nuanced)

Taken together, classroom assessment options are needed that align with data needs within contemporary frameworks of service delivery, meaning data that can be used to inform everyday teaching decisions for all students (i.e., core instruction, Tier 1) as well as targeted use related to more intensive student needs (i.e., students receiving small group or individualized supports, Tiers 2 and 3). Direct behavioral indicators can serve an important role in contemporary assessment, which necessitates efficient and timely measurement for the purposes of monitoring responsiveness and identifying gaps in current versus expected performance. Direct behavioral indicators of academic (e.g., oral reading fluency) and physical health (e.g., vision and hearing, body mass index) are commonly used in schools to proactively screen students to identify those who may need strengthened teaching and learning supports (Briesch, Chafouleas, Dineen, McCoach, & Donaldson, 2021). For example, using oral reading fluency assessments at fall, winter, and spring periods can quickly benchmark performance of all students in a grade, providing immediate data regarding which individuals, groups, and/or classrooms exhibit gaps in expected performance, directing teaching and learning supports to facilitate improvements. Although not yet widespread in use in comparison to academic indicators (Briesch et al., 2021), potential for direct behavioral indicators such as DBR exists with regard to noncognitive skill assessment as science and practice strive for consensus on the "what" regarding targets of measurement. In the next section, we expand on the work that has been conducted to expand the concepts of direct behavioral indicators to social, emotional, and behavioral domains through development and validation of DBR.

● Development and Validation of DBR

As previously reviewed, the past 20 years have brought an assessment shift in many U.S. schools from a largely diagnostic model of service delivery to one in which the need for additional services is determined through responsiveness to intervention. That is, students who are found to not meet expected performance through proactive screening efforts are provided with evidence-based intervention supports, and their progress is frequently monitored to determine whether the intervention results in intended change in performance. Although such an approach helps to ensure that students' struggles are not the result of inadequate instruction or supports, a major challenge was the lack of tools available for the assessment of student behavior within such models (Kim, Anthony, & Chafoulas, 2021; Chafoulas, Volpe, Gresham, & Cook, 2010). Although behavior rating scales had long been a popular assessment method in school-based settings, the scales largely served a diagnostic assessment purpose given origins within clinical psychology for use to assess psychopathology and confirm diagnoses in reference to a normative comparison. In addition, rating scales typically consisted of a large number of items (e.g., 20 or more for a measure assessing a single domain; 100 or more for a measure assessing multiple domains), and thus were not designed for frequent administration. Finally, directions asked respondents to provide their general perceptions of behavior over an extended period of time (e.g., 1–3 months), meaning a long latency between occurrence and recording. Thus, although targets of measurement were generally well-defined *a priori* and easy to rate by a variety of respondents (self, parent, teacher), capacity of rating scales as a direct behavioral indicator was greatly limited with regard to repeated use and detection of small changes in behavior, as well as potential for increased subjectivity in interpretation. At the other end of the spectrum lies systematic direct observation, in which a trained observer systematically records operationally defined behaviors at the time of occurrence. Systematic direct observation offers a highly objective snapshot of behavior at a single point in time, and easily meets the two criteria needed to be considered a direct behavioral indicator (i.e., a prior definition, short latency). At the same time, however, systematic direct observation procedures could be highly labor intensive to carry out, as an external observer in the classroom was typically necessary. Therefore, there was a need to harness the strengths of each method to meet the needs of contemporary classroom behavioral assessment—that is, offering some of the directness of systematic direct observation while maintaining the applied feasibility of behavior rating scales (Chafoulas, 2011).

Given the positioning of DBR as filling gaps in available school-based direct behavioral indicators for social, emotional, and behavioral domains, DBR development specifically attended to four key measurement strengths: flexibility, efficiency, repeatability, and defensibility. As previously noted, these characteristics parallel the recommendations offered by Jones and colleagues (Introduction, this volume). First, DBR is highly flexible, meaning that it can be adapted to meet the demands of many different situations. With regard to the targets of measurement, DBR is only limited to those that can be readily observed by a rater. It is therefore possible to assess not only behavioral excesses (e.g., aggression) and deficits (e.g., inattention) but also student strengths and skills (e.g., prosocial behavior). DBR affords additional flexibility, however, with regard to such aspects as how often the rating occurs (e.g., once daily, multiple times per day) and the type of scale used (e.g., Likert-type scale, checklist). This level of flexibility means that the assessment protocol can be tailored to meet the unique demands of a situation (e.g., whole-class expectations, age of the student, focus and intensity of presenting concerns). A checklist of key considerations for selecting behavior targets can be found in Table 7.1.

The one caveat to flexibility is that decisions and definitions are determined *a priori*. Initial work in development of DBR attended to the literature on classroom behavior expectations and common challenges and involved studies to evaluate variations in definitions of targets of measurement (Chafouleas, 2011). The resulting work focused future research on establishing evidence around three targets of measurement, defined as core school-based behavioral competencies, or those behaviors expected to maintain a positive classroom environment conducive to learning. Operational definitions, including examples and non-examples, were determined with regard to the following behaviors: (1) disruptive, (2) academically engaged, and (3) respectful (see Table 7.2 for definitions and examples).

TABLE 7.1. Checklist for Selecting DBR Targets

☐ 1. Determine appropriate level of assessment or intervention.
The scope and specificity of behavioral targets will vary depending on the level of interest. Global indicators may be most appropriate at the universal level whereas individualized targets should be selected at the intensive level.

☐ 2. Determine appropriate level of behavioral molarity.
DBR may be used to target global constructs (e.g., disruptive behavior, social competence) or specific indicators (e.g., calling out, expresses frustration appropriately).

☐ 3. Ensure behavior can be reliably measured.
DBR is best used to target those behaviors that can be directly observed by the rater and do not require a high degree of inference.

☐ 4. Ensure behavior is socially valid.
Target behaviors should be considered important to stakeholders within a particular context and relevant to both instruction and intervention planning.

☐ 5. Consider inclusion of positive behavioral targets.
If the goal of intervention is to both reduce negative behaviors and increase positive behaviors, it is important to ensure that the DBR includes these replacement behaviors.

TABLE 7.2. DBR-SIS Core Behavioral Competencies: Definitions and Examples

Core behavioral competency	Examples
Academically engaged: Actively or passively participating in the classroom activity	*Examples:* writing, raising his/her hand, answering a question, talking about a lesson, listening to the teacher, reading silently, or looking at instructional materials
	Non-examples: doodling, looking around the room, staring, aimless flipping through materials, activity unrelated to instructional task
Disruptive: Action that interrupts regular school or classroom activity	*Examples:* out of seat, fidgeting, calling out, talking/yelling about things that are unrelated to classroom instruction, acting aggressively, playing with objects
	Non-examples: staying in seat, raising hand, waiting to be called upon before responding, keeping hands/feet to self, using objects appropriately, working quietly
Respectful: Compliant and polite behavior in response to adult directions, and/or interactions with peers and adults	*Examples:* follows teacher directions, prosocial interaction with peers, positive response to adult request, verbal or physical disruption without a negative tone/connotation
	Non-examples: refusal to follow teacher directions, talking back, eye-rolling, inappropriate gesture, inappropriate language and/or social interactions, disruption with negative tone/connotation

Note. From Briesch, Chafouleas, and Riley-Tillman (2016). Copyright © 2016 The Guilford Press. Reprinted by permission.

In brief, the rationale for these targets of measurement as core school-based behavioral competencies was driven by what has been referred to as a keystone approach. A keystone approach offers a solution to classroom management that addresses the range of behavioral needs. Such an approach is practical given that teachers can focus on teaching and reinforcing a specific set of skills that are foundational to a range of related behaviors. When keystone behaviors are modified, positive changes are expected not only for the targeted behaviors but for others as well, which results in overall broader improvement in child outcomes and overall classroom environment (Ducharme & Shecter, 2011). It is expected that teaching and reinforcing of keystone behaviors can be realistically incorporated into classroom routines, with reduction of problem behaviors that also can lead to reduced use of exclusionary disciplinary practices. In short, these three targets of measurement were selected as core school-based behavioral competencies given that they represent targets that can improve interactions within and between the learner (i.e., student) and classroom environment.

Assessment using direct indicators of core school-based behavioral competencies provides the data necessary to inform decision making regarding classroom management practices at the individual student and/or classwide level, with proactive and positive classroom management leading to improved short-, medium-, and long-term outcomes for the learner and the classroom environment. See Figure 7.2 for a visual representation of this keystone approach to the identification of direct behavioral indicator targets of measurement within DBR.

Second, DBR is efficient, in that it requires minimal time and resources to implement. Ratings are conducted by individuals who are already within the assessment setting (i.e., classroom teacher or assistant as opposed to external observers). The rater can be anyone who has had sufficient opportunity to observe the target behavior during the prespecified period—older students have even served to rate themselves. The only caveat is that ratings must be completed by the same person for the same student across occasions, given the potential for anchoring of scores to differ across raters. DBR is also efficient in that ratings are designed to take only a few seconds to complete, given the limited number of total items. In this way, assessment is minimally intrusive. See Figure 7.3 for example DBR scale formats.

Third, the instrumentation and efficiency of rating procedures of DBR lends itself to be repeatable, meaning that it can be administered across multiple occasions. In this way, data can be used to create the formative behavior streams necessary in progress monitoring and to evaluate responsiveness to intervention. These features of efficiency and repeatability become particularly important as intensity of behavior and requisite intervention supports increase, given the increased need for data to rapidly respond to adaptations in support.

Finally, DBR is defensible, in that there are psychometric data supporting its use across screening and progress-monitoring purposes. Many studies have been conducted over the past two decades to establish evidence of accuracy, reliability/dependability, validity, and sensitivity to change (Briesch et al., 2016). To date, the strongest psychometric support exists for the DBR Single-Item Scale (DBR-SIS). See Figure 7.3 for an example. Using this scale format, informants are asked to rate student behavior in relation to a single construct that is globally worded (e.g., academic engagement). Raters are provided with an operational definition that includes specific behavioral examples (e.g., raising hand as an indicator of academic engagement) to help guide their judgments; however, only one overall rating occurs. Furthermore, although an individual student may be rated across multiple DBR-SISs, data interpretation occurs at the item level. The most common scale format asks informants to rate the percentage of time that a student exhibited a target behavior using an 11-point scale ranging from 0 to 100%.

Direct Indicators of Core School-Based Behavioral Competencies

Disruptive—Student action that interrupts regular school or classroom activity.

Examples:
Getting out of seat, fidgeting or playing with objects, acting aggressively, talking or yelling about things unrelated...

Non-Examples:
Staying in seat, raising hand, waiting to be called on before responding, keeping body parts to self, working quietly....

Academically Engaged—actively or passively participating in the classroom activity.

Examples:
Writing, raising hand, answering a question, talking about a lesson, listening to the teacher, reading silently....

Non-Examples:
Doodling, looking around the room, staring into space, aimlessly flipping through materials, activity unrelated...

Respectful—compliant and polite behavior in response to adult direction and/or interactions with peers and adults.

Examples:
Following adult direction, prosocial interaction with peer(s), positive response to adult request, disruption without a negative tone...

Non-Examples:
Refusal to follow adult direction, talking back, eye rolling, inappropriate gesture, language, disruption with a negative tone

Improved Classroom Management Decision Making

- Use direct indicator data to identify gaps in performance
- Timely implementation of intervention strategy
- Use direct indicator data to monitor response to intervention
- Continue, adapt, or terminate strategy

Improved Classroom Outcomes for Learner and Environment

Short-term	Medium-term	Long-term
Decreased problem behaviors	Reduced reliance on exclusionary disciplinary practices	Improved outcomes for learning and overall well-being
Increased social–emotional skills	Increased engagement in learning activities	
	Increased social connectedness (adult–student, student–student)	

FIGURE 7.2. A keystone approach linking use of direct indicators of core school-based behavioral competencies to improved classroom outcomes for both learner and environment.

DBR Single Item-Scale

Directions: Place a mark along the line that best reflects the percentage of total time that the student was academically engaged during the observation period.

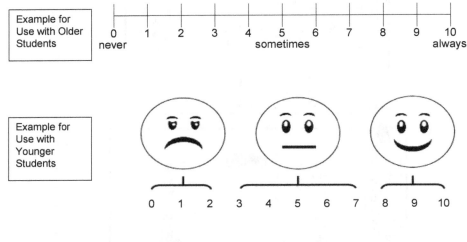

DBR Multi-Item Scale

Directions: Read each item below, and circle the number that represents the degree to which the behavior was a problem during the observation using the following scale:

1—Not at all; 2—Minor; 3—Moderate; 4—Substantial

Following rating of all items, sum scores to create a total score for Disruptive Behavior.

Behavior—Disruptive Behavior	Rating			
Student called out	1	2	3	4
Student was out of seat without permission	1	2	3	4
Student talked to peers when inappropriate	1	2	3	4
Total:				

FIGURE 7.3. Example formats for DBR scales.

Because many of us have come to associate longer with better or more reliable when it comes to assessment, the idea of a single-item scale may at first appear somewhat unusual. It has been argued, however, that much like the way we aggregate data across multiple subjects in a research study in order to arrive at a more generalizable finding, data may also be aggregated across multiple occasions in order to reduce measurement error that occurs as a result of fluctuations over time (Epstein, 1983). Research has shown that dependable estimates of student engagement and disruptive behavior may be obtained using 7–10 DBR-SIS ratings (e.g., Chafouleas, Briesch, et al., 2010), and has documented moderate to high correlations (i.e., associations between variables, convergent validity) with data collected using systematic direct observation (e.g., Chafouleas, Riley-Tillman, Sassu, LaFrance, & Patwa, 2007; Chafouleas, Sanetti, Jaffery, & Fallon, 2012). Additionally, and most important when monitoring student progress over time, research has documented that DBR-SIS is sensitive to changes in student behavior that result from implementation of typical classroom interventions (e.g., DBRC; Chafouleas, Sanetti, Kilgus, & Maggin, 2012; Sims, Riley-Tillman, & Cohen, 2017).

Although much of the research conducted on DBR over the past two decades has focused on use of DBR-SIS to assess the three core behavioral competencies, it is important to again emphasize that one of the aforementioned strengths of DBR is its inherent flexibility, as "DBR is not defined by a single scale, form, or number of rating items" (Chafouleas et al., 2009, p. 196). In recent years, extensions have been noted with regard to the types of behaviors assessed using DBR-SIS. In addition to broadening the scope of DBR-SIS targets to include additional dimensions of social competence (e.g., "appropriate social interaction with teacher" "appropriate social interaction with peers"; Kilgus, Riley-Tillman, Stichter, Schoemann, & Bellesheim, 2016), extensions have been noted into the realm of internalizing behavior (e.g., academic anxiety; von der Embse, Scott, & Kilgus, 2014). Additionally, Kilgus, Kazmerski, Taylor, and von der Embse (2017) developed a DBR-SIS that would provide information both about the target behavior (e.g., disruptive behavior) and the potential reasons why it was occurring, to best inform intervention choices based on function (e.g., adult attention, escape/avoidance). For example, calling-out behavior during math instruction may be happening because the student is trying to escape a task that is too difficult or because the student is seeking attention from the teacher. Thus, adding this layer of understanding of behavior based on function can help determine directions for intervention supports that are more likely to be effective given match to the reason for occurrence. Most recently, Bruhn, Barron, Fernando, and Balint-Langel (2018) used DBR-SIS to assess the degree to which student behavior was consistent with three established schoolwide expectations (i.e., "be respectful," "be responsible," "be ready") during classroom instruction. Given that schoolwide expectations are already familiar and recognizable to all students and staff in the building, there is rationale for aligning targets of measurement to enhance connections in assessment and intervention.

Yet another extension of the DBR method has been the development of multi-item scales (i.e., DBR Multi-Item Scale, or DBR-MIS; see Figure 7.3 for an example). Using DBR-MIS, informants are asked to rate several specific indicators relevant to a global construct, and the individual item scores are then summed to produce a composite score. For example, a DBR-MIS designed to assess academic engagement included five items: "finishes work on time," "actively participates in class," "raises hand when appropriate," "works hard," "stays on task" (Volpe & Briesch, 2012). One of the advantages of a DBR-MIS is that it is possible to customize the scale to address the unique concerns of an individual student. For example, whereas one student's noncompliant behavior may involve laying their[1] head on the desk instead of engaging in assigned tasks, another student may engage in more verbally aggressive noncompliance. Additionally, use of DBR-MIS allows for assessment and monitoring to occur at two levels—that of the item and that of the scale. In this way, it is possible to detect day-to-day changes with regard to specific target behaviors while simultaneously monitoring more global progress over time. Research conducted to date has supported the construct validity and dependability (e.g., Daniels, Briesch, Volpe, & Owens, 2019; Volpe, Chaffee, Yeung, & Briesch, 2020) of DBR-MIS for measuring both academic enabling (i.e., academic engagement, interpersonal skills, organizational skills) and problem (i.e., disruptive, oppositional, socially withdrawn) behaviors. In addition, sensitivity to change has been demonstrated for academic engagement, interpersonal skills, organizational skills, and disruptive behavior (Matta, Volpe, Briesch, & Owens, 2020).

Taken together, the foundation for DBR has been established as a direct behavioral indicator relevant to social, emotional, and behavioral functioning. DBR instrumentation and procedures have tremendous potential for adaptability to fit a diverse range of assessment options. For example, a whole school may choose to adopt DBR for classwide use to inform everyday decisions (i.e., Tier 1 in a multi-tiered service framework) that are aligned with schoolwide positive behavior expectations or the keystone approach defined by DBR-SIS core behavior competencies. In contrast, student support teams or teachers may recommend use of DBR to monitor individual student behavior when gaps exist in expected performance and more intensive supplemental supports are needed (i.e., Tier 2 or 3 in

---

[1] We use "they" as a generic, singular, third-person pronoun as recommended in the 7th edition of the *Publication Manual of the American Psychological Association*.

a multi-tiered service framework). In these individualized cases, targets of measurement may be defined based on specific issues identified and directions for support strategies, such as a strategy to reduce verbal aggression toward peers during recess and transitions. Decisions about choices for use of direct behavioral indicators are flexible and determined by the assessment context. Once the focus of the assessment is determined (e.g., individual student for intensive behaviors, classwide assessment of schoolwide expectations), steps for setting up the DBR instrumentation and procedures can be followed to establish a highly usable system that is flexible, efficient, defensible, and repeatable. See Table 7.3 for a summary checklist of considerations when using DBR.

TABLE 7.3. Summary Checklist for Using DBR in Student Assessment

☐ 1. Determine the appropriateness of DBR.
Although use of DBR is supported in screening and progress-monitoring contexts, high stakes decision making necessitates the use of supplemental measures.

☐ 2. Identify target behavior(s).
Single- or multi-item scales may be used to assess target behaviors that require minimal inference on the part of the rater. Attention should be paid to the wording of target behaviors, given that changes may differentially influence rating accuracy.

☐ 3. Develop an operational definition for each target behavior.
Strong operational definitions describe the target behavior in observable, measurable terms and pass the "stranger test," meaning that the definition should be clearly understandable to someone who has no familiarity with the student or problem.

☐ 4. Determine who will conduct ratings.
The individual best suited to conduct DBR ratings is the one who has sufficient opportunity to observe the target behavior(s). This may be the classroom teacher, an instructional aide, or even the student themself.

☐ 5. Determine where, when, and how often ratings will occur.
Ratings may be limited to one particular setting/time of day or conducted across multiple contexts depending on data collection needs and the number of opportunities available for data collection.

☐ 6. Determine appropriate scale and develop the DBR form.
Although most work to date has focused on the use of an 11-point Likert-type scale, additional options include use of dichotomous ratings, categorical scales, and behaviorally anchored scales.

☐ 7. Conduct rater training.
Training should review behavioral definitions, model how rating should be conducted, and allow for practice and immediate feedback.

Note. From Briesch, Chafouleas, and Riley-Tillman (2016). Copyright © 2016 The Guilford Press. Reprinted by permission.

• DBR: Directions Forward for Dual Purpose in Research and Practice

As discussed throughout the chapters in this book, it is commonly accepted that a gap exists between research and practice with regard to measurement of noncognitive skills, and direct behavioral indicators are not exempt from this challenge. Strong psychometric evidence is insufficient to ensure that assessment tools are actually used in practice as intended, as determinants of actual use in schools include key factors such as consumer understanding and ease of use. Ease of use becomes particularly important in the context of progress monitoring, in which repeated, frequent measurement is necessary for timely evaluation of response to intervention. For these reasons, the DBR method as a direct behavioral indicator was purposefully developed to maximize rater usability. Research on initial development of DBR-SIS focused on establishing instrumentation and procedures that required minimal training and minimal burden to use (i.e., ratings take only a few seconds to complete), while also meeting defensible standards around technical adequacy. Research directions in DBR evaluation have been intentional in balancing interests of both science and practice, resulting in a highly usable behavioral assessment method that possesses desirable features of direct behavioral indicators.

A parallel issue relates to establishing agreement regarding the targets of measurement to advance a cohesive body of research and inform recommendations for practice. Although interest in social, emotional, and behavioral intervention has seen tremendous expansion in recent decades, a noted concern is defining desired outcomes in a measurable way, and then determining those indicators that serve to provide immediate and defensible data important to driving intervention decisions. As previously noted, the history of behavioral assessment research has not been marked by consensus around these issues, leaving gaps in recommended directions for practice. Although school personnel are highly familiar, and engage at high rates, with direct indicators of other domains of student functioning, such as academic (e.g., reading inventories) and physical health (e.g., vision screenings), traditionally less emphasis has been placed on the use of direct indicators in social, emotional, and behavior domains. For example, a recent survey found that whereas the majority of school building administrators reported conducting academic and health screenings to identify those students at risk, similar screening for social, emotional, or behavioral risk were carried out in only 10% of school buildings (Briesch et al., 2021). Yet, wide support for the role for schools in identifying and supporting student social, emotional, and behavioral needs exists across constituents including school administrators, teachers, student support personnel, and parents (Briesch et al., 2020, 2021; Dineen et al., 2020). In summary, it appears that practice is poised to incorporate direct behavioral indicators—and thus it is incumbent upon researchers to do the work that facilitates directions regarding salient targets of measurement.

Finally, we offer comment related to the current and future status of direct behavioral indicators for research purposes. Assessment feasibility is paramount in practice, yet it also represents a central advantage when extended to a research context. Within the context of single-case design studies, for example, it is necessary to collect time-series data in order to assess change from baseline to intervention phases. Although systematic direct observation has often been used as an outcome measure in single-case studies, this assessment method can be highly labor-intensive, thus limiting the number of participants whose behavior can reasonably be measured at one time. Shifting to the use of participant observers—rather than an external observer—offers the potential to incorporate larger and more robust samples within single-case studies. Several research studies using single-subject research designs have been published in recent years that utilized DBR as a primary outcome measure to determine the effectiveness of interventions targeting both externalizing (e.g., Chafouleas, Sanetti, Jaffrey, & Fallon, 2012) and internalizing behaviors (e.g., Dart et al., 2014).

The benefits of direct behavioral indicators such as DBR, however, are not limited to the realm of single-case studies. Within large-N research, estimates of behavior pre- and postintervention are often limited to a single data point. In some cases, student behavioral outcomes may be measured using observations, such as those conducted in the classroom or on the playground. Although use of systematic direct observation provides for an objective snapshot of behavior at a single point in time, concerns arise regarding the generalizability of the limited number of obtained estimates. For example, even under highly standardized assessment conditions, it is likely that performance may be influenced in subtle ways by factors such as the time of day, events occurring in the community, or even the weather. As discussed previously in this chapter, aggregating data across multiple occasions—such as by collecting repeated DBR data—offers one way to reduce the random measurement error associated with collecting data at a single point in time (Epstein, 1983). It is perhaps even more common, however, for researchers to collect pre-post data using standardized rating scales, which presents potential for increased error given the degree of latency between when the behavior occurs and when it is measured. Use of DBR as an outcome measure reduces this latency, thereby minimizing the degree of inference needed. Thus, future research may assist in more complete exploration of psychometric adequacy given different configurations of data that are aggregated over time and under varied situationally specific conditions.

A final consideration that must be contended with returns to defining the targets of measurement—or which noncognitive skills should be assessed. Although we have presented an argument for three core behavioral competencies, we acknowledge that other direct indicators of social, emotional, and behavioral competencies may be added depending on key considerations within the context (e.g., developmentally salient, aligned with schoolwide systems). Given the foundations to the work on DBR were drawn from behavioral assessment, we acknowledge perspectives that may be added from other fields to further strengthen the use of direct behavioral indicators in both research and practice. Thus, we fully support the expansion of work to facilitate stronger agreement regarding core noncognitive competencies that may be measured using direct behavioral indicators. We suggest there is sound potential for this direction given the close alignment of the desirable features of direct behavioral indicators such as DBR with the key considerations in measurement outlined by Jones, Lesaux, and Barnes (Introduction, this volume).

REFERENCES

Briesch, A. M., Chafouleas, S. M., Dineen, J. N., McCoach, D. B., & Donaldson, A. (2021). Reported screening practices across academic, behavioral, and physical health domains. *Journal of Positive Behavior Interventions*.

Briesch, A. M., Chafouleas, S. M., & Riley-Tillman, T. C. (2016). *Direct Behavior Rating: Linking assessment, communication, and intervention*. Guilford Press.

Briesch, A. M., Cintron, D. W., Dineen, J. N., Chafouleas, S. M., McCoach, D. B., & Auerbach, E. (2020). Comparing stakeholders' knowledge and beliefs about supporting students' social, emotional, and behavioral health in schools. *School Mental Health, 12*(2), 222–238.

Bruhn, A., Barron, S., Fernando, J., & Balint-Langel, K. (2018). Extending the Direct Behavior Rating: An examination of schoolwide behavior ratings and academic engagement. *Journal of Positive Behavior Interventions, 20*, 31–42.

Chafouleas, S. M. (2011). Direct Behavior Rating: A review of the issues and research in its development. *Education and Treatment of Children, 34*, 575–591.

Chafouleas, S. M., Briesch, A. M., Riley-Tillman, T. C., Christ, T. C., Black, A. C., & Kilgus, S. P. (2010). An investigation of the generalizability and dependability of Direct Behavior Rating Single Item Scales (DBR-SIS) to measure academic engagement and disruptive behavior of middle school students. *Journal of School Psychology, 48*, 219–246.

Chafouleas, S. M., Johnson, A. H., Riley-Tillman, T. C., & Iovino, A. A. (2020). *School-based behavioral assessment informing instruction and intervention* (2nd ed.). Guilford Press.

Chafouleas, S. M., Riley-Tillman, T. C., Sassu, K. A., LaFrance, M. J., & Patwa, S.

S. (2007). Daily Behavior Report Cards (DBRCs): An investigation of consistency of on-task data across raters and method. *Journal of Positive Behavior Interventions, 9,* 30–37.

Chafouleas, S. M., Sanetti, L. M. H., Jaffery, R., & Fallon, L. (2012). Research to practice: An evaluation of a class-wide intervention package involving self-management and a group contingency on behavior of middle school students. *Journal of Behavioral Education, 21,* 34–57.

Chafouleas, S. M., Sanetti, L. M. H., Kilgus, S. P., & Maggin, D. M. (2012). Evaluating sensitivity to behavioral change across consultation cases using Direct Behavior Rating Single-Item Scales (DBR-SIS). *Exceptional Children, 78,* 491–505.

Chafouleas, S. M., Volpe, R. J., Gresham, F. M., & Cook, C. (2010). School-based behavioral assessment within problem-solving models: Current status and future directions. *School Psychology Review, 34,* 343–349.

Christ, T. J., Riley-Tillman, T. C., & Chafouleas, S. M. (2009). Foundation for the development and use of Direct Behavior Rating (DBR) to assess and evaluate student behavior. *Assessment for Effective Intervention, 34,* 201–213.

Cone, J. D. (1978). The behavioral assessment grid (BAG): A conceptual framework and a taxonomy. *Behavior Therapy, 9,* 882–888.

Daniels, B., Briesch, A. M., Volpe, R. J., & Owens, J. S. (2019). Content validation of Direct Behavior Rating multi-item scales for assessing problem behaviors. *Journal of Emotional and Behavioral Disorders.* Advance online publication.

Dart, E. H., Furlow, C. M., Collins, T. A., Brewer, E., Gresham, F. M., & Chenier, K. H. (2014). Peer mediated check-in/check-out for students at-risk for internalizing disorders. *School Psychology Quarterly, 30,* 229–243.

Dineen, J. N., Chafouleas, S. M., Briesch, A. M., McCoach, D. B., Newton, S. D., & Cintron, D. W. (2021). Exploring social, emotional, and behavioral screening approaches in U.S. public school districts. *American Education Research Journal.*

Ducharme, J. M., & Shecter, C. (2011). Bridging the gap between clinical and classroom intervention: Keystone approaches for students with challenging behavior. *School Psychology Review, 40,* 257–274.

Epstein, S. (1983). Aggregation and beyond: Some basic issues on the prediction of behavior. *Journal of Personality, 51,* 360–392.

Hulac, D., & Briesch, A. M. (2017). *Effective classroom management: An evidence-based approach.* Guilford Press.

Kilgus, S. P., Kazmerski, J. S., Taylor, C. N., & von der Embse, N. P. (2017). Use of Direct Behavior Ratings to collect functional assessment data. *School Psychology Quarterly, 32,* 240–253.

Kilgus, S. P., Riley-Tillman, T. C., Stichter, J. P., Schoemann, A. M., & Bellesheim, K. (2016). Reliability of Direct Behavior Ratings—Social Competence (DBR-SC) data: How many ratings are necessary? *School Psychology Quarterly, 31,* 431–442.

Kim, E. K., Anthony, C. J., & Chafouleas, S. M. (2021). Social, emotional, and behavioral assessment within tiered decision-making frameworks: Advancing research through reflections on the past decade. *School Psychology Review.*

Lane, K. L., Menzies, H. M., Ennis, R. P., & Oakes, W. P. (2015). *Supporting behavior for school success: A step-by-step guide to key strategies.* Guilford Press.

Losen, D., C. Hodson, C., Keith, M. A., Morrison, K., & Belway, S. (2015). "Are we closing the school discipline gap?" The Civil Rights Project at UCLA and the Southern Poverty Law Center. Retrieved from *http://civilrightsproject. ucla.edu/resources/projects/center-for-civil-rights-remedies/school-to-prison-folder/federal-reports/are-we-closing-the-school-discipline-gap/losen-are-we-closing-discipline-gap-2015-summary.pdf.*

Matta, M., Volpe, R. J., Briesch, A. M., & Owens, J. S. (2020). Five Direct Behavior Rating Multi-Item Scales: Sensitivity to the effects of classroom interventions. *Journal of School Psychology.*

Silva, B. (1993). *Psychometric foundations and behavioral assessment.* Sage.

Sims, W. A., Riley-Tillman, T. C., & Cohen, D. R. (2017). Formative assessment using Direct Behavior Ratings: Evaluating intervention effects of Daily Behavior Report Cards. *Assessment for Effective Intervention, 43,* 6–20.

Volpe, R. J., & Briesch, A. M. (2012). Generalizability and dependability of single-item and multiple-item Direct Behavior Rating scales for engagement and disruptive behavior. *School Psychology Review, 41,* 246–261.

Volpe, R. J., Chaffee, R. K., Yeung, T. S., & Briesch, A. M. (2020). Initial development of multi-item Direct Behavior Rating measures of academic enablers. *School Mental Health.* Advance online publication. *https://doi.org/10.1007/s12310-019-09338-w*

Von der Embse, N. P., Scott, E. C., & Kilgus, S. P. (2014). Sensitivity to change and concurrent validity of Direct Behavior Ratings for academic anxiety. *School Psychology Quarterly, 30,* 244–259.

Wright, J. (2010). The RIOT/ICEL matrix: Organizing data to answer questions about student academic performance & behavior. Retrieved from *www.interventioncentral.org/sites/default/files/rti_riot_icel_data_collection.pdf.*

Ysseldkye, J. E., & Christenson, S. L. (1987). Evaluating students' instructional environments. *Remedial and Special Education, 8*(3), 17–24.

CHAPTER 8

Using Behavior Incident Data for Program and Classroom Decision Making

Addressing Issues of Equity and Exclusionary Discipline Responses

Lise Fox, Myrna Veguilla, and Mary Louise Hemmeter

Early care and education settings (e.g., child care, public school PreK, Head Start) are a context in which young children learn social skills, emotional competencies, and expectations related to being in educational settings. These settings are each unique in terms of their funding streams, teacher qualifications, ratios, and access to support services (e.g., special education, mental health). They are often a child's first experience in settings with groups of children. The first 5 years of life is a period of rapid development and key to children's success in school and beyond. During this time, children begin to learn peer relationship skills, social problem solving, emotional literacy, self-regulation, and how to engage and participate in group settings. Children who have a strong foundation in social skills and emotional competencies are more likely to be successful in school and have more positive post-school outcomes (Denham et al., 2003; Jones, Greenberg, & Crowley, 2015).

During the early years, evidence of difficulties in social-emotional competence often appears in the form of challenging behaviors (e.g., aggression toward self or others, running from adults, screaming, biting) or internalizing behaviors (e.g., withdrawal, lack of peer interactions). Research indicates that when social-emotional challenges are not addressed during the early years, a trajectory of poor outcomes can begin (e.g., Brennan, Shaw, Dishion, & Wilson, 2012; Bulotsky-Shearer & Fantuzzo, 2011; Hauser-Cram & Woodman, 2016). While many of these behaviors are developmentally expected (e.g., some preschoolers tantrum and hit when frustrated), when they become persistent or intense, they often result in exclusionary discipline practices that are counterproductive to the child's social-emotional competence. Developmentally inappropriate and exclusionary discipline practices include removing the child from the classroom, sending the child home, using time-out or corporal punishment, or asking the child to leave the program (Nese & McIntosh, 2016).

Over the last 15 years, there has been growing knowledge about the rate at which preschool children are suspended or expelled from PreK programs. Research from the early 2000s indicates that preschool children were three times more likely to be suspended or expelled than children in K–12 (Gilliam, 2005). There are multiple factors that might contribute to these findings, including practitioners with limited training on how to address challenging behavior effectively, policies that allow suspensions and expulsions rather than supporting children to be included, lack of support personnel (i.e., school psychologist, mental health consultant) who can assist early childhood educators with developing interventions, and attitudes that view punishment or exclusion as effective approaches for "dealing" with challenging behavior. More recent data have confirmed these findings and further indicate that these exclusionary discipline practices have been disproportionately used with boys and Black children (U.S. Department of Education, 2014, 2016).

The use of exclusionary discipline with young children is a national concern (American Academy of Pediatrics, 2013; Meek & Gilliam, 2016; U.S. Commission on Civil Rights, 2019; U.S. Department of Health and Human Services & U.S. Department of Education, 2014), and is particularly troubling as the practice removes children from instruction and the interventions that are needed to promote the development of social, emotional, and behavioral skills. Moreover, its use may cause family hardship through the loss of child care or preschool enrollment. In addition, research in schools has shown that early expulsion and suspension predicts later expulsion and suspension and is predictive of contact with the juvenile justice system, unemployment, and dropping out of high school (Darney, Reinke, Herman, Stormont, & Ialongo, 2013; Skiba, Arredondo, & Williams, 2014). Many advocates have referred to this phenomenon as the "school-to-prison pipeline" (Ginwright, 2004) with early childhood advocates asserting that the data on early childhood suspension and expulsion points to a "cradle to prison pipeline" (Meek & Gilliam, 2016).

Concurrent with these findings and recommendations has been a focus on the preparation of early childhood teachers to meet the needs of all children in early childhood settings. Early childhood teachers consistently report that challenging behavior is their most significant training need and that they lack preparation about how to intervene effectively with children who have persistent challenging behavior (Reinke, Stormont, Herman, Puri, & Goel, 2011; Snell, Berlin, Voorhees, Stanton-Chapman, & Hadden, 2012; Stormont, Lewis, & Smith, 2005). Over the last 10 years, research has demonstrated that training followed by coaching can be effective for supporting teachers to implement prevention and promotion practices (e.g., Conroy et al., 2019; Hemmeter, Snyder, Fox, & Algina, 2016; Snyder et al., 2018).

We have a growing body of evidence that when teachers receive training and coaching to use prevention and promotion practices, they report improvements in children's social skills and challenging behavior (Hemmeter et al., 2016; Hemmeter, Fox, et al., 2021). Most of this work has focused on teachers' classroomwide use of the practices but it has not looked at the extent to which teachers apply these practices to all children equitably. It is important that we examine how we support teachers to use effective behavior support practices with all children while at the same time reducing their disproportional use of exclusionary discipline practices with boys and Black children. The use of equitable disciplinary practices cannot begin at the teacher level, rather it will take a program/schoolwide effort that includes a commitment to implementing effective practices equitably, a commitment to ensuring that all children get the support they need to be successful in the program, strategies for supporting teachers and families around children with the most persistent problem behaviors, and engagement and partnership with families that focuses on hearing, supporting, and learning from them. Further, programs must have a process in place for monitoring their disciplinary practices to ensure that they are positive, focused on prevention, and applied equitably across children. What is needed at the program level are measures related to the ecological context in which challenging behavior occurs and the factors related to the practices used by program staff to address challenging behavior.

In this chapter, we describe a measure that can be used by programs engaged in initiatives focused on promoting young children's social-emotional competence, reducing the use of exclusionary discipline practices, and using data for decision making in support of teachers and children. The measure we describe, the Behavior Incident Report System (BIRS), provides a practical approach for measuring, summarizing, and analyzing challenging behavior in the program, and how adults respond to those incidents, with the goal of improving program practices to more effectively support teachers and the children in their classrooms. The BIRS provides data relevant to the ecology or context in which challenging behavior occurs and how adults respond to those behaviors. The BIRS allows the program to use an approach that steps away from defining challenging behavior as a deficit within an individual child to identifying how to make changes in the environment and practices in a manner that promotes social-emotional skills. In this chapter, we describe the measure and how it was developed and then describe how the data are collected and summarized. We follow our introduction to the measure with a description of how programs use the data to support teachers to prevent and address challenging behavior more effectively, examine their data for issues related to equity, and engage in actions for program improvement.

• Measuring Behavior Incidents and Responses to Behavior

Without a data system to track how staff are responding to behavior challenges, early childhood programs are unlikely to systematically determine how they address challenging behavior, the use of exclusionary discipline, and if there are issues of disparities in responses to behavior. In some states, public preschool services that are delivered through public school systems might use the data systems provided to K–12 schools. However, most early childhood classrooms and programs do not systematically collect data on challenging behavior, or the responses teachers and programs use to address those behaviors (Garrity & Longstreth, 2020; Garrity, Longstreth, & Linder, 2017; Meek & Gilliam, 2016). In many early childhood programs, the only behavior data gathered are related to an injury or safety concern that might be noted on an incident report required by child care licensing or program policy.

The BIRS was developed in 2003 to provide a data system for early care and education programs to use for tracking and analyzing incidents of challenging behavior and the responses teachers and administrators use to address those behaviors within a program. The data system was developed for programs that were implementing the *Pyramid Model for Promoting the Social and Emotional Competence of Infants and Young Children* (Fox, Dunlap, Hemmeter, Joseph, & Strain, 2003; Hemmeter, Ostrosky, & Fox, 2006; Hemmeter, Ostrosky, & Fox, 2021) program-wide. The Pyramid Model is a multi-tiered framework of evidence-based practices for promoting social and emotional skills, preventing challenging behavior, and intervening with children who have persistent challenging behavior. Program-wide implementation of the Pyramid Model involves being systematic about the implementation support needed to guide classroom teachers in implementing the evidence-based social-emotional teaching practices that are defined by the approach. There is clear evidence across multiple studies that high-quality implementation is vital to the effective use of an intervention or curriculum and positive program outcomes (Durlak, 2015; Durlak & DuPre, 2008; Metz, Halle, Bartley, & Blasberg, 2013). A consideration of implementation means that programs consider the infrastructure needed for a program to implement a particular approach or innovation. In early education programs, that infrastructure might include teacher training, ongoing coaching, family engagement strategies, and the use of data tools to monitor implementation and outcomes. In program-wide implementation of the Pyramid Model, early childhood programs form a leadership team comprising an administrator or director, teachers, other support staff, and a family member who meet monthly and use data to make decisions about implementation progress, intervention fidelity, professional development, behavior intervention, and teacher and child outcomes.

The BIRS was designed to provide leadership teams with information related to when challenging behaviors are occurring, who behaviors occur with, the types of behaviors, and how teachers and programs respond to each incident. The measure is designed to provide information that is summarized visually for teams to use in analysis and problem solving as they consider how to prevent and address child challenging behavior using evidence-based practices.

Teachers use a form to record information surrounding the challenging behavior incident, and the forms are entered into a database management system. Prior to teachers using the system they are trained on how challenging behaviors are defined and what types of behaviors should be documented on the form. For young children, some amount of challenging behavior can be developmentally expected. For example, it is common for 2-year-olds to have a tantrum when frustrated and the tantrum might include hitting and kicking. We also expect that, for many children, when adults redirect them or offer them comfort, the challenging behavior is resolved. In determining incidents that might be documented on a behavior incident report (BIR), teachers are guided to consider if the behavior is occurring with intensity, frequency, or duration that is not developmentally expected, and if the behavior involves injury or harm to the child or others or is otherwise dangerous. Data gathered from the system are aggregated and displayed in graphs to provide the program leadership team with information to use as they analyze patterns and factors relating to the occurrence of behavior incidents and determine actions for addressing challenging behavior in the program.

Field Testing

In 2003, the BIRS was field-tested in early childhood programs that were receiving training and technical assistance in the implementation of the Pyramid Model to determine if the system was feasible and informative. Teachers were able to complete forms easily, and data from the system were used by the program to identify teachers who needed classroom support to address challenging behavior, identify children in need of more intensive intervention, and identify modifications that might be needed in staffing, activity structure, and materials within activities. Program-level data from the system were used by teams in data decision-making conversations about what actions might be taken to prevent challenging behavior and in implementing strategies to promote prosocial skills. For example, one program identified that many incidents, across classrooms, were occurring on the playground. As a result, the program increased supervision on the playground and increased the number of toys that were available to children to reduce behavior incidents. In another program, the data showed teachers in multiple classrooms were frequently responding to disruption during large-group activities by using time-out although they had noted that the possible motivation for the behavior was to avoid the activity. In response, the program provided training to teachers on how to design large-group activities to increase the likelihood that children would be engaged and how to respond to children when they had behavior challenges during large-group instruction. In addition, they clarified their intention that classroom teachers should not use time-out unless it was part of an approved behavior plan. The field-testing of the BIRS continued in 2006–2008 with 32 programs that were receiving training and technical assistance in the program-wide implementation of the Pyramid Model. However, a formal evaluation of the reliability or social validity of the BIRS has not yet been conducted.

The BIRS was initially offered to programs for their use through federal training and technical assistance centers (i.e., Center on the Social and Emotional Foundations for Early Learning, Technical Assistance Center on Social Emotional Intervention) that were funded to assist states and programs in promoting social and emotional skill development and addressing challenging behavior. Many programs reported that they used the BIRS as one of their data decision-making tools. In 2016, the BIRS was redesigned to include fields that would allow for an analysis of behavior incidents by race, ethnicity, gender, special education status, and dual-language learner status. In addition, definitions were added so that the BIRS could provide data on the use of exclusionary discipline (i.e., suspension and expulsion).

BIRS 2.0

The revised system is offered to early childhood programs through a national technical assistance center (National Center for Pyramid Model Innovations: *www.challengingbehavior.org,* 2018) funded by the U.S. Office of Special Education Programs to improve and support the capacity of state systems and local programs to implement an early childhood multitiered system of support to improve the social, emotional, and behavioral outcomes of young children with, and at risk for, developmental disabilities or delays. Programs are encouraged to use the BIRS 2.0 to collect data on behavior incidents and make program-level decisions about supporting children and teachers.

The core components of the BIRS package include a PDF form for recording a single behavior incident, online training, an Excel spreadsheet to input BIRs, and the BIRS Data-Based Decision-Making Guide (von der Embse, Ferro, Binder, Veguilla, & Fox, 2018). Each component is described below.

BIR Form

The BIR form is designed for teachers to quickly complete after a behavior incident occurs (e.g., completion times of 30 seconds to 1 minute). The form provides check boxes to capture information about the behavior, the activity in which the behavior occurred, who was interacting with the child when the behavior occurred, the teacher's perception of the purpose of the behavior, and adult and program responses to the behavior (see Figure 8.1). Codes are used for teacher and child names so that the forms and data summaries lack identifiable information. The selections within each category are specifically designed to capture the kinds of behaviors, activities, and responses that commonly occur within an early childhood setting. Examples in the problem behavior category include physical aggression, social withdrawal, destroying materials, and running away from the adult, and examples in the activity category include activities diapering, small-group activity, and center play. The items on the form are operationally defined so that teachers have instructions on the item to select within each category. At the bottom of the form, a child's demographic information (i.e., gender, race, and ethnicity) and whether they have an individualized education program (IEP) and are a dual-language learner (DLL) are recorded the first time a teacher completes a BIR. This information is essential for using the system to identify issues of disproportionality, which will be discussed later in the chapter.

The form includes a list of the responses that a teacher might apply in the classroom (e.g., redirection, teach a new skill) and the administrative actions that might occur following the incident (e.g., call to family, sent home for remainder of the day, sent home for multiple days). Administrative actions and teacher responses that are considered suspensions and expulsions are also listed on the form so that data on exclusionary discipline actions can be collected. The form does not include the nomenclature of "suspension" or "expulsion," as that terminology is not commonly used by early educators. Instead, the form lists the responses that are descriptive of exclusionary discipline actions. In-school suspensions include responses of "time in a different classroom or adult outside of classroom" and "temporary removal from classroom." Out-of-school suspensions are identified as "sent home for 1 or more days" and "sent home for remainder of day." Expulsion from a program is listed as a "dismissal from program."

Behavior Incident Report

Program ID: _____

Classroom ID:	Child ID:	Date	Time:

Behavior Description:

Problem Behavior (check most intrusive)

❑ Physical aggression	❑ Noncompliance	❑ Repetitive behaviors
❑ Disruption/Tantrums	❑ Social withdrawal/Isolation	❑ Hurting self
❑ Inconsolable crying	❑ Running away	❑ Trouble falling asleep
❑ Verbal aggression	❑ Breaking/Destroying objects or items	❑ Other:_____
❑ Inappropriate language	❑ Unsafe behaviors	

Activity (check one)

❑ Arrival	❑ Outdoor play	❑ Departure
❑ Circle/Large group activity	❑ Special activity	❑ Therapy
❑ Small group activity	❑ Field trip	❑ Quiet time/Nap
❑ Centers/Indoor play	❑ Self-care/Bathroom	❑ Transportation
❑ Diapering	❑ Transition	❑ Individual activity
❑ Meals	❑ Clean-up	❑ Other:_____

Others Involved (check one)

❑ Teacher	❑ Family Member	❑ Transportation driver
❑ Assistant Teacher	❑ Support/Administrative staff	❑ Kitchen staff
❑ Peers	❑ Substitute	❑ None
❑ Therapist	❑ Classroom volunteer	❑ Other:

Possible Motivation (check one)

❑ Obtain desired item	❑ Gain adult attention/comfort	❑ Avoid sensory
❑ Obtain desired activity	❑ Avoid adults	❑ Don't know
❑ Gain peer attention	❑ Avoid task	❑ Other:_____
❑ Avoid peers	❑ Obtain sensory	

Response (check one or the most intrusive)

❑ Verbal reminder	❑ Provide physical comfort	❑ Teacher contact family
❑ Redirect to different activity/toy	❑ Curriculum modification	❑ Time out
❑ Move within group	❑ Re-teach/Practice expected behavior	❑ Physical guidance
❑ Remove from activity	❑ Loss of activity	❑ Physical hold/Restrain
❑ Remove from area	❑ Time with a teacher	❑ Other:_____
❑ Remove item	❑ Time in a different classroom or adult outside of classroom	

Administrative Follow-Up (check one or most intrusive)

❑ Not applicable	❑ Targeted group intervention	❑ Conditional enrollment
❑ Talk with child	❑ Temporary removal from classroom	❑ Transfer to another program
❑ Contact family	❑ Sent home for remainder of day	❑ Reduce hours in program
❑ Family meeting	❑ Sent home for 1 or more days	❑ Dismissal from program
❑ Arrange behavioral consultation/team		❑ Other:_____

Comments:

If this is the <u>first BIR</u> for the child, please select the following demographic Information:	__ Male __ Female	__ Dual-language learner __ IEP in place	Ethnicity: __ Hispanic or Latino of any race __ Not Hispanic or Latino
			Race: __ Native American or Alaskan Native __ Asian __ Black or African American __ Native Hawaiian or Other Pacific Islander __ Two or more races __ White

FIGURE 8.1. BIR form.

BIRS Online Training

Teachers are trained how to complete a BIR through an online training module. The 1-hour training explains when and how to complete a BIR and includes video examples of children's challenging behavior for practice on completing the form using the operational definitions for selection. Programs that implement the system are encouraged to conduct additional training with all staff about the value of using the system, the use of the form, how forms will be completed and submitted for data entry, and how data will be used in the program to provide support to children and teachers, and to make program changes.

Excel Spreadsheet

Completed BIR forms are entered into an Excel spreadsheet that is provided as part of the BIR system. The Excel spreadsheet provides an in-depth analysis of incidents occurring at the program, classroom, and individual-child level. It also provides metrics to assess disproportionality at the program level and alerts the user to possible concerns of overrepresentation in BIR identification by race/ethnicity, gender, IEP, and DLL status.

The BIRS Data-Based Decision-Making Guide

The BIRS Data-Based Decision-Making Guide (von der Embse et al., 2018) supports program-wide leadership teams in analyzing their data. The guide encourages teams to review data using visual analysis, consider factors that might influence data patterns, and make decisions on action steps (referred to as look–think–act). The guide provides steps for reviewing and analyzing data at the program, classroom, and individual-child level. The guide also helps users identify potential actions that might be implemented in response to concerns identified from the data review.

● Using Behavior Incident Data to Address Challenging Behavior

The BIRS provides a program with summary data that are graphically displayed and can be used to make data-informed decisions related to addressing challenging behavior. In programs without a systematic way to collect and summarize these data, decisions are often made based on a program leader's sense of what might be happening (e.g., "It seems like we are having a lot of problem behavior on the playground"), in response to family concerns (e.g., "My child's teacher responded inappropriately to my child's challenging behavior"), or in response to teacher issues (e.g., "I need help to manage the challenging behavior in my classroom"). The BIRS allows program leadership teams to review data on critical information to make a data-informed statement about what is occurring at their program. Teams will better understand the incidents that are happening in their program by having BIR data that identify the challenging behaviors that are occurring most frequently, the classrooms and children who are involved, teachers' perceptions of the motivation of the challenging behavior, and how teachers and administrators respond to behavior incidents.

Data collected through the BIRS are reviewed and discussed at monthly leadership team meetings using the BIRS Data-Based Decision-Making Guide and worksheets for data discussion. The data decision-making process begins by looking at data at the program level and answering the questions in Table 8.1.

In the monthly review of data, the program leadership team examines the graphs generated by the spreadsheet and uses the look–think–act

TABLE 8.1. BIRS Questions

Questions	Data source	Excel tab name
Is problem behavior increasing or decreasing?	Average number of incidents per day	• Program Summary
Who are the children that are experiencing challenging behavior?	Incidents by child Incidents by classroom ID	• Monthly BIRs by Child ID • Monthly BIRs by Classroom ID
Who are others involved with incidents?	Incidents by others involved	• Others Involved
When does problem behavior occur—routine/activity?	Incidents by activity	• Activity
Where does problem behavior most frequently occur—location?		
What behaviors are most frequently reported?	Incidents by problem behavior	• Problem Behavior
Why are children engaging in challenging behavior?	Incidents by possible motivation	• Possible Motivation
What social, emotional, or communication skills need to be taught?		
How are we responding to challenging behavior?	Incidents by response Incidents by administrative follow-up	• Response • Admin Follow-Up

process that is outlined in the guide. The core graphs provide the data to address the questions presented in Table 8.1. This data review process begins at the program level by examining how many BIRs were completed for a particular month and how that compares to prior months. In the examination of those data, the team will also review how many children there are with a BIR each month. The number of BIRs might fluctuate just as the number of children with a BIR. It is possible that the number of BIRs could have an upward trend, but a review of the data might show a decrease in the number of children and an increase in the number of BIRs for a small number of children. Throughout the "look" process, attention to trends and responses of concern (e.g., suspensions, expulsions, use of restraint) should be identified.

The next step in the data analysis process is "think." In this step, the trends identified during the "look" process should be questioned. For example, if there was an increase in the number of BIRs in October in the program, the team might wonder if another event contributed to the increase (e.g., construction on the playground led to no outdoor time for 2 days). Similarly, when examining a classroom summary and noting that the numbers of children with challenging behavior are high in one classroom, the team might consider if the teacher had received training and coaching or if there are other factors that are related to the larger number of children with challenging behavior. During the "think" process, a team might note that a particular environment or activity had a higher number of incidents and wonder if there are common factors related to those environments or activities that identify a need for professional development. For example, if the data indicated that across all classrooms, most BIRs were occurring during large-group, teacher-directed activities, the program leadership team might decide to conduct professional development on effective strategies for using small- and large-group instructional activities. During this second step of data analysis, these types of questions are asked and answered through a thorough review of the data.

The "act" step in the process of data analysis is unique to each program and concern. After reviewing and interpreting the data, the leadership team then engages in conversation about what action plan steps are needed in response to the conclusions from the previous steps. The team might decide more data collection is needed or to provide professional development. Action steps should match "think" questions.

The data analysis process might result in the identification of an individual classroom or child that needs additional support (i.e., is associated with a greater number of BIRs). In these cases, the focus from program-level data analysis to classroom- or child-level analysis is more appropriate. When the data indicate that higher numbers of BIRs are associated with an individual child or classroom, the classroom coach or behavior specialist can use the BIRS to examine the data at that level and identify patterns that might be addressed using the look–think–act process. For example, if the team notes that a high number of BIRs is associated with an individual child, the team might check to see if the child has an active behavior support plan and if the plan is being implemented as intended. The classroom coach or behavior specialist might meet with the teacher to learn more about the behavior and initiate the steps need to design a more effective intervention. Similarly, if the team notices that two or three classrooms account for the majority of the BIRs in the program, the classroom coach might schedule an observation in those classrooms to see if those teachers are using the social-emotional promotion and prevention practices in their teaching.

After the program leadership team has addressed the questions for their program, they will use the BIRS data to develop a precision statement that is a data-based description of a situation or concern (von der Embse et al., 2018). For example, a team could examine their data and initially conclude that "most of the challenging behavior in the program is noncompliance." In the development of a precision statement, the team digs more deeply into their data and develops the following statement: "BIRs are most commonly completed for noncompliance during transitions when children are trying to avoid moving to the new activity and the most common response from teachers is to provide physical guidance." By creating a precision statement (see Figure 8.2), the team can articulate a data-based conclusion to their analysis. These precision statements can be thought of as focused responses to the "think" questions. As the team goes through the

---

BIRs are most commonly completed for _____ [Problem Behavior]

in _____ [Activity] with _____ [Others Involved]

to _____ [Possible Motivation]. The most common response

is _____ [Response] with _____ [Administrative Follow-Up].

BIRs are most commonly completed for _Physical aggression_ _____

in _Centers/Indoor play_ _____ with _peers_ _____

to _obtain a desired item._ _____ The most common response

is _Verbal reminder_ _____ with _no administrative follow-up._ _____

FIGURE 8.2. Precision statement template and example.

look–think–act process, they address their precision statements by creating an action plan. For example, the program leadership team might develop an action plan for the precision statement that was presented above that includes providing a training workshop focused on structuring transitions and the use of transition strategies and follow-up coaching for teachers to support implementation.

The BIRS problem-solving process encourages team members to use their data to understand contextual information related to behavior incidents and design actions that will prevent or address behavior more effectively. For example, a program leadership team in their monthly review of data saw that most of their behavior incidents were aggression, and those incidents most often occurred toward peers on the playground. The data summary also showed that teachers were coding the motivation of physical aggression as gaining a desired item/activity/material. In the problem-solving discussion, a team member pointed out that there were very few materials (e.g., balls, sand toys) and pieces of equipment (e.g., trikes, swings) on the playground to keep the number of children who were on the playground engaged all at the same time. The team decided to make a change in the number of classrooms that were scheduled for the playground at the same time and purchased additional materials so that all children were more likely to be actively engaged. During the next review of the data, the playground incidents were decreased.

Programs should also conduct a quarterly equity review. Equity profiles of demographic variables in the system (i.e., race, ethnicity, gender, IEP status, DLL status) provide BIRS users with metrics to assess possible disproportionality, guiding users to assess whether actions are equitable across groups and if so, how large the disparities are. There are three sets of equity profiles by demographic variable: by frequency across all behavior incidents regardless of response, by frequency across all behavior incidents that result in an in-school suspension, by frequency across all behavior incidents that result in an out-of-school suspension, and by frequency across all behavior incidents that result in an expulsion. As data are entered, these metrics are calculated. If there is disproportionality, the system provides an equity alert and identifies the data on the disparities. For example, an equity alert might indicate that children who are Hispanic or Latino are twice as likely to have an in-school suspension in comparison to all other children or that boys are more likely to be suspended than girls, even when controlling for the relative proportion of students in that category. Review of the alerts will help to identify overrepresentation in incident reporting and incidents resulting in an exclusionary discipline action by each demographic variable. Teams are encouraged to review their equity data quarterly and to use the worksheet on the BIRS Data-Based Decision-Making Guide to review each alert and identify possible actions.

● Addressing Exclusionary Discipline and Equity Concerns

The BIRS provides an important tool for programs that are making a commitment to the elimination of exclusionary discipline practices, addressing equity, and providing effective and culturally responsive multi-tiered systems of support in their program (i.e., the Pyramid Model). The BIRS provides teams with data that can identify what exclusionary discipline actions are occurring (i.e., in-school suspension, out-of-school suspension, dismissal) and data on other responses to behavior (e.g., restraint, time-out) that might be of concern. In addition, the equity alert generated by the system can make a program aware of disproportionality in incidents or exclusionary discipline that should trigger the team to examine their data through an equity lens.

The problem-solving process for the equity alert requires that the team consider the magnitude of the issue by examining the provided risk ratio, composition values, and other measures of disproportionality and then engage in problem analysis. In the analysis, the team determines that a small number of classrooms account for much of the issue of concern (e.g., in-school suspension that is disproportionately used with boys) and develops an action plan related to those classrooms, or the data might indicate that the concern is occurring across all classrooms and requires program-wide strategies to address the concern.

Teams are also encouraged to consider what other data might be used to help understand the factors that contribute to the broader issues related to the use of exclusionary discipline responses and equity concerns. Other sources of data that might be relevant include measures of classroom implementation of social-emotional teaching practices (e.g., Teaching Pyramid Observation Tool; Hemmeter, Fox, & Snyder, 2014), program climate survey, family engagement survey, or overall classroom quality measures (e.g., CLASS; Pianta, LaParo, & Hamre, 2008).

Actions for Exclusionary Discipline Concerns

The analysis of BIR data might reveal that the program is using suspension or expulsion to address challenging behavior across classrooms or within a smaller number of classrooms. In programs that are using a multi-tiered system of support such as the Pyramid Model, it will be important for teams to examine the fidelity of their implementation and strengthen any weaknesses in their promotion and prevention practices. Additional decisions that might address this issue include: developing an explicit policy that exclusionary discipline is not permitted; designing procedures to provide teachers with immediate assistance and support when they feel there is a behavior crisis; developing efficient and responsive procedures for assisting a teacher with the development of behavior intervention strategies by a behavior specialist, school psychologist, or mental health consultant; providing coaching to teachers around the implementation of behavior intervention strategies and behavior support plans; or using functional behavioral assessment and positive behavior support to collaborate with families in the development of behavior support plans. It should be noted that these are only a sample of the program actions that might address the specific issue identified through analysis of the data. The most important aspect of this decision-making approach is the use of data (i.e., BIRs, practice implementation fidelity) to pinpoint contextual factors related to exclusionary discipline and the development of proposed actions that are aligned to the data observations and precision statement.

Actions for Equity Concerns

If the analysis of the BIRS data indicate equity concerns across all classrooms in the program, the program leadership team (e.g., program director, teachers, families, behavior support/mental health staff) should consider what actions might be used to address the issue (National Association for the Education of Young Children, 2019). Those actions might include conducting an equity audit to examine the commitment of the program to culturally responsive practices and equitable outcomes for all children (Skrla, Scheurich, Garcia, & Nolly, 2004); examining program policies, procedures, and curricula approaches to assess the cultural fit with the children, families, community, and staff; creating a professional development plan to provide training and coaching in the use of culturally responsive practices; offering a regular opportunity for staff and administrators to meet and learn more about advancing equity in the program; expanding opportunities for bringing diverse perspectives to the leadership team; or establishing collaborative partnerships with mental health and other community service providers to offer more comprehensive services to vulnerable children and their families.

Addressing equity concerns across the program will require a commitment to implementing change over time, processes to gain staff investment in the change process, and continual dialogue with staff, families, and community stakeholders. In the design of the action plan to address equity concerns, the program will start with actions that seem to be clearly needed and then expand with additional actions as the program engages in the systems change process. For example, a program might start with making a concerted effort to recruit and hire staff that reflect the diversity of the children and families in the program and ensure that translators are available for all family meetings and family–teacher conferences. In addition, they might provide ongoing professional development to staff in understanding implicit bias, using antibias and culturally responsive practices, and strengthening relationships with families. As the program implements those strategies, they learn more about the supports that families need and the need to offer different ways for all families to engage in the program and they learn more about staff perspectives and their needs for new practices to support children with behavioral difficulties and team with families. Thus, as the program begins its work in addressing equity, they learn more about what needs to be addressed.

In addition, equity issues will need to be addressed with individual teachers. All teachers should have foundational training in social-emotional teaching practices, culturally responsive practices, interventions to address challenging behavior, and implicit bias (Allen & Steed, 2016). Classroom coaching will be needed to support teachers as they engage in the process of practice change (Snyder, Hemmeter, & Fox, 2015). When exclusionary discipline occurs with disproportionality, the leadership team should consider whether a teacher's implicit bias or the lack of culturally responsive practices might be related to those actions or whether it is a program issue that should be addressed. Actions to address implicit bias might build upon a training event to guide teachers to become aware of concerns related to implicit bias, although it is highly likely that a training event will be insufficient for practice change, especially as it relates to implicit biases. In programs where classroom coaches have developed strong collaborative and trusting relationships with teachers, the classroom coach is in the best position to guide the teacher toward practice-change goals related to equity issues and behavior responses (Ferro, Fox, Binder, & von der Embse, 2017).

The classroom coach can be an important support for a teacher as the teacher engages in reflection on their own biases and how those biases are demonstrated in their interactions with children and families. The classroom coach can help teachers see when their practices or interactions might reflect bias or neglect to be culturally responsive. For example, a classroom coach might note that a teacher is more likely to respond positively to the children who speak English in the class and to engage in conversations about their interests. The coach also observes that the teacher is more often directive and punishing with children who are dual-language learners when they fail to follow directions or are perceived as noncompliant. Once the coach has identified a concern, the coach can guide the teacher in reflection and help the teacher identify the problem. The coach can use the goal-setting and action plan process with the teacher to develop some strategies for implementation to address the concern and use the coaching process to assist the teacher in strengthening practices. In the previous example, the teacher and coach might include an action plan goal around having at least two conversations with children who are dual-language learners each day and creating visuals of the children's interests and a list of phrases in the children's home language for the teacher to use in the conversations. In addition, the coach might help the teacher identify strategies to use to support children when they fail to follow a direction or seem noncompliant.

● Summary and Next Steps

In this chapter, we have provided information on a tool that early childhood programs can use to summarize and analyze data related to behavior incidents with the intention of strengthening the ability of the program to prevent challenging behavior, provide effective intervention to children, and improve instructional and program practices. The BIRS is still in a developmental process, and research related to reliability, feasibility, and the value of the use in early childhood programs is needed.

The system is available in two formats. The Excel spreadsheet for inputting BIR forms and analyzing data is available on the National Center for Pyramid Model Innovations' website. This spreadsheet is free to download and use. An alternative to this system is the online platform provided by *www.PBISApps,* the Early Childhood School-Wide Information System (EC-SWIS) that is available for a fee. The online system allows for the same analyses of data provided by the Excel spreadsheet, so the functionality is equivalent.

We believe that the BIRS provides early childhood programs with a vital tool to understanding behavior incidents, using data to make decisions that improve practices and outcomes, and monitoring and responding to disciplinary actions that are applied disproportionately. Without these data, program personnel might make decisions related to behavior based on their instincts, on assumptions about effective approaches, on bias-based beliefs, or in other ways that might be harmful to children and families (e.g., use of exclusionary discipline).

REFERENCES

Allen, R., & Steed, E. A. (2016). Culturally responsive Pyramid Model practices: Program-wide positive behavior support for young children. *Topics in Early Childhood Special Education, 36*(3), 165–175.

American Academy of Pediatrics, Council on School Health. (2013). Out-of-school suspension and expulsion. *Pediatrics, 131*(3), e1000–e1007. Available at *https://pediatrics.aappublications.org/content/131/3/e1000.*

Brennan, L. M., Shaw, D. S., Dishion, T. J., & Wilson, M. (2012). Longitudinal predictors of school-age academic achievement: Unique contributions of toddler-age aggression, oppositionality, inattention, and hyperactivity. *Journal of Abnormal Child Psychology, 40*(8), 1289–1300.

Bulotsky-Shearer, R. J., & Fantuzzo, J. W. (2011). Preschool behavior problems in classroom learning situations and literacy outcomes in kindergarten and first grade. *Early Childhood Research Quarterly, 26*(1), 61–73.

Conroy, M. A., Sutherland, K. S., Algina, J., Ladwig, C., Werch, B., Martinez, J., . . . Gyure, M. (2019). Outcomes of the BEST IN CLASS intervention on teachers' use of effective practices, self-efficacy, and classroom quality. *School Psychology Review, 48,* 31–45.

Darney, D., Reinke, W. M., Herman, K. C., Stormont, M., & Ialongo, N. S. (2013). Children with co-occurring academic and behavior problems in first grade: Distal outcomes in twelfth grade. *Journal of School Psychology, 51*(1), 117–128.

Denham, S. A., Blair, K. A., DeMulder, E., Levitas, J., Sawyer, K., Auerbach-Major, S., & Queenan, P. (2003). Preschool emotional competence: Pathway to social competence? *Child Development, 74*(1), 238–256.

Durlak, J. A. (2015). What everyone should know about implementation. In J. A. Durlak, C. E. Domitrovich, R. P. Weissberg, & T. P. Gullota (Eds.), *Handbook of social emotional learning: Research and practice* (pp. 395–405). The Guilford Press.

Durlak, J. A., & DuPre, E. P. (2008). Implementation matters: A review of research on the influence of implementation on program outcomes and the factors affecting implementation. *American Journal of Community Psychology, 41,* 327–350.

Ferro, J., Fox, L., Binder, D. P., & von der Embse, M. (2017). *Pyramid Model equity coaching guide.* Retrieved from *https://challengingbehavior.cbcs.usf. edu/docs/Pyramid-Model-Equity-Coaching-Guide.pdf.*

Fox, L., Dunlap, G., Hemmeter, M. L., Joseph, G. E., & Strain, P. S. (2003). The teaching pyramid: A model for supporting social competence and preventing challenging behavior in young children. *Young Children, 58*(4), 48–52.

Garrity, S. M., & Longstreth, S. L. (2020). Using the teaching and guidance policy checklist to develop culturally and linguistically appropriate guidance policies. *Early Childhood Education Journal, 48*(1), 71–77.

Garrity, S. M., Longstreth, S. L., & Linder, L. K. (2017). An examination of the quality of discipline policies in NAEYC-accredited early care and education programs. *Topics in Early Childhood Special Education, 37*(2), 94–106.

Gilliam, W. S. (2005). *Prekindergartners left behind: Expulsion rates in state prekindergarten systems.* Yale University Child Study Center.

Ginwright, S. (2004). *Black in school: Afrocentric reform, urban youth and the promise of hip-hop culture.* Teachers College Press.

Hauser-Cram, P., & Woodman, A. C. (2016). Trajectories of internalizing and externalizing behavior problems in children with developmental disabilities. *Journal of Abnormal Child Psychology, 4*(4), 811–821.

Hemmeter, M. L., Fox, L., & Snyder, P. (2014). *Teaching Pyramid Observation Tool (TPOT) for preschool classrooms, Research edition.* Brookes.

Hemmeter, M. L., Fox, L., Snyder, P., Algina, J., Hardy, J., Bishop, C., & Veguilla, M. (2021). Corollary child outcomes from the Pyramid Model professional development intervention efficacy trial. *Early Childhood Research Quarterly, 54,* 204–218.

Hemmeter, M. L., Ostrosky, M. M., & Fox, L. (2006). Social and emotional foundations for early learning: A conceptual model for intervention. *School Psychology Review, 35*(4), 583–601.

Hemmeter, M. L., Ostrosky, M. M., & Fox, L. (2021). *Unpacking the Pyramid Model: A practical guide for preschool teachers.* Brookes.

Hemmeter, M. L., Snyder, P., Fox, L., & Algina, J. (2016). Evaluating the implementation of the Pyramid Model for promoting social-emotional competence in early childhood classrooms. *Topics in Early Childhood Special Education, 36*(3), 133–146.

Jones, D. E., Greenberg, M., & Crowley, M. (2015). Early social-emotional functioning and public health: The relationship between kindergarten social competence and future wellness. *American Journal of Public Health, 105*(11), 2283–2290.

Meek, S. E., & Gilliam, W. S. (2016). *Expulsion and suspension as matters of social justice and health equity.* National Academy of Medicine. Retrieved from *https://nam.edu/wp-content/uploads/2016/10/Expulsion-and-Suspension-in-Early-Education-as-Matters-of-Social-Justice-and-Health-Equity.pdf.*

Metz, A., Halle, T., Bartley, L., & Blasberg, A. (2013). The key components of successful implementation. In T. Halle, A. Metz, & I. Martinez-Beck (Eds.), *Applying implementation science in early childhood programs and systems* (pp. 21–42). Brookes.

National Association for the Education of Young Children. (2019). Advancing equity in early childhood education. Retrieved from *www.naeyc.org/resources/position-statements/equity.*

National Center for Pyramid Model Innovations. (2018). *Using the behavior incident report system.* Retrieved from *http://challengingbehavior.cbcs.usf.edu/docs/BIR_FAQ.pdf.*

Nese, R. N. T., & McIntosh, K. (2016). Do school-wide positive behavioral interventions and supports, not exclusionary discipline practices. In B. G. Cook, M. Tankersley, & T. J. Landrum (Eds.), *Advances in learning and behavioral disabilities* (pp. 175–196). Emerald Group.

Pianta, R. C., LaParo, K., & Hamre, B. (2008). *Classroom Assessment Scoring System—PreK* [CLASS]. Brookes.

Reinke, W. M., Stormont, M., Herman, K. C., Puri, R., & Goel, N. (2011). Supporting children's mental health in schools: Teacher perceptions of needs, roles, and barriers. *School Psychology Quarterly, 26*(1), 1–13.

Skiba, R. J., Arredondo, M., & Williams, N. T. (2014). More than a metaphor? The contribution of exclusionary discipline to a School-to-Prison Pipeline. *Equity and Excellence in Education, 47*(4), 546–564.

Skrla, L., Scheurich, J. J., Garcia, J., & Nolly, G. (2004). Equity audits: A practical leadership tool for developing equitable and excellent schools. *Educational Administration Quarterly, 40*(1), 133–161.

Snell, M. E., Berlin, R. A., Voorhees, M. D., Stanton-Chapman, T. L., & Hadden, S. (2012). A survey of preschool staff concerning problem behavior and its prevention in Head Start classrooms. *Journal of Positive Behavior Interventions, 14*(2), 98–107.

Snyder, P., Hemmeter, M. L., & Fox, L. (2015). Supporting implementation of evidence-based practices through practice-based coaching. *Topics in Early Childhood Special Education, 35*(3), 133–143.

Snyder, P., Hemmeter, M. L., McLean, M., Sandall, S., McLaughlin, T., & Algina, J. (2018). Effects of professional development on preschool teachers' use of embedded instruction practices. *Exceptional Children, 84*(2), 213–232.

Stormont, M., Lewis, T. J., & Smith, S. (2005). Behavior support strategies in early childhood settings: Teachers' importance and feasibility ratings. *Journal of Positive Behavior Interventions, 7*(3), 131–139.

U.S. Commission on Civil Rights. (2019). *Beyond suspensions: Examining school discipline policies and connections to the school-to-prison pipeline for students of color.* Retrieved from *www.advancingstates.org/sites/nasuad/files/07-23-Beyond-Suspensions.pdf.*

U.S. Department of Education, Office of Civil Rights. (2014, March). Data snapshot: Early childhood education. (Issue Brief No. 2). Retrieved from *www2.ed.gov/about/offices/list/ocr/data.html.*

U.S. Department of Education, Office of Civil Rights. (2016, October). *2013–2014 Civil Rights Data Collection: A First Look.* Retrieved from *www2.ed.gov/about/offices/list/ocr/docs/2013-14-first-look.pdf.*

U.S. Department of Health and Human Services & U.S. Department of Education. (2014). *Policy statement on expulsion and suspension policies in early childhood settings.* Retrieved from *www.acf.hhs.gov/sites/default/files/ecd/expulsion_suspension_final.pdf.*

von der Embse, M., Ferro, J., Binder, D. P., Veguilla, M., & Fox, L. (2018). Behavior incident report system: Data-based decision-making guide. Retrieved from *http://challengingbehavior.cbcs.usf.edu/Implementation/data/index.html.*

CHAPTER 9

Defining and Measuring Quality of Early Childhood Education in Low- and Middle-Income Countries

Abbie Raikes

Children in low- and middle-income countries (LMIC) face notable threats to healthy development, including greater risk of exposure to violence, inadequate nutrition and health care, and fewer opportunities for stimulating care at home and in school (Britto et al., 2017). Access to quality early childhood education (ECE) has been identified as an important avenue for addressing and ameliorating negative environmental impacts on child development (Britto et al., 2017; Rao, Sun, Chen, & Ip, 2017) and is included in the Sustainable Development Goals' Target 4.2 (Raikes et al., 2017).

Although expansion of ECE has been rapid in many parts of the world, ECE quality has often received less attention than ensuring children have access to ECE (Raikes, Davis, & Burton, 2019). There is a great deal of variability in ECE quality, within and across countries (for example, see Bidwell & Watine, 2016, on sub-Saharan Africa). Large-scale estimates of ECE quality are difficult to come by in many countries, because government monitoring systems may not include all types of settings and often do not collect key indicators of ECE quality, such as whether teachers are trained and have adequate materials. However, there are several reasons to wonder whether quality is adequate: Investments in ECE are still low in many LMIC (Neuman & Okeng'o, 2019), and as a result, many ECE systems are struggling to ensure ECE is well staffed and resourced with trained teachers. Many countries have a mix of private and public settings, and oversight and investments in private settings may be outside of the scope of government agencies. As enrollment increases, existing problems—such as overcrowded classrooms and limited materials—may be exacerbated.

• Preschool Classroom Quality
and Children's Social and Emotional Learning in LMIC

Despite the challenges in ensuring access to quality ECE, results from several interventions suggest positive associations between ECE attendance and children's development (Rao et al., 2017), ranging from small to moderate effect sizes. Few studies have sought to identify associations between ECE and children's social and emotional skills, but the expansion of ECE creates an opportunity to focus more heavily on the role of ECE in promoting social and emotional skills. Effectively integrating social and emotional learning (SEL) into preschool classrooms, especially training and supporting teachers, requires measurement that accurately captures the classroom environments that are most conducive to SEL, beginning with a shared understanding of what *quality* in preschool means and how that definition is both consistent and varied across settings.

In this chapter, I outline and address key issues in measuring quality in early childhood settings in low- and middle-income countries. Throughout the chapter, I offer examples of how one initiative, the Measuring Early Learning Quality and Outcomes (MELQO) project, addressed these concerns, concluding with pathways forward for ensuring reliable, relevant measurement. As described below, there are several tools available to measure quality in ECE, and it is not uncommon for tools from high-income countries to be adapted for use in LMIC. However, as countries invest in and expand ECE, it becomes increasingly important to consider how to define and build measurement tools for LMIC. To balance between globally defined and locally relevant definitions of quality, MELQO proposed an adaptable measure of quality, the Measuring Early Learning Environments scale (MELE; see Raikes et al., 2019, for a review of MELQO). The MELE scale outlined a set of global constructs that were intended to be adapted by local stakeholders, to ensure alignment with policy and context. As a result, there are several versions of the MELE scale in use now, with some common and some unique elements in each setting, based on the adaptation process and priorities of country stakeholders (see Raikes et al., 2019, for a review). Throughout this chapter, examples from MELE are used to provide an example of ECE quality measurement in LMIC.

Defining and Measuring ECE Quality in LMIC

Is there a common definition of *ECE quality* that is relevant across settings, or should we think of quality as contextually determined? Definitions of ECE quality in high-income countries have been influenced by theoretical viewpoints on child development as well as empirical work outlining associations between quality and child development. In the United States, current definitions of ECE quality focus on multiple aspects of children's environments, with emphasis on teacher–child interactions; having age-appropriate materials available; curriculum and activities appropriate for children; and healthy and safe conditions (Burchinal, 2018). The two main quality instruments used in the United States—the Early Childhood Environment Ratings Scales (e.g., ECERS; Harms, Clifford, & Cryer, 1980; ECERS-R; Harms, Clifford, & Cryer, 1998; ECERS-E, Sylva, Siraj-Blatchford, & Taggart, 2003; ECERS-3; Harms, Clifford, & Cryer, 2015) and the Classroom Assessment Scoring System (CLASS-PreK; Pianta, La Paro, & Hamre, 2008)—reflect several key assumptions about quality, including the centrality of teacher–child interactions in which teachers provide sensitive and supportive scaffolding for children's learning; children's abilities to exercise autonomy and choice within their environments; and the importance of rich language interactions that give children ample opportunities to express themselves and engage in dialogue with teachers and peers.

Variants of these measures have been used frequently in studies of ECE quality and child development in LMIC (Fernald, Prado, Kariger, & Raikes, 2017). As one example among many variations of the ECERS in LMIC, Moore, Akhter, and Aboud (2008) found that children who attended higher-quality classrooms in Bangladesh had higher scores on measures of child development. As noted above, McCoy and Wolf (2018) reported positive associations between quality as measured by the Teacher Instructional Practices and Processes System (TIPPS), a variation of the CLASS designed for LMIC, and child development over the course of a school year.

However, other work questions the value of a "universal" definition of quality that is expressed in uniform instruments applied across settings. Myers (2004) argued that quality is inherently sensitive to context, and thus should be defined and measured in ways that are culturally relevant and do not assume the existence of underlying constructs with similarities across settings. A relativistic and postmodern view of quality that deprioritizes measurement and monitoring in lieu of the development of shared "meaning making" has also been articulated as a more impactful route toward improving quality than relying on a universal and imposed definition of quality (Dahlberg, Moss, & Pence, 2007). These two viewpoints were echoed by Tobin (2005), who argued that universal definitions of quality, such as those that are embedded in global measures of ECE quality, run the risk of displacing local definitions of quality that are more aligned and sensitive to unique cultural contexts. Using examples of France and Japan, Tobin maintained that preschool settings would be considered problematic by U.S. standards, but these ECE settings are successful in preparing French and Japanese citizens for educational systems (and lifelong well-being) within their countries. The definitions of quality may also have significance for how the data from the measures are used: In his anthropo-logical analyses of quality measurement, Tobin (2005) stated that measures should be locally generated to ensure maximum cultural applicability and value. This may especially be the case in settings where ECE systems are just beginning, and resources for materials, classrooms, and teacher train-ing are limited.

Perhaps because there are so few cross-country studies on ECE qual-ity, only a small amount of work to date has focused on identifying specific aspects of quality that may vary from one place to the next, especially process quality focusing on teacher–child interactions and children's engagement with materials, peers, and other daily experiences. Yet there may be sub-stantial cultural and contextual variation in how process quality is defined and experienced. Regarding one element that often is included in quality measurement, the extent to which children have choice and autonomy in their daily activities, Keller (2012) documented the influence of sociocul-tural context in affecting the development and manifestation of autonomy in young children. In Indonesia, for example, children are given culturally appropriate tools (including large knives) to practice cutting vegetables on their own. Such a degree of autonomy would be considered unsafe and inappropriate in the United States. Appropriate levels of autonomy in one setting may not be viewed as such in another, and this is perhaps especially the case as many families in LMIC transition between rural and urban environments. Dialogue between teachers and children is another central element of existing quality measures; the extent to which adults encour-age children's verbal self-expression and discussion of their internal states has also been posited to be reflective of the larger sociocultural context in which children grow up, specifically adults' exposure to formal education (Keller, 2012). In sum, while empirical work demonstrates the importance of ECE quality for child development in LMIC, more work is needed to identify aspects of quality that may vary according to setting, and to docu-ment the specific differences in how quality is defined as a critical step in improving the accuracy and value of ECE quality measurement.

Because quality standards are nascent in many LMIC (UNICEF, 2019), the question of how to define quality—and who defines it—is relevant from parents through to government officials. For example, when considering what should be taught in ECE, parents in Ghana articulated views of quality that had elements that can be considered generally consistent with theories and empirical findings, such as the importance of both academic preparation for school and play, but also noted that children should learn greetings in school, which is specific to Ghanaian context (Kabay, Wolf, & Yoshikawa, 2017). Kabay and colleagues also hypothesized that there may be stronger commonalities in definitions of quality among rural versus urban parents, regardless of country of origin. Teachers and parents may also hold different definitions of ECE quality, with parents less likely to endorse play as a mechanism of learning than teachers (Avornyo & Baker, 2018). Yet parents, and even teachers, may not consistently be included in the design and implementation of government quality standards. The lack of engagement of ECE professionals and parents in defining ECE can lead to conflict between parents, teachers, and government officials on what should be prioritized and measured in ECE settings, leading to measures that are not especially valued because they miss key elements of ECE quality. Definitions of ECE quality in relation to SEL may be especially important to view in cultural context. As mentioned by McCoy (Chapter 3, this volume), the variations in cultural definitions of SEL will naturally lead to diversity in the definitions of ECE quality: Physical punishment, for example, may be considered a marker of extremely low quality in some settings, but viewed as necessary for children's healthy development in others. At the same time, it is also important to differentiate practices that arise because teachers define quality differently, and practices that arise (or do not take place) because teachers face too many barriers to their implementation. For example, in some settings in sub-Saharan Africa, teachers may agree with definitions of quality that emphasize children's play, teacher–child interactions, and access to materials, but because so few resources are available to achieve quality ECE, they have few opportunities to implement such practices (Davis et al., 2021).

As one example of how scales can be aligned to local settings, the MELE scale combines a core of common items along with guidance on adapting items to match local context. Adaptation processes include reviewing standards and convening workshops of stakeholders to discuss and prioritize items for measurement. As a result, MELE scales may have some common elements across sites, but have variation that reflects decisions made by local stakeholders. Looking across countries, we have often found that the core MELE constructs, many of which emerged from global research literature, are valued by country stakeholders (e.g., Raikes, Koziol, Davis, & Burton, 2020), but there are also important variations, such as the degree of autonomy children receive, the structure of the classroom day, and the type and amount of materials available. Yet despite the potential value of building locally relevant quality measures, few studies have reported on the feasibility and psychometric validity of this approach, or the impact that such measures can have on improving teaching and learning. The variation in scales could maximize local value, but also creates challenges in examining psychometric properties and comparing results across sites. Next we turn to a brief overview of what we know about ECE quality in LMIC, to help us evaluate quality measures—or said another way, how we know whether ECE quality measures are actually capturing critical elements of ECE quality.

ECE Quality and Child Development in LMIC

Evaluation of quality measurement in ECE is largely driven by the relationship with child development: Quality measurement is important if it can help identify the environments that best promote children's development. A first step, then, is to examine empirical work on the associations between ECE quality and child development in LMIC.

While research on quality and child development is not as plentiful in LMIC countries as it is in high-income countries, there is a growing body of work documenting associations between ECE quality and child development across many contexts. Using a variety of study designs and measures of ECE quality and child development, higher quality ECE, defined by both "structural" variables such as teacher/child ratios and class sizes, and "process" variables such as children's access to materials and teacher–child interaction, has been associated with child development in several countries, for example in India (Rao, 2010), Cambodia (Rao, Richards, Sun, Weber, & Sincovich, 2019), Bangladesh (Aboud & Hossain, 2011), Ghana (McCoy & Wolf, 2018), Indonesia (Brinkman et al., 2017), Kenya (Malmberg, Mwaura, & Sylva, 2011), and Colombia (Andrew et al., 2019). To date, thresholds of quality—or what levels of quality must be reached for children to benefit from ECE—have not been clearly established. As noted above, standards for quality have been designed mostly with high-income country settings in mind, with emphasis on materials and spaces that require substantial resources. Yet some research suggests that even settings that are deemed "low quality" by high-income country standards can have a positive impact on child development (e.g., Rao, 2010; Rao et al., 2012). Recent work has also documented that ECE quality is meaningfully related to growth in child development over the course of a school year (e.g., in Ghana; McCoy & Wolf, 2018), and ECE participation, dosage, and intensity have been associated with cognitive, language, and social–emotional development in Mongolia, China, Vanuatu, and Cambodia (Rao et al., 2019).

Measurement of child development creates one challenge in exploring the associations between quality and child development across countries. As outlined by McCoy (see Chapter 3, this volume), cultural and contextual influences on the development and measurement of child development preclude reliance on a "universal" set of skills, but there is also evidence to suggest that some skills are relevant across contexts, which strengthens the argument that ECE quality and child outcomes are associated. For example, using items indexing Ghanaian preschool and kindergarten children's social cognition, such as perspective taking, empathy, and emotion identification, McCoy and Wolf (2018) found that social–emotional skills were associated with early academic skills in Ghana and both were associated with ECE quality, and in Kenya, Willoughby and colleagues (Willoughby, Piper, Kwayumba, & McCune, 2019) found associations between executive functioning, literacy, and mathematics, but no association with ECE participation was found. When reviewing these results, it is important to note that measurement invariance in cross-country child development measures has not yet been established, meaning that we may not yet be able to say that a score in one setting means the same thing as it does in another (e.g., Halpin et al., 2019). When measures are invariant, if we see child development and quality associated in two countries, we can assume that the results are telling us similar information about the role of ECE quality in child development. That said, the available body of evidence points toward the importance of ECE quality in child development, thus justifying a deeper look at how quality is conceptualized and measured, and at the psychometric properties of the tools.

• Evaluating Measures: Psychometrics and Facilitating Change

Results from quality measurement can play an important role in shaping monitoring systems and supporting teacher improvement (OECD, 2015). An important barometer of a measure's value is whether results can be used to help promote professional development, investments in ECE, and other changes that lead to better experiences for children. Psychometric properties of measurement tools, especially their proneness to measurement error, are important (Mashburn, 2017). Despite the widespread use of ECERS and CLASS in the United States, it is not clear whether these two measures consistently meet standards of validity, or said another way, if the measures are accurately and consistently measuring "quality" across settings. Several studies have questioned the psychometric properties of these tools, such as inconsistent factor structures, item disordering, and small effect sizes in relation to child development (Brunsek et al., 2017; Perlman et al., 2016; Gordon et al., 2015). This could be because there is not "one" definition of quality, as noted above—and suggests we may also want to evaluate scales based on the value of the results for promoting improvement. The frequent use of ECERS and CLASS adaptations in LMIC thus raises questions on not only the cultural implications of relying on measures from high-income countries, but also on the accuracy of these scales. Because contexts in LMIC are more diverse and there may be classrooms with very few characteristics of quality as defined by these scales, measurement error may be replicated and even increased when using the scales in these contexts.

Therefore, despite the potential limitations of relying on psychometrics alone to judge the quality of scales, psychometric analyses provide one window into scale functioning. The available evidence upon which to base psychometric evaluations of ECE quality measurement in LMIC is limited, especially when looking beyond associations between ECE quality measures and child development. Addressing internal structure, McCoy and Wolf (2018) found a three-factor solution using data from the TIPPS in Ghana, with small but expected associations between the factors and child development. Using ECERS scores from Colombia, Mariano and colleagues (2019) found multiple factor solutions, but they did not report on associations between these factors and other variables. Many studies using adaptations of the ECERS and CLASS scales do not report on internal structures, leading to limited insight on the internal structures of quality scales in LMIC. At a minimum, ECE quality scales used in LMIC should meet basic psychometric standards, including demonstration of internal validity and structure, demonstrated through internal coherence and the presence of predicted factor structures; concurrent validity, demonstrated through predicted associations with child development and teacher characteristics; and predictive validity, demonstrated by documenting the positive associations between ECE quality and child development over time.

The MELE scale provides one of the first opportunities to evaluate the psychometric properties of a scale designed for cultural adaptation. Results suggest that culturally adapted scales demonstrate scale properties that are generally in line with global scales like ECERS. Ponguta et al. (2019) reported on the adaptation process in Colombia, including a detailed matching of scale items to quality constructs outlined in policy documents, which led to modifications to the scale to better match policy priorities. For example, new domains were added to capture the importance of transition from preprimary to primary school and the presence of integrated teams to address health, nutrition, and psychosocial development, in addition to modifications to specific items to ensure cultural and contextual applicability. Raikes et al. (2020) have also documented psychometric properties of MELE when used in one context among a typical sample of preschools. Of note was the small association between quality factors and child development, although quality was associated with teacher characteristics.

Another key element of psychometric functioning is relevance, or the extent to which data that emerge from ECE quality scales are viewed as useful and applicable to ECE policy and programs. To date, there are few systematic investigations of the role of ECE quality data in encouraging improvement in LMIC, but this is clearly an area for further investigation given the challenges facing many ECE settings. In sum, more research is needed to determine the psychometric properties and patterns of associations of adapted quality measures when used in LMIC, and centrally, to determine whether the origin and process for creating the tools has an impact on data use.

• Next Steps in ECE Quality Measurement in LMIC

Deciding if and how to define quality in a standardized manner depends heavily on how the resulting data will be used. There are several possible uses for data on ECE quality, ranging from large-scale monitoring of quality across countries (Yoshikawa, Wuermli, Raikes, Kim, & Kabay, 2018); focused feedback to teachers to improve ECE quality settings; and research to generate more information on what works and for whom. Requirements for measurement vary based on the purpose (Fernald et al., 2017). Monitoring systems are in place to ensure basic levels of quality provision in many high- and middle-income countries (see OECD, 2015, for a review), but many low-income countries are still in the early stages of developing effective monitoring systems (UNICEF, 2019). The early stages of monitoring systems in many countries means that there is still ample opportunity to think critically about how to generate useful and impactful data, beginning with the process of defining and measuring quality and extending to the use of data to improve teaching and learning. It is not yet clear if and how the content of quality measures influences their impact on ECE provision and policy: More locally grounded measures could be more effective in creating change if they articulate concepts on quality that resonate more deeply across stakeholders, especially ECE professionals, where quality improvement efforts are likely focused (Cottle & Alexander, 2012). But it is also important to recognize the importance of constructs that may not yet be fully integrated into a local culture yet have a profound impact on child development, such as the transition to ECE environments that emphasize dialogue and autonomy.

Viewing from a "glass half full" perspective, quality measurement tools from high-income countries can provide a starting point for country adaptation; the "glass half empty" perspective suggests that reliance on these scales runs the risk of repeating multiple types of measurement error and cultural misalignment (e.g., Mashburn, 2017; Tobin, 2005). There are several paths forward in ECE quality measurement in LMIC. One path is to continue reliance on globally generated measures: This path potentially provides a faster route in the short term, as these measures are developed and may have been adapted to better match the context. However, this path runs the risk of producing measures with a great deal of error. Another path is to invest in locally generated tools, likely requiring a greater investment of time, but potentially producing data and measurement systems with greater applicability to the local setting, with strong emphasis on defining how the data are used to support teaching and learning. This route may delay attention to quality in some settings, as resources for ECE overall are limited (Neuman & Okeng'o, 2019), and research may not be a high priority in many countries. Finally, it may also be possible to invest in the careful and systematic documentation of the adaptations and local variations that are used to measure quality now, with the long-term goal of establishing how well these scales measure child development.

To date, we know very little about how data can facilitate change in ECE. Given the nascent monitoring systems in many countries, it is likely that few teachers receive objective feedback on their performance using ECE quality measures. And further, as noted earlier, many ECE settings are private or informal, so they may not even be formally registered as part of the ECE system. Measurement must begin where ECE settings are, with straightforward and easily digestible feedback along with resources for improvement. Beyond the content and structure of the measures, for data to lead to change, we also must build a culture of trust. This culture includes trust in measures of quality and child development and trust in how the data will be used—for improvement rather than punishment, and for inclusion rather than to exclude children and teachers from the ECE system. If key stakeholders do not feel that measures accurately index the unique and valued aspects of children or their environments, or if there is distrust in how the data will be used, the tremendous effort that goes into collecting and analyzing data may go to waste.

Quality measurement has an important role to play in creating effective and equitable ECE systems. Measures development can be a time-intensive and lengthy endeavor, yet these investments may result in a stronger, more data-driven system that ensures ECE quality for all children.

REFERENCES

Aboud, F. E., & Hossain, K. (2011). The impact of preprimary school on primary school achievement in Bangladesh. *Early Childhood Research Quarterly, 26*(2), 237–246.

Andrew, A., Attanasio, O., Bernal, R., Sosa, L. C., Krutikova, S., & Rubio-Codina, M. (2019). *Preschool quality and child development* (No. w26191). National Bureau of Economic Research.

Avornyo, E. A., & Baker, S. (2018). The role of play in children's learning: The perspective of Ghanaian early years stakeholders. *Early Years,* 1–16.

Bidwell, K., & Watine, L. (2014). *Exploring early education programs in peri-urban settings in Africa*. Innovations for Poverty Action.

Brinkman, S. A., Hasan, A., Jung, H., Kinnell, A., Nakajima, N., & Pradhan, M. (2017). The role of preschool quality in promoting child development: evidence from rural Indonesia. *European Early Childhood Education Research Journal, 25*(4), 483–505.

Britto, P. R., Lye, S. J., Proulx, K., Yousafzai, A. K., Matthews, S. G., Vaivada, T., . . . MacMillan, H. (2017). Nurturing care: Promoting early childhood development. *Lancet, 389*(10064), 91–102.

Brunsek, A., Perlman, M., Falenchuk, O., McMullen, E., Fletcher, B., & Shah, P.

S. (2017). The relationship between the Early Childhood Environment Rating Scale and its revised form and child outcomes: A systematic review and meta-analysis. *PLoS ONE, 12*(6), e0178512.

Burchinal, M. (2018). Measuring early care and education quality. *Child Development Perspectives, 12*(1), 3–9.

Cottle, M., & Alexander, E. (2012). Quality in early years settings: Government, research and practitioners' perspectives. *British Educational Research Journal, 38*(4), 635–654.

Dahlberg, G., Moss, P., & Pence, A. (2007). *Beyond quality in early childhood education and care: Languages of evaluation.* Routledge.

Davis, D., Miller, D., Mrema, D., Matsoai, M., Mapetla, N., Raikes, A., & Burton, A. (2021). Understanding perceptions of quality among early childhood education stakeholders in Tanzania and Lesotho: A multiple qualitative case study. *Social Sciences & Humanities Open, 4*(1), 100153.

Fernald, L. C., Prado, E., Kariger, P., & Raikes, A. (2017). *A toolkit for measuring early childhood development in low and middle-income countries.* World Bank.

Gordon, R. A., Hofer, K. G., Fujimoto, K. A., Risk, N., Kaestner, R., & Korenman, S. (2015). Identifying high-quality preschool programs: New evidence on the validity of the Early Childhood Environment Rating Scale–Revised (ECERS-R) in relation to school readiness goals. *Early Education and Development, 26*(8), 1086–1110.

Halpin, P. F., Wolf, S., Yoshikawa, H., Rojas, N., Kabay, S., Pisani, L., & Dowd, A. J. (2019). Measuring early learning and development across cultures: Invariance of the IDELA across five countries. *Developmental Psychology, 55*(1), 23.

Harms, T., Clifford, R. M., & Cryer, D. (1980). *Early Childhood Environment Rating Scale.* Teachers College Press.

Harms, T., Clifford, R. M., & Cryer, D. (1998). *Early Childhood Environment Rating Scale—Revised.* Teachers College Press.

Harms, T., Clifford, R., & Cryer, D. (2015). *Early Childhood Environment Rating Scale* (3rd ed.). Teachers College Press.

Kabay, S., Wolf, S., & Yoshikawa, H. (2017). "So that his mind will open": Parental perceptions of early childhood education in urbanizing Ghana. *International Journal of Educational Development, 57*, 44–53.

Keller, H. (2012). Autonomy and relatedness revisited: Cultural manifestations of universal human needs. *Child Development Perspectives, 6*(1), 12–18.

Malmberg, L. E., Mwaura, P., & Sylva, K. (2011). Effects of a preschool intervention on cognitive development among East-African preschool children: A flexibly time-coded growth model. *Early Childhood Research Quarterly, 26*(1), 124–133.

Mariano, M., Caetano, S. C., Ribeiro da Silva, A., Surkan, P. J., Martins, S. S., & Cogo-Moreira, H. (2019). Psychometric properties of the ECERS-R among an epidemiological sample of preschools. *Early Education and Development, 30*(4), 511–521.

Mashburn, A. J. (2017). Evaluating the validity of classroom observations in the Head Start designation renewal system. *Educational Psychologist, 52*(1), 38–49.

McCoy, D. C., & Wolf, S. (2018). Changes in classroom quality predict Ghanaian preschoolers' gains in academic and social-emotional skills. *Developmental Psychology, 54*(8), 1582.

Moore, A. C., Akhter, S., & Aboud, F. E. (2008). Evaluating an improved quality preschool program in rural Bangladesh. *International Journal of Educational Development, 28*(2), 118–131.

Myers, R. G. (2004). In search of quality in programs of early childhood care and education. Background paper for Education for All, Global Monitoring Report 2005. UNESCO, Paris. Retrieved from *www.unesco.org/education/gmr_download/references_2005.pdfS*.

Neuman, M. J., & Okeng'o, L. (2019). Early childhood policies in low-and middle-income countries. *Early Years Journal, 39*(3), 233–238.

Organisation for Economic Co-operation and Development. (2015). *Starting strong IV: Monitoring quality in early childhood education and care*. OECD Publishing.

Perlman, M., Falenchuk, O., Fletcher, B., McMullen, E., Beyene, J., & Shah, P. S. (2016). A systematic review and meta-analysis of a measure of staff/child interaction quality (the classroom assessment scoring system) in early childhood education and care settings and child outcomes. *PloS One, 11*(12), e0167660.

Pianta, R. C., La Paro, K. M., & Hamre, B. K. (2008). *Classroom Assessment Scoring System™: Manual Pre-K*. Paul H Brookes Publishing.

Ponguta, L. A., Maldonado-Carreño, C., Kagan, S. L., Yoshikawa, H., Nieto, A. M., Aragón, C. A., . . . Escallon, E. (2019). Adaptation and application of the measuring early learning quality and outcomes (MELQO) framework to early childhood education settings in Colombia. *Zeitschrift für Psychologie*.

Raikes, A., Davis, D., & Burton, A. (2019). Early childhood care and education in the era of sustainable development: Balancing local and global priorities. In L. E. Sutter, E. Smith, & B. D. Denman (Eds.), *The SAGE handbook of comparative studies in education*. Sage New York.

Raikes, A., Koziol, N., Davis, D., & Burton, A. (2020). Measuring quality of preprimary education in sub-Saharan Africa: Evaluation of the Measuring Early Learning Environments scale. *Early Childhood Research Quarterly, 53*, 571–585.

Raikes, A., Sayre, R., Davis, D., Anderson, K., Hyson, M., Seminario, E., & Burton, A. (2019). The Measuring Early Learning Quality & Outcomes initiative: Purpose, process and results. *Early Years*, 1–16.

Rao, N. (2010). Preschool quality and the development of children from economically disadvantaged families in India. *Early Education and Development, 21*(2), 167–185.

Rao, N., Sun, J., Pearson, V., Pearson, E., Liu, H., Constas, M. A., & Engle, P. L. (2012). Is something better than nothing? An evaluation of early childhood programs in Cambodia. *Child Development, 83*(3), 864–876.

Rao, N., Sun, J., Chen, E. E., & Ip, P. (2017). Effectiveness of early childhood interventions in promoting cognitive development in developing countries: A systematic review and meta-analysis. *Hong Kong Journal of Paediatrics, 22*(1), 14–25.

Rao, N., Richards, B., Sun, J., Weber, A., & Sincovich, A. (2019). Early childhood education and child development in four countries in East Asia and the Pacific. *Early Childhood Research Quarterly, 47,* 169–181.

Sylva, K., Siraj-Blatchford, I., & Taggart, B. (2003). *Assessing quality in the early years: Early childhood environment rating scale: Extension (ECERS-E), four curricular subscales.* Trentham Books.

Tobin, J. (2005). Quality in early childhood education: An anthropologist's perspective. *Early Education and Development, 16*(4), 421–434.

Wolf, S., Halpin, P., Yoshikawa, H., Dowd, A. J., Pisani, L., & Borisova, I. (2017). Measuring school readiness globally: Assessing the construct validity and measurement invariance of the International Development and Early Learning Assessment (IDELA) in Ethiopia. *Early Childhood Research Quarterly, 41,* 21–36.

UNICEF. (2019). *Defining, monitoring and improving quality: Guidelines for stronger quality assurance systems in early childhood education.* UNICEF.

Yoshikawa, H., Wuermli, A. J., Raikes, A., Kim, S., & Kabay, S. B. (2018). Toward high-quality early childhood development programs and policies at national scale: Directions for research in global contexts. *Social Policy Report, 31*(1), 1–36.

CHAPTER 10

Capturing the Social and Emotional Classroom

Using Setting-Level Measures to Drive Improvements
in Teaching and Learning

Sophie P. Barnes, Rachel M. Abenavoli, and Stephanie M. Jones

A majority of efforts in the field of social and emotional learning (SEL) rely on programs, curricula, and interventions as a mechanism for improving children's outcomes (e.g., Jones, Brush, et al., 2017). These approaches typically include targeted activities, games, and lessons that require children and youth to learn about and practice skills or behaviors within a particular skill area (e.g., learning about and practicing the steps to conflict resolution). Setting-level features and processes, such as the daily practices and strategies that teachers use in their classroom, are also common targets of interventions designed, ultimately, to have positive impacts on children. As described in other chapters (Obradović & Steyer, Chapter 1, and McKown, Chapter 2, this volume), these programs typically use measures of individual student outcomes that are aligned with the program target to assess changes in children's skills as a result of the program or intervention. For example, an intervention with an emphasis on emotion knowledge and understanding might use a measure that asks the child to identify how children feel in various photos (e.g., sad, mad, surprised; Schultz, Izard, & Bear, 2004). Though these direct skill-building efforts have evidence of moderate effectiveness (Durlak, Weissberg, Dymnicki, Taylor, & Schellinger, 2011; Jones, Barnes, Bailey, & Doolittle, 2017), interventions and measurement approaches at the individual level neglect the settings in which these interventions take place and the influence that these environments have on the delivery of an intervention and ultimately children's outcomes. In this chapter, we describe the need to measure the social and emotional setting, including the specific teacher practices and social processes that support children's outcomes, and we describe an array of observational tools designed for this purpose. We then discuss in more detail one of these tools, the Adapted Teaching Style Rating Scale (A-TSRS), with a focus on its use across research and practice and its potential for driving improvements in teaching and learning.

• *Why* Should We Measure the Social and Emotional Setting?

Reliable, valid, and precise measurement of children's development and outcomes is necessary but not sufficient when it comes to understanding and promoting social, emotional, and behavioral development. As highlighted in setting-level and bioecological theories (Bronfenbrenner & Morris, 2006; Seidman & Cappella, 2017; Tseng & Seidman, 2007), the broader contexts in which children spend their time—and the regular, daily interactions they have with adults and peers within those contexts—are key drivers of children's social and emotional development. Despite this robust theoretical grounding, most measurement approaches in both research and practice focus squarely on largely decontextualized assessments of individual children (e.g., direct assessments of children's skills or state standardized testing).

To illustrate this basic notion, consider what happens when baking a cake. We know that both the individual ingredients that make up the recipe *and* the settings on the oven matter; even with the right amounts of flour, milk, and sugar, a cake won't come together if the oven temperature is too high or low, the rack is in the wrong place, or the timer is set for too much or too little baking time. Tweaking the ingredients of a recipe without considering the settings of the oven is like focusing solely on the individual child without considering features of the social contexts in which they grow and learn. Although it is possible to make improvements to the recipe that offset the impact of the oven settings, achieving the desired outcome actually requires identifying and resolving issues with the oven, or, in other words, careful attention to the setting. Shifting attention from a narrow focus on student outcomes to a broader acknowledgement of the complex, multilevel factors that contribute to those outcomes aligns with recent calls for greater attention to equity in the field of social and emotional learning (SEL; Duchesneau, 2020; Gregory & Fergus, 2017; Jagers, Rivas-Drake, & Williams, 2019). Models that situate SEL "deficits" within the child, rather than focus on root causes and inequities outside the child that shape and constrain development, are insufficient for reducing socioeconomic and racial/ethnic disparities at best, and may reinforce the norms and conditions that create and sustain disparities at worst (Duchesneau, 2020).

Adapting features of the setting is a mechanism for improvement at both the individual and setting levels, just like changing the features of an oven can improve the function of the oven itself *and* the outcome of the recipe within it. To bring about change, knowledge of the possible levers for change, or the features within a setting that one can adapt, is critical. Tseng and Seidman (2007; see also Seidman & Cappella, 2017) outline a framework for setting-level outcomes, consisting of resources (e.g., physical or personnel), allocation of resources (e.g., where and how the resources are deployed), and social processes (e.g., interactions between people and groups). In this framework, the organization and allocation of resources can facilitate change, but the outcomes of a setting are unlikely to change without targeting social processes, defined by Tseng and Seidman as norms, relationships, and participation in activities.

Social processes are manipulable and well suited to the world of SEL because most SEL practices begin with (or filter through) adults and are the vehicle driving student outcomes (Jennings & Greenberg, 2009; Jones, Bouffard, & Weissbourd, 2013). Adults attend professional development, implement interventions, model relevant behavior, and create the norms and routines that guide children's daily lives. Even if a teacher receives an SEL curriculum (resources) and blocks off time in their schedule to implement the SEL lessons (allocation of resources), a change in the setting or individual outcomes will not likely happen in a sustained manner unless teachers actually change their practices, for example, by implementing the SEL lessons and embedding opportunities to practice in daily classroom activities (social processes).

Social processes exist "in the social and temporal space among individuals," meaning that understanding and measuring social processes requires focusing on the "inter-relationships," or the dynamic relationship between more than one thing (Tseng & Seidman, 2007, p. 219). This suggests classroom observations, which focus on teachers, students, and, importantly, the interactions between them, are an aligned measurement approach to capture the dynamic interactions, activities, and norms in a setting. Of course, theoretically grounded and nuanced measurement at both levels—student *and* setting—is needed to more fully understand developmental pathways, identify (and evaluate) promising avenues for intervention, and drive improvements in teachers' daily practices.

• *What* Should We Measure in the Social and Emotional Setting?

Although many features of the school setting—including financial resources, the physical environment, school policies, climate—contribute to children's outcomes, in this chapter, we focus on social processes that are most salient and proximal (i.e., direct) drivers of children's learning and development (Bronfenbrenner & Morris, 2006; Tseng & Seidman, 2007). In particular, we focus on teacher practices because they meet three criteria (McKown, 2017): (1) they are meaningful—that is, they promote children's social, emotional, and behavioral outcomes, (2) they are measurable—concrete and definable, and (3) they are malleable—changeable through intervention and professional development.

Several theoretical frameworks and research traditions highlight (and emphasize to different degrees) a few key dimensions of teacher practice that specifically support children's social, emotional, and behavioral development. For example, grounded in attachment theory and its application to teacher–student relationships, one area of work focuses on the role of emotionally supportive interactions. Interactions characterized by warmth, sensitivity, and support for children's autonomy have been shown to facilitate positive teacher–child relationships and promote children's sense of safety, willingness to explore and engage in the classroom, and social and emotional outcomes (Downer, Sabol, & Hamre, 2010; Pianta, Hamre, & Allen, 2012).

Other frameworks emphasize the role of classroom management practices. Teachers' use of consistent routines, clear instructions and expectations, positive and proactive (versus harsh or directive) behavior management strategies, and strategies for supporting attention and engagement provide the necessary conditions and supports for children to learn to regulate their behavior in the service of positive, prosocial goals (Everston & Weinstein, 2006; Webster-Stratton & Herman, 2010; Webster-Stratton, Reid, & Stoolmiller, 2008). These practices, and interventions targeting these practices, have been shown to improve children's executive functioning and behavior regulation and to reduce dysregulated or aggressive behavior (Dominguez, Vitiello, Maier, & Greenfield, 2010; Rimm-Kaufman, Curby, Grimm, Nathanson, & Brock, 2009; Morris, Millenky, Raver, & Jones, 2013; Raver et al., 2009).

Finally, modeling and teaching social and emotional skills—whether this occurs formally or informally, in the context of a planned lesson or during naturally occurring teachable moments—also play an important role in children's skill development. Providing explicit instruction in emotion vocabulary and using feeling words in everyday interactions build children's emotion awareness and understanding. Validating and supporting children when they express positive or negative emotions, and modeling strategies to manage distress, calm down, or marshal positive energy when needed promote children's emotion regulation skills. Using peer interactions or conflict as opportunities for learning, with developmentally appropriate support from the teacher, can build children's capacity for perspective taking and problem solving (Ahn, 2005; Denham, Bassett, & Zinsser,

2012; Domitrovich, Cortes, & Greenberg, 2007; Morris, Denham, Bassett, & Curby, 2013).

• *How* Should We Measure the Social and Emotional Setting?

A common approach to measuring teacher practices with reliability and validity is for trained observers to visit a classroom during regular instructional time and follow a structured protocol to rate specific features of the setting (Pianta & Hamre, 2009). While many classroom observation tools focus on global quality or content-specific instruction in academic domains (e.g., literacy or math practices; Kane & Staiger, 2012), a few capture one or more aspects of the social and emotional setting described above. Although they share a focus on the social and emotional setting, these observational tools vary along a number of additional dimensions worth noting. First, because they are grounded in different theoretical frameworks and/or intervention models, the tools differ in terms of which specific features of the setting are measured, and the extent to which those features are more global or specific in nature. For example, some tools focus on the overall emotional climate of the classroom, whereas others focus on specific behavior management and/or instructional practices. The tools also differ in terms of the length and number of observation cycles conducted (e.g., multiple 20-minute cycles versus one 3-hour observation), and in terms of the rating scale, with some measures requiring observers to make ratings using 5- or 7-point Likert scales and others requiring observers to note the presence or absence of a practice using a checklist. We highlight a few tools below, primarily used in early childhood contexts, to illustrate the range of setting-level measurement approaches; readers are referred to other sources for more exhaustive reviews (e.g., Praetorius & Charalambous, 2018; Halle, Vick Whittaker, & Anderson, 2010).

The Early Childhood Environment Rating Scale (ECERS; Harms, Clifford, & Cryer, 2014) is a measure of global quality that has been used in child care, Head Start, and PreK settings for decades. The current version of the tool, the ECERS-3, is designed to measure the physical learning environment, program structure, health and safety routines, literacy/language practices, learning activities, and interactions among teachers and children. Trained observers rate the quantity and quality of 35 items on a 7-point scale following a 3-hour classroom observation. ECERS scores have been shown to predict children's outcomes, including prosocial and on-task behavior (Halle et al., 2010; Peisner-Feinberg et al., 2001).

Another commonly used classroom observation tool in research and practice/policy contexts is the Classroom Assessment Scoring System (CLASS; Pianta, LaParo, & Hamre, 2008). The CLASS is designed to measure the quality of teacher–student interactions in PreK to 12th-grade classrooms across three domains: Emotional Support, which encompasses positive and negative climate, teacher sensitivity, and regard for student perspectives; Classroom Organization, which includes behavior management strategies, productive use of time, and instructional formats/facilitation; and Instructional Support, which encompasses concept development, quality of feedback, and language use. Observers conduct multiple 20-minute cycles per classroom, and at the conclusion of each cycle, they rate each of 10 dimensions on a 7-point scale. Prior research demonstrates that the tool is reliable, captures three related domains of teacher–student interactions, and is related to children's social–emotional, behavioral, and academic outcomes (Hamre et al., 2013; Hamre, Hatfield, Pianta, & Hamil, 2014; Mashburn et al., 2008).

A third tool, the Teaching Pyramid Observation Tool (TPOT), was developed to measure implementation of practices directly aligned to the Pyramid Model (see Fox, Veguilla, & Hemmeter, Chapter 8, this volume), a tiered promotion–prevention–intervention framework for supporting children's social–emotional development (Hemmeter, Snyder, Fox, & Algina, 2016; Snyder, Hemmeter, Fox, Bishop, & Miller, 2013). The tool captures environmental arrangements, "red flags," and key practices, which range from schedules and routines to explicit emotion skills instruction. Observers mark whether each of 131 indicators was "present" or "not present" during the observation. Research shows that inter-rater agreement on the TPOT is high, that the tool is sensitive to changes in teacher practice resulting from targeted professional development, and that scores on the TPOT are related to children's social and emotional outcomes (Snyder et al., 2013).

We focus the rest of this chapter on a fourth observational tool, the Teaching Style Rating Scale (TSRS; Domitrovich, Cortes, & Greenberg, 2000; Raver, Domitrovich, Greenberg, Morris, & Mattera, 2012). The TSRS was initially developed to measure practices closely aligned with the Preschool Promoting Alternative Thinking Strategies (Preschool PATHS) intervention model (Domitrovich et al., 2007, 2009) and was then refined and expanded in the national Head Start CARES demonstration trial to capture a broader range of practices—used across different classroom settings and different intervention models (Preschool PATHS, Incredible Years, and Tools of the Mind—Play [Tools–Play])—that support children's social and emotional skill development (Adapted-TSRS [A-TSRS]; Morris et al., 2014; Raver et al., 2012). The tool has been further adapted and used across early childhood and elementary school settings (Jones, Imm, & HopeLab, 2016). The A-TSRS complements tools that measure more global aspects of quality, like the ECERS and CLASS, and provides further nuance by capturing specific practices that enable children to practice and develop self-regulation, emotion vocabulary, emotion regulation strategies, perspective taking, and problem solving. After observing a classroom for 15–20 minutes, observers rate the quantity and quality of specific teaching behaviors relating to classroom structure and management and social–emotional skill instruction using a 5-point scale. In the remaining sections, we provide more information about the A-TSRS, illustrate how classrooms vary in their A-TSRS practices, and describe how the A-TSRS has and can be used in research and practice/policy settings to drive improvements in teaching and learning.

The Adapted Teaching Style Rating Scale

Different sets of items have been included in different versions of the A-TSRS, but two core modules have been used mostly frequently. The first, Classroom Structure and Management (CSM), focuses on practices that create predictable, safe, and supportive environments that facilitate children's self-regulation and positive social behavior. These include teachers' consistency of practice and routines (e.g., transition routines), classroom awareness practices (e.g., monitoring the room), positive behavior management strategies (e.g., praise, redirection), low use of negative behavior management strategies (e.g., harsh discipline practices), attention support strategies (e.g., verbal and nonverbal cues), and preparedness. A second module, Social and Emotional Opportunities (SEO), focuses on instructional strategies teachers may use during social–emotional lessons or activities as well as organically throughout the day during naturally occurring opportunities for skill building. These include practices that support children's emotion understanding (e.g., modeling, using feeling words), emotion expression (e.g., validating and encouraging children to share emotions), emotion regulation (e.g., reminding students to take a deep breath to calm down), social awareness (e.g., asking one child to think about how another child might be feeling), and social problem solving (e.g., helping children work through a conflict). Additional items used in some versions of the A-TSRS measure teachers' scaffolding of peer interactions, scaffolding of children's dramatic play, and talk aloud (e.g., teacher verbalizes their planning or thought process when problem solving).

To support consistency in ratings across observers, the A-TSRS includes concrete behavioral anchors for each item as well as a set of observable actions to look for in the classroom. For example, the behavioral anchor for a "5" (the highest score) for Emotion Modeling notes that the teacher "consistently finds opportunities to teach children about their emotions by identifying and labeling children's emotional experiences." Observable actions related to Emotion Modeling might include using emotion vocabulary while reading a book, using "I" statements to describe the teacher's own emotions, facilitating an activity about emotions (e.g., a Feelings

Tree), or asking children to describe what it feels like when they are sad, happy, angry, etc. Examples of observable actions can be added or removed when using the tool with different grade levels or in settings where specific actions are more or less relevant. The flexible and modularized format of the A-TSRS also makes it easy to adapt the tool (e.g., add or remove items) to maximize its relevance in a particular setting or study, depending on a school system's priorities or programming (e.g., curriculum or teacher professional learning) or set of research questions to be examined.

Prior research using the A-TSRS has demonstrated that the tool is reliable across raters and settings, can detect subtle changes in teacher practice resulting from targeted professional development not captured by other tools, and may be associated with children's social, emotional, and behavioral outcomes (Domitrovich et al., 2009; Morris et al., 2014; Raver et al., 2012; Rojas, Mattera, Morris, & Raver, 2021). In addition, scores on the A-TSRS are moderately correlated with other measures of the social and emotional setting, including the CLASS, suggesting that it captures both overlapping and distinct features of the classroom context (Rojas et al., 2021). In a trial of Preschool PATHS (an early childhood SEL curriculum) combined with a literacy curriculum (Head Start REDI), teachers who received training and coaching in the PATHS model showed improvements on several TSRS items relative to teachers in the control group who did not receive training; children in PATHS classrooms also showed theoretically aligned improvements in emotion understanding, social problem solving, and social behavior relative to control children, providing initial support for the hypothesized causal pathway from specific teacher practices to specific and aligned children's skills (Bierman et al., 2008; Domitrovich et al., 2009). In the Head Start CARES evaluation of three distinct preschool social–emotional programs (Preschool PATHS, Incredible Years, and a 1-year adaptation of Tools of the Mind [Tools–Play]), results indicated that the A-TSRS detected impacts on theoretically aligned domains of teacher practice. For example, relative to control teachers, Preschool PATHS teachers showed improvements in social and emotional instructional practices, Incredible Years teachers showed improvements in classroom management practices, and Tools–Play teachers showed improvements in scaffolding practices. In addition, Preschool PATHS and Incredible Years led to improvements in children's social and emotional skills and behavior, again lending support to the notion that use of specific teacher practices drives improvements in specific social and emotional skills (Morris et al., 2014).

Three Very Different Ovens: An Example of the A-TSRS in Practice

While specific A-TSRS practices have been shown to predict improvements in specific and aligned child outcomes, it is also instructive to understand how different practices come together within a classroom to shape children's holistic experiences, with implications for their social, emotional, and behavioral development. To illustrate the A-TSRS and the variability it can capture, below we present data from three elementary-age classrooms in British Columbia, Canada, collected in January 2019, at the beginning of an intervention study. All classrooms were engaged in typical classroom practice (a math lesson). We present these data to illustrate three profiles of classrooms that we have noticed across hundreds of A-TSRS observations: high scoring across both CSM and SEO domains, low scoring across both domains, and a combined high CSM/low SEO classroom. Note that possible scores range from 1 to 5, with higher scores in all of the categories indicating a more positive classroom environment.

As shown in Table 10.1, the teacher in classroom 1 scored high across the CSM and SEO domains, meaning that the teacher was consistently aware of the classroom environment, had the classroom operating smoothly with predictable rules and routines, and used positive behavioral management techniques (e.g., use of eye contact, clear and logical consequences). The

TABLE 10.1. Profiles of Three Classrooms Using the A-TSRS

	Classroom 1: High CSM/SEO	Classroom 2: Low CSM/SEO	Classroom 3: High CSM/ Low SEO
Classroom structure and management (CSM)			
Classroom awareness	5	1	4
Positive behavior management	5	1	5
Negative behavior management[a]	5	2	5
Attention support	4	1	3
Consistency/routine	5	1	4
Preparedness	5	2	4
Mean CSM score	4.83	1.33	4.17
Social and emotional opportunities (SEO)			
Emotion modeling	4	1	1
Emotion expression	5	1	2
Emotion regulation	4	1	1
Social awareness	5	1	1
Social problem solving	4	1	1
Mean SEO score	4.40	1	1.20

[a]Negative behavior management has been reverse-scored so that higher scores indicate lower levels of negative behavior management.

teacher also found opportunities to teach children about their emotions by identifying and labeling children's emotional experiences and encouraging and supporting children to both express and regulate their emotions, as appropriate. Finally, the teacher made efforts to draw children's attention to the emotional experiences of others and the interpersonal consequences of behavior, and approached problem solving as an opportunity for learning.

By contrast, the teacher in classroom 2, engaged in a similar instructional activity, scored very low across all items. In this classroom, the teacher was consistently unaware of the classroom environment, may have used punitive discipline techniques (e.g., shame or yelling) to address student behavior and to gain and maintain the attention of the class, and spent a significant amount of time on noninstructional activities. The teacher also did not use emotion language or create a validating emotional environment (i.e., discouraged students from communicating how they feel). A key distinction here from other tools is that a low score on an item or in a domain does not necessarily reflect poor quality or negative interactions; instead, it may indicate that the teacher did not use a practice or set of practices during the observation period.

Classroom 3 represents a blend of classrooms 1 and 2, scoring relatively high in CSM, and low in SEO. What's notable is that we did not have any classrooms in the sample with the opposite pattern, meaning classrooms that scored low on CSM and high in SEO (see Figure 10.1 on p. 216), suggesting that a well-managed classroom environment with clear rules, activities, and routines (Jones, Bailey, & Jacob, 2014) is foundational to other instruction practices and activities.

Though we use data from real classrooms, this example is designed to be heuristic, representing the profiles of classrooms in which children learn and grow. Though additional work is needed to link these diverse classroom profiles to children's outcomes, thinking back to the oven example above, these classrooms are three very different "ovens," providing children with distinct experiences and interactions and very different orientations toward and opportunities to practice and develop their own social and emotional skills. In classrooms 1 and 3, children have consistent and clear routines and expectations, with opportunities to practice self-regulation and engage in well-prepared activities in a "smooth" classroom environment. However, students in classroom 3 have fewer opportunities to build emotion awareness, perspective taking, and problem-solving skills than do students in classroom 1. We might then hypothesize, for example, that a child in classroom 1 will have higher levels of SEL skills given the scaffolded opportunities to practice provided by their teacher, and that a child in classrooms 2 or 3 may have lower levels of SEL skills given the absence of teacher practices that intentionally foster those skills. Attempting to understand children's skills without taking into account the different environments in which they are embedded provides a narrow and incomplete view of a child's skill development. These profiles also highlight the need for tailored support for teachers, with some classrooms benefiting from support in particular domains (e.g., classrooms 2 and 3 need additional support in SEO).

A-TSRS in Action: Two Case Studies

Given its flexibility and relevance, the A-TSRS has the potential to bridge research, practice, and policy. Below we illustrate two uses of the tool across these spheres. The first case study describes the integration of the A-TSRS into New York City (NYC)'s PreK for All system at scale in the context of a partnership between university researchers and the NYC Department of Education. The second case study approaches the A-TSRS through a research lens and highlights potential ways to learn from collected data, drawing on typical data "checks" employed in research studies. These illustrations highlight key considerations for measurement—one emphasizes issues of relevance and gathering actionable data at scale, the other focuses on ensuring psychometrically sound use of the A-TSRS in particular contexts.

A-TSRS in NYC's Universal PreK System, PreK for All

One setting in which the A-TSRS has been used recently, and at scale, is NYC, where the district's free, universal PreK program, PreK for All, currently serves about 70,000 4-year-olds each year in a mixed-delivery system of over 1,800 district schools and community-based organizations. From the start, the NYC Department of Education's Division of Early Childhood Education (DECE) has demonstrated a strong commitment not only to expanding children's *access* to PreK, but to ensuring access to *high-quality* PreK experiences, by providing programs with a set of research-based quality standards and providing tailored professional learning and on-site support from instructional coordinators and social workers to all PreK programs. In addition, DECE has built a robust quality-monitoring and accountability system, in which each PreK program is observed with both the CLASS and ECERS-R at least once every 3 years by trained observers employed by DECE. With an internal data team and support from research partners at New York University (NYU) and other NYC universities and institutes, DECE brings data and research to bear as they identify priorities, make decisions, and allocate resources to continually strengthen the PreK for All system.

DECE first decided to adapt and use the A-TSRS within their system in an effort to understand the impacts of three distinct professional learning models they provide to PreK programs on targeted teacher practices. The "Explore" and "Create" professional learning series focus on developmentally appropriate math- and arts-based instruction, respectively. A third series, "Thrive," builds on years of research on the ParentCorps intervention (Brotman et al., 2011) and focuses on supporting children's SEL through classroom management practices, use of feeling words in the classroom, and family engagement practices (Brotman et al., 2021). Together with researchers at NYU's Steinhardt Institute of Human Development and Social Change and NYU's Langone Center for Early Childhood Health and Development, DECE considered various observation tools and ultimately chose to use the A-TSRS for several reasons: (1) The items were well-aligned with the setting-level social and emotional processes targeted in the teacher professional learning DECE wanted to evaluate, (2) the flexible nature of the tool meant that modules could be dropped or added given the goals of data collection, and (3) the tool could be used as an "add-on" to the CLASS as part of DECE's existing quality-monitoring system. These partnership studies are ongoing, but preliminary findings from an evaluation of the Thrive series suggest that items on the A-TSRS (particularly in the SEO domain) appear to capture emerging differences following Thrive professional learning that were not detected by other observation tools. Notably, the SEO items that were sensitive to change were observed fairly infrequently overall and may represent an important area of growth in many classrooms. These results are critical to DECE leadership as they continue to refine and strengthen professional learning opportunities for PreK for All teachers and program leaders, which are expected to translate to high-quality experiences and greater impacts for children.

Over the last few years, NYC has continued to expand early childhood services (e.g., 3K for All) and DECE has developed a new strategic vision that prioritizes a focus on equity across the system and infuses a trauma-informed lens across all aspects of their work. These shifts have led to parallel shifts in DECE's quality-monitoring system, including more frequent CLASS observations (every other year rather than every 3 years) and the collection of additional data on classroom environments. In addition to using the A-TSRS to test the impact of professional learning, DECE is now planning to use the CSM and SEO modules more broadly across the PreK for All system to measure practices that align with DECE's new emphasis on trauma-informed practice (once it is safe to resume in-person observations after the COVID-19 pandemic). Given its focus on practices that support children's social, emotional, and behavioral development, the A-TSRS is well-aligned with trauma-informed approaches and may provide DECE with useful descriptive information about teacher practice, broadly, and how to improve practice through new policies or programs. For the first time in NYC, program leaders and teachers—along with their instructional coordinators and social workers who provide on-site coaching and consultation—will also receive timely feedback and recommendations based on the results of their A-TSRS observations, which they can use to improve the quality and consistency of practices that support children's social, emotional, and behavioral development.

DECE's use of the A-TSRS in the context of a robust quality-monitoring system in NYC underscores a number of key considerations, highlighted by Jones and colleagues (Introduction, this volume), for measuring the social and emotional setting. First, the A-TSRS was iteratively adapted by research and policy partners to increase its *relevance* in NYC, first to evaluate the impact of teacher professional learning, and then to measure practices aligned with DECE's increased commitment to a trauma-informed lens across a wider pool of programs. Second, the A-TSRS focuses on *developmentally salient practices* that support young children's emerging social, emotional, and behavioral skills, and it is inherently *contextualized* in that it focuses on setting-level features and processes; this focus is well aligned with DECE's focus on inputs—that is, program quality and teacher practice—rather than outputs—that is, child outcomes—as this is the level at which DECE policy leaders have leverage and can intervene. In addition, because the A-TSRS has demonstrated *sensitivity* to change in other studies of professional development (and ongoing work is examining sensitivity in the NYC context), the A-TSRS provides *actionable* information to research and policy partners in NYC about the effects of teacher professional learning and trauma-informed supports, and ways these might be strengthened to maximize impact. And, given the behavioral focus and concrete anchors of the A-TSRS, frontline program leaders, coaches, and teachers can use A-TSRS results to identify areas for growth and improve practice at the local level. Finally, training, ongoing supervision, and data checks throughout the data cycle, as described in the second case study, ensure that the tool is and remains *psychometrically sound* in the NYC context over time. Importantly, and in contrast to other studies in which A-TSRS observers are employed by a research team and function largely "outside" the practice/policy system in which the studies take place, A-TSRS observations in NYC are embedded within the PreK for All quality-monitoring system (with NYU and Harvard researchers providing training and supervision on the A-TSRS), and are conducted by DECE-employed observers who also conduct routine CLASS observations. Embedding the A-TSRS within DECE's existing quality-monitoring system as a complement to CLASS and ECERS facilitates *feasibility, scalability, and sustainability* of the tool, with the potential for improving the quality of the settings across a large, diverse, and complex system of early childhood education in NYC in which thousands of children learn and grow each year.

A-TSRS in Research Studies: An Example from British Columbia

In contrast to the case study of the A-TSRS in NYC DECE in which teachers receive timely, individualized feedback, the A-TSRS in research contexts focuses on improving practices for large groups of teachers over time. The use of data for research purposes typically falls into the following categories of purpose: (1) the accumulation of evidence for a phenomenon or empirical relationship (e.g., evidence for the role of classrooms in children's outcomes over time), (2) evaluating the impact of an intervention (e.g., PATHS, described above), and (3) tweaking and improving the measure itself to grow its relevance, precision, and psychometric properties. Across these examples, the focus is on broad trends, patterns, and measure development rather than on improving outcomes for individual teachers, classrooms, or schools.

Research studies often refer to the measures used in their studies as "reliable" or "valid," suggesting that this is a property of the tool itself. However, reporting that the A-TSRS is valid and reliable applies to its use in that context and for a particular purpose. This is particularly important to keep in mind when making judgments about reliability and validity estimates from research studies, which are typically small scale and have a high degree of control (e.g., a small team of graduate student observers conducting observations over a short period of time).

Understanding how a measure operates in a particular setting is imperative, particularly when (1) the measure has not been used in a similar setting or with a similar population of teachers or students, (2) a different version of the tool is used (e.g., A-TSRS provides users with the flexibility to add or remove modules), and (3) the tool is used over time (e.g., embedded into a longitudinal measurement plan).

A number of straightforward analytic techniques typically used in research studies can guide the implementation and monitoring of setting-level measures, like the A-TSRS, in practice. Using data collected from a recent study in British Columbia, below we outline a set of four simple data "checks" school-based personnel can employ to examine the functioning of a measure in their setting:

1. *What is the distribution of scores in the sample?* Examine the data looking at the means (average scores across classrooms), the standard deviation (spread or stretch of the data), and the minimum and maximum scores. Table 10.2 shows the average scores for the study in British Columbia. In this sample, we see that classrooms score relatively high in the CSM domain and relatively low in the SEO domain. Researchers might also examine the data by grade, school, or any other meaningful groupings.

TABLE 10.2. Mean A-TSRS Scores

Scale	Number of observations	Mean	Standard deviation	Minimum	Maximum
CSM	81	4.01	0.59	2	5
SEO	81	2.19	0.82	1	4.4
Full A-TSRS	81	3.13	0.61	1.67	4.75

Looking at the scores visually with a histogram (Figure 10.1) enables us to see the distribution of scores. Ideally variation will exist in scores between classrooms, suggesting that the measure captures differences between classrooms. If all of the observations received the same score, the measure would provide very little information about which classrooms to target for improvement. Ideally there are no floor or ceiling effects, meaning that classrooms are either "topping" or "bottoming" out and the measure is not capturing classrooms that are either very high or very low. In our sample, we see that the observation scores are relatively normally distributed (i.e., shaped like a mountain) and that for both scales (CSM and SEO) there are scores across the distribution and not clustered at the highest or lowest ends.

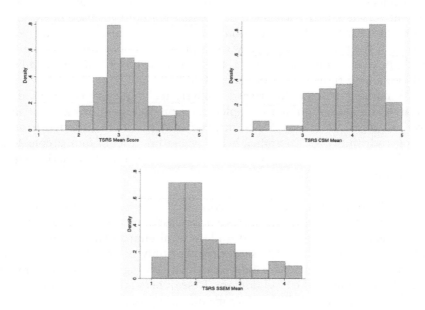

FIGURE 10.1. Histograms of A-TSRS scores.

2. *Are observers aligned?* In theory, classrooms will receive the same score regardless of the observer. Ensuring parity and alignment across multiple raters requires (1) determining a plan for assessing reliability, and (2) establishing a threshold for reliability, or how much observer scores need to align. We typically double code 20% of observations, meaning that two observers will be present and their scores will be compared. Our threshold is within one point (above or below) 80% of the time. In our most recent evaluation, 17 classrooms (21%) were double coded, and interrater reliability (IRR) across all items was high (95%) (see Table 10.3).

3. *Do these items "hang together" in the setting?* Internal consistency, a form of reliability assessed by Cronbach's alpha, refers to whether a measure is assessing what it is intended to measure, or the degree to which a set of items measure a single construct. In this study, Cronbach's alpha for the full scale is 0.83 and the alphas for each subscale are adequate, at 0.80. Another interpretation of Cronbach's alpha is to say that 80% of the variance in scores can be accounted for by *true* variance (or actual differences between classrooms) rather than error.

4. *Do scores on the A-TSRS correlate with other meaningful outcomes?* Validity refers to how a measure correlates with other measures and outcomes of interest in a particular setting. To understand validity, researchers examine associations (typically using correlational analyses) between the A-TSRS (or measure of interest) and (1) other measures intended to assess the same or similar constructs (e.g., other measures that capture the social–emotional setting, like the CLASS) and (2) key child

TABLE 10.3. A-TSRS inter-rater reliability

Item	Exact match (%)	Within one match (%)
Classroom awareness	65	94
Positive behavior management	53	94
Negative behavior management	65	100
Attention support	24	88
Consistency/routine	59	94
Preparedness	65	94
Emotion modeling	82	94
Emotion expression	71	100
Emotion regulation	65	94
Social awareness	53	94
Social problem solving	76	94

outcomes such as social and emotional skills, academic achievement, and discipline.

• Applications and Future Directions

The examples above illustrate how the A-TSRS can be used in research and practice to gather reliable, valid, and nuanced information about the social and emotional settings children experience, and how that information might be used to drive improvements in real-world educational contexts. At the local level, teachers, principals, and coaches can use classroom-level A-TSRS ratings to understand areas of strength and areas for growth. The behaviorally focused A-TSRS anchors and observable actions can empower teachers to identify specific behaviors to weave into their daily practice, set concrete goals for improving practice, and track progress toward those goals. At a more macro level, district leaders can work with research and data partners to embed the A-TSRS within existing data collection streams and leverage the modularized format to adapt and align the tool with specific priorities, programs, or needs in the district (e.g., by adding or removing modules, items, or observable actions) (Abenavoli, Barnes, & Jones, 2019). They then can use A-TSRS ratings in aggregate to understand social and emotional setting-level processes broadly across the entire district, and the extent to which children's access to high-quality social and emotional settings is equitably distributed across the system. Examining mean-level A-TSRS scores, trends over time, and variability across schools or centers within the district can help policy leaders evaluate whether existing interventions are working effectively, as well as identify ways to target or strengthen supports for teachers (e.g., professional learning, coaching, curricula) that drive improvements in practice and, ultimately, improvements in children's social, emotional, and behavioral development.

Setting-level observational tools, and the A-TSRS in particular, represent a practical, feasible, and promising measurement approach for informing local (i.e., classroom) and macro-level (i.e., district) efforts that aim to improve setting, teacher, and student outcomes. As we advocate for tools that bridge research and practice, as in the NYC DECE illustration, we note that additional work is needed to advance the use and utility of the A-TSRS for research and practice/policy purposes. Future directions include continuing to adapt the tool itself, expanding its application in practice, understanding associations between various classroom "profiles" and children's outcomes, and examining relevance across cultures and contexts. In addition, more knowledge is needed to make strategic decisions (i.e., determine number of raters, number of observation cycles) that balance precision and feasibility (i.e., time, cost). A precise and nuanced understanding of the broader settings in which children spend their time—and the interactions they have with adults and peers within those settings—is necessary to contextualize and most effectively support children's social and emotional development. Identifying and building measures that capture and promote improvements in these settings (like an oven thermometer and corresponding troubleshooting guide) represents an important mechanism for growth in teaching and learning.

REFERENCES

Abenavoli, R., Barnes, S. P., & Jones, S. M. (2019). *Adapted Teaching Style Rating Scale (A-TSRS) overview.* New York University.

Ahn, H. J. (2005). Teachers' discussions of emotion in child care centers. *Early Childhood Education Journal, 32,* 237–242.

Bierman, K. L., Domitrovich, C. E., Nix, R. L., Gest, S. D., Welsh, J. A., Greenberg, M. T., . . . Gill, S. (2008). Promoting academic and social-emotional school readiness: The Head Start REDI program. *Child Development, 79,* 1802–1817.

Bronfenbrenner, U., & Morris, P. A. (2006). The bioecological model of human development. In R. M. Lerner & W. Damon (Eds.), *Handbook of child psychology: Theoretical models of human development* (pp. 793–828). Wiley.

Brotman, L. M., Calzada, E., Huang, K.-Y., Kingston, S., Dawson-McLure, S., Kamboukos, D., . . . Petkova, E. (2011). Promoting effective parenting practices and preventing child behavior problems in school among ethnically diverse families from underserved, urban communities. *Child Development, 82,* 258–276.

Brotman, L., Dawson-McClure, S., Rhule, D., Rosenblatt, K., Hamer, K., Kamboukos, D., . . . Huang, K. (2021). Scaling early childhood evidence-based interventions through RPPs. *The Future of Children, 31,* 57–74.

Denham, S. A., Bassett, H. H., & Zinsser, K. (2012). Early childhood teachers as socializers of young children's emotional competence. *Early Childhood Education Journal, 40,* 137–143.

Dominguez, X., Vitiello, V. E., Maier, M. F., & Greenfield, D. B. (2010). A longitudinal examination of young children's learning behavior: Child-level and classroom-level predictors of change throughout the preschool year. *School Psychology Review, 39,* 29–47.

Domitrovich, C. E., Cortes, R., & Greenberg, M. T. (2000). *The Teacher Style Rating Scale* Unpublished research instrument, Pennsylvania State University.

Domitrovich, C. E., Cortes, R. C., & Greenberg, M. T. (2007). Improving young children's social and emotional competence: A randomized trial of the preschool "PATHS" curriculum. *The Journal of Primary Prevention, 28,* 67–91.

Domitrovich, C. E., Gest, S. D., Gill, S., Bierman, K. L., Welsh, J. A., & Jones, D. (2009). Fostering high-quality teaching with an enriched curriculum and professional development support: The Head Start REDI program. *American Educational Research Journal, 46,* 567–597.

Downer, J. T., Sabol, T. J., & Hamre, B. (2010). Teacher–child interactions in the classroom: Toward a theory of within- and cross-domain links to children's developmental outcomes. *Early Education & Development, 21,* 699–723.

Duchesneau, N. (2020). Social, emotional, and academic development through an equity lens. *Education Trust.*

Durlak, J. A., Weissberg, R. P., Dymnicki, A. B., Taylor, R. D., & Schellinger, K. B. (2011). The impact of enhancing students' social and emotional learning: A meta-analysis of school-based universal interventions. *Child Development, 82*(1), 405–432.

Evertson, C. M., & Weinstein, C. S. (Eds.). (2006). *Handbook of classroom management: Research, practice, and contemporary issues.* Erlbaum.

Gregory, A., & Fergus, E. (2017). Social and emotional learning and equity in school discipline. *The Future of Children, 27*(1), 117–136.

Halle, T., Vick Whittaker, J. E., & Anderson, R. (2010). *Quality in early childhood care and education settings: A compendium of measures* (2nd ed.). Child Trends.

Hamre, B. K., Pianta, R. C., Downer, J. T., DeCoster, J., Mashburn, A. J., Jones, S. M., . . . Hamagami, A., (2013). Teaching through interaction: Testing a developmental framework of teacher effectiveness in over 4,000 classrooms. *The Elementary School Journal, 113,* 461–487.

Hamre, B., Hatfield, B., Pianta, R., & Jamil, F. (2014). Evidence for general and domain-specific elements of teacher–child interactions: Associations with preschool children's development. *Child Development, 85,* 1257–1274.

Harms, T., Clifford, R. M., & Cryer, D. (2014). *Early Childhood Environment Rating Scale.* Teachers College Press.

Hemmeter, M. L., Snyder, P. A., Fox, L., & Algina, J. (2016) Evaluating the implementation of the Pyramid Model for promoting social–emotional competence in early childhood classrooms. *Topics in Early Childhood Special Education, 36,* 133–146.

Jagers, R. J., Rivas-Drake, D., & Williams, B. (2019). Transformative social and emotional learning (SEL): Toward SEL in service of educational equity and excellence. *Educational Psychologist, 54*(3), 162–184.

Jennings, P. A., & Greenberg, M. T. (2009). The prosocial classroom: Teacher social and emotional competence in relation to child and classroom outcomes. *Review of Educational Research, 79,* 491–525.

Jones, S. M., Bailey, R., & Jacob, R. (2014). Social-emotional learning is essential to classroom management. *Phi Delta Kappan, 96,* 19–24.

Jones, S. M., Barnes, S. P., Bailey, R., & Doolittle, E. J. (2017). Promoting social and emotional competencies in elementary school. *The Future of Children, 27*(1), 49–72.

Jones, S. M., Bouffard, S. M., & Weissbourd, R. (2013). Educators' social and emotional skills vital to learning. *Phi Delta Kappan, 94*(8), 62–65.

Jones S. M., Brush, K., Bailey, R., Brion-Meisels, G., McIntyre, J., Kahn, J., . . . Stickle, L. (2017). Navigating social and emotional learning from the inside out: Looking inside and across 25 leading SEL programs: A practical resource for schools and OST providers (elementary school focus). Wallace Foundation.

Retrieved from *www.wallacefoundation.org/knowledge-center/Documents/Navigating-Social-and-Emotional-Learning-from-the-Inside-Out.pdf.*

Jones, S. M., Imm, P., & HopeLab. (2016). *Brain Games 2015–2016 pilot study, South Carolina final report.* Harvard Graduate School of Education.

Kane, T. J., & Staiger, D. O. (2012). *Gathering feedback for teaching: Combining high-quality observations with student surveys and achievement gains.* Bill and Melinda Gates Foundation, MET Project Research Paper.

Mashburn, A. J., Pianta, R. C., Hamre, B. K., Downer, J. T., Barbarin, O. A., Bryant, D., . . . Early, D. M. (2008). Measures of classroom quality in prekindergarten and children's development of academic, language, and social skills. *Child Development, 79,* 732–749.

McKown, C. (2017). Social–emotional assessment, performance, and standards. *The Future of Children, 27,* 157–178.

Morris, C. A., Denham, S. A., Bassett, H. H., & Curby, T. W. (2013). Relations among teachers' emotion socialization beliefs and practices, and preschoolers' emotional competence. *Early Education and Development, 24,* 979–999.

Morris, P., Mattera, S. K., Castells, N., Bangser, M., Bierman, K., & Raver, C. C. (2014). *Impact findings from the Head Start CARES demonstration: National evaluation of three approaches to improving preschoolers' social and emotional competence.* MDRC.

Morris, P., Millenky, M., Raver, C. C., & Jones, S. M. (2013). Does a preschool social and emotional learning intervention pay off for classroom instruction and children's behavior and academic skills? Evidence from the Foundations of Learning Project. *Early Education & Development, 24,* 1020–1042.

Peisner-Feinberg, E., Burchinal, M., Clifford, R., Culkin, M., Howes, C., Kagan, S. L., & Yazejian, N. (2001). The relation of preschool child-care quality to children's cognitive and social developmental trajectories through second grade. *Child Development, 72,* 1534–1553.

Pianta, R. C., & Hamre, B. K. (2009). Conceptualization, measurement, and improvement of classroom processes: Standardized observation can leverage capacity. *Educational Researcher, 38,* 109–119.

Pianta, R. C., Hamre, B. K., & Allen, J. P. (2012). Teacher-student relationships and engagement: Conceptualizing, measuring, and improving the capacity of classroom interactions. In S. L. Christenson, A. L. Reschly, & C. Wylie (Eds.), *Handbook of research on student engagement* (pp. 365–386). Springer Science + Business Media.

Pianta, R. C., La Paro, K. M., & Hamre, B. K. (2008). *The Classroom Assessment Scoring System manual, K–3.* Brookes.

Praetorius, A. K., & Charalambous, C. Y. (2018). Classroom observation frameworks for studying instructional quality: Looking back and looking forward. *ZDM: The International Journal on Mathematics Education, 50,* 535–553.

Raver, C. C., Domitrovich, C. E., Greenberg, M. T., Morris, P. A., & Mattera, S. K. (2012). *Adapted Teaching Style Rating Scale* [Unpublished research instrument]. MDRC.

Raver, C. C., Jones, S. M., Li-Grining, C., Zhai, F., Metzger, M. W., & Solomon, B. (2009). Targeting children's behavior problems in preschool classrooms: A cluster-randomized controlled trial. *Journal of Consulting and Clinical Psychology, 77,* 302–316.

Rimm-Kaufman, S. E., Curby, T. W., Grimm, K. J., Nathanson, L., & Brock, L. L. (2009). The contribution of children's self-regulation and classroom quality to children's adaptive behaviors in the kindergarten classroom. *Developmental Psychology, 45,* 958–972.

Rojas, N. M., Mattera, S., Morris, P., & Raver, C. (2021). Measuring preschool teachers' social-emotional practices: A comparison of two measures. *Early Education and Development.*

Schultz, D., Izard, C. E., & Bear, G. G. (2004). Children's emotion processing: Relations to emotionality and aggression. *Development and Psychopathology, 16,* 371–387.

Seidman, E., & Cappella, E. (2017). Social settings as loci of intervention. In M. A. Bond, I. Serrano-García, & C. B. Keys (Eds.), *APA handbook of community psychology: Vol. 2. Methods for community research and action for diverse groups and issues* (pp. 235–254). American Psychological Association.

Synder, P., Hemmeter, M. L., Fox, L., Bishop, C. C., & Miller, M. D. (2013). Developing and gathering psychometric evidence for a fidelity instrument: The Teaching Pyramid Observation Tool—Pilot Version. *Journal of Early Intervention, 35,* 150–172.

Tseng, V., & Seidman, E. (2007). A systems framework for understanding social settings. *American Journal of Community Psychology, 39*(3–4), 217–228.

Webster-Stratton, C., & Herman, K. C. (2010). Disseminating Incredible Years Series early-intervention programs: Integrating and sustaining services between school and home. *Psychology in the Schools, 47,* 36–54.

Webster-Stratton, C., Reid, M. J., & Stoolmiller, M. (2008). Preventing conduct problems and improving school readiness: Evaluation of the Incredible Years Teacher and Child Training Programs in high-risk schools. *Journal of Child Psychology and Psychiatry, 49,* 471–488.

PART III

POPULATION-LEVEL TOOLS TO GUIDE PRACTICE AND POLICY

CHAPTER 11

Cross-Cutting Issues for Measuring Social–Emotional Competency in Context

General Opportunities and Challenges
with an Illustration of the Washoe County School District
Social and Emotional Competency Assessment

Rachel A. Gordon and Laura A. Davidson

This chapter offers guidance to school districts who are considering or already engaged in assessing students' social–emotional competencies (SECs). We begin by laying out general opportunities and challenges of SEC assessments—that is, opportunities to make SECs visible and to generate formative and summative feedback, challenges of measuring ethically, precisely, and fairly, and of choosing among formats, avoiding reifying scales, and tailoring to local needs (see Figure 11.1). We then describe specific strategies for enhancing the opportunities and limiting the challenges, suggesting how districts can assess needs and establish partnerships in order to engage in continuous measure improvement, multifaceted evidence building, and cocreation measure development (see Figure 11.2). We exemplify the strategies by describing the Washoe County School District Social and Emotional Competency Assessments (WCSD-SECAs) and the related coequal research–practice partnership in which we developed the strategies. The WCSD-SECAs are free, open-source student self-report measures designed for districtwide assessment of 5th- to 12th-grade students' SECs. We discuss how the WCSD-SECA approach to develop, study, refine, and use SEC assessments offers a compelling model aligned with principles outlined in the introduction of this book and in other recent guidance (Assessment Work Group, 2019). We offer a vision for the future of SEC measure development, advocating for greater emphasis on assessments built on continuous improvement within strong research–practice–student partnerships, reporting multiple forms of reliability and validity evidence, and making assessment systems open-source and freely available to facilitate greater access, networked learning, and tailoring to local contexts.

• General Opportunities and Challenges

The opportunities and challenges of assessing SECs districtwide (see Figure 11.1) were at the forefront of our work together within a researcher–practitioner partnership funded by the Institute of Education Sciences (IES) that included an array of researchers and practitioners from within and across the school district (WCSD[1]), a university (the University of Illinois at Chicago), and a national organization (the Collaborative for Academic, Social, and Emotional Learning, CASEL; Crowder, Gordon, Aloe,

---

Opportunities

☐ Making SECs *visible* (potentially on par with "ABCs" over time)

☐ Giving students, parents, and teachers feedback on student progress (*formatively*)

☐ Helping teachers and leaders gauge outcomes (*summatively*)

Challenges

☐ The full body of evidence is not always weighed before each use (*measurement ethics*)

☐ Scores are not exactly equal to "true" SEC levels (*measurement error*)

☐ Items may not mean the same thing across subgroups and contexts (*measurement invariance*)

☐ Different strategies for assessment have strengths and limits (*measurement formats and informants*)

☐ Scales and subscales may be treated as more "real" than they are (*measurement dimensionality*)

☐ Assessments may not be easily tailored for local needs (*measurement adaptations*)

FIGURE 11.1. Opportunities and challenges of assessing students' SECs in districts.

---

[1]WCSD is a large school district of 64,000 students and 104 schools located in northwestern Nevada. The majority of students are White (43%) and Hispanic (42%), with small populations of students who are Asian (4%), African American (3%), Pacific Islander (1%), and multiracial (6%). Over half (51%) of students qualify for free or reduced-price lunch.

Davidson, & Domitrovich, 2019; Gordon, Crowder, Aloe, Davidson, & Domitrovich, 2021; Davidson et al., 2018; Schamberg et al., 2017). We developed the WCSD-SECA approach (described below) to elevate the assessment opportunities while tackling the challenges head on.

Opportunities

Assessing SECs offers a considerable opportunity for school districts given that *what is tested is made visible to teachers, students, parents, and administrators* (Assessment Work Group, 2019). A well-known example is the outsized attention to academic standardized test scores spurred by school accountability policies (Figlio & Loeb, 2011; Wang, Beckett, & Brown, 2010). An opportunity exists, therefore, to elevate SECs to a more equal footing with academics ("ABCs") through SEC assessment, although this must be carefully done while learning lessons and avoiding challenges evident in the history of academic testing (discussed in the next section). The goal of integrating social and emotional learning (SEL; the process by which growth in SECs is supported) into classroom instruction, teacher education, school policies, and state standards, side-by-side with academics, has also been fostered by efforts to expand SEL in schools across the United States and internationally (Domitrovich, Durlak, Staley, & Weissberg, 2017). For instance, SEL played a critical role in helping WCSD teachers support students experiencing substantial frustration with then newly adopted Common Core State Standards in English Language Arts, especially with close reading exercises and engaging with complex texts. WCSD's SEL Department partnered with the Curriculum and Instruction Department to map the SECs students needed to persist with the more difficult reading material (e.g., emotion self-management when they experience stress while encountering unfamiliar vocabulary, empathy for peers struggling with the exercises), and develop strategies to help build students' social and emotional capacity to engage with the new common core standards and expectations. This greater emphasis on teaching students strategies to be aware of and to manage their own emotions and their interactions with others prompts a desire to assess their learning in these areas, be they in comprehensive districtwide SEL initiatives or in activities adopted by individual teachers. Just as districts test what they teach in math and reading skills so too can they test what they teach in SECs.

As in academics, such testing of SECs can be implemented in formative and summative ways, each of which offer opportunities (Assessment Work Group, 2019). *Formative assessments* of SECs allow teachers to gauge students' progress, adjust their teaching strategies to meet student needs, and develop plans for SEL prior to implementation. *Summative assessments* of

SECs allow more formal evaluations of student growth, including when teachers, schools, and districts adopt SEL curricula or interventions and when reporting to stakeholders (e.g., funders, community members, district or state leadership) about SEL initiatives (Taylor et al., 2018). Modern technology facilitates the integration of both types of assessments into learning management systems, simplifying tracking and reporting. Dashboards from such systems can help teachers and counselors identify students in need of support and can help leaders monitor where more systemic investments and adjustments may help subgroups of students and educators. In WCSD, SEC data are disaggregated at the school, grade level, and student population levels, and provided to schools midyear to help inform course corrections and planning for the next school year. WCSD uses a three-pronged approach to SEL that includes direct instruction supported by adopted SEL curriculum, academic integration of SEL into all academic courses, and a focus on building a positive climate and culture. SEC data support all three areas of SEL implementation and are primarily used by principals and site leadership teams to inform school performance planning process. For example, if a school's students had reported struggling most with self-awareness of emotions in the annual spring survey, teachers might frontload those lessons toward the beginning of the next school year. Or, if data indicated that students in a particular grade level reported a substantial decline in self-management of schoolwork coinciding with declines in math achievement relative to the prior year, schools may deploy targeted SEL supports embedded in math content at that grade level. Summative uses can be higher stakes, though, raising the importance of the challenges discussed next. For instance, other districts might move in a higher stakes direction by providing students and parents periodic feedback in class, conferences, and report cards to identify areas of current strength and future growth. As another exmaple, other districts might wish to aggregate SECs into school report cards so that superintendents, policymakers, and the public may identify contexts needing more funding and assistance.

Challenges

Challenges to testing are well known, many salient for assessing ABCs as well as SECs, and some exacerbated for SEC assessment, requiring caution as districts consider how to measure SECs and for what uses (Duckworth & Yeager, 2015; Melnick, Cook-Harvey, & Darling-Hammond, 2017; West, 2016; see also Hamilton, Chapter 13, this volume). We next discuss several of these challenges, including measurement ethics, error, invariance, formats/informants, dimensionality, and adaptations (see Figure 11.2). Each reflects the tension of meeting current practice needs while following modern measurement standards and using rigorous psychometric models.

Getting Started

☐ Identify needs and goals for assessing SECs (considering opportunities and challenges).

☐ Examine local capacity for SEC research and practice, and reach out to partners to complement strengths and fill gaps.

☐ Ask questions about existing evidence and commit to building local evidence.

Continuous Measure Improvement

☐ Recognize that measures are not static products taken off the shelf with fixed reliability and validity that work consistently across time and space.

☐ View measures as dynamic tools requiring continual updating of evidence, including that they work in consistent and meaningful ways locally.

Multifaceted Evidence Building

☐ Use multiple types of evidence when choosing assessments and when improving them over time.

☐ Draw on numerous methodologies to offer a richly textured portrait of how assessments work within the district.

Cocreation Measure Development

☐ Engage students, parents, teachers, staff, and leaders as coequals in measure development.

☐ Recognize that no single contributor owns the items or measure.

☐ Share items and measures openly with others.

FIGURE 11.2. WCSD-SECA approach to emphasize opportunities and reduce challenges when assessing SECs in districts.

Measurement Ethics

Modern measurement standards emphasize that the full body of evidence should be considered relative to each potential use of an assessment (AERA/APA/NCME, 2014; APA, 2017). As an example, the bar of reliability and validity (i.e., psychometric) evidence would be set higher for summative than formative assessment, and especially for high-stakes accountability uses. Yet, historically, the psychological and educational sciences, and the testing industry, have established reliability and validity in more static ways, with decision makers often citing the same evidence from a manual, test review, or marketing materials for multiple types of uses (Gordon, 2015). This general disconnect between modern testing standards and on-the-ground practice is heightened when measuring SECs. The evidence base for SEC tests is wide, reflecting many definitions, yet thin, reflecting their recency and still accumulating research on best practices for their use in real-world applications (Jones, Bailey, Brush, & Nelson, 2019; Merrell & Gueldner, 2010). Sometimes, existing measures developed for other purposes have been retooled to align with SEL frameworks in order to meet assessment needs sparked by the SEL movement. Justification for such uses has tended to rest on the broader evidence base for the original test and its underlying constructs rather than its re-expression.

For instance, the Social Skills Improvement System (SSIS; Gresham & Elliott, 2008) and its earlier versions have been widely used in schools since the 1980s and 1990s. Although its original subscales used a different framework, the SSIS developers recently reorganized its existing items into an SEL version (Gresham et al., 2020). Such tests also often are sold by publishers and can be expensive for schools (e.g., the SSIS costs about $3.50 per student for administration, scoring, and reporting). Some measures have also been released specifically to measure the SECs, yet often again resting on existing literatures and item sets with limited reliability and validity evidence for their specific SEC uses. As companies aim to fill schools' need to assess SECs, a challenge has been to translate the reliability and validity evidence in digestible ways and to make it easy to integrate SEC assessments into learning management systems without leapfrogging over the evidence. As an example, the data analytics company Panorama Education contracts with states, districts, and schools to administer, score, and report on student SEC surveys. These surveys are marketed online as research-backed but do not provide extensive details about the multifaceted aspects of reliability and validity evidence discussed below (Panorama Education, n.d., 2016). As a result, districts may assume the evidence fits their context, unless they have capacity to engage in the kinds of strategies discussed below (e.g., asking about multifaceted evidence relative to their local context and building psychometrically rigorous district evidence). Continually emphasizing measurement ethics helps districts follow recommended practice of considering the full body of evidence for an assessment before each potential use.

Measurement Error

Test scores are not identical to true scores. Rather, test scores are observable yet imperfect manifestations of unobservable constructs, reflecting measurement error in addition to true levels. As an example of measurement error, when a person steps on and off a bathroom scale multiple times, the measured weight will fluctuate to some degree, as each measure reflects momentary differences in the inner workings of the scale and in the environment. Although measurement error is well recognized by researchers, error bars—as when a political poll reports that the percentage planning to vote for a candidate is estimated within 3 points—are not always used when presenting students' test scores, including from SEC assessments. Partly, the exclusion of error bars seems to reflect an assumption that they would confuse nonresearch stakeholders trying to interpret results. Partly, their exclusion seems to reflect default displays catching up with modern computational capabilities, where error bars require more programming effort. Partly, their exclusion seems to reflect a general reliance on simpler scoring strategies—basic sums, means, or proportions—rather than scoring based on modern psychometric models. As we show with the WCSD-SECAs example below, we have found that it is possible to bridge this divide and to explain scores and their error bands in ways that practitioners, policymakers, parents, and students can understand. Doing so is important given that measurement error is especially critical in helping test makers and test takers recognize the trade-offs of using shorter versus longer tests. Since longer tests take more time to complete (including time away from instruction), districts and students often prefer shorter versions. As examples, an SEC assessment used by the state of Delaware included just three items for each subdomain (Mantz, Bear, Yang, & Harris, 2018), and those used by California's CORE districts have four to nine items per subscale (West, Buckley, Krachman, & Bookman, 2018). Below, we discuss how we have illustrated the implications for measurement error of such short tests in the WCSD-SECAs and how psychometric linking strategies can be used to balance test length and measurement error.

Measurement Invariance

Advanced psychometric models are also needed to fully demonstrate whether a test operates consistently for students across subcontexts and subcultures (referred to as measurement invariance). When the meanings of constructs and their expressions instead vary across subgroups (referred to as measurement noninvariance) simple sums, means, or proportions cannot be fairly compared across subgroups. In these cases, psychometrically adjusted scores are essential (Millsap, 2011).

Such adjustments are likely to be needed for SEC assessments. For instance, whereas we may be able to get educators (as well as students, their parents, and the broader public) to agree upon what multiplication entails and which multiplication problems are easier and harder, it is difficult to get them to agree upon whether and when certain emotions should be regulated and what adequate emotion regulation looks like. The reason for this challenge is that norms about SECs are socially constructed and socially situated (Castro-Olivo & Merrell, 2012; Hecht & Shin, 2015; Shweder, Minow, & Markus, 2002). Thus, the definition of SECs and the associated expressions and understandings that signal them differ from place to place, time to time, and group to group. As an example, historically in U.S. society, it was more socially acceptable for educated White men to display anger than for others to do so. In contemporary society, it is increasingly recognized that lingering bias may restrict expressions and alter interpretations of anger displayed by some groups of students. Such social variation in the definition of what it means to "appropriately" regulate anger complicates attempts to measure SECs that involve expression of emotions. As another example, if questioning the teacher means intellectual engagement in one culture, and disrespect of elders in another culture, then an SEC assessment item about engaging in debate with teachers during class may have different meaning across cultures. For these reasons, districts must test for whether items operate differently across groups (such as by student gender, race/ethnicity, and socioeconomic status) and take any differences into account (in the ways we illustrate with the WCSD-SECA below).

Considering measurement noninvariance is also a priority given the depth with which contemporary educators and schools across the United States embrace diversity, equity, and inclusion—and the increasing attention paid to transformative SEL, the process of students and staff building respectful relationships while acknowledging similarities and differences, examining inequities, and codeveloping solutions to community and social problems (Aspen Institute, 2018; Jagers, 2016; Jagers, Rivas-Drake, & Borowski, 2018; Jagers, Rivas-Drake, & Williams, 2019). Yet doing so requires helping schools move beyond historical approaches to identifying measurement invariance. Although psychometricians in academia and the testing industry have developed a suite of strategies to test for measurement invariance, four common practices mean that the results may not always meet the needs of districts and their stakeholders.

- *A first problem with the standard approach is its default goal— generally, to identify items that work in the same way across subgroups.* As we note below, instead, schools might draw upon practices developed in fields such as cross-cultural and indigenous psychology to flip the goal and begin by considering subgroup-centric perspectives (Denzin, Lincoln, & Smith, 2008; Paris, 2012; Smith, Spillane, & Annus, 2006). As an example, the Mexican American Socialization Scale was developed using ethnographic and pilot studies that revealed the construct of *Bien Educado,* which encompassed young children's comportment, cooperation, meeting role obligations, obedience, and respect; for instance, children are taught *respeto* for themselves and others, which reinforces patterns of authority stemming from heritage cultures (Bridges et al., 2012, p. 557).

- *A second problem with the standard approach is that the implications of having many more students in some subgroups than others are not always considered.* The importance of this issue is that true differences can be harder to detect if sample sizes are small in certain subgroups (in statistical terms, the statistical test may be *underpowered;* Yoon & Lai, 2018). This second issue can go hand-in-hand with the first, if analysts gloss over small sample sizes when their goal is to identify items that work the same way across subgroups.

- *A third problem is that the focus can be on the invariance of the test as a whole, that is, all of its items as a set.* As a result, noninvariance of a few items may be overlooked—again an issue that may be exacerbated by a goal of finding invariance and the presence of small sample sizes. Recently developed approaches offer alternatives, as we illustrate below (Cheung & Lau, 2012; Muthén & Asparouhov, 2014).

- *A fourth problem reflects the predominance of certain psychometric approaches in past research with SECs, particularly factor analytic approaches that were developed for continuous items.* Item response theory approaches, in contrast, are designed for categorical items—the form of most SEC assessments' multicategory response structures (Likert-type, such as 1 = never to 5 = always; Gordon, 2015; Liu et al., 2017). In the WCSD-SECAs example below, we demonstrate how this concern is not merely technical; instead, it gets at the heart of what we mean conceptually when we say subgroups may differently interpret items and has great relevance for our interpretation of average differences among subgroups.

Measurement Formats and Informants

Another challenge to districts is that they can choose among many different formats and informants for SEC assessments, such as performance tasks or self, peer, teacher, and parent reports. Here, it is important to remember that all types have strengths and limitations (Duckworth & Yeager, 2015). Their trade-offs (along with their full body of psychometric evidence) should be considered before any given use. For instance, teacher and student reports can have the authenticity of allowing stakeholders to hear directly about classroom experiences, yet can be vulnerable to *reference point biases* and *social desirability biases. Reference points* come to mind when teachers are asked to rate the approximate frequency (never, sometimes, often, always) that a student "Does what you ask," or, when students are asked to make similar choices about a statement like "I do my schoolwork on time." The reference points might be students in their current class, students they have known in the past, students they see in the media, or students they've read about or studied. Using a different reference point can affect how any individual teacher or student interprets the questions and the response options. *Social desirability bias* happens when individuals consider how others would react to their responses, and adjust their choices accordingly—for example, a student may say to themselves "I only sometimes do my schoolwork on time, but I should do it more often, so I'll say often." Although such limitations might steer stakeholders toward performance tasks—where students are asked to demonstrate their competencies directly—such tasks are vulnerable to their own biases. *Stereotype threat,* for instance, occurs when a task primes a student to a belief that their subgroup doesn't perform well in the tested area—for example, a student may anticipate, consciously or subconsciously, "People think students like me aren't able to control our emotions." Our WCSD-SECAs example focuses on student self-report, although the strategies we demonstrate can be used across formats and informants for SEC assessments, including when using or comparing assessments across multiple formats and informants.

Measurement Dimensionality

The constructs featured in assessments can be reified—treated as though they are real—and as a result start to drive educators' conversations and practice. For instance, the Classroom Assessment Scoring System (CLASS) has become a dominant measure of classroom practices, and teachers are sometimes described as beginning to use "CLASS-speak"—using the subscales and items to describe their practices (Delaney & Krepps, 2021). Given these ways in which a scale's subscales and items may filter into practice, a crucial first step is to demonstrate evidence that the items well reflect those subscales (including when an assessment is designed to operationalize a certain SEL framework or repurposed to align with a framework). In other words, districts need to ask: Is there evidence that an assessment's items reflect its proposed subscales or subdomains (referred to as measure dimensionality)? Answering this question is important given the already noted plethora of SEL frameworks that originate from various subfields, such as personality psychology, character development, clinical psychology, and bullying prevention, each using labels that have related but distinct implications for practice (Berg et al., 2017; Jones et al., 2019; Ura, Castro-Olivo, & d'Abreu, 2019). These frameworks are increasingly codified into state, district, and school SEL standards (Berg et al., 2017; DePaoli, Atwel, & Bridgeland, 2017; Jordan & Hamilton, 2020; Tyton Partners, 2020).

Yet evidence that SEL assessments reflect their theoretical constructs is lacking (Gordon et al., 2021). Reports to practitioners do not always acknowledge that the psychometric evidence for the proposed constructs is weak (e.g., acknowledging the implications of *fit statistics* being less than adequate when reporting and explaining how well the expected model is reflected in the data). When evidence about dimensionality is reported, it often is incomplete. The most rigorous testing would consider whether an SEC assessment's items better represent its proposed constructs than alternatives (such as those in some of the alternative frameworks just mentioned). Doing so requires reporting comparisons (with fit statistics) among multiple models. Rigorous testing would also consider an assessment's full framework (such as presenting fit statistics when all of the subscales of a multiconstruct measure are considered in a single model rather than considering each subscale's items one at a time). Below, we use the WCSD-SECAs example to illustrate how researchers and practitioners can work together to conduct, interpret, and act on such tests both by learning how to scrutinize existing evidence and by building local evidence about whether an assessment's items reflect its theoretical framework in their districts.

Measurement Adaptations

The final challenge we consider relates to educators' likely desire to adapt assessments for their local context, given the already noted potential for contextual and cultural variation, the variety of SEL frameworks, and desires to align with local SEL standards. Part of the reason such adaptation is challenging is that district staff may not have the time and training needed for local adaptation, replication, and improvement. As a result, districts may need to collaborate with consultants, scholars, and companies or across schools, districts, and states. These collaborations bring their own challenges, however, such as ambiguous ownership of cocreated items and scorings, a topic educational scholars and practitioners have only begun to consider (Gordon & Superfine, 2021). In the present SEC assessment landscape, items and their scoring are also sometimes considered proprietary, which restricts local adaptation (as in the SSIS example mentioned above; Gresham et al., 2020). Other times, items are openly available, but platforms to administer, score, and report them are sold to schools (as in the Panorama Education example mentioned above; Panorama Education, n.d.). In these cases, ownership of the platforms, scorings, algorithms, and items may sometimes be proprietary or ambiguous (Gordon & Superfine, 2021). We discuss next how we have aimed to make the WCSD-SECAs openly available and to continuously learn about sustainable and transparent strategies for adaptation, replication, and improvement.

• WCSD-SECAs Example

The development and use of the WCSD-SECAs exemplifies three approaches that we developed in our partnership and that others could adopt to emphasize the opportunities and reduce the challenges of assessing SECs in districts: (1) a continuous measure improvement approach, (2) a multifaceted evidence-building approach, and (3) a cocreation measure development approach.

*First, the WCSD-SECAs underscores some of the primary advantages of using a **continuous measure improvement approach*** (Davidson et al., 2018; Gordon, 2015). Under this approach, measures are not seen as static products taken off the shelf with fixed reliability and validity that apply consistently across time and space. Rather, measures are viewed as dynamic tools requiring continual updating of evidence demonstrating that the measures work in consistent and meaningful ways in local contexts. Notably, the WCSD-SECAs were developed iteratively over a 5-year period, with regular revisions as new evidence about its reliability and validity in practice emerged. As noted, the measures are free and open-source, and the authors have actively encouraged researchers and practitioners to continue to work to refine and adapt the measures to meet their cultural, logistical, and data use needs, leading to the creation of innovative, locally aligned adaptations, and a pooling of knowledge about how the measures work across multiple contexts. This continuous measure improvement approach is aligned with the current standards for educational and psychological testing, mentioned above, in which reliability and validity evidence are viewed as constantly building and in which ethical practice evaluates the full body of current evidence in relation to each potential use (AERA/APA/NCME, 2014; APA, 2017; Davidson et al., 2018; Gordon, 2015).

*Second, the WCSD-SECAs exemplified a **multifaceted evidence-building approach**, going beyond common yet limited approaches for building evidence about how well assessments work*. Again, this approach is consistent with modern standards, by drawing on multiple sources of evidence (AERA/APA/NCME, 2014). This approach contrasts with what has been standard practice, in which scholars and districts developing SEC assessments report few and limited types of reliability and validity evidence for an assessment's fixed set of items (often from what is referred to as a *classical test theory approach*). For instance, developers might focus on a summary measure of how associated test items are with one another (a statistic called *Cronbach's alpha*, which reflects the average item correlation and number of items). In contrast, the WCSD-SECAs used multiple kinds of psychometric models, including detailed statistics that capture more fine-grained information about how well each item works (referred to as an *item response theory approach*). As we worked on iterative item development, we created a large list of items with these statistics (referred to as an *item bank*), providing ourselves and other potential users ready information to support selecting or modifying items to be aligned with district practice, curricula, and student populations (referred to as *locally adapted*). These item response theory analyses also allow for more nuanced study of measurement invariance, pinpointing how items perform with different population groups (which as already noted identifies areas in which cultural and social norms may influence interpretation of items and, when considered across grade levels, offers fairer insights into the developmental trajectory of SECs from elementary to high school).

*Third, we modeled a **cocreation measure development approach** in developing the WCSD-SECAs in which researchers and practitioners were equal partners in the development of the measure, subsequent research, and dissemination of tools to ensure WCSD-SECA results were accessible to all stakeholders.* Our core team contained researchers and practitioners whose input was mutually respected. A primary goal of the partnership was to transfer knowledge about item response theory approaches such that all team members could draw meaning from results. Students and educators were critical collaborators in this work, helping to write and refine items, as well as regularly providing feedback on how to improve the quality of survey administration. Teams of students and educators also served as partners in the dissemination of research findings, helping to facilitate thoughtful conversations with other students and educators about the meaning of complex statistical findings in ways that were engaging and relevant for practice and improvement. The open-source dissemination of the WCSD-SECAs was consistent with this cocreation commitment, as no single contributor was seen as owning the items or measures.

The Instrument and Its Origins

The original goal of developing the WCSD-SECAs was to help educators identify social and emotional needs and strengths along students' pathway to graduation and, as a result, to better inform SEL implementation and school improvement decisions in the district. The project resulted in the development of a bank of items and two instruments aligned to the CASEL 5 areas of core competencies (self-awareness, self-management, relationship skills, social awareness, and responsible decision making) and WCSD SEL standards. A 138-item bank has been used by WCSD and other districts to provide examples of the types of student competencies teachers might see in their classrooms, make adaptations to local contexts, or create pre/post versions. A 40-item long-form assessment encompasses subcomponents of the CASEL 5 in eight subscales (with self-awareness assessed in two subdomains of emotions and of strengths and weaknesses [formerly "self-awareness of self-concept"], and self-management assessed in three specific subdomains of emotions, goals, and schoolwork). A short-form assessment's 17 items capture global SEC.

The instruments ask students to rate how difficult or easy various competencies are for them. A series of statements follow the instructions "Please tell us how easy or difficult each of the following are for you."

Students respond on a 4-point scale with labels 1 = very difficult, 2 = difficult, 3 = easy, and 4 = very easy. For example, one statement assessing relationship skills asks students about "Sharing what I am feeling with others." Another statement, assessing self-awareness of emotions, asks about "Knowing ways I calm myself down."

The WCSD-SECAs started from an evaluation tool created by the American Institutes for Research (AIR) and CASEL to evaluate the impact of the Collaborating Districts Initiative (CDI). This initiative, funded by CASEL and the NoVo Foundation, sought to build the capacity of eight large urban school districts, including WCSD, to systematically provide support for SEL to all PreK–12 educators. It proposed to demonstrate that large districts could implement SEL with fidelity at scale and systemwide, and also sought to develop and refine practical tools that promote the effective implementation and assessment of SEL. To strengthen the research base around this work, AIR conducted an evaluation that included the collection of student self-report ratings of SEC from within each CDI participating district (AIR & CASEL, 2013). This CDI instrument was the starting point for the development of the SECA measures. In 2013, WCSD, CASEL, and researchers from the University of Illinois at Chicago began the IES-funded researcher–practitioner partnership grant, mentioned above, to study the relationship between students' risk for dropout and their self-reported SECs, iteratively developing a refined and expanded set of items.

Since its initial release, over 200 national and international researchers, school district staff, and community organization leaders have requested the WCSD-SECAs from the authors, and dozens have reported having adapted the measure to better meet their local needs. These adaptations have included adding items from the larger item bank that better met local standards and curriculum goals, creating alternate test forms to reduce testing effects in pre/post assessment administrations, translating the measure into multiple languages, and adapting measures for use with adults wanting to assess their own SECs. As noted previously, one of the primary advantages of the continuous improvement approach is that it allows for this networked approach to collective measure adaptation and evidence accumulation.

As one example of the benefits of WCSD-SECA approaches in practice, the Nevada Department of Education ultimately adopted the short-form WCSD-SECA as part of its SEC measure for all districts in the state in its required annual student climate survey. This decision was made, in part, because the measure aligned with WCSD's SEL standards, which the state had also adopted statewide (called "Social, Emotional, and Academic Development (SEAD) Competencies" to avoid the Nevada requirement that teachers must grade all "Standards," a high-stakes accountability practice the reliability and validity evidence to date does not support). District SEC data are used by the Nevada Department of Education (NVDOE) to assign grant funds, monitor grant programming, and to identify statewide professional learning and SEL programming needs. The WCSD, NVDOE, and its survey vendor, AIR, meet periodically, including with other state Departments of Education, like Massachusetts, which uses the WCSD-SECA, to update each other about reliability and validity findings, and new reporting and data use strategies. This networked approach to learning has helped inform our own knowledge of the WCSD-SECAs psychometric properties, including its performance across much larger and diverse samples than WCSD's. WCSD has since been able to share this updated reliability and validity information with new districts and organizations hoping to administer the survey with populations different from WCSD, like rural areas and larger urban cities like Las Vegas.

Iterative Item Development to Align with Local Practice and to Reduce Measurement Error

One of the first challenges the partnership faced was a substantial ceiling effect in the original CDI instrument, meaning many of the 5th–12th graders chose the top category ("very easy") across most items. Although on the one hand this could be a good result—most students perceive themselves as highly competent in the assessed SECs—from a measurement perspective such a ceiling effect suggests that the instrument might not offer a strong signal of students' true competency along the underlying constructs like self-awareness of emotions and relationship skills. On the contrary, conceptually, we would expect a measure to pick up variation in SECs as students grew and learned from the end of elementary school through high school and that within each grade students would demonstrate varying levels of skills across the CASEL 5. If instead most students received the top score, then the instrument was not picking up such expected variation. The ceiling effect also suggested that the instrument was not sensitive enough to pick up growth related to any SEL curricula or interventions, since students would already be maxing out the test at the start.

The team used a multipronged approach to examine this issue. Of particular interest was distinguishing the kinds of social desirability and reference point biases noted above from a need for more items that better captured the higher levels of competencies. In other words, possibly some students chose the highest category because they thought that was what was expected of them rather than truly feeling the competencies were easy for them. If we wanted to deeply understand these possibilities, we knew we needed to engage with students directly, building on the student voice and knowledge cocreation that was already present in WCSD when our partnership began and expanded over time. We started by analyzing the preliminary data, finding different subgroups among students who selected the top score on every item. Some had other signals of high SECs. Yet others seemed to be choosing the top categories on all items because they were bored or because they struggled with understanding item wording (Davidson et al., 2018). To better understand these challenges, we designed a series of focus groups with students that mirrored the preliminary data. As part of these group activities, students helped write items for the survey that reflected skills important to them using everyday language they would use with their classmates (Davidson et al., 2018). For example, students described "good relationship skills" as someone who "doesn't leave anyone out" and "walks over to invite someone who is lonely to play," which ultimately inspired the development of the item "Being welcoming to someone I don't usually eat lunch with." Students also described someone without good relationship skills as someone who "had to be 'right' in any argument," helping us to craft the item "Respecting a classmate's opinions during a disagreement." To support buy-in, WCSD also created a proctoring video in which students described why the survey was being administered and where students could see the results online, and, the district continues to regularly engage with students around the survey including during annual data summits (Davidson et al., 2018; WCSD, 2020b).

Another aspect of our approach that helped to reduce the ceiling effect, and to adapt locally, was alignment of items with the local standards taught in WCSD. In the partnership, we designed activities for our research–practice team to crosswalk against the standards to ensure full item coverage, including at the most difficult competencies at the highest grades. This approach also helped the instrument keep a strong foothold in the CASEL 5 framework while resonating with the local SEL standards used by practitioners in WCSD. In other words, the alignment ensured that the instrument used language that parallels what educators hear during professional development, and what they use to guide and monitor SEL implementation locally. As noted previously, when the NVDOE adopted WCSD's SEL standards and the WCSD-SECAs, this further helped ensure that statewide SEL policy and funding priorities were aligned with common SEL standards, and monitored by the same SEC assessment statewide (NV Department of Education, 2017). In response to the SEL field's greater call for transformative SEL approaches, the NVDOE has established a statewide workgroup, of which WCSD SEL and research staff are members, to draft a second version of SEAD Competencies that reflect a greater lens toward equity using some of the information WCSD learned about the measure's validity across student population groups. This work will in turn help to inform the next version of WCSD-SECAs, ensuring that the measure and standards evolve together to reflect new programmatic needs and measure uses.

Specifically, developing the WCSD-SECAs, we wrote items to align with standards that described the skills, attitudes, knowledge, and behaviors expected within the CASEL 5 at each of the district's five grade bands (combining two or three grade levels). These standards were used as guides when the team refined and added items, but with language tailored to reading levels appropriate for students in grades 5–12, and also supplemented with items based on broader research and practice knowledge. For instance, a WCSD-SECA self-awareness of emotion item, "Knowing the emotions I feel," directly corresponds to a WCSD elementary school SEL standard, "Recognize and accurately name personal feelings." However, a WCSD-SECA item "Helping to make my school a better place" was not directly identified in the SEL standards, but was added because the team recognized it to be an important indicator of social awareness in practice and research literature for older students. Once initial items were developed, pairs of team members, one practitioner and one researcher, were assigned to each competency domain in order to review and refine items to ensure readability, alignment to WCSD standards, and coverage of broader research and practice knowledge bases. Later, practitioners and researchers generated predictions about when, developmentally, each competency would be rated "easier" by students (e.g., in elementary vs. high school) to ensure the measure covered a broad range of developmental milestones from grades 5–12.

Although built on this strong theoretical model and practice guidance, it was important for the research–practice team to validate whether the items that the students' responses indicated were easiest and hardest matched our original expectations. Doing so also helped us translate results to stakeholders, including around measurement error. The team used Rasch modeling, a type of item response theory approach that allowed us to estimate where the items were located along their underlying (latent) competency domains. Doing so was useful because we could then assess whether the positioning of items aligned with expectations based on the developmental standards—that is, that "easier" items corresponded to elementary versus middle or high school standards (Crowder et al., 2019). We found that the Rasch model facilitated translation to students, teachers, leaders, and other stakeholders because, when its assumptions hold, item distributions can be presented graphically, analogous to the ticks on a ruler. Figure 11.3 illustrates how we adapted the traditional research presentation of this ruler to be engaging for students, parents, teachers, and leaders. The figure shows, for instance, that "Sharing what I am feeling with others" is the hardest item, whereas "Forgiving classmates when they upset me" falls closer to the middle.

One way we used this ruler was to consider whether the grade level of standards correctly predicted the observed item ordering (Crowder et al., 2019). That is, the relative order of items can be interpreted in relation to expected developmental or grade-level progressions, as in which competencies would emerge first, which next, and so on. We looked to see whether

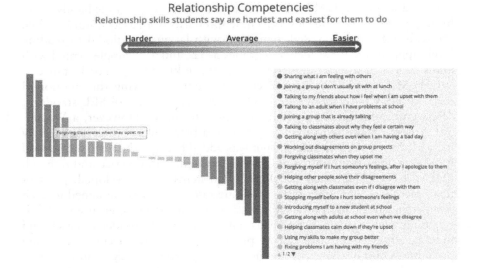

FIGURE 11.3. Relationship competencies.

the items our team placed at elementary levels were ordered in the Rasch results lower than those at middle and high school levels. Although many items matched expectations, we found the empirical item ordering differed from what we expected for about half of the subdomains. These results are important not only for iterative item development but also for both practice and research. For continuous measure improvement, we reevaluated items to see if they needed further refinement. Practitioners can also use the results to see if standards require revision—was a standard placed at a particular grade band, although it really reflects a skill, attitude, knowledge, or behavior that would emerge for most students at earlier or later grades? Researchers can similarly use the results to help inform theory—do certain SECs reflect developmental progressions where some knowledge and skill is foundational to achieving other knowledge and skill?

Another way WCSD leverages the ruler analogy is when it reports the results of its Rasch analyses and other SEC assessment research on its public-facing dashboard, *www.WCSDdata.net,* where staff, families, and students gain access to districtwide data and research to help inform conversations about the SECs (this dashboard is the source of Figure 11.3). Through close collaboration between the district's SEL and Accountability Offices, WCSD created several training modules to support school staff's use of this dashboard. For example, in one training, educators review the Rasch results that indicate which competencies are ordered highest and lowest by students, learning about how this ordering offers a signal of which competencies students feel are hardest and easiest to accomplish. During one training, educators reviewed the data showing that students regularly report that sharing their feelings with others is difficult for them, and developed strategies for supporting students with the competencies they report struggling with most often, including by teachers sharing their own feelings with students more frequently to better model the competency.

Another way we have used the Rasch approach is to shine a light on the importance of having a sufficient number of items corresponding to the full continuum of underlying SECs evident across students in the district. The Rasch model formalizes the effect on measurement error of the kinds of ceiling effects described above, helping us to visualize these ceilings and to demonstrate greater error in estimating SECs for students located above those ceilings (as discussed next). It also extends beyond the lack of items at the extremes (ceilings and floors) by reinforcing the problem when there are large gaps between item locations (i.e., the ticks on the ruler) even in midrange. A strength of the Rasch approach over simple sums, means, and proportions is that the item distribution can be graphed alongside the student distribution, allowing for such gaps in items where students are located to be clearly evident. For instance, Figure 11.4 shows how fewer items were at the top of the scale (a ceiling effect) and there were also some internal gaps between items (such as between item 2 and items 3 and 4). (Note that in this figure each # represents 56 students and each dot 1–55 students; each number reflects an item; Davidson et al., 2018).

Person	Item
.####	
.	
.	
.	
.	
.	
.	
.#	
.#	
.	
.#	
.#	
.#	
.#	
.#	
.#	1
.#	2
.#	
.##	
.##	3 4
.###	5
.##	
.##	6
.#	7 8 9 10 11
.##	12 13 14
.##	15
.##	16 17 18 19 20
.#	21
.#	22
.#	23 24
.#	
.#	25
.	26
.	
.	27
.	
.	
.	28
.	

FIGURE 11.4. Distribution of students and items for the Relationship Skills domain from a Rasch model.

In general, we will have a noisy signal of a student's SEC level when few items are located at their competency level. To make this idea concrete, we can think of a math test that included questions about addition and division but not about subtraction and multiplication. Students in the midrange of math competency will likely be poorly distinguished from one another on such a test, as they would all be expected to get all the addition questions right and all of the division questions wrong. Subtraction and multiplication items would be needed to separate their midrange competency levels. For SEC assessments, districts can use graphs like Figure 11.4 to ensure they haven't inadvertently overlooked items at certain levels. For instance, based on Figure 11.4, we knew we had more work to do in creating harder items (at the top of the scale) and filling some internal gaps. Numbers of items also matter. More items can cover a greater range of competency than fewer items. Psychometrically, measurement error is also reduced as the number of items increase. In our item development work, we quantified that even in our long-form assessment that had 4–6 items per subdomain the level of measurement error was considerable (half or more the full score range; Crowder et al., 2019). Our current collaborations are developing linked item sets to reduce measurement error without lengthening the test. In other words, different sets of items can target different competency levels with some common items linking across the sets, as in computerized adaptive academic testing (Gordon, Wang, Nguyen, & Aloe, 2021). For instance, to the extent that data confirm the items that align with elementary, middle, and high school standards, different versions of an SEC assessment can be created for each level. The majority of items in each version would correspond to that version's grade levels, although some items would be present in all versions. These common items would be selected from those that are relevant across levels, for instance items that fall at the boundaries between elementary and middle school and between middle and high school.

Examining Constructs (Dimensionality) and Considering Fairness (Invariance)

The WCSD-SECAs' development process also tested whether the CASEL 5 framework, the theoretical framework on which the measure and WCSD's SEL standards are based, was supported empirically. Indeed, though one of the most used frameworks in the SEL field and providing a useful common language for understanding SEL, the CASEL 5 framework has stronger theoretical and practice roots than empirical confirmation (as do many other SEL frameworks). Using an item factor analysis appropriate for categorical items, we did not find support for all five of the CASEL domains in two school years of WCSD data using the 40 items of the WCSD-SECA long form. Instead, we found greater evidence for three underlying constructs of intrapersonal skills, interpersonal skills, and emotion knowledge, consistent with broader band intrapersonal/interpersonal and knowledge/skill constructs related to the CASEL 5 and other SEL frameworks (e.g., Pellegrino & Hilton, 2012). These three constructs were evident across subgroups defined by grade level and gender/ethnicity, with statistically equivalent factor loadings (Gordon et al., 2021). WCSD is reflecting further on these findings to determine what they may indicate about needs for future survey, or perhaps even standards, revision.

Developing and testing of the WCSD-SECAs also attempted to respond to the concerns noted above about whether SEC measures are fair and equitable (Aspen Institute, 2018; Assessment Work Group, 2019; Jagers et al., 2018). Responding to this call, we have extensively reported on various indicators of measurement invariance to more deeply comprehend subgroup differences in SECs, analyzing whether measurement invariance is stronger for certain subpopulations and how subgroup levels of SECs and their SECs' associations with outcomes change before and after adjusting for any measurement invariance. These analyses have indicated infrequent, but meaningful, noninvariance across population groups, specifically between elementary and high school students, and among White females and Hispanic females. Adjusting for noninvariance was consequential (Gordon et al., 2021). General patterns of SEC levels showed that, in the higher grades, all gender/ethnic groups tended to report lower intrapersonal SECs and higher interpersonal SECs. Girls, and especially girls who identified as White, also endorsed greater intrapersonal and interpersonal skills than did boys. Boys endorsed greater emotion knowledge SEC than did girls, particularly in high school. Yet the differences among groups were understated when using simple item averages. The reason is that these simple averages couldn't adjust for the ways students in different subgroups responded differently to items, despite having equivalent latent competencies (i.e., the simple item averages did not adjust for noninvariance). Importantly, the few prior studies of measurement noninvariance within SEC assessments have not considered the issues our results uncovered because they have used methods that assume the items are continuous—that is, can take on many values like measuring weight in ounces. Doing so misses the fact that most SEC assessments, like the WCSD-SECAs, instead have items that are categorical—that is, have just a few possible responses for each item, such as the four WCSD-SECAs' responses of *very difficult, difficult, easy,* and *very easy.* The methods we used allowed us to better detect differences in how students selected choices from among these four response options. Our findings showed that doing this was important, because it was the different ways various subgroups chose among the response options (despite having equivalent underlying competency) that affected fair assessments of subgroups' average levels of SECs (Gordon et al., 2021).

As discussed above, discovering measurement noninvariance between student groups on SEC assessments may uncover social and cultural differences that may be important to equitable implementation of SEL and writing of standards. Rather than removing noninvariant items from the measures (as is common in academic testing), uncovering differential SEC item interpretations among population groups provides opportunities for rich conversations to explore potential gender, culture, and developmental differences in the ways SECs are understood, expressed, and experienced across populations and contexts. In relation to the WCSD-SECA example, the population differences we identified have served as the basis for designing follow-up projects and local WCSD studies to better understand how boys, girls, and nonbinary students, different age groups, and different races and ethnicities experienced the district's SEL curriculum. We also continue to test for noninvariance, and encourage other users of the SECA to do so, in order to see the extent to which our findings replicate. Doing so is a particularly important aspect of continuous measure improvement given the dearth of measurement invariance studies in the field of SEC assessment yet the emphasis on fairness, equity, and transformative SEL (Aspen Institute, 2018; Jagers, 2016; Jagers et al., 2018, 2019).

Informing Practice

One of the primary goals of the WCSD-SECAs researcher–practitioner partnership was to develop innovative ways to ensure data collected about student SECs were useful, understandable, and provided actionable guidance to educators without glossing over the limitations of the data. This happens through the dashboard and activities already discussed, and in other ways. At the beginning of each year, WCSD's Office of Accountability produces a large Data Profile Book for each school, which includes academic, behavior, absenteeism, climate, and social and emotional assessment data from the WCSD-SECAs to guide schools' development of their annual School Performance Plans. Accountability staff help schools identify links among the data points. For example, if a school notices increased behavioral incidences among freshman students, who also report higher difficulty getting along with their teachers and classmates (relationship competencies assessed on the WCSD-SECAs), schools might consider ways to adjust their SEL curriculum to include more peer-to-peer relationship building for freshman at the beginning of the school year to promote better adjustment.

WCSD also hosts annual Data Summits about WCSD-SECAs data, featuring the results of the research–practice partnerships' research efforts in ways that are approachable to the district staff, boards of trustees, community members, and students who participate in the events. During a recent Student Voice Data Summit (the fifth such event the district has hosted), 150 students explored age, gender, and cultural differences in how students rate their emotion management, a presentation inspired by the measurement noninvariance generated by the research–practice results (Crowder et al., 2019). Students provided incredible insights into why measurement noninvariance may have occurred on items. For example, students thought different patterns of socialization influenced why high school boys were more likely than high school girls to endorse "Staying calm when stressed" as easy, believing that boys were less likely to admit feeling stress compared to girls, who are more freely encouraged to discuss their emotions. Following findings indicating measurement noninvariance between Hispanic males and non-Hispanic females, WCSD's research and SEL teams partnered on a project to better understand how useful and relevant their SEL curriculum was, which led to several adaptations of lessons incorporating students' feedback for improvement.

• Conclusions

The WCSD-SECAs are student self-report SEC assessments designed for schoolwide and districtwide use with 5th–12th graders. Developed in a research–practice partnership, the WCSD-SECAs are openly and freely available for other schools, districts, and states to use and adapt (WCSD, 2020a). We share the strategies we have used in our continuous measure improvement efforts so that others can likewise build local reliability and validity evidence and can adapt items where evidence suggests improvements are needed. These strategies also embrace a modern view of tests as dynamic rather than static, evolving to reflect new theory, practice, and research and to adjust to local contextual and cultural needs. From this perspective, we aim to be transparent about the evidence base of the WCSD-SECAs, which reflects both their current strengths and their room for growth. Our current efforts include continuing to replicate evidence, understand results, and revise items in relation to the ways items operate differently across student populations, related efforts to develop linked item sets that are tailored to subgroups and that can precisely estimate student SECs without undo test length, and support and encouragement of multiformat and multi-informant studies in order to help schools understand the differential utility of different score types for various uses. We also continue to embrace networked research–practice collectives that support sustainable, transparent, and open-license development and sharing of SEC items, scorings, algorithms and platforms such that all students, parents, teachers, and leaders have access to assessments that are fair and meaningful and that support teaching and learning across schools regardless of location or resources.

ACKNOWLEDGMENTS

This chapter rests upon collaborative research that began with an IES researcher–practitioner partnership grant (No. R305H130012). We gratefully acknowledge the entire partnership team, including Celene Domitrovich, Marisa Crowder, Randy Brown, Ben Hayes, Ann McKay-Bryson, Robert Schamberg, Trish Shaffer, Roger Weissberg, and Jeremy Taylor, as well as more recent collaboration with Ariel Aloe. Throughout, we cite papers and websites that readers can consult to learn more about the partnership and collaborators. We are saddened to have lost this past year Ben Hayes, Washoe County School District's Chief Accountability Officer, and Roger Weissberg, a co-founder and Chief Knowledge Officer of the Collaborative for Academic, Social, and Emotional Learning. Both were champions for students and practitioners, innovators in the engaged use of knowledge to guide social and emotional learning, and invaluable mentors to us. The funding source was not involved in the research study design or the decision to submit this manuscript. The content does not necessarily reflect the views or policies of the IES or the U.S. Department of Education, nor does mention of trade names, commercial products, or organizations imply endorsement by the U.S. government. Note that WCSD contracts with Panorama Education to administer the WCSD-SECAs and other assessments.

REFERENCES

American Educational Research Association, American Psychological Association, & National Council on Measurement in Education. (2014). *Standards for educational and psychological testing.* American Educational Research Association.

American Institutes for Research & Collaborative for Academic, Social, and Emotional Learning. (2013). *Student self-report of social and emotional competencies.* Authors.

American Psychological Association. (2017). *Ethical principles of psychologists and code of conduct: Section 9: Assessment.* Author.

Aspen Institute. (2018). *Pursuing social and emotional development through a racial equity lens: A call to action.* Author.

Assessment Work Group. (2019). *Student social and emotional competence assessment: The current state of the field and a vision for its future.* Collaborative for Academic, Social, and Emotional Learning.

Berg, J., Osher, D., Same, M. R., Nolan, E., Benson, D., & Jacobs, N. (2017). *Identifying, defining, and measuring social and emotional competencies: Final Report.* American Institutes for Research.

Bridges, M., Cohen, S. R., McGuire, L. W., Yamada, H., Fuller, B., Mireles, L., & Scott, L. (2012). *Bien educado*: Measuring the social behaviors of Mexican American children. *Early Childhood Research Quarterly, 27,* 555–567.

Castro-Olivo, S. M., & Merrell, K. W. (2012). Validating cultural adaptations of a school-based social-emotional learning program for use with Latino immigrant adolescents. *Advances in School Mental Health Promotion, 5,* 78–92.

Cheung, G. W., & Lau, R. S. (2012). A direct comparison approach for testing measurement invariance. *Organizational Research Methods, 15,* 167–198.

Crowder, M. K., Gordon, R. A., Brown, R. D., Davidson, L. A., & Domitrovich, C. E. (2019). Linking social and emotional learning standards to the Social–Emotional Competency Assessment: A Rasch approach. *School Psychology Quarterly, 34,* 281–295.

Davidson, L. A., Crowder, M. K., Gordon, R. A., Domitrovich, C. E., Brown, R., & Hayes, B. (2018). A continuous improvement approach to social and emotional competency measurement. *Journal of Applied Developmental Psychology, 55,* 93–106.

Delaney, K. K., & Krepps, K. (2021). Exploring Head Start teacher and leader perceptions of the Pre-K Classroom Assessment Scoring Systems as part of the Head Start Renewal System. *Early Childhood Research Quarterly, 55,* 214–229.

Denzin, N. K., Lincoln, Y. S., & Smith, L. T. (2008). *Handbook of critical and indigenous methodologies.* Sage.

DePaoli, J. L., Atwel, M. N., & Bridgeland, J. (2017). *Ready to lead: A national principal survey on how social and emotional learning can prepare children and transform schools.* CASEL.

Domitrovich, C. E., Durlak, J. A., Staley, K. C., & Weissberg, R. P. (2017). Social–emotional competence: An essential factor for promoting positive adjustment and reducing risk in school children. *Child Development, 88,* 408–416.

Duckworth, A. L., & Yeager, D. S. (2015). Measurement matters: Assessing personal qualities other than cognitive ability for education purposes. *Educational Researcher, 44,* 237–251.

Figlio, D., & Loeb, S. (2011). School accountability. *Handbook of the Economics of Education, 3,* 383–421.

Gordon, R. A. (2015). Measuring constructs in family science: How can IRT improve precision and validity? *Journal of Marriage and Family, 77,* 147–176.

Gordon, R. A., Crowder, M. K., Aloe, A. M., Davidson, L. A., & Domitrovich, C. E. (2021). *Student self-ratings of social-emotional competencies: Dimensional structure and outcome associations of the WCSD-SECA among Hispanic and non-Hispanic White boys and girls in elementary through high school.* Manuscript under review.

Gordon, R. A., & Superfine, B. (2021). Who owns educational products developed with federal funds? Intellectual property rights in preK–12 education. *Journal of Educational Policy, 36,* 557–575.

Gordon, R. A., Wang, T., Nguyen, H., & Aloe, A. M. (2021). *Using the alignment method to account for measurement invariance among many groups: A tutorial and R package to facilitate interpretation.* Manuscript under review.

Gresham, F., Elliott, S., Metallo, S., Byrd, S. Wilson, E., Erickson, M., . . . Altman, R. (2020). Psychometric fundamentals of the Social Skills Improvement System: Social–emotional learning edition rating forms. *Assessment for Effective Intervention, 45,* 194–209.

Gresham, F. M., & Elliott, S. N. (2008). *Social Skills Improvement System Rating Scales.* Pearson Assessments.

Hecht, M. L., & Shin, Y. (2015). Culture and social and emotional competencies. In J. A. Durlak, C. E. Domitrovich, R. P. Weissberg, & T. P. Gullotta (Eds.), *Handbook of social and emotional learning: Research and practice* (pp. 50–64). Guilford Press.

Jagers, R. J. (2016). Framing social and emotional learning among African-American youth: Toward an integrity-based approach. *Human Development, 59,* 1–3.

Jagers, R. J., Rivas-Drake, D., & Borowski, T. (2018). *Equity & social and emotional learning: A cultural analysis.* CASEL.

Jagers, R. J., Rivas-Drake, D., & Williams, B. (2019). Transformative social and emotional learning (SEL): Toward SEL in service of educational equity and excellence. *Educational Psychologist, 54,* 162–184.

Jones, S. M., Bailey, R., Brush, K., & Nelson, B. (2019). *Introduction to the taxonomy project: Tools for selecting and aligning SEL frameworks.* CASEL.

Jordan, P. W., & Hamilton, L. S. (2020). *Walking a fine line: School climate surveys in state ESSA plans.* FutureEd.

Liu, Y., Millsap, R. E., West, S. G., Tein, J., Tanaka, R., & Grimm, K. J. (2017). Testing measurement invariance in longitudinal data with ordered-categorical measures. *Psychological Methods, 22,* 486–506.

Mantz, L. S., Bear, G. G., Yang, C., & Harris, A. (2018). The Delaware Social-Emotional Competency Scale (DSECS-S): Evidence of validity and reliability. *Child Indicators Research, 11,* 137–157.

Melnick, H., Cook-Harvey, C. M., & Darling-Hammond, L. (2017). *Encouraging social and emotional learning in the context of new accountability.* Learning Policy Institute.

Merrell, K. W., & Gueldner, B. A. (2010). *Social and emotional learning in the classroom: Promoting mental health and academic success.* Guilford Press.

Millsap, R. E. (2011). *Statistical approaches to measurement invariance.* Routledge.

Muthén, B., & Asparouhov, T. (2014). IRT studies of many groups: The alignment method. *Frontiers in Psychology, 5,* 978.

Nevada Department of Education. (2017). Nevada statewide social and emotional competencies. Retrieved from *www.doe.nv.gov/uploadedFiles/ndedoenvgov/content/Boards_Commissions_Councils/State_Board_of_Education/2017/November/nvstatesocialcompetencies.pdf.*

Panorama Education. (n.d.). Support the whole student with research-backed SEL assessments for students and adults. Retrieved from *www.panoramaed.com/social–emotional-learning-sel.*

Panorama Education. (2016). Preliminary report: Reliability and validity of Panorama's social–emotional learning measures. Retrieved from *https://panorama-www.s3.amazonaws.com/files/sel/SEL-Validity-Report.pdf.*

Paris, D. (2012). Culturally sustaining pedagogy: A needed change in stance, terminology, and practice. *Educational Researcher, 41,* 93–97.

Pellegrino, J. W., & Hilton, M. L. (2012). *Education for life and work: Developing transferable knowledge and skills in the 21st century.* National Academies Press.

Schamberg, R., Domitrovich, C. E., Davidson, L. A., Hayes, B., Shaffer, T., Gordon, R. A., . . . Weissberg, R. P. (2017). Implementing effective partnerships: Case study of creating a monitoring system for school districts to promote social and emotional learning: A researcher-practitioner partnership. In J. W. Owen & A. M. Larson (Eds.), *Researcher-Policymaker Partnerships: Strategies for Launching and Sustaining Successful Collaborations* (pp. 52–71). Routledge.

Shweder, R., Minow, M., & Markus, H. R. (Eds.). (2002). *Engaging cultural differences: The multicultural challenge in liberal democracies.* Russell Sage Foundation.

Smith, G. T., Spillane, N. S., & Annus, A. M. (2006). Implications of an emerging integration of universal and culturally specific psychologies. *Perspectives on Psychological Science, 1,* 211–233.

Taylor, J. J., Buckley, K., Hamilton, L. S., Stecher, B. M., Read, L., & Schweig, J. (2018). Choosing and using SEL competency assessments: What schools and districts need to know. Retrieved from *https://measuringsel.casel.org/pdf/practitioner-guidance.pdf.*

Tyton Partners. (2020). *Finding your place: The current state of K–12 social emotional learning.* Author.

Ura, S. K., Castro-Olivo, S. M., & d'Abreu, A. (2019). Outcome measurement of school-based SEL intervention follow-up studies. *Assessment for Effective Intervention [online first].*

Wang, L., Beckett, G. H., & Brown, L. (2010). Controversies of standardized assessment in school accountability reform: A critical synthesis of multidisciplinary research evidence. *Applied Measurement in Education, 19,* 305–328.

Washoe County School District. (2020a). WCSD's Social and Emotional Competency Assessment. Available at *www.washoeschools.net/Page/10932.*

Washoe County School District. (2020b). Data Summits. Available at *www.wcsd-data.net/data-summits.*

West, M. R. (2016). *Should non-cognitive skills be included in school accountability systems? Preliminary evidence from California's CORE districts (Evidence Speaks Reports, Vol. 1, #13).* Brookings.

West, M. R., Buckley, K., Krachman, S. B., & Bookman, N. (2018). Development and implementation of student social-emotional surveys in the CORE districts. *Journal of Applied Developmental Psychology, 55,* 119–129.

Yoon, M., & Lai, M. H. C. (2018). Testing factorial invariance with unbalanced samples. *Structural Equation Modeling, 25,* 201–213.

CHAPTER 12

Measuring and Monitoring Children's Social and Emotional Competence and Well-Being in Schools, Families, and Communities at the Population Level

The Middle Years Development Instrument

Kimberly A. Schonert-Reichl

The true measure of a nation's standing is how well it attends to its children—their health and safety, their material security, their education and socialization, and their sense of being loved, valued, and included in the families and societies into which they are born.
—UNICEF (*Innocenti Report Card 7*, 2007)

What kind of education do we need in an interconnected 21st century to prepare young people across the globe to flourish individually, and to contribute to solving the social and ecological challenges that confront the entire globe today? What are the skills, attitudes, and competencies that our future generation will need to become happy, productive, and healthy citizens that are fully prepared for their adult roles as citizens, employees, parents, and volunteers? In the face of current societal, economic, environmental, and social challenges, identifying the social and emotional competencies (SECs) that our young people need for the future is critical now more than ever before (Schonert-Reichl & Weissberg, 2014). As we contemplate the future of education at this important inflection point in our collective history, it is useful, as the quote from the UNICEF report reminds us, to direct our attention to creating the conditions where all children can feel loved, safe, and cared for across multiple contexts and ecologies.

This chapter focuses on efforts to assess children's SECs and well-being within school systems and communities at the level of the population.

Population-level data refers to data gathered from a set of individuals across an entire population who share characteristics, such as grade level or age. A population can be determined by geographies, such as all children in one school district or all students in one school, a neighborhood or community. Gathering data at the level of the student population can be used for assessing and monitoring developmental changes in children's SEC's over time and across schools and neighborhoods as well to assess the effectiveness of SEL programs and practices.

The chapter begins by providing a rationale for measuring and monitoring the SECs of children, highlighting the importance of assessment. Then, the Middle Years Development Instrument (MDI)—a population-level measure of children's social and emotional development and well-being in middle childhood inside and outside of school—is described. In this section, the research-to-action project that led to the collaborative creation of the MDI through a partnership among researchers, community leaders, and educators is delineated. Next, a review of the development and validation of the MDI is outlined. Following this, examples of the knowledge mobilization strategies that have been developed to report MDI data back to the schools and communities are provided. Finally, MDI outcomes and impact are illustrated through stories of how the MDI data have been used to catalyze action to improve students' SECs and well-being.

● Measuring and Monitoring Children's SEC

The promotion of SEL into the education system at all levels requires a systematic perspective and approach (Mahoney et al., 2020). Widespread acceptance and "buy-in" regarding the importance of SEL to children's lifelong health, well-being, and achievement is one of the vital first steps. And underpinning this acceptance with solid data/evidence and ongoing research about the power of SEL is critical. Indeed, an essential ingredient is the ongoing capture of relevant and useful data, at both an individual and a population level, that holds the focus in the right places, that provides a foundation for evaluation, and that gives an ongoing measure of progress at the level of the population toward the larger goal of overall improved child SEC and well-being.

SEL involves the processes through which individuals acquire and effectively apply the knowledge, attitudes, and skills necessary to understand and manage their emotions, feel and show empathy for others, establish and achieve positive goals, develop and maintain positive relationships, and make responsible decisions (Collaborative for Academic, Social, and Emotional Learning [CASEL], 2013; Weissberg, Payton, O'Brien, & Munro, 2007). That is, SEL teaches the personal and interpersonal skills we all need to handle ourselves, our relationships, and our work effectively and ethically. As such, SECs are viewed as "mastery skills" underlying virtually all aspects of human functioning. SEL emphasizes active learning approaches in which skills can be generalized across curriculum areas and contexts when opportunities are provided to practice the skills that foster positive attitudes, behaviors, and thinking processes.

Recent discussions of systemic SEL emphasize the importance of taking into account the key settings in which the development of children's SECs occur (see Mahoney et al., 2020). These key settings include classrooms, schools, homes, and the community. Moreover, it should be emphasized that effective SEL interventions and skill development should occur in an environment that is safe, caring, supportive, participatory, and well-managed, an environment that supports students' development and provides opportunities for practicing skills. Communication styles; high performance expectations; classroom structures and rules; school organizational climate; commitment to equity and the academic success of all students; student voice, identity, and engagement; district policies; and parental and community involvement are all important components of a system-wide approach to SEL (Emerson, Masse, Ark, Schonert-Reichl, & Guhn, 2018; Jagers et al., 2019; Magee, Guhn, Schonert-Reichl, & Oberle, 2019; Mahoney et al., 2020; Oberle, Guhn, Gadermann, Thomson, & Schonert-Reichl, 2018).

Greenberg, Domitrovich, Weissberg, and Durlak (2017) have cogently argued that SEL should be conceptualized as a public health approach to education, positing:

> The ultimate goal of public health is to improve the general population's well-being. That means not only preventing diseases, disorders, injuries, and problem behaviors, but also nurturing positive outcomes that improve quality of life. To achieve this goal, public health researchers and practitioners begin by documenting the epidemiology of the problems they target, tracking the rates at which a problem occurs and who is most affected. They also study the risk and protective factors associated with a problem—that is, factors that increase or decrease the likelihood that the problem will develop among certain groups. (p. 14)

Greenberg and colleagues go on to contend that one reason for a public approach to SEL is that the implementation of *universal* SEL interventions in schools could significantly impact public health at the level of the population. In this vein, it follows that it is important to take a public health approach when assessing SEL and monitoring it at a population level. For example, population-level data on child well-being and SECs can provide researchers, educators, and policymakers with opportunities to discover answers to questions that cannot be found with studies of subgroups of children or youth that may not be representative of the larger population of all children and youth.

• An Essential Step to Advance the Field of SEL: Evaluating and Monitoring

Building on milestones in the field of SEL, educators, scholars, and policymakers collectively have discussed essential steps for advancing a future agenda of supporting students' well-being and social and emotional needs and making the promotion of students' social and emotional development in schools and communities a priority (Weissberg, Durlak, Domitrovich, & Gullotta, 2015). One essential step in this endeavor involves the development and implementation of psychometrically sound and developmentally appropriate measurement tools to evaluate and monitor students' SEC and development in schools, families, and communities. See Chapter 1, this volume, for further discussion on this topic.

As conveyed in the widely known axiom "What gets assessed gets addressed"—we now know that a systematic monitoring and evaluation framework is critical for creating accountability systems in which a priority is given to the promotion of students' SECs and skills. That is, in order to determine how and when to intervene, one must first have data that can inform what is working, and what interventions or programs should be put into place to foster students' SEC, well-being, and resiliency to promote thriving and to prevent adjustment problems later in life.

Nonetheless, although there has been much progress in the field of SEL in the past decade, there exist significant gaps in our understanding of the best ways in which to measure, evaluate, and monitor children's SECs. As noted by Clark McKown, a renowned researcher and pioneer in the field of SEL assessment, "In the push to boost young people's social and emotional learning (SEL), assessment has lagged behind policy and practice. We have few usable, feasible, and scalable tools to assess children's SEL. And without good assessments, teachers, administrators, parents, and policymakers can't get the data they need to make informed decisions about SEL" (2017, p. 157).

This latter point is particularly noteworthy—there is a dire need for the identification of scientifically sound assessment tools that are cost-effective and easy to use if we hope to promote a more comprehensive understanding of children's SEC and the mechanisms and processes that influence it at the population level. Given this, I draw through a public health lens and a deep dive into an example of monitoring children's SEC at the population level. Population-level assessment tools measure developmental change or trends in populations at varied geographies. This allows the study of variations in children's well-being and SECs across time and location.

• Measuring and Monitoring Children's SEC and Well-Being at a Population Level: The Middle Years Development Instrument

The most contemporary child well-being indicator on a global
level is the Middle Years Development Instrument (MDI) . . .
which is applied in Vancouver, British Columbia.
—LERIOU, KAZANI, KOLLIAS, & PARASKEVOPOULOU (2021)

In the section that follows, the Middle Years Development Instrument (MDI) is briefly described, and a delineation of the MDI's origins in the context of a research-to-action university–community partnership is put forth. This is then followed by a detailed section outlining the MDI's development and validation process that includes a description of the MDI's conceptual framework, and alignment with British Columbia's (BC's) curriculum framework. This section ends by briefly outlining the ways in which the MDI aligns with CASEL's framework of SEL.

The MDI is a student self-report measure for students in fourth and seventh grades (now expanded to include grade 8) to collect data about children's social and emotional development; physical health and well-being; connectedness to adults at home, in school, and in community; school experiences; and after-school time use. The MDI is used by school–community–university partnerships to collect data at a population level, so that schools and communities can translate MDI findings into actions that promote children's SEC and well-being.

The development of the MDI began in 2007 as a university–community partnership and, as the above quote describes, has grown to be seen as a key assessment tool of child well-being worldwide. Indeed, the pilot study of the MDI took place in 2010 with 3,026 fourth-grade students from 201 classrooms in 72 elementary schools in a diverse, urban public school district (with a total student population of over 50,000) in Vancouver, British Columbia (BC), Canada, and has grown considerably in the last decade. Specifically, the MDI has expanded throughout most of the 60 school districts in BC, and to date, over 190,000 fourth- and seventh-grade students across hundreds of classrooms and schools have completed the MDI. Moreover, the MDI has expanded across Canada, and has been implemented in Alberta, Ontario, Nova Scotia, Manitoba, the Yukon, and the Northwest Territories. And the MDI has expanded beyond Canada into the United States, Australia, Switzerland, France, Germany, Peru, Croatia, the United Kingdom, and Israel, with new projects beginning in Japan and Pakistan.

How the MDI Began: A Research-to-Action Community Partnership

Recognizing the increasing importance of SEL and its assessment in the United States (e.g., McKown, 2017), educators and community members in Vancouver became interested in assessing children's SECs and well-being inside and outside of school. One of the community stakeholders deeply committed to promoting the well-being of children during the middle childhood years was the United Way of the Lower Mainland (UWLM), which provided funding to myself and colleagues at the University of British Columbia (UBC) to conduct a large-scale cross-sectional study examining children's social and emotional development and well-being inside and outside of school (Schonert-Reichl et al., 2007). The study included over 1,400 children in fourth through seventh grades across eight school districts in the Lower Mainland of BC and was supported by stakeholders invested in identifying key ecological factors and developmental assets in schools and communities associated with children's SEC and healthy development. The partnerships developed with key stakeholders was central to the success of the research project. Indeed, over the course of the research from its initial design to data collection and analysis, the project team met regularly with a university–community advisory group developed specifically for the project to engage in rich discussions regarding every step of the process. This process led to a true collaborative effort in which relational trust was developed and nurtured and which a common goal of understanding the well-being and SECs of children was at the core.

The study, titled "The Psychological and Social Worlds of Canadian Children Ages 9–12," found that sixth- and seventh-grade students' social and emotional well-being, sense of belonging at school, and connectedness to adults at school, at home, and in the neighborhood was significantly lower than that of fourth and fifth graders. Moreover, sixth and seventh graders spent significantly less time participating in structured after-school activities and more time alone at home after school compared to fourth and fifth graders (Schonert-Reichl et al., 2007). For the stakeholders who served as advisors for the study, the findings raised the question of how they could help local schools and communities support children's SEC and well-being during the middle childhood years. Additionally, the study findings surfaced the need to investigate students' social and emotional development and well-being inside and outside of school across time and regional boundaries. This resulted in a call for a longitudinal and a representative *population*-level approach to assessing and monitoring children's social and emotional development in schools and communities.

Development and Validation of the MDI

In 2007, after the completion of the middle childhood study described above, we engaged in further partnership with the UWLM, along with educators in BC and other stakeholders, to use the data from the study to lead to the creation of a populationwide, recurring monitoring tool on children's social and emotional development, well-being, and social contexts, thus leading to the development of the MDI. We recognized that despite the growing body of research on population-level indicators of child well-being, there was a relative paucity of measures that (1) allowed for an examination of associations between indices of children's social and emotional well-being and assets across multiple contexts, (2) were focused on the developmental period identified as "middle childhood," (3) included dimensions of both positive and negative outcomes, and (4) were obtained from the children themselves. With regard to this latter dimension, it has been argued (Ben-Arieh, 2005) that children should be involved "in measuring and monitoring their own well-being" (p. 574). This approach is aligned with the United Nations Convention on the Rights of the Child (*www.unicef.org/crc*), Article 12, which states "children are full-fledged persons who have the right to express their views in all matters affecting them and requires that those views be heard and given due weight in accordance with the child's age and maturity." Following this recommendation, one of our primary aims was to develop a reliable and valid instrument, using children as informants.

Hence, the MDI was designed as a survey tool to collect information on children's social and emotional development, health, and well-being, and key contextual assets deemed as important for child development outcomes (e.g., Scales, Benson, & Mannes, 2006; Theokas & Lerner, 2006). Furthermore, the MDI was designed to feasibly be administered at large scale, so that stakeholders in communities and schools can obtain representative population-level data on five dimensions of children's social and emotional development, physical health and well-being, connectedness, school experiences, and after-school time use to inform their respective programs, actions, and services. In order to meet these criteria for the MDI, our team of researchers and community partners engaged in a 5-year development, piloting, and validation research process.

Conceptual Framework

The conceptual framework that informed the development of the MDI was derived from the literature on SEL and development (Greenberg et al., 2003), positive psychology (Huebner, Gilman, & Furlong, 2009; Seligman & Cszikzentmihalyi, 2000), resiliency and competence (Luthar, 2006; Masten & Coatsworth, 1998), and a strengths- and asset-based approach to child development (Lerner, Fisher, & Weinberg, 2000; Theokas & Lerner, 2006). Moreover, the development of the MDI was informed by bioecological theories on human development (Bronfenbrenner, 1979, 2005) and theories that emphasize the developmental primacy of social relationships (Ainsworth & Bowlby, 1991; Ryan & Deci, 2000; Thompson, 1999). These theories illustrate how social, biological, and cultural factors in different ecological contexts (e.g., family, school, community) jointly influence children's development. Accordingly, the MDI was designed to obtain information on children's relationships across multiple contexts (peers, adults in schools and neighborhoods), their experiences and activities in their primary social ecologies (family, school, community), and their social and emotional development, physical health, and well-being.

The Stages of the MDI Development

The first stage for the MDI project team was to conduct an extensive literature review. The aim of the literature review was to identify the constructs and developmental domains that are, conceptually and empirically, considered to be essential in middle childhood and adolescence (e.g., Del Giudice, 2014; Eccles, 1999; Masten & Coatsworth, 1989). The review specifically focused on capturing constructs and domains that are relevant to the development of competence and well-being in middle childhood and adolescence. In addition, we consulted (via focus groups or surveys) with educational staff and community program and service providers, to find out what type of self-report information from children would be particularly informative for their respective practices and programs.

Resulting from this process, six broad domains were identified: (1) social and emotional development; (2) physical health and well-being; (3) connectedness (relationships with adults and peers); (4) school experiences; (5) after-school time use; and (6) academic skills and achievement. The domain of academic skills and achievement was eventually, however, not considered for inclusion in the MDI, because schools in BC regularly collect students' grades and data from standardized achievement tests (*www.bced.gov.bc.ca/assessment/fsa*).

In a second step, it was determined which constructs within the remaining five domains should be included. This step involved the identification of reliable and valid items and/or scales for the identified constructs. The criteria for consideration were (1) reliability (i.e., strong internal consistency of items on the subscales), (2) validity (research evidence that the construct measures what it is supposed to measure), and (3) age appropriateness (ages 9–12) of the questions' content and wording. The original list of candidates included more than 300 items, from more than 100 scales. These included scales that the researchers in the MDI project had used in their previous research (Schonert-Reichl et al., 2007; Hymel, White, & Ishiyama, 2004), as well as scales that have been used in other large-scale research projects on middle childhood and adolescence. From this list, scales that did not meet the above criteria were excluded. Also, when two or more scales assessed very similar constructs and correlated highly (according to published research of our own data), only the scale with the better/best psychometric properties and broadest validity evidence was kept. Throughout this process, decisions were made in consultation with all MDI project partners, to draw on their respective expertise. Among the researchers on the MDI team, there were individuals with expertise in psychometric research, assessment, questionnaire development, developmental theory, and child development. Among the school board and the community organization partners, there were individuals with the insights to anticipate which items and scales would be considered to have face validity and would be of particular interest to or potential conflict to parents, teachers, school administrators, policymakers, and Ministry of Education delegates. The resulting selection of items and scales was circulated among a group of parents, educational staff, and school board administrators who were not directly involved in the development of the MDI. According to their feedback, a few additional revisions were made (e.g., rewording instructions; adding definitions of the words *bullying* and *community/neighborhood*). One key lesson learned throughout this entire process was the importance of an interdisciplinary team who possessed expertise on many aspects of survey development coupled with engagement of key stakeholders who could provide invaluable information and direction.

From its inception, the purpose of the MDI was to yield findings that can facilitate meaningful change in children's environments and enhance their SEC and well-being. Informed by what has been called the "science and practice of knowledge translation" (Straus et al., 2011), the MDI was developed in accordance with recommended best practices for encouraging stakeholders' use of the data. This included engaging knowledge users throughout the entire research process, from determining what items should be measured on the MDI, to how data should be reported, and how we could facilitate sustained use of the data over time (Baumbusch et al., 2008; Green et al., 2009; Straus et al., 2011).

After a series of pilot tests, the final MDI contained six demographic questions (gender, birth date, family/household members, first language(s) learned, language(s) spoken at home, English reading proficiency) and 72 items that assessed five domains of children's development and well-being: (1) social and emotional development, (2) connectedness with parents, schools, peers, and neighborhoods, (3) school experiences, (4) physical health and well-being, and (5) constructive use of after-school time. Each domain is comprised of several subscales or of individual items (Schonert-Reichl, 2011; Thomson et al., 2018). Because the questionnaire asks questions about peer relationships, bullying/victimization, and school climate, children may indicate at the end of the questionnaire—on a separate, detachable sheet—whether they "want help with problems [they] are having with other students." For the list of each dimension with related constructs, see Table 12.1.

TABLE 12.1. MDI Dimensions and Measures

MDI dimensions	Measures	Measures in the grade 7 MDI only
Social and emotional development	*Optimism* Empathy Prosocial behavior *Self-esteem* *Happiness* *Absence of sadness* Absence of worries Self-regulation (short term) Self-regulation (long term)	Responsible decision making Self-awareness Perseverance Assertiveness Citizenship/social responsibility
Physical health and well-being	*General health* **Eating breakfast** **Meals at home with family** Junk food **Frequency of good sleep** Help-seeking for emotional well-being Transportation to and from school	
Connectedness	**Adults at school** **Adults in the neighborhood** **Adults at home** **Peer belonging** **Friendship intimacy** Important adults	

Use of after-school time	**Organized activities**
	  Educational lessons or activities
	  Youth organizations
	  Sports
	  Music or arts
	How children spend their time
	After-school people/places
	Children's wishes and barriers	

School experiences	Academic self-concept School climate School belonging Motivation Future goals Victimization and bullying	

Note. Measures in the Well-Being Index are shown in *italics*; measures in the Assets Index in **bold**.

A final step in the development of the MDI was the later expansion of the survey for children in seventh grade. Three years after the grade 4 MDI was initially implemented in schools, a grade 7 version was introduced. The grade 7 MDI enables educators to monitor students' social and emotional well-being during a developmental period when children begin to face greater pressures socially and academically (Eccles, 2004; Eccles & Roeser, 2013) and when many chronic mental health issues related to social and emotional health begin to be observed (Kessler, Berglund, Demler, Jin, & Walters, 2005). Furthermore, in Canada, grade 7 is the last year of elementary school before children graduate to high school and therefore a last opportunity to assess social–emotional trends in the same population of students longitudinally. The grade 7 survey contains all of the items in the grade 4 measure and an additional five constructs that are either more relevant to older children's experiences (i.e., "citizenship and social responsibility" including volunteering experiences and graduation plans) or constructs that are only validated as a self-report scale for children in grades 6 or higher (i.e., "self-awareness" [Moilanen, 2007] and "responsible decision making" [Fuligni & Eccles, 1993; Wentzel, 1993]). Other constructs ("perseverance" [Kern, Benson, Steinberg, & Steinberg, 2016] and "assertiveness" [Springer & Phillips, 1997]) are developmentally appropriate at both ages, but had been cut from the grade 4 version to keep the survey a manageable length for younger children as determined in the feasibility studies.

Relevance of the MDI within the BC Assessment Landscape

As noted above, an essential component in the development of the MDI was inclusion of school and community partners. This was important in order to garner buy-in for MDI implementation in schools and communities, as well as to promote the usability of MDI data. Given that stakeholders in schools and communities had a voice regarding core questions and concepts to address within the MDI, many of those involved were eager to implement the survey to learn how the children in their jurisdictions were doing with regard to their social and emotional skills and their social contexts. Furthermore, stakeholders were keen to implement the MDI specifically with fourth and seventh graders because it measured dimensions of children's development not currently being measured elsewhere in the system, but that complemented existing student data (i.e., measures of academic ability, and school readiness in kindergarten). In BC, academic skills are routinely assessed in grade 4 and grade 7 using the standardized Foundation Skills Assessment exam (FSA; British Columbia Ministry of Education, 2016). In this context, many schools were experienced with implementing large-scale assessment systems. Furthermore, several school district and ministry administrators had personally participated in past collaborations with the

MDI research team on the EDI survey, which had already been administered provincewide for the past decade. Stakeholders therefore saw the MDI as a valuable expansion of the established assessment routine in BC in several ways: (1) It was the first time children could routinely self-report on their own well-being; (2) It provided insight into development during middle childhood and early adolescence; (3) The MDI was strengths-based; and (4) It was linkable to children's kindergarten school readiness and grades 4 and 7 academic achievement data to provide a more fulsome picture of children's development in BC and better understanding of associations between early childhood development, academic success, and social and emotional well-being (Gadermann et al., 2016; Gregory et al., 2020; Guhn, Gadermann, Almas, Schonert-Reichl, & Hertzman, 2016).

In 2015, the BC Ministry of Education redesigned the K–12 education curriculum to include "personal and social competency" as one of three core competencies for all students attending public and independent schools in BC (*https://curriculum.gov.bc.ca/competencies;* British Columbia Ministry of Education, 2015). This curriculum change reflects the increasing weight policymakers place on children's social–emotional development in BC. Additionally, the new curriculum further enhances the potential role of the MDI in school-based assessments, because the criteria for "success in school" now explicitly include positive personal and cultural identity, personal awareness and responsibility, and social responsibility—dimensions that are specifically assessed on the MDI. The policy change presents a unique opportunity in that it serves as a natural experiment via which one could evaluate the impacts of the SEL-focused curriculum on children's MDI scores at a population level.

Alignment with CASEL's SEL Framework

After identifying these five broad MDI domains, connections were drawn with measurement frameworks developed by leading experts in children's social and emotional skills, specifically the CASEL (*www.casel.org*) framework for SEL—a framework used in school districts across BC, Canada, and internationally, and one which research has demonstrated to be associated with positive outcomes for students (Durlak, Weissberg, Dymnicki, Taylor, & Schellinger, 2011). Particularly within the grade 7 version of the MDI (which allowed for the inclusion of more items), all of the MDI subscales can be linked to abilities and skills outlined in CASEL's core SECs (i.e., self-awareness, social-awareness, self-management, relationship skills, and responsible decision making; CASEL, 2013; Elias at al., 1997). A comparison of CASEL's core competencies and the constructs measured on the MDI is presented in Table 12.2, including both the CASEL 5 competencies and CASEL Key Settings.

TABLE 12.2. Comparison of CASEL's Core Competencies and the MDI Constructs

Core SEL competencies defined by CASEL (*www.CASEL.org*)	MDI constructs
Self-awareness: The abilities to understand one's own emotions, thoughts, and values and how they influence behavior across contexts. This includes capacities to recognize one's strengths and limitations with a well-grounded sense of confidence and purpose.	Optimism Self-awareness Academic self-efficacy Self-esteem (self-concept)
Social awareness: The abilities to understand the perspectives of and empathize with others, including those from diverse backgrounds, cultures, and contexts. This includes the capacities to feel compassion for others, understand broader historical and social norms for behavior in different settings, and recognize family, school, and community resources and supports.	Empathy
Self-management: The abilities to manage one's emotions, thoughts, and behaviors effectively in different situations and to achieve goals and aspirations. This includes the capacities to delay gratification, manage stress, and feel motivation and agency to accomplish personal/collective goals.	Short-term self-regulation Long-term self-regulation Perseverance Health habits
Relationship skills: The abilities to establish and maintain healthy and supportive relationships and to effectively navigate settings with diverse individuals and groups. This includes the capacities to communicate clearly, listen actively, cooperate, work collaboratively to problem solve and negotiate conflict constructively, navigate settings with differing social and cultural demands and opportunities, provide leadership, and seek or offer help when needed.	Assertiveness Prosocial behavior Friendship intimacy Help-seeking Peer belonging
Responsible decision making: The abilities to make caring and constructive choices about personal behavior and social interactions across diverse situations. This includes the capacities to consider ethical standards and safety concerns, and to evaluate the benefits and consequences of various actions for personal, social, and collective well-being.	Responsible decision making Citizenship and social responsibility

Moving from Data to Action with the MDI

The increasingly widespread recognition of children's SEC as a foundational component of life-course success and well-being is a significant accomplishment of collaborative efforts between researchers, practitioners, and policymakers (Humphrey, 2013; Weissberg et al., 2015). That said, assessment systems that fail to involve key stakeholders or fail to present data in an accessible format are unlikely to have meaningful impacts (Baumbusch et al., 2008; Green, Ottoson, García, & Hiatt, 2009). Clearly, any successful reform effort needs to involve administrators, teachers, and students together in creating a high-quality and respectful educational environment in which they feel motivated and supported (see Table 12.3 for a list of environments where SEL can be fostered and the associated MDI measures; Schonert-Reichl, 2017). Indeed, we must take heed of the words of Seymour Sarason (1982) who so wisely posited: "To the extent that the effort at change identifies and meaningfully involves all those who directly or indirectly will be affected by the change, to that extent the effort stands a chance to be successful" (p. 294).

Obtaining Buy-In: Highlighting the Unique Properties of the MDI

Central to the MDI are three unique properties that have greatly contributed to acceptance and usefulness of the MDI in schools and communities across the world. First, because the MDI is a self-report survey, it provides children with voice in reporting how they feel, how they spend their time, and what they would want to see changed within their schools and communities that is aligned with Article 12 of the United Nations Convention on the Rights of the Child (United Nations, 1989). Hence, the MDI enables children to participate in shaping their environments and emphasizes the value of listening to children's perspectives (Schonert-Reichl et al., 2012). Second, the survey gathers data at a population level; all children within participating school districts take part in the MDI unless they, or their parent, opt out. This method avoids common sampling pitfalls including underrepresentation of children from ethnic minorities or families with lower educational attainment (Anderman et al., 1995; Ellwood et al., 2010). It also promotes stakeholder interest in the results, as the survey data represent actual children within a local context as opposed to a statistic derived from a sample of children in another community (Guhn et al., 2012). Third, implementation of the survey requires collaboration between schools, school districts, and community partners, which facilitates the use of the data once results are reported. Systematic evaluation of MDI knowledge-translation activities have identified that knowledge

TABLE 12.3. Environments for Fostering SEL and Associated MDI Measures

Environments for fostering SEL as identified by CASEL	MDI Measures

Communities	Help-seeking for emotional well-being
	Transportation to and from school
	Connectedness to adults in the neighborhood/community
	Important adults in the neighborhood/community
	Organized activities
	    Educational lessons or activities
	    Youth organizations
	    Sports
	    Music or arts
	How children spend their time
	After-school people/places
	    Safe places in neighborhood/community to hang out
	    Neighborhood/community programs for children their age
	Volunteering

Families and caregivers	Connectedness to adults at home Meals at home with family Help-seeking for emotional well-being
Schools	School climate School belonging Connectedness to adults at school Important adults at school Help-seeking for emotional well-being Victimization and bullying After-school people/places

users including policymakers, community stakeholders, and school administrators value the MDI as a "common language" that facilitates resource allocation and goal setting between otherwise isolated departments and organizations invested in children's healthy development.

Reporting Data to Schools and Communities

As a population-level measure, the MDI data are used in a systemic capacity in supporting schools, out-of-school programs, and government. From this perspective, four key knowledge user audiences were considered of particular importance for effective knowledge translation: (1) policymakers, (2) educators and education administrators, (3) community planners, and (4) children. Although the MDI reporting structure was developed with these primary groups in mind, it is important to note that parents have also been engaged in the results through public presentations and Parent

Associate Committee meetings and free online accessibility to MDI community reports and maps. Furthermore, specifically designed resources for educators, community members, and other stakeholders, including parents, can be found in an online toolkit—Discover MDI (*www.discovermdi.ca*). The toolkit features shareable, plain-language walk-throughs of key MDI concepts, tools and tips for presenting MDI data, and recommendations for using the MDI to initiate change in schools and communities. It is aimed at a diverse set of users: those new to the MDI and those who want to deepen their work with their MDI data.

In consultation with members of each of the stakeholder groups, a variety of knowledge visualizations and syntheses were developed, and knowledge products and tools that would best meet their needs, including comprehensive reports, neighborhood and school district maps packages, webinars, networking events, and development of an online knowledge user toolkit. This process was highly interactive and iterative. Although researchers began to make meaning of the MDI data, the way in which data users were absorbing and interpreting the data informed improved approaches that had increased relevance and resonance. This process of adaptation and improvement has continued since 2010 and is an essential aspect of our ongoing community engagement and knowledge-translation strategy.

Data Visualization and Dissemination Strategies

Relevance and usability are regarded as two of the most important aspects of whether or not research results translate into practice (Green et al., 2009). As such, knowledge-translation products were designed according to the criteria of being clear, yet complex enough to be useful for our diverse key audiences. Based on our previous research collaborations with knowledge users, we had learned that (1) educators were motivated to see the practical relevance of the data for their own day-to-day activities, (2) administrators wished to recognize or envision the data's potential benefit for their schools, and (3) policymakers wished to obtain research evidence that enhanced their political mandates (Guhn et al., 2012). Timeliness of data reporting (i.e., receiving MDI results prior to budget decisions for the following fiscal year) was also identified as an important factor for determining uptake within schools and communities.[1] Consequently, two levels of reporting were developed to meet these diverse needs.

---

[1] Because MDI data are aggregated at the school rather than classroom level, timeliness of reporting has been a consideration primarily for planning and programming decisions at the school level. Data are collected in November and reported the following March.

At the first reporting level, confidential school reports created separately for grade 4 and grade 7 are provided to each participating school. These reports feature a variety of visual representations of each school's data (i.e., children's average scores across SEL indicators) compared to the school district average. The purpose of these reports is to help school staff identify areas of social and emotional development and assets in each grade level (i.e., adult relationships, peer relationships, nutrition and health, constructive use of after-school time, school experiences) in which their children fared well or excelled, and areas in which their social and emotional development and assets needed to be enhanced and supported. Grade-4 and grade-7 surveys contain slightly different items and are used by slightly different audiences. For example, high school principals will often request the grade-7 reports from the principals of elementary or middle school "feeder" schools in their area. We also developed a series of infographics to communicate summary statistics that would be easily interpretable and engaging for students to be able to participate in the unpacking of their MDI results with their teachers.

Figures 12.1 to 12.4 provide examples of these infographics illustrating how data on children's average self-reported social and emotional development within a school compared with the school district average; well-being and assets indices; connectedness to adults at school, at home, and the neighborhood; and other school experiences are presented. Based on consultation with educators and administrators, it was determined that the

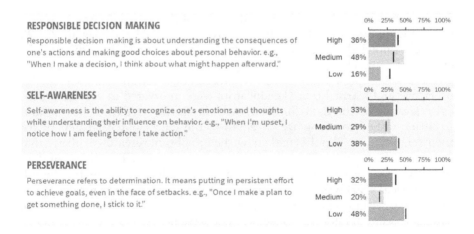

FIGURE 12.1. Examples of MDI graphs for students' SECs. Image courtesy of the Human Early Learning Partnership, University of British Columbia, School of Population and Public Health, April 2021 (*http://earlylearning.ubc.ca/mdi*).

Well-Being Index

 **High Well-Being (Thriving)**
Children who score in the high range on at least 4 of the 5 measures of well-being and have no low-range scores.

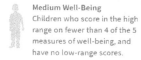 **Medium Well-Being**
Children who score in the high range on fewer than 4 of the 5 measures of well-being, and have no low-range scores.

 **Low Well-Being**
Children who score in the low range on at least 1 of the 5 measures of well-being.

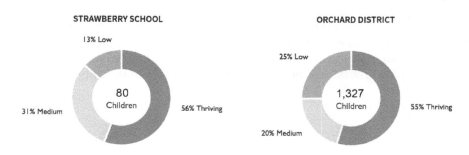

STRAWBERRY SCHOOL

13% Low

80 Children

31% Medium

56% Thriving

ORCHARD DISTRICT

25% Low

1,327 Children

55% Thriving

20% Medium

Assets Index

Percentage of children reporting the presence of an asset

<70%   70-79%   80-89%   90%>

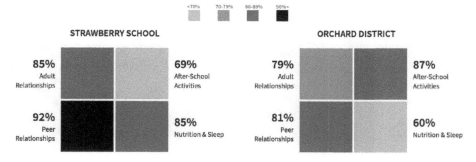

STRAWBERRY SCHOOL

85% Adult Relationships

69% After-School Activities

92% Peer Relationships

85% Nutrition & Sleep

ORCHARD DISTRICT

79% Adult Relationships

87% After-School Activities

81% Peer Relationships

60% Nutrition & Sleep

FIGURE 12.2. The MDI well-being and assets indices. Image courtesy of the Human Early Learning Partnership, University of British Columbia, School of Population and Public Health, April 2021 (*http://earlylearning.ubc.ca/mdi*).

school-level reports remain confidential to each school and school district in order to avoid public comparisons or rankings of schools. This decision also addressed a public reaction to previously perceived misuse of provincially collected academic achievement data that had been used for purposes other than intended, by publicly ranking schools according to students' scores on standardized achievement tests, and without contextualizing the school achievement data (that is, without, for example, taking into account socioeconomic status differences).

A key strategy supporting the uptake of the information in these reports, thus ensuring a higher degree of translation into action, has been a direct and concerted knowledge-brokering strategy. This function has been described in a range of public health settings (Ward, House, & Hamer, 2009) and has been employed broadly by the Human Early Learning Partnership (HELP) across a number of years to facilitate uptake of research. In the case of the MDI, this has included a range of activities that include direct contact face-to-face with school users (including workshops and presentations), training and discussion webinars, and smaller strategic discussions. This process has proven extremely valuable in developing ongoing

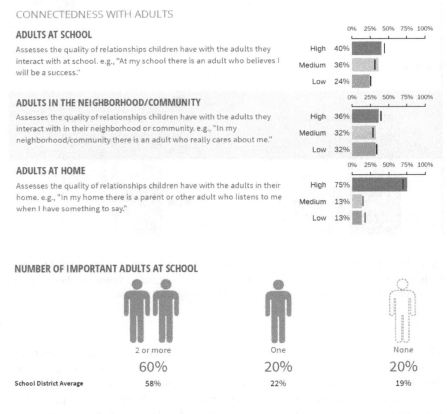

FIGURE 12.3. MDI infographics for connectedness with adults at school, in the neighborhood/community, and at home, and for number of important adults. Image courtesy of the Human Early Learning Partnership, University of British Columbia, School of Population and Public Health, April 2021 (*http://earlylearning.ubc.ca/mdi*).

Percentage of children who feel it is **very important** to:

56%	36%	40%
make friends	get good grades	learn new things

I plan to graduate from high school.

96%   4%

Yes   No

Percentage of children who **agree a little** or **agree a lot** that:

I plan to graduate from college, university, or some other training after high school.

When I grow up, I have goals and plans for the future.   I feel I have important things to do in the future.

84%   16%

78%   68%   Yes   No

FIGURE 12.4. Sample infographics. Image courtesy of the Human Early Learning Partnership, University of British Columbia, School of Population and Public Health, April 2021 (*http://earlylearning.ubc.ca/mdi*).

relationships with knowledge users and in understanding more fully how MDI data can be used more effectively in a school context. This has fed directly into the process of ongoing adaptation and improvement as reporting approaches are increasingly focused on the needs of users.

At the second reporting level, school district and community reports are provided aggregate children's MDI scores by the total school district, and by neighborhood (accessible from *www.earlylearning.ubc.ca/mdi*). Similar to the confidential school reports, scores for each neighborhood can be compared against the school district total to identify areas of relative strength and weakness. In addition, one of the most important features of the MDI reports is geospatial data mapping that reports MDI data using "heat maps" defined by existing recognized neighborhood boundaries (see Figure 12.5). Data are mapped according to children's block-level residential address rather than the school address, thereby maintaining the relevance of the data for neighborhood communities while discouraging school comparisons, as many children attend school outside their school catchment area. The maps in Figure 12.5 illustrate two composite scores that were developed to quickly summarize child outcomes at the neighborhood level. The well-being index (top of figure) is an aggregate measure of children's optimism, self-esteem, happiness, sadness, and general health. Darker shades indicate a higher level of overall well-being (thriving). The after-school time asset (bottom of figure) is one of four contextual assets (including adult relationships, peer relationships, and nutrition and sleep). Darker shades

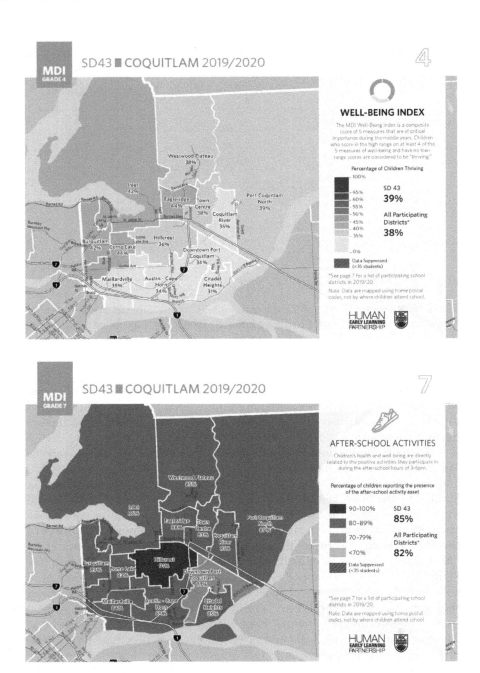

FIGURE 12.5. MDI maps by school district/community for well-being and participation in after-school activities. Image courtesy of the Human Early Learning Partnership, University of British Columbia, School of Population and Public Health, April 2021 (*http://earlylearning.ubc.ca/mdi*).

indicate that a greater proportion of children in that neighborhood reported participating in structured after-school programs between 3 to 6 P.M.

The maps have been powerful in their ability to effectively create awareness around the large neighborhood-to-neighborhood variability in foundational child well-being indicators and social context factors (inequities are easily visible). The maps also provide representative research evidence about children and their environmental context for *local communities* (as opposed to aggregated at a provincial level) that engages audiences differently and allows knowledge users to engage in meaning-making. That is, community members can relate their own knowledge of their children and their community contexts to the research findings presented to them. As a result, the MDI community maps have been particularly useful to community planners and policymakers for quickly identifying geographic areas within their municipalities where children are experiencing strengths and assets and where they are experiencing challenges. MDI maps can also support efforts to increase equity for children in schools and community. That is, the neighborhood maps provide a visual representation of how the assets that are present in children's lives are distributed throughout the neighborhoods in a community. These maps and the accompanying reports for each neighborhood can help illuminate inequities present in a community and provide a starting point for work to improve equity in a community. For example, in the case of the map for after-school time (see Figure 12.5, bottom), educators and other decision makers can identify neighborhoods in which there is a low proportion of children participating in structured after-school activities, and then find ways to make programs more accessible for children, by first identifying the barriers, such as cost and transportation, in those neighborhoods.

Furthermore, because the data can be collected every year, these maps and reports can also be used to track children's well-being and social contexts over time to evaluate impacts of interventions at local and municipal levels. Unlike the school reports that are only available to schools, the community-level reports are publicly available and make it possible to compare results across neighborhoods and across districts. These comparisons can be useful if the purpose is to find similarities and differences within regions that can help explain the data. For example, accompanying neighborhood-level data presented within the reports further enables knowledge users to unpack the data to identify which particular indicators (e.g., peer belonging, friendship intimacy) are driving social and emotional development outcomes. Engaging stakeholders in these discussions has been helpful in promoting collaboration toward the common purpose of improving children's well-being, rather than creating competition. A similar strategy of knowledge brokering used with schools has also unfolded with community organizations and collaborative structures. This has been essential in ensuring that MDI data are used to connect schools with the broader after-school sector so that more seamless and comprehensive approaches to supporting children can be developed.

• MDI Outcomes and Impacts

An increasingly important part of knowledge-translation activities in the MDI project has been the collection of community stories about how MDI data have been used and how it has impacted children. These stories are essential in connecting MDI users with each other so that learning about how to move to action happens at a peer-to-peer level. Stories have been shared with other knowledge users through an online toolkit, the MDI Field Guide, to inspire engagement in similar initiatives (see an online toolkit, *www.discovermdi.ca*).

We know that "it takes a village to raise a child" so it is best not to attempt change without engaging stakeholders at all levels. That's why the MDI Field Guide has been designed to be a collaborative space where users can ask questions, submit their ideas, and share their stories with others who are using MDI data and concepts in their work in BC and across Canada. The Field Guide features shareable, plain-language walkthroughs of key MDI concepts, "Quicksheets" that describe key MDI domains, tools and tips for presenting MDI data, and recommendations for using the MDI to initiate change in schools and communities. It is aimed at a diverse set of users: those new to the MDI and those who want to deepen their work with their MDI data.

One example of the way in which the MDI data have been used to catalyze action is illustrated by work in Revelstoke, a small rural school district in BC in which educational leaders and stakeholders have engaged collaboratively to work with MDI data to improve the well-being of their students. The Revelstoke School District has been collecting MDI data with their fourth-grade students since 2010 and seventh-grade students since 2013. Their "District Achievement Contract" has focused on supporting student's health and well-being as one of three areas of focus. Subsequently, all schools in the district are tracking MDI results in their annual school plans.

As a result of tracking MDI results over time, educators and community partners in Revelstoke's schools have been able to identify areas of strength and improvement. By incorporating MDI data into their planning, they are working toward building a wide variety of activities and programs to help to improve the presence of assets in children's lives and build students' SECs. Examples of the district's initiatives include: (1) "Healthy

Habits" programs at the elementary level that involve multi-age groupings with students studying specific themes on health and SECs in small-group settings with the support of all staff; (2) Action Schools projects taking place at each of the elementary schools that are engaging students in leadership roles and providing opportunities for staff to engage in healthy activities; (3) An elementary school breakfast program pilot that is currently providing healthy breakfast for students before school two mornings per week, a program receiving significant support from the community and from the Parent Advisory Council; and (4) "Neighborhood of Learning Spaces" that are occupied by community service providers including "youth liaisons" and mental health workers and facilitate on-site access for students.

Another example of how the MDI data have catalyzed action in schools comes from another school district in BC. The Alberni School District on Vancouver Island was an early adopter of the MDI. In this district, the MDI is seen as more than a data collection tool to track children's well-being and SECs. Instead, it is seen as a mechanism to support increased understanding of, and commitment to, their students' social and emotional well-being, and a leverage point for building district-wide initiatives. During their first year of MDI participation in 2013, students' relationships and connections with educators and staff within the school was highlighted as an area of significant concern. For example, the percent of seventh-grade students indicating the presence of two or more important adults in their school was low, at only 34%, and the number of students reporting no adults as important at school was high at 53%. Informed from research provided by the MDI team at UBC demonstrating that adult connections in school, including the quality of relationships children have with the adults at their school, predicts well-being and prosocial behavior (Oberle, Schonert-Reichl, Guhn, Zumbo, & Hertzman, 2014), the educators in the Alberni School District developed an increased awareness of both the issue and its implications. This sparked the district's commitment to developing intentional strategies to fostering caring and supportive relationships between educators and students. Using MDI to monitor their intentional and explicit efforts to connect with students on a regular basis, subsequent MDI data suggested that, through collective effort, some substantial improvements were seen. Specifically, MDI data showed a significant change of seventh-grade students' reporting of important adults from 34% in 2013 to 2014 to 51% in 2015 to 2016. Similarly, the percent of seventh-grade students indicating that they do not have an important adult at school decreased from 53% to 30% for the same years. This is one of a number of case studies that illustrate the power of the MDI to catalyze action to improve the well-being of students. (Note that these and other stories can be found in the MDI Field Guide, *www.discovermdi.ca*).

● Conclusions

Initial buy-in to the MDI may have been influenced by the novelty of social and emotional assessment in BC, ability of data to be linked to other assessment tools, or familiarity with our existing research including the EDI school readiness measure. Its staying power, however, is likely creditable to the value schools and communities see in the results. While evaluating the effectiveness of our knowledge translation activities remains a priority, initial feedback indicates that the data are presented in a way that is accessible and interpretable to our key audiences, including children themselves. The MDI has been well-received by participants and stakeholders and is garnering more national and international interest. Knowledge users also report high satisfaction with the reports and maps. Furthermore, from an academic standpoint, data collected from the MDI have significantly contributed to an improved understanding of the importance of social and emotional well-being in the middle years and identification of factors that predict children's health and well-being throughout childhood and adolescence (Gadermann et al., 2015; Guhn et al., 2016; Guhn et al., 2013; Oberle, Schonert-Reichl, Guhn, Zumbo, & Hertzman, 2014).

From its very inception, the central goal of the MDI was to develop an assessment tool that reliably and validly measured children's SECs and at the same time facilitated improvements to children's environments by identifying modifiable, "actionable" factors such as adult and peer connectedness, sleep and nutrition, and after-school opportunities (Oberle, Guhn, Gadermann, Thomson, & Schonert-Reichl, 2018; Oberle, Ji, Guhn, Schonert-Reichl, & Gadermann, 2019; Oberle, Ji, Kerai, Guhn, et al., 2020; Oberle, Ji, Magee, Guhn, et al., 2019). Some remaining questions pertain to whether the MDI data are consistently being used and the degree to which MDI data are leading to positive change for children. As illustrated by the stories presented earlier, we have witnessed examples of the MDI's usefulness, including serving as a catalyst for improved services for children and as a way in which to unite stakeholders around a common goal, or initiate a process of further inquiry. However, we have also heard stories in which administrators who do not share their results with their educators, either because of a lack of confidence in the veracity of child self-report data or because they do not want to share any findings that might challenge educators' current practices.

Over the past several years, there has been a growing interest in and literature identifying the necessity of assessing and measuring the SECs of children and youth. With ever increasing demands for accountability, it appears that we can no longer rely on our "common sense" or "good hunches" in knowing what does or does not work (Schonert-Reichl, 2019). As noted by Slavin (2008), "throughout the history of education, the adoption of instructional programs and practices has been driven more by ideology, faddism, politics, and marketing than by evidence" (p. 5). As SEL becomes integrated into education systems throughout Canada, the United States, and worldwide, it will be critical that population-level assessment systems engage schools and communities early and meaningfully in their evaluations in order to facilitate the full utilization of the data and to promote collaborative initiatives that optimize the chances of improving social and emotional outcomes for all children.

REFERENCES

Ainsworth, M. D. S., & Bowlby, J. (1991). An ethological approach to personality development. *American Psychologist, 46,* 333–341.

Anderman, C., Cheadle, A., Curry, S., Diehr, P., Shultz, L., & Wagner, E. (1995). Selection bias related to parental consent in school-based survey research. *Evaluation Review, 19,* 663–674.

Baumbusch, J. L., Kirkham, S. R., Khan, K. B., McDonald, H., Semeniuk, P., Tan, E., & Anderson, J. M. (2008). Pursuing common agendas: A collaborative model for knowledge translation between research and practice in clinical settings. *Research in Nursing & Health, 31,* 130–140.

Ben-Arieh, A. (2005). Where are the children? Children's role in measuring and monitoring their wellbeing. *Social Indicators Research, 74,* 573–596.

British Columbia Ministry of Education. (2015). Curriculum core competencies. Retrieved September 23, 2016, from *https://curriculum.gov.bc.ca/competencies*.

British Columbia Ministry of Education. (2016). Foundation skills assessment. Retrieved September 23, 2016, from *www.bced.gov.bc.ca/assessment/fsa*.

Bronfenbrenner, U. (1979). *The ecology of human development: Experiments by nature and design.* Harvard University Press.

Bronfenbrenner, U. (Ed.) (2005). *Making human beings human. Bioecological perspectives on human development.* Sage.

Collaborative for Academic, Social, and Emotional Learning. (2013). *2013 CASEL guide: Effective social and emotional learning programs—Preschool and elementary school edition.* Author.

Del Giudice, M. (2014). Middle childhood: An evolutionary-developmental synthesis. *Child Development Perspectives, 8*(4), 193–200.

Durlak, J. A., Weissberg, R. P., Dymnicki, A. B., Taylor, R. D., & Schellinger, K. B. (2011). The impact of enhancing students' social and emotional learning: A meta-analysis of school-based universal interventions. *Child Development, 82,* 405–32.

Eccles, J. S. (1999). The development of children ages 6 to 14. *Future of Children, 9*(2), 30–44.

Eccles, J. S. (2004). Schools, academic motivation, and stage-environment fit. In R. M. Lerner & L. Steinberg (Eds.), *Handbook of adolescent psychology* (2nd ed., pp. 125–153). Wiley.

Eccles, J. S., & Roeser, R. W. (2013). Schools as developmental contexts during adolescence. In I. Weiner (Ed.), *Handbook of psychology: Vol. 6. Developmental psychology* (pp. 321–337). Wiley.

Elias, M. J., Zins, J. E., Weissberg, R. P., Frey, K. S., Greenberg, M. T., Haynes, N. M., . . . Shriver, T. P. (1997). *Promoting social and emotional learning: Guidelines for educators.* ASCD.

Ellwood, P., Asher, M. I., Stewart, A. W., Aït-Khaled, N., Anderson, H. R., Beasley, R., . . . Nilsson, L. (2010). The impact of the method of consent on response rates in the ISAAC time trends study. *International Journal of Tuberculosis and Lung Disease, 14,* 1059–1065.

Emerson, S. D., Mâsse, L. C., Ark, T. K., Schonert-Reichl, K. A., & Guhn, M. (2018). A population-based analysis of life satisfaction and social support among children of diverse backgrounds in British Columbia, Canada. *Quality of Life Research, 27*(10), 2595–2607.

Fuligni, A. J., & Eccles, J. S. (1993). Perceived parent-child relationships and early adolescents' orientation toward peers. *Developmental Psychology, 29,* 622–632.

Gadermann, A. M., Guhn, M., Schonert-Reichl, K. A., Hymel, S., Thomson, K., & Hertzman, C. (2016). A population-based study of children's well-being and health: The relative importance of social relationships, health-related activities, and income. *Journal of Happiness Studies, 17*(5), 1847–1872.

Green, L. W., Ottoson, J. M., García, C., & Hiatt, R. A. (2009). Diffusion theory and knowledge dissemination, utilization, and integration in public health. *Annual Review of Public Health, 30,* 151–174.

Greenberg, M. T., Domitrovich, C. E., Weissberg, R. P., & Durlak, J. A. (2017). Social and emotional learning as a public health approach. *Future of Children, 27*(1), 13–32.

Greenberg, M. T., Weissberg, R. P., O'Brien, M. U., Zins, J. E., Fredericks, L., Resnik, H., & Elias, M. J. (2003). Enhancing school-based prevention and youth development through coordinated social, emotional, and academic learning. *American Psychologist, 58,* 466–474.

Gregory, T., Dal Grande, E., Brushe, M., Engelhardt, D., Luddy, S., Guhn, M., . . . Brinkman, S. (2020). Associations between school readiness and student well-being: A six-year follow up study. *Child Indicators Research, 14,* 369–390.

Gregory, T., Engelhardt, D., Lewkowicz, A., Luddy, S., Guhn, M., Gadermann, A., . . . Brinkman, S. (2019). Validity of the Middle Years Development Instrument for population monitoring of student wellbeing in Australian school children. *Child Indicators Research, 12*(3), 873–899.

Guhn, M., Gadermann, A., Almas, A., Schonert-Reichl, K. A., & Hertzman, C. (2016). Associations of teacher-rated social, emotional, and cognitive development to self-reported wellbeing, peer relations, and academic test scores in middle childhood. *Early Childhood Research Quarterly, 35,* 76–84.

Guhn, M., Schonert-Reichl, K. A., Gadermann, A. M., Marriott, D., Pedrini, L., Hymel, S., & Hertzman, C. (2012). Well-being in middle childhood: An assets-based population-level research-to-action project. *Child Indicators Research, 5*(2), 393–418.

Huebner, E. S., Gilman, R., & Furlong, M. J. (2009). A conceptual model for research in positive psychology in children and youth. In E. S. Huebner, R. Gilman, & M. J. Furlong (Eds.), *Handbook of positive psychology in schools* (pp. 3–8). Routledge/Taylor & Francis.

Humphrey, N. (2013). *Social and emotional learning: A critical appraisal*. Sage.

Hymel, S., White, A., & Ishiyama, I. (2004). *Safe School Student Survey*. West Vancouver School District.

Jagers, R. J., Rivas-Drake, D., & Williams, B. (2019). Transformative social and emotional learning (SEL): Toward SEL in service of educational equity and excellence. *Educational Psychologist, 54*(3), 162–184.

Janus, M., & Offord, D. R. (2007). Development and psychometric properties of the Early Development Instrument (EDI): A measure of children's school readiness. *Canadian Journal of Behavioral Science/Revue Canadienne des Sciences du Comportement, 39,* 1–22.

Kern, M. L., Benson, L., Steinberg, E. A., & Steinberg, L. (2016). The EPOCH measure of adolescent well-being. *Psychological Assessment, 28,* 586–597.

Kessler, R. C., Berglund, P., Demler, D., Jin, R., & Walters, E. E. (2005). Lifetime prevalence and age-of-onset distributions of DSM disorders in the National Comorbidity Survey Replication. *Archives of General Psychiatry, 62, 593–602.*

Leriou, E., Kazani, A., Kollias, A., & Paraskevopoulou, C. (2021). Understanding and measuring child well-being in the region of Attica, Greece: Round one. *Child Indicators Research, 14*(1), 1–51.

Lerner, R. M., Fisher, C. B., & Weinberg, R. A. (2000). Toward a science for and of the people: Promoting civil society through the application of developmental science. *Child Development, 71,* 11–20.

Luthar, S. S. (2006). Resilience in development: A synthesis of research across five decades. In D. Cicchetti & D. J. Cohen (Eds.), *Developmental psychopathology: Risk, disorder, and adaptation* (pp. 740–795). Wiley.

Magee, C., Guhn, M., Schonert-Reichl, K. A., & Oberle, E. (2019). Mental well-being among children in foster care: The role of supportive adults. *Children & Youth Services Review, 102,* 128–134.

Mahoney, J., Weissberg, R., Greenberg, M., Dusenbury, L., Jagers, R., Niemi, K., . . . Yoder, N. (2020). Systemic social and emotional learning: Promoting educational success for all preschool to high school students. *American Psychologist,* 1–16

Masten, A. S., & Coatsworth, J. D. (1998). The development of competence in favorable and unfavorable environments: Lessons from research on successful children. *American Psychologist, 53,* 205–220.

McKown, C. (2017). Social-emotional assessment, performance, and standards. *The Future of Children, 27*(1), 157–178.

Moilanen, K. L. (2007). The Adolescent Self-Regulatory Inventory: The development and validation of a questionnaire of short-term and long-tern self-regulation. *Journal of Youth and Adolescence, 36,* 835–848.

Oberle, E., Guhn, M., Gadermann, A. M., Thomson, K., & Schonert-Reichl, K. A. (2018). Positive mental health and supportive school environments: A population-level longitudinal study of dispositional optimism and school relationships in early adolescence. *Social Science and Medicine, 214,* 154–161.

Oberle, E., Ji, X. R., Guhn, M., Schonert-Reichl, K. A., & Gadermann, A. M. (2019). Benefits of extracurricular participation in early adolescence: Associations with peer belonging and mental health. *Journal of Youth and Adolescence, 48*(11), 2255–2270.

Oberle, E., Ji, X. R., Kerai, S., Guhn, M., Schonert-Reichl, K. A., & Gadermann, A. M. (2020). Screen time and extracurricular activities as risk and protective factors for mental health in adolescence: A population-level study. *Preventive Medicine, 141,* 106291.

Oberle, E., Ji, X. R., Magee, C., Guhn, M., Schonert-Reichl, K. A., & Gadermann, A. M. (2019). Extracurricular activity profiles and wellbeing in middle childhood: A population-level study. *PLOS ONE, 14*(7), e0218488.

Oberle, E., Schonert-Reichl, K. A., Guhn, M., Zumbo, B. D., & Hertzman, C. (2014). The role of supportive adults in promoting positive development in middle childhood: A population-based study. *Canadian Journal of School Psychology, 29*(4), 296–316.

Ryan, R. M., & Deci, E. L. (2000). Self-determination theory and the facilitation of intrinsic motivation, social development, and well-being. *American Psychologist, 55,* 68–78.

Sarason, S. B. (1990). *The predictable failure of educational reform: Can we change course before it's too late?* Jossey-Bass.

Sauve, J. A., & Schonert-Reichl, K. A. (2019). Creating caring classroom and school communities: Lessons learned from social and emotional learning programs and practices. In J. A. Fredricks, A. L. Reschly, & S. L. Christenson (Eds.), *Handbook of student engagement interventions* (pp. 279–295). Academic Press.

Scales, P. C., Benson, P. L., & Mannes, M. (2006). The contribution to adolescent well-being made by nonfamily adults: An examination of developmental assets as contexts and processes. *Journal of Community Psychology, 34,* 401–413.

Schonert-Reichl, K. A. (2011). *Middle childhood inside and out: The psychological and social worlds of Canadian children ages 9–12. Full report.* Human Early Learning Partnership—University of British Columbia.

Schonert-Reichl, K. A. (2017). Social and emotional learning and teachers. *Future of Children, 27*(1), 137–155.

Schonert-Reichl, K. A. (2019). Advancements in the landscape of social and emotional learning and emerging topics on the horizon. *Educational Psychologist, 54*(3), 222–232.

Schonert-Reichl, K. A., Buote, D., Jaramillo, A., Foulkes, K., Rowcliffe, P., Calbick, J., . . . (2007). *Middle childhood inside and out: The psychological and social world of children 9–12.* University of British Columbia/United Way of the Lower Mainland.

Schonert-Reichl, K. A., Guhn, M., Gadermann, A., Hymel, S., Sweiss, L., & Hertzman, C. (2012). Development and validation of the Middle Years Development Instrument (MDI): Assessing children's well-being and assets across multiple contexts. *Social Indicators Research, 114*(2), 345–369.

Schonert-Reichl, K. A., & Weissberg, R. P. (2014). Social and emotional learning during childhood. In T. P. Gullotta & M. Bloom (Eds.), *Encyclopedia of primary prevention and health promotion* (2nd ed., pp. 936–949). Springer.

Seligman, M. E. P., & Csikszentmihalyi, M. (2000). Positive psychology. *American Psychologist, 55,* 5–14.

Slavin, R. E. (2008). Perspectives on evidence-based research in education. *Educational Researcher, 37,* 5–14.

Springer, J. F., & Phillips, J. L. (1997). *Individual Protective Factors Index (IPFI): A measure of adolescent resiliency.* Saint Louis: Evaluation Management Training Associates Inc.

Straus, S. E., Brouwers, M., Johnson, D., Lavis, J. N., Legare, F., Majumdar, S. R., . . . KT Canada Strategic Training Initiative in Health Research (STIHR). (2011). Core competencies in the science and practice of knowledge translation: Description of a Canadian strategic training initiative. *Implementation Science, 6,* 127.

Theokas, C., & Lerner, R. M. (2006). Observed ecological assets in families, schools, and neighborhoods: Conceptualization, measurement, and relations with positive and negative developmental outcomes. *Applied Developmental Science, 10,* 61–74.

Thompson, L. S. (1999). Creating partnerships with government, communities, and universities to achieve results for children. *Applied Developmental Science, 3,* 213–216.

Thomson, K. C., Oberle, E., Gadermann, A. M., Guhn, M., Rowcliffe, P., & Schonert-Reichl, K. A. (2018). Measuring social-emotional development in middle childhood: The Middle Years Development Instrument. *Journal of Applied Developmental Psychology, 55,* 107–118.

UNICEF. (2007). *Child poverty in perspective: An overview of child well-being in rich countries. Innocenti Report Card 7.* UNICEF Innocenti Research Centre.

United Nations. (1989). *Convention of the Rights of the Child.* Retrieved September 20, 2016, from *www.ohchr.org/en/professionalinterest/pages/crc.aspx.*

Ward, V. L., House, A. O., & Hamer, S. (2009). Knowledge brokering: Exploring the process of transferring knowledge into action. *BMC Health Serv Res, 9,* 12.

Weissberg, R. P., Durlak, J. A., Domitrovich, C. E., & Gullotta, T. P. (2015). Social and emotional learning: Past, present, and future. In J. A. Durlak, C. E. Domitrovich, R. P. Weissberg, & T. P. Gullotta (Eds.), *Handbook of social and emotional learning* (pp. 3–19). Guilford Press.

Weissberg, R. P., Payton, J. W., O'Brien, M. U., & Munro, S. (2007). Social and emotional learning. In F. C. Power, R. J. Nuzzi, D. Narvaez, D. K. Lapsley, & T. C. Hunt (Eds.), *Moral education: A handbook: Vol. 2. M–Z* (pp. 417–418). Greenwood Press.

Wentzel, K. R. (1993). Motivation and achievement in early adolescence: The role of multiple classroom goals. *Journal of Early Adolescence, 13,* 4–20.

Zins, J. E., Weissberg, R. P., Wang, M. C., & Walberg, H. J. (2004). *Building academic success on social and emotional learning: What does the research say?* Teachers College Press.

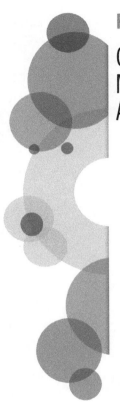

PART IV

CROSS-CUTTING METHODOLOGICAL AND POLICY ISSUES

Cross-Cutting Methodological Considerations for Measuring and Assessing Noncognitive Skills

Laura S. Hamilton

The authors who contributed to this volume have described a diverse set of assessments that have the potential to promote data-informed teaching and learning of skills that are essential for student success. Each of the assessment approaches discussed in this volume shows promise as a way to gather timely, instructionally relevant data on students' noncognitive skills.[1] The growing number and variety of assessments is a welcome development, especially in light of the widespread interest among educators in assessing their students' noncognitive skills (Atwell & Bridgeland, 2019; Hamilton & Doss, 2020). Thoughtful use of classroom-based assessments can improve instruction and student learning (Heritage & Wylie, 2020), but it needs to be informed by a careful consideration of the technical quality and appropriateness of an assessment for a particular use. In this chapter I discuss several of the most significant methodological challenges that will need to be overcome to support the use of these assessments in classrooms and ensure that educators have access to high-quality, relevant data to inform instruction.

Although documentation of the technical quality of assessments is typically the responsibility of developers and researchers, it is crucial that users of assessments—including educators who interpret and make decisions based on scores—have a basic understanding of methodological

---

[1] Throughout this chapter, I use *noncognitive skills* to describe the set of competencies that this volume addresses. I use this phrase to ensure alignment with the title of the volume, while recognizing that preferences regarding what to call these competencies vary.

considerations that might influence their use. This understanding is crucial for ensuring that assessments are well aligned with users' needs and that their use leads to benefits for students. Moreover, well-designed, methodologically sound assessments combined with informed data use can have positive effects beyond the educational context in which they are used, by encouraging policymakers and other stakeholders to prioritize noncognitive skills. Poorly designed assessments and uninformed use, by contrast, create a potential for harm, including for individual learners and for the broader effort to support noncognitive skill development. Advances in the field of noncognitive assessment will require constructive collaboration among researchers, policymakers, and practitioners, and this collaboration in turn will benefit from a shared understanding of these key methodological issues.

Detailed guidance regarding evaluation of the psychometric properties of assessment scores is beyond the scope of this chapter. Other sources of such guidance are widely available (see, e.g., American Educational Research Association, American Psychological Association, & National Council on Measurement in Education [AERA, APA, & NCME], 2014; Buros Center for Testing, n.d.; Council of Chief State School Officers and Education Counsel, 2019; Soland, Hamilton, & Stecher, 2013, and Taylor et al., 2018). In this chapter, I return to the discussion of key features of noncognitive skills assessments provided in the Introduction and discuss the methodological considerations that are most relevant to evaluating these features. I then highlight a small number of important methods-related topics and provide brief discussions of their implications for practice, policy, and future research.

● Revisiting the Key Features of Noncognitive Skills Assessments

In the Introduction, Jones, Lesaux, and Barnes described six features of noncognitive skills assessments that contribute to their utility for informing teaching and learning. One of these—"psychometrically sound"—is directly relevant to the focus of this chapter. But psychometric quality should not be evaluated in isolation from other criteria, and each of the six key features discussed earlier deserves attention when assessing the methodological quality of any assessment. The authors of the Introduction described psychometric soundness as consisting of two broad categories— reliability and validity. As they noted, and as I discuss in more detail below, reliability and validity pertain to specific uses of scores and are not inherent characteristics of measures.

Each of the other five features is in some ways related to the overarching concept of validity. Measurement and assessment that are *relevant and contextualized* involve providing opportunities for children and youth to demonstrate their skills in contexts that reflect the settings in which they typically engage. Accurately capturing evidence of these contextualized skills depends on approaches that are *developmentally salient* and that are sufficiently *sensitive and nuanced*. And appropriate use of scores for the intended purposes of informing teaching and learning depends on information that is *actionable* for those purposes. In the remainder of this chapter, I discuss key methodological issues and refer to these features where applicable.

Gathering Evidence of Validity and Reliability for Intended Uses

Any use of an assessment should be guided by the foundational considerations of validity, reliability, and fairness (AERA, APA, & NCME, 2014; Soland, Hamilton, & Stecher, 2013). I discuss the first two of these topics in this section and address fairness in the next. Assessment developers and publishers often provide technical documentation or other information that includes evidence of validity and reliability, though it can be challenging to interpret this information and to evaluate its relevance to a specific assessment context. Validity is sometimes narrowly interpreted as referring to whether an assessment measures what it is supposed to measure, but the concept of validity is much more complex and nuanced. The *Standards for Educational and Psychological Testing* (AERA, APA, & NCME, 2014; hereafter referred to as "the *Standards*") defined *validity* as "the degree to which evidence and theory support the interpretations of test scores for proposed uses of tests" (p. 11).

A few parts of this definition are especially noteworthy. Validity should be conceptualized in terms of degrees rather than as a yes/no decision (in other words, users should be wary of claims that an assessment "is valid"), and it involves a process of using both evidence and theory to support interpretations. When assessment users are evaluating validity evidence, it is essential to understand the extent to which that evidence supports a specific use. Evidence that is relevant to a large-scale monitoring of group performance might not be relevant if the goal is to use the data to inform instructional decisions about individual students. Some scholars have suggested the value of developing a "validity argument" (Bell et al., 2012; Kane, 2006) in which test developers or users present claims that describe the inferences and decisions that assessment data are intended to support and then systematically gather and present evidence from multiple sources to back up those claims. For most instructional uses, it is not necessary to develop an elaborate validity argument, but the suggestion to identify the relevant claims and the evidence needed to support them is worth heeding. For example, if a school adopts a new assessment that is intended to evaluate whether implementation of a new curriculum is associated with improvements in students' self-efficacy, a validity argument would probably include claims that the assessment accurately measures students' self-efficacy, that it is sensitive to changes in self-efficacy (so that it can capture any improvements resulting from the curriculum), and that the way that it conceptualizes self-efficacy is reasonably well-aligned with how the curriculum presents this construct. A validation effort would involve seeking evidence to support each of these claims.

The *Standards* described five broad categories of validity evidence, as shown in Table 13.1. Not every assessment use requires evidence from all five categories, but these categories can be helpful for thinking about what type of evidence is most relevant and where there might be gaps in available information about validity.

Noncognitive measures can be used for a variety of purposes—as outcome measures or predictors in research studies, in large-scale monitoring systems, or to inform day-to-day instructional decisions, to name a few. This volume focuses on use of measures to improve teaching and learning, but even within that broad category, specific purposes and decisions might vary to include individualizing instruction or informing curriculum purchases, among others. In addition, the setting where teaching and learning takes place might include schools, child care centers, after-school or summer programs, other community organizations, and of course, the home and neighborhood. The approach to gathering validity and reliability evidence must be informed by the specific setting and purpose, including the decisions that the user hopes to make and the kinds of information needed to support those decisions. For instance, if test users wish to situate a student's performance within a national distribution—perhaps by using a national percentile rank that indicates the percentage of the national sample that received scores lower than the student's score—validity evidence should include information on the composition of the national sample and the extent to which it is truly representative of the nation's student population. Such evidence is not needed in cases that do not involve the use of national norms or comparisons with a national sample. A well-thought-out validity argument that describes the desired inferences and decisions can be a helpful guide to understanding what validity evidence is most important for a given purpose.

The *Standards* defined *reliability* as "the degree to which test scores for a group of test takers are consistent over repeated applications of a measurement procedure and hence are inferred to be dependable and consistent for an individual test taker; the degree to which scores are free of random errors of measurement for a given group" (AERA, APA, & NCME, 2014, pp. 222–223). Put more simply, reliability is about consistency, and

TABLE 13.1. Categories of Validity Evidence

Category of evidence	Brief description	Example evidence
Evidence based on *content*	Wording and format of items, tasks, and scoring rubrics.	Expert ratings of items indicate that their content is aligned with the standards that the assessment was designed to measure.
Evidence based on *response processes*	The cognitive or other processes in which examinees engage while completing the assessment, and whether these processes are consistent with developers' intentions.	Interviews with students indicate that an assessment designed to measure critical thinking actually requires students to engage in critical thinking as they complete the items.
Evidence based on *internal structure*	Relationships among items, scales, or domains that are consistent with theory and intended use.	On an assessment that includes four subscores, the correlations among items within the same subscore are higher than the correlations among items on different subscores (see Gordon & Davidson, Chapter 11, this volume, for a discussion of dimensionality and related concepts)
Evidence based on *relationships with other variables*	Correlations with other measures of the same competency or different competencies.	Scores on a student self-report assessment of social awareness correlate positively with teacher ratings of students' social interactions and don't correlate too highly with students' reading achievement (a high correlation might suggest the student assessment is heavily dependent on reading skills).
Evidence related to *consequences*	Consideration of how the actual consequences of test use (e.g., changes to curriculum, interventions for students) are aligned with the intended claims and supported by other validity evidence.	Documentation of how assessment scores are used and the extent to which those uses are consisted with what the developer intended and with the available evidence.

Note. Data from AERA, APA, and NCME (2014); Taylor et al. (2018).

measurement error can result in lack of consistency. Reliability information is often shared via a "reliability coefficient," sometimes with information about how that coefficient was calculated and what aspect of reliability it refers to. A key consideration is that error can come from many different sources, and typical reliability coefficients only capture one source. For example, a commonly used measure of reliability is "coefficient alpha," which measures the extent to which scores on individual items relate to one another. A high coefficient alpha is helpful for assuring users that performance on the individual items that comprise an assessment score produce relatively consistent information, but it doesn't tell us anything about the sources of error beyond items, such as the likelihood that scores will differ depending on the time of day when the assessment is administered. Another potential source of measurement error that applies to some assessments is a result of differences in raters, so having an indicator of rater consistency is important for such assessments but would be irrelevant for assessments that don't involve raters.

Because no assessment has perfect score reliability, any individual score should be interpreted as an estimate of the student's true performance, and where possible, users should be given information about the precision of that estimate. One way to convey this information is through the construction of "error bands" around a score. These can help users understand the likely range of scores for an individual on a specific measure, and this information in turn can inform decision making. A score report might, for instance, show that the error around a total score on an assessment is quite small, and that therefore it can be interpreted as being a reasonably precise estimate. But on that same assessment, error bands around subscores that are constructed from subsets of items on the assessment might be larger, in which case users would need to apply greater caution to their use of those scores for making decisions about students. Moreover, users will need guidance on the extent to which reliability is relevant to specific assessments. A measure of emotional state, for instance, would be expected to produce different responses over time, even within a single day, so users should not interpret lack of stability of scores over time as an indication of problematic levels of score reliability.

As Gordon and Davidson (Chapter 11, this volume) pointed out, and as the variety of assessments that authors discussed in this volume makes clear, evaluating validity and reliability of scores on noncognitive skills assessments can in many cases require advanced measurement training due to the nontraditional nature of the items and tasks used in these assessments. Close collaboration with researchers, such as through a researcher–practitioner partnership like the one that Gordon and Davidson described, can be an essential support for ensuring that evidence of technical quality is appropriate and sufficient for intended uses.

What Educators Can Do

- Carefully review available evidence of validity and reliability and evaluate its relevance to your context (e.g., characteristics of students, purpose of assessment). The more limited the evidence, the more judicious you should be in making inferences and decisions based on scores.
- Engage partners (e.g., local university faculty or technical assistance providers) or refer to resources listed earlier to help make sense of the evidence.
- If needed, work with researchers or assessment developers to gather new validity and reliability evidence that will help you evaluate the degree of support for your intended uses.
- Whenever possible, gather data from multiple sources rather than relying on a single assessment. For example, a direct assessment of student skills could be supplemented with a self-report survey that measures similar skills. Use of multiple measures reduces the likelihood that lack of technical quality in one assessment will influence decision making.

• Fairness and Equity in Noncognitive Skills Assessment

Fairness is in many ways an aspect of validity; for example, the *Standards* defined *fairness* as "the validity of test score interpretations for intended use(s) for individuals from all relevant subgroups" (AERA, APA, NCME, 2014, p. 219). But it is worth highlighting as a separate consideration because of the importance fairness plays in promoting beneficial uses of assessments and because of the related equity implications of noncognitive skills assessment. Without evidence that an assessment generates scores that are fair to all subgroups who will participate in it, there is a risk that use of the scores will result in inappropriate inferences about, and adverse consequences for, members of specific groups. It is important to recognize group differences on an assessment are not, by themselves, evidence of lack of fairness. They could instead reflect differences in opportunities to develop the skills being assessed. But when such differences are observed, it is incumbent upon assessment developers and users to try to identify their sources and work to ensure that assessments that reflect inequities in opportunities to learn do not deny students opportunity to learn in the future (e.g., through use of a single test score to assign students to more- or less-rigorous instructional programs).

Evidence related to fairness takes several forms. One set of methods that are used to evaluate fairness focuses on identifying individual items that might produce inaccurate estimates for one or more groups. A commonly used collection of approaches referred to as differential item functioning (DIF; Walker, 2011) methods examines whether scores for two or more groups on a single item are different, after matching those groups on their total score. DIF analysis would typically be conducted for each item on an assessment. If a DIF analysis finds, for example, that males and females achieve the same total score but that females strongly outperform males on one item, we would flag that item as having DIF and would want to examine it further to decide whether it should be omitted from the assessment. DIF analyses are routinely carried out by professional assessment developers.

A limitation of DIF methods is that if the entire test is biased against a group, DIF will not identify that overall bias. Other approaches, such as examining measurement invariance (the extent to which an assessment functions the same way across groups, especially in terms of how item scores are related to one another and to other measures) can provide evidence of fairness that pertains to the assessment as a whole rather than just to individual items (Millsap, 2011). Gordon and Davidson (Chapter 11, this volume) provided a more detailed discussion of measurement invariance and its limits as a way of understanding how assessments function for different groups.

Considerations related to fairness and equity also require an examination of how the underlying construct is defined, whether the definition is appropriate for all groups, and the extent to which the construct reflects the student's own attributes or capabilities versus other factors. Obradović and Steyer (Chapter 1, this volume) provided a good illustrative example: "We conceptualize student motivation to engage and persist on challenging learning tasks not as a character or personality trait, but rather as a product of various socialization processes and situational factors that are cognitively and emotionally internalized by students" (p. 19). Gordon and Davidson (Chapter 11, this volume) provided another example, drawing on differences in what are considered acceptable ways to regulate emotions across different cultures. Absent an understanding of the ways in which students' performance on an assessment reflects these sociocultural differences and other situational conditions, users of assessment data might make inferences or decisions that are unwarranted and potentially harmful. Users of assessments also need to identify potential mismatches between how noncognitive constructs are defined and the needs and experiences of the populations being assessed. Jagers, Rivas-Drake, and Borowski (2018) described the five competencies in CASEL's framework through an "equity lens," discussing ways in which common conceptualizations of these competencies reflect the biases of dominant cultures, and offering strategies for reinterpreting these competencies to ensure their relevance to other communities.

Fairness also requires careful consideration of accessibility—that is, to what extent are all examinees able to access the assessment so that they can demonstrate their competencies? Accessibility is an especially prevalent concern when assessing non-native speakers of the language of the assessment as well as students with disabilities. Such examinees might require accommodations (e.g., screen magnification, text to speech) to participate fully in the assessment (Kettler, 2012). Developers and users should also examine individual items for accessibility and fairness issues, as students' responses to certain content might be influenced by their ability to access specific experiences (e.g., asking a student with deafness about their responses to songs or their enjoyment of concerts).

Obradović and Steyer (Chapter 1, this volume) listed some additional factors that could affect fairness, including the characteristics and actions of the assessor (for assessments that involve an assessor), the dynamics in the classrooms where assessments are administered, and the ways in which assessments are described when they are introduced to students. Because the concept of fairness is so multifaceted, it is difficult to offer clear guidance regarding the specific types of evidence that are needed to evaluate fairness and equity beyond the standard psychometric approaches (e.g., DIF) discussed above. Instead, users should carefully consider all the potential threats to fairness in light of their specific use case and context, and work with assessment developers, researchers, or others to devise a plan for investigating the fairness of scores and the broader equity implications of assessment use.

As McCoy (Chapter 3, this volume) discussed in detail, technical considerations about how assessments function are a necessary but not sufficient consideration when interpreting data from students whose cultural contexts vary. Without adequate attention to the appropriateness of noncognitive skill definitions for students from different backgrounds (including race/ethnicity, culture, and language, among others), assessment use might result in a misunderstanding of student needs and strengths and to students feeling alienated by the assessment process (Jagers et al., 2018). This risk can be mitigated through efforts by educators to learn about students' backgrounds and to understand the structural barriers and other experiences that have shaped their development. Educators might also consult with diverse groups of students and other stakeholders to ensure that the assessments themselves, and the definitions of skills that they measure, are appropriate for all groups and whether adaptations are warranted. Moreover, using data on opportunity to learn, including the structural barriers to that opportunity, can help assessment users interpret information about performance differences and use this information to design constructive next steps. This discussion also has implications for score reporting. The way that a construct is defined in a score report, and the information provided to users regarding how to contextualize the reported information, can substantially influence the kinds of inferences users make.

What Educators Can Do

- Seek evidence of fairness of the assessment for any groups who will participate in the assessment, aligning sources of evidence with the specific assessment context and intended uses.

- Learn about your students' backgrounds, histories, interests, and hopes for the future so that your use of assessment data can be informed by a full understanding of how the data fit within the broader context of each child's life experiences. Systematic data on students' prior learning opportunities can be especially helpful for informing decision making.

- Consult with a diverse group of stakeholders, including other educators and students themselves, to help interpret assessment results.

• Being Clear about What You're Measuring

One of the most significant challenges facing the field is a lack of consensus on what "noncognitive" skills are, or even on what to call this category of skills. Several phrases, including *social and emotional competencies, 21st-century skills, employability skills,* and *inter-* and *intrapersonal skills,* are in widespread use. Harvard's Explore SEL project (*http://exploresel. gse.harvard.edu*) provides a compelling illustration of the large number of frameworks that researchers and practitioners have developed to organize the skills, along with the often overlapping terms used to describe individual constructs. Moreover, educators can promote noncognitive skills not just through stand-alone instruction on those skills but by integrating them into academic instruction or other activities (Aspen Institute, 2019). In these cases, educators might want to measure how students' noncognitive skills are developing in response to that instruction, but which skills to focus on might not be immediately clear.

Another relevant consideration is whether to refer to these constructs as "skills" in all cases. The word *skill* is typically used to describe someone's ability to carry out a task or apply expertise. In the noncognitive realm, for instance, Soto, Napolitano, and Roberts (2020) define social, emotional, and behavioral skills as "capacities" that people can draw on in specific situations and that can be improved through interventions. Some of the assessment methods discussed in this volume measure emotional states, attitudes, beliefs, or other constructs that aren't truly "skills." Although the use of "skills" as shorthand might work well in some contexts, it is important for educators and other users of assessments to understand when they are evaluating a skill and when the construct being measured is something else.

In the context of instructional uses of assessments, the primary value of clearly defining and understanding the construct being measured is to ensure the utility and relevance of the assessment for informing decisions about teaching and learning. If a teacher is using an assessment to gauge whether students are learning the content of a lesson, it is imperative that the assessment measures the skills that the lesson is aiming to promote. Moreover, if an assessment captures information about a construct that is not a "skill"—such as an emotional state or attitude—a clear understanding of how the scores are relevant to an instructional effort will be needed.

What Educators Can Do

- Before using an assessment, make sure you understand not only the names of the constructs it measures but how they are defined, operationalized, and scored, to ensure that the data will serve their intended purposes.
- When searching for an assessment, refer to available frameworks and guidance on connecting them to make sure you are aware of assessments that might suit your needs but that use different construct names.

• Understanding Strengths and Limitations of Assessment Methods

The assessments discussed in the chapters of this volume incorporated numerous approaches to eliciting responses from students. These include self-report, observer-report (e.g., a teacher report about a students' behavior), biometric data, and direct, technology-based formats, among others. Each of these broad approaches can include a wide variety of specific assessment and task types and strategies. For example, observer-report measures include measures in which observers record data on relatively objective indicators such as the direct behavioral indicators described by Chafouleas and Briesch (Chapter 7, this volume). Other assessments in this category involve more subjective, higher-inference rating scales such as the ones used by the CORE Districts (Toch & Miller, 2019), which ask students to rate their own skills by responding to statements such as "I remembered and followed directions" and questions such as "How carefully did you listen to other people's points of view?" (see CORE Districts, n.d.).

Some of these formats lends themselves better to certain constructs than others do. For instance, McKown (n.d.-a) wrote that in general, self-report measures are best-suited to eliciting beliefs and attitudes; observer-report measures are ideal for documenting observable behaviors; and direct assessments are especially relevant to assessments of skills. Soto, Napolitano, and Roberts (2020) discussed the value of performance-based measures (similar to McKown's "direct assessments" category) that engage students in tasks that require them to apply a skill. These authors also discussed situational judgment tests (SJTs), which ask students to respond to hypothetical scenarios, as a promising approach. A general principle here is that users need to consider the types of responses an assessment elicits and from whom, and ensure that the inferences they make from scores reflect this understanding.

Beyond the constructs they measure, each of these formats has advantages and disadvantages that need to be weighed. Important considerations include cost, development time, training requirements, administration burden, accessibility supports available to ensure all students can participate, and acceptability to stakeholders. A Web-based assessment might work well in a school in which all students have access to Internet-connected devices but not in a school that lacks those resources. An assessment that requires teacher ratings of student behaviors might be more or less acceptable to teachers depending in part on how much time they have to complete the ratings and how this activity fits into the rest of their workload.

These formats also vary in their susceptibility to different threats to validity. For self-report and observer-report measures, various types of response bias can arise, including social desirability (a tendency to respond in ways that reflect positively on the respondent), reference bias (responses are affected by the characteristics of a comparison group, even if the respondent was not asked to make such a comparison), and cultural bias (responses are influenced by respondents' cultural background and experiences) (Schweig, Hamilton, & Baker, 2019). Slavin (2017) described such measures as being subject to "parroting," in which respondents answer in ways that reflect what they might have heard or read about. Consider the parallels in academic assessment; we generally place greater reliance on direct assessments of student knowledge and skills than on self-reports (e.g., "I'm good at solving multiplication problems") or observer reports (e.g., "this student is good at solving multiplication problems"). Clearly, a well-designed assessment that requires students to solve multiplication problems would provide a more accurate assessment of students' skills in this area. At the same time, direct assessments of noncognitive skills can be expensive and infeasible, and very few are available for use in schools and classrooms. It is likely that assessment users will confront trade-offs in their decisions about what assessments to adopt.

What Educators Can Do

- Once you have identified the constructs you are interested in measuring, examine the various methods used by available measures and select an approach that balances feasibility and cost concerns with the need for a method that produces high-quality data on the construct of interest.

- Interpretation of scores should be informed by an understanding of possible sources of bias or other threats to validity associated with a particular format.

Measuring Change

Many instructional uses of assessment involve measures of change in performance over time. Users might be interested in examining changes in scores before and after a new intervention is implemented, or they might want to monitor changes in students' noncognitive skills over the course of several years. As noted in the earlier discussion of validity, it is important for users to gather validity evidence that is relevant to an intended use. Ideally, any use of an assessment to measure change over time should be supported by evidence of validity of the scores on the assessment for that use (Millsap & Cham, 2012). Because that evidence hasn't been gathered for many assessments, users sometimes must rely on less-than-optimal information to guide their use of assessments for measuring change. Users must be especially aware of potential threats to the validity of inferences based on measures of change. In particular, if the same form (i.e., the same set of items or tasks) is administered to the same students more than once, there is a risk that students' responses might be influenced by their prior exposure to it, thereby producing inaccurate evidence of change. This concern can be addressed if the developer has provided multiple forms (i.e., a different set of items or tasks on each administration), but in those cases it is important to seek evidence that scores on the different forms are directly comparable to one another as well as across student subgroups. Another consideration is score reliability, as measures of change typically have more measurement error and therefore lower score reliability than the separate scores on which they are based.

In the absence of high-quality evidence to support the use of change measures based on noncognitive skills assessments, users should tread cautiously when interpreting those measures, recognizing that they might be distorted or highly imprecise. Nonetheless, measures of change can be informative for instructional purposes, and can be especially helpful for estimating growth at the group (e.g., classroom or grade) level, as group-level scores are less subject to concerns about imprecision compared with individual scores.

What Educators Can Do

- Seek validity and reliability evidence to support any use of noncognitive skills assessments to measure change over time. If such evidence is unavailable, either avoid making inferences based on change scores or seek supplemental information to corroborate those inferences.

● Keep in mind that group-level change scores can be less subject to measurement error than individual-level ones, but can still be affected by other factors discussed above, such as the effects of previous exposure to the items.

● Understanding the Implications of Novel Uses of Technology

Use of technology-based educational assessments and learning software has grown rapidly, fueled in part by the rapid shift to remote learning in spring 2020 and by innovations in areas such as artificial intelligence. Several of the assessments described in this volume rely on tablets or other forms of technology. A 2017 "design challenge"[2] launched by the Assessment Work Group resulted in numerous submissions of innovative assessment ideas, including using response-process data from academic assessments to make inferences about noncognitive skills (Soland, Zamarro, Cheng, & Hitt, 2019). Noncognitive skills assessments can also be embedded in gamelike learning environments like the one used for Zoo U (DeRosier & Thomas, 2018). This approach to assessment has the potential to facilitate a seamless connection between instruction and assessment and to ensure that students are adequately engaged in the assessment.

Obradović and Steyer (Chapter 1, this volume) provided another example of how such assessments can contribute to enhanced understanding of students' competencies:

> Leveraging students' engagement metrics during digitized academic assessments, researchers can identify students whose quick response patterns suggest that they did not carefully consider the test items. Soland and colleagues have conceptualized such rapid responding as an index of low effort (response time effort [RTE]) and linked it to lower levels of student-reported self-efficacy and self-management among middle and high school students (Soland, Zamarro, Cheng, & Hitt, 2019; Soland & Kuhfeld, 2019). (p. 22)

Technology can not only expand the scope of what we're able to measure; it can also introduce cost savings and other efficiencies into the assessment process. One example comes from a technology-based assessment of executive functioning described by Obradović, Sulik, Finch, and Tirado-Strayer (2018), which can be administered to groups of students while producing evidence that is comparable to what is typically obtained from individually administered assessments. Moreover, technology can be

---

[2] Available at the CASEL website (*https://measuringsel.casel.org/?s=design+challenge*).

leveraged to make assessments more accessible to all students (e.g., those with disabilities), as noted earlier. However, it is equally important that these new testing accommodations be considered when using timing data and other process data that may be different for those who are using additional supports (see Laitusis, 2022, for a discussion of how accommodations can influence scoring of process data).

An additional benefit of technology is that these assessments lend themselves to deeper investigations of validity and fairness. One particularly promising approach to evaluating fairness for technology-delivered assessments involves analyzing response-process data. Information that digital tools can gather on response times, clicking sequences, likelihood of accessing available resources (e.g., glossaries), and other actions in which students engage can shed light on how members of different groups might approach the assessment differently. This information, in turn, can inform our understanding of whether group differences in performance on assessments might be affected by differences in constructs other than what the assessment was designed to measure (Ercikan, Huo, & He, 2020). Even though educators might only use the final scores in their decision making, evidence of differences in how students engage in the assessment can be important for score interpretation.

Although these applications of technology are promising, they pose numerous technical and logistical challenges related to availability of devices and Internet access, data-privacy concerns, and differences in students' familiarity and comfort with the technology being used. The general guidance regarding selection and evaluation of assessments presented so far in this chapter applies to both technology-based and non-technology-based assessments, but the introduction of technological requirements creates a need for additional scrutiny to ensure the assessments will function as intended and that students and educators are protected from any harms that might stem from the use of technology.

What Educators Can Do

- Before adopting a technology-based assessment, confirm that you and your students have access to the necessary infrastructure and devices and that your students are able to use the platform.
- Ensure assistive technologies can be used with the technology-based assessment or appropriate accommodations are provided.[3]
- Check with the developer or provider to understand how data will be stored and shared; ensure that privacy protections are in place.

---

[3] This can be done using the Voluntary Product Accessibility Template (VPAT) to evaluate compliance with the revised 508 Standards (*www.section508.gov/sell/vpat*).

● Other Considerations

This chapter has described some of the more significant and widespread methodological challenges educators face as they adopt assessments to monitor students' noncognitive skills. A few additional considerations are worth mentioning briefly.

● *Understanding consequences.* Whenever a new assessment is adopted, it is crucial not only to monitor how well the assessment works in terms of providing the desired information to inform instruction, but also to identify any consequences stemming from the use of the test, whether intended or unintended. Of particular concern in the noncognitive realm, given the relative lack of experience most educators have in this area and the novelty of many of the proposed methods, is potential misuse of data in ways that will harm students (e.g., by assigning inappropriate labels or sharing the scores with others who do not need access to them).

● *Deciding whether to build, adapt, or buy.* Decisions about whether to use an existing assessment as is, to adapt an existing assessment, or to create an assessment from scratch need to be informed by several factors, including the availability of a suitable assessment; the need for documented evidence of validity, reliability, and fairness; and costs. As McKown (n.d.-b) pointed out, it is easy to underestimate the time and other burdens associated with developing a new assessment and ensuring that it works as intended. It can also be helpful to explore ways to use informal data, such as teachers' observations or discussions with students, to provide some insight into students' noncognitive skills (Hamilton & Schwartz, 2019).

● *Balancing assessments of student skills with measures of the learning environment.* Data on student competencies that are not accompanied by evidence of students' opportunities to learn and develop those competencies provide incomplete information for making instructional decisions. Newman, Osher, Moroney, and Neiman (Chapter 14, this volume) will discuss the value of measuring conditions for learning; Barnes, Abenavoli, and Jones (Chapter 10, this volume) emphasized the need to capture setting-level features of the classroom environment; and McKown (Chapter 2, this volume) advocated for using implementation measures in conjunction with measures of outcomes. Indicators of school or classroom climate, exposure to curriculum and instruction, and other learning conditions are important parts of a comprehensive instructional improvement effort.

● *Promoting effective data use.* McKown (Chapter 2, this volume) briefly described features of effective use of data for decision making. Assessment scores cannot improve instruction on their own; educators need guidance and other supports (e.g., time for collaborative planning, access to coaching) to help them make sense of the data and use the information in ways that will benefit students.

● Linking Methodological Research to the Needs of Practitioners

Finally, although many of the methodological considerations discussed in this chapter are primarily the responsibility of the assessment developer, users must understand these issues and draw on their best judgment combined with other available resources and guidance to interpret the evidence provided by the developer and to evaluate its implications for their intended uses and interpretations of assessment scores. Few educators receive comprehensive training in psychometrics, so these efforts can benefit from partnerships with researchers and developers (see Gordon & Davidson, Chapter 11, this volume, for a detailed description of such a partnership). In particular, future research on noncognitive skills assessments should be informed by practitioners' needs and interests. A continuous-improvement approach to assessment research and development, with practitioners engaged in every phase of design, development, evaluation, and refinement, could have benefits for the broader researcher and practitioner communities. Because the contexts in which learning happens are always changing, and because new approaches to developing, administering, and using assessments are frequently being developed, an effort to ensure the technical quality of an assessment is likely to require an ongoing strategy in which new evidence is gathered and modifications are made to the assessment itself or to administration and use guidance in response to that evidence. It will be critical to document lessons learned from the uses of assessments in new populations or for new purposes. These lessons can inform validity arguments and point to areas where additional evidence is needed. Close collaboration between researchers and practitioners will be key to advancing the field of noncognitive assessment in ways that benefit all learners.

REFERENCES

American Educational Research Association, American Psychological Association, & National Council on Measurement in Education. (2014). *Standards for educational and psychological testing.* American Educational Research Association. Retrieved March 5, 2021, from *www.testingstandards.net/open-access-files.html.*

Aspen Institute. (2019). *From a nation at risk to a nation at hope: Recommendations from the National Commission on Social, Emotional, and Academic Development.* National Commission on Social, Emotional, and Academic Development.

Atwell, M. N., & Bridgeland, J. M. (2019). *Ready to lead: A 2019 update on principals' perspectives on how social and emotional learning can prepare children and transform schools.* Collaborative for Academic, Social, and Emotional Learning.

Bell, C., Gitomer, D. H., McCaffrey, D. M., Hamre, B. K., Pianta, R. C., & Qi, Y. (2012). An argument approach to observation protocol validity, *Educational Assessment, 17,* 62–87.

Buros Center for Testing. (n.d.). SEL assessment technical guidebook. Author. Retrieved February 15, 2021, from *https://buros.org/sel-assessment-technical-guidebook.*

CORE Districts. (n.d.). Social-emotional skills. Author. Retrieved February 15, 2021, from *https://coredistricts.org/wp-content/uploads/2021/01/SEL-Metrics-update_1.5.21.pdf.*

Council of Chief State School Officers & Education Counsel. (2019). *Measuring school climate and social and emotional development: A navigation guide for states and districts.* Author.

DeRosier, M. E., & Thomas, J. M. (2018). Establishing the criterion validity of Zoo U's game-based social emotional skills assessment for school-based outcomes. *Journal of Applied Developmental Psychology, 55,* 52–61.

Ercikan, K., Huo, H., & He, Q. (2020). Use of response process data to inform group comparisons and fairness research. *Educational Assessment, 25,* 179–197.

Hamilton, L. S., & Doss, C. J. (2020). *Supports for social and emotional learning in American schools and classrooms* (RR-A397). RAND.

Hamilton, L. S., & Schwartz, H. L. (2019). *Get smart about social and emotional learning measurement.* American Enterprise Institute.

Heritage, M., & Wylie, E. C. (2020). *Formative assessment in the discipline: Framing a continuum of professional learning.* Harvard Education Press.

Jagers, R. J., Rivas-Drake, D., & Borowski, T. (2018). *Equity and social and emotional learning: A cultural analysis.* Collaborative for Academic, Social, and Emotional Learning.

Kane, M. T. (2006). Validation. In R. L. Brennan (Ed.), *Educational measurement* (4th ed., pp. 17–64). Praeger.

Kettler, R. J. (2012). Testing accommodations: Theory and research to inform practice. *International Journal of Disability, Development and Education, 59,* 53–66.

Laitusis, C. C. (2022). Fairness and accessibility: Challenges and solutions in scoring performance assessments. In J. Jonson & K. Geisinger (Eds.), *Fairness in educational and psychological testing: Examining theoretical, research, practice, and policy implications of 2014 Standards.* Washington, DC: AERA.

McKown, C. (n.d.-a). Show and tell: Two kinds of social emotional learning (SEL) assessment tools. Retrieved February 15, 2021, from *https://xsel-labs.com/blog/show-tell-assessments-sel.*

McKown, C. (n.d.-b). Social emotional learning (SEL) assessment: Build or buy? Retrieved from *https://xsel-labs.com/blog/social-emotional-learning-sel-assessment-build-or-buy.*

Millsap, R. E. (2011). *Statistical approaches to measurement invariance.* Routledge.

Millsap R. E., & Cham, H. (2012). Investigating factorial invariance in longitudinal data. In B. Laursen, T. D. Little, & N. A. Card (Eds.), *Handbook of developmental research methods* (pp. 109–127). Guilford Press.

Obradović, J., Sulik, M. J., Finch, J. E., & Tirado-Strayer, N. (2018). Assessing students' executive functions in the classroom: Validating a scalable group-based procedure. *Journal of Applied Developmental Psychology, 55,* 4–13.

Schweig, J., Hamilton, L. S., & Baker, G. (2019). *School and classroom climate measures: Considerations for use by state and local education leaders* (RR-4259-FCIM). RAND.

Slavin, R. (2017). *MOOSES: Measureable, observable, objective social emotional skills.* Retrieved February 23, 2021, from *https://robertslavinsblog. wordpress.com/2017/05/25/reviewing-social-and-emotional-learning-for-essa-mooses-not-parrots.*

Soland, J., Hamilton, L. S., & Stecher, B. M. (2013). *Measuring 21st-century competencies: Guidance for educators.* Asia Society.

Soland, J., Zamarro, G., Cheng, A., & Hitt, C. (2019). Identifying naturally occurring direct assessments of social-emotional competencies: The promise and limitations of survey and assessment disengagement metadata: *Educational Researcher, 48*(7), 466–478.

Soto, C. J., Napolitano, C. M., & Roberts, B. W. (2020). Taking skills seriously: Toward an integrative model and agenda for social, emotional, and behavioral skills. *Current Directions in Psychological Science, 30,* 26–33.

Taylor, J. J., Buckley, K., Hamilton, L. S., Stecher, B. M., Read, L., & Schweig, J. (2018). *Choosing and using SEL competency assessments: What schools and districts need to know.* Collaborative for Academic, Social, and Emotional Learning.

Toch, T., & Miller, R. (2019). *CORE Lessons: Measuring the social and emotional dimensions of student success.* FutureEd.

Walker, C. W. (2011). What's the DIF? Why differential item functioning analyses are an important part of instrument development and validation. *Journal of Psychoeducational Assessment, 29*(4), 364–376.

CHAPTER 14

Thriving Matters

Policies and Assessment That Foster Equity and Thriving

Jessica Newman, David Osher, Deborah Moroney,
and Samantha Neiman

The assessment of social and emotional competency (SEC) is not just about skills or technical matters. Educators and mental health professionals often treat assessment as an objective and technical process in which they think about assessment in terms of the mechanics and procedures—what the assessment measures, the data that the assessment yields—but sociocultural factors (including the rater's own subjectivity) affect assessment as well. Social and emotional learning (SEL) assessment should be functional to produce helpful information that contributes to thriving and equity. Assessment of SECs, specifically, is about how we support and equip individuals with the portable competencies and dispositions that enable them to thrive in life and to support the thriving of others (Osher et al., 2020). SEL assessment should be functional and produce helpful information that contributes to thriving and equity.

Assessment is never neutral. As described in other chapters in this volume, there are many measurement and assessment issues that stem from the fact that assessment is a culturally embedded process that is often fraught with implications for people's life course and implemented in a society and world marked by inequality, privilege, and unpredictability (Osher & Cantor, in press; Spencer, Offidani-Bertrand, Harris, & Velez, 2020). For example, assessment measures and instruments have often been developed and normed based on dominant groups, so assessment and instruments have an inherent assumption regarding "others." Examples include phrenology (Greenblat, 1995)—measuring the size and shape of people's brains—and the origins of IQ testing, which treated intelligence as an invariant trait, possessed by some people and not others, which could be measured by a singular test. Assessment must be approached with caution; assessment is—at best—inferences about people's competencies and how those competencies will develop and play out in different contexts, both in the present and in the future (e.g., Correa-Chavez, Rogoff, & Mejía Aruz, 2005; Nesselroade & Molenaar, 2016). All forms of assessment— and especially SEL assessment—must be approached with humanity and humility, both because assessment has limits and because assessment errors can affect people's lives.

Policies can affect what types of data are collected, from whom, and in what context, along with the ways the data are used and the consequences ("stakes") of their use. Policies mandate, authorize, or prohibit behavior and transfer resources to enable types of activities. Assessment policies matter because they influence whether and how we go about assessment. Although policies occur and have influence at multiple levels (federal-, state-, local-, individual-, and school-level policies and practices; we dive more into this later in the chapter), all policies have the power to enable, encourage, legitimize, incentivize, prohibit, and sanction system, organizational, group, and individual behavior. Policies related to the assessment of social and emotional competencies and skills affect *how* we focus on and measure the development of SEC. To put this in the context of education, when policies enable, encourage, and legitimize assessment, SEL practices may be seen as useful. Or when policies incentivize assessment this may lead to quality improvement. But when there are no formal policies, informal policy may govern behavior such as using assessment with no purpose or for purposes the assessment is not designed to support (Chudnovsky & Trujillo, 2019). Examples of informal policy interpretation are on-the-job socialization by professional peers, for example teachers telling other teachers "what social and emotional skill looks like" or how to assess SEL.

Across the chapters in this volume, the authors have described the myriad complex measurement and assessment issues. Throughout this chapter, we elevate or reinforce key contextual factors that must be considered when interpreting policy and engaging in assessment. We describe policy history that underpins current SEL assessment practice and offer considerations for policy implementation at the local level. We go beyond a focus on competence assessment to consider first the foundational elements for effective SEL: implementation readiness and school climate or conditions for learning and how those may be measured instead of or in addition to SEC.

● How Policies Influence SEL Assessment

Policies are purposive social actions that seek to produce or prevent social outcomes. These outcomes may or may not be valued by or benefit all stakeholders—some may leverage the policy in practice, some may not care, and some may actually oppose the policy, or view or experience its effects as hurtful (Mills, 1959). The ways in which policies are brought to bear is likely also influenced from the level at which they are established (e.g., federal, state, local) and their relevance to the stakeholders the policies will affect.

Although policies are the outcome of purposive and sometimes deliberative social action, they have collateral as well as unanticipated consequences (Merton, 1957). "Unanticipated consequences" can occur either because the consequences are unforeseeable, because policies are insufficiently clear or poorly operationalized, or because planning did not sufficiently include the perspectives and voices of stakeholders who could have anticipated the harmful consequences (Mayo, Moroney, & Huff, 2019). Assessment-related consequences include the reinforcement of stereotypes, stigma, self-fulfilling prophecies (e.g., learner-learned helplessness and provider sense of inefficacy), and goal displacements such as "teaching to the test." For instance, teachers may perceive data on students' ability to self-regulate as indicative of immutable traits and may then make pedagogical choices based on that (mis)perception. This array of challenges can be mitigated or even averted in three ways, and ideally a combination: (1) by focusing on policy clarity; (2) by leveraging longitudinal data collection, which can identify sleeper effects (Kumkale & Albarracin, 2004); and (3) through inclusive planning and monitoring processes that incorporate the perspectives of diverse stakeholders and end users—forming cross-functional teams in schools, for example (Barbour, LaTurner, & Osher, 2018; Butler et al., 2018), and actively engaging culturally and linguistically diverse students, families, and community members in the development of SEL assessment policies. Good policies anticipate the previously unanticipated.

If assessment policies are to be realized on the ground and at scale, they must be realized with quality policy implementation—that is, how one goes about making decisions or engaging in policy-related practices matters. Implementation always involves different contexts (Dymnicki, Wandersman, Osher, Grigorescu, & Huang, 2014) and is affected by policy clarity, readiness to implement the policy, decentralization, and the way in which people "on the ground" interpret and implement the policies. These individuals function as "street-level bureaucrats" as they work to interpret and implement the policies, perhaps while grappling with the ambiguities and misalignment that comes from implementing policy in real-world contexts (Lipsky, 1980; Maynard-Moody & Musheno, 2000; May & Winter, 2009). An example of this is when there is a policy for teachers to assess student-level SECs. The street-level bureaucrat in this case is the school administrator, counselor, or teacher who must navigate the practicalities of putting that policy into practice—what gets measured, how, with whom, and to what end? These are all complex decisions that must be made to bring the policy to life.

While these complexities are observed in centralized bureaucracies (such as Beijing, China, where street-level bureaucrats undermined policies focused on inclusive education; Osher, 2014), they are particularly profound in the highly decentralized U.S. education system, where states, school districts, principles, and even some teachers have high degrees of freedom. Readiness to implement policies, no matter the level of policy origin or policy implementation, is a product of individual motivation, organizational priorities, implementation-specific capacity, and general organizational capacity (Mayo, Moroney, & Huff, 2019; Osher, 2018). Readiness to implement assessments of SECs, for example, is affected by, among other things, whether implementers see SEL as important, the organizational capacities that can support the effective collection and reporting of assessment data (e.g., the data infrastructure), and adult technical and social and emotional capacities in implementing assessments and using the data. We discuss this in greater detail later in this chapter.

Although policies that promote and support assessment of SECs must overcome challenges, there still are systemic, pedagogical, and developmental reasons for engaging in assessment of social and emotional competencies and skills as well. The systemic reasons include focusing educators, policymakers, funders, voters, families, and students on SEL and SEL outcomes: What gets counted contributes to what people see as counting, and what gets assessed is more likely to be addressed. Reporting on the acquisition of SECs can focus stakeholders' attention on SEL, and the assessment of SEL may help counter the policy-driven focus on a narrow band of academically focused outcomes like grades and test scores.

Once policies ensure that people attend to SEL, it is important to support SEL implementation. Effective assessment can help educators, families, and students gather and use data to improve the SEL process. The key here is attending to (1) what gets measured, (2) how, and (3) with whom, as well as (4) how the results are used. Attention to these key decisions can, in turn, affect individual and group learning and developmental outcomes. We offer considerations and recommendations for navigating this complex process later in this chapter.

• But First, Do No Harm: Policy Considerations for SEL Assessment

Assessment practices can contribute to the social reproduction of inequality (Artiles, Kozleski, Trent, Osher, & Ortiz, 2010; Broadfoot, 1986; Helms, 2007). Although there are good reasons for engaging in SEL assessment, there are risks—many of which can be mitigated by good policy. It is important to avert or at least buffer against any potential harm. Technical assessment issues such as reliability and validity play a key role here, but so do political, ideological, and ethical issues. In fact, fairness (a fundamental, if often underaddressed criterion; Curtin, Cahill, Hall, O'Sullivan, & Özerk, 2019); intellectual, cultural, and professional humility; and ethical responsibility of assessment are key to doing no harm. Fairness is particularly important since culture and context affect which competencies are exhibited and how (e.g., Coppens, Corwin, & Alcalá, 2020; Fernández, 2015), how meaningful they are to the people who are being assessed, and how they are rewarded or punished in different settings.

In the case of assessing SEC, *fairness* is avoiding universalizing some groups' norms and culturally grounded behaviors and/or ignoring the ways in which those behaviors can be demonstrated and realized in different cultural contexts (Helms, 2006). For example, African American students may demonstrate adaptive competencies, such as how they manage the risks and stressors they face both in and out of school. Those competencies may either be ignored or viewed negatively in formal or informal assessment processes that do not recognize cultural values and contextual demands that go beyond the experience or intellectual frames of those who develop, create standards for, interpret, or otherwise use SEL assessments (Gaylord-Harden, Barbarin, Tolan, & Murry, 2018; Spencer et al., 2020).

Intellectual humility includes being aware of the limits of what can be learned from any measurement, for example acknowledging and addressing the role that families can play in helping identify social and emotional strengths that are valued and displayed outside of school. Likewise, *cultural humility* involves an awareness of how our cultural lenses and position in social structures affect what we see and don't see as well as what we value and devalue, and the willingness to learn from individuals whose experiences and cultural perspectives are different than one's own—even if it is intellectually and emotionally hard. Both types of humility entail intentionally reaching out to others who may know more about a child or the child's context, listening deeply, and acting upon what is learned. In other words, it is important to value and address other sources of information beyond the assessment, knowing and elevating that other data sources, when used in tandem with assessment modeling or data, can provide a more robust and potentially accurate picture of what we are trying to assess. Humility can be displayed and strengthened by meaningfully seeking out and utilizing critical feedback from diverse colleagues, youth, and community members before one develops or applies standards and measures. *Professional humility* involves displaying respect for the time, perspective, and experiences of the end users of assessment, including those who are assessed.

Ethical responsibility involves taking responsibility to proactively avoid negative consequences that may stem from the assessment or the data and subsequent actions the assessment generates. Ethical responsibility means that the developer's or assessors' moral obligations do not end with the assessment, but also extend to how assessments are used and the consequences of their use (e.g., the development of negative identities; Salinger & Osher, 2018).

Even a good assessment can only provide one lens for viewing reality. No matter how well designed an assessment is, it bakes in some elements of instrument and measurement bias, and this includes the biases that every type of informant brings to the assessment process. Teachers provide an example. Teachers' judgment is often privileged over children's subjectivity and teachers are seen as "natural raters," who informally and formally rate students regularly (Kellam & Rebock, 1992; Pas & Bradshaw, 2014). But teachers are still human, and their perceptions can be affected by implicit biases, stress, job press, and the limits of what they see and where and how they see it. It is not necessarily something that teachers are doing intentionally but it is their singular view and that in itself is a signal about the data, the perspective it represents, and the ways in which it can and should be used.

Good multi-informant assessments or performance-based assessments of SECs should also reflect the jaggedness of learning. In other words, the development of SECs is different for each individual because development is jagged, not linear. This jaggedness is in part due to each individual's unique characteristics, role models, or feedback they receive from significant others or from reference groups (Merton, 1957), or the audiences that would witness or observe their behavior (Goffman, 1974). The concept of jaggedness reflects the multidimensional nature of learning and the many indicators that can be used to develop a student's learning profile (Cantor, Osher, Berg, Steyer, & Rose, 2018; Rose, 2016). Just as emergent readers may be strong in some areas (e.g., narrative skills) and weaker in others (e.g., print awareness or word find), so children may display strong interpersonal skills while struggling with aspects of self-regulation.

The learning of SECs, their appropriation, demonstration, and reinforcement is context- and emotion-dependent (see Sliwinski, 2008, for summary of research on variability). That is, the context, including the particular tasks or practices that are the context for assessment, the peers who are present, who administers the assessment, and the assessment context, matters. While this is likely to be the case for many or all areas of SEL assessment, research in the area of self-regulation that involves the famous "marshmallow test" provides an example of what is a more general phenomenon. The original marshmallow test explored children's ability to self-regulate for a delayed reward (i.e., if you wait for the researcher to return before eating your marshmallow you will then be able to eat two marshmallows rather than one). In the new marshmallow test, researchers examined the impact of trust or distrust, by creating a situation prior to the marshmallow task where some assessors demonstrated their untrustworthiness by not delivering the new crayons that they had promised to deliver. If a child trusted the adult to bring them the marshmallow later, they were more likely to be able to wait, but if they did not trust the adult, they were less likely to wait. This new experiment and others suggest that children's response to a simple test of self-regulation appears to be affected not only by children's self-regulation (what the original study was designed to measure along with the strategies children deploy to regulate), but also by children's sense of the reliability of the commitment and tester (based on the child's prior experience and observations; Watts, Duncan, & Quan, 2018). As such, the context of the assessment, and children's prior experiences (both immediately proximate and in the longer-run) are key to understanding how they do on the assessment. This provides a clear example of how external factors influence assessment and should be considered as well.

Although policies can be examined in a theoretically grounded objective manner, they are finalized (and in some cases, developed) through political processes and adapted by street-level bureaucrats who implement policy with varied levels of readiness and knowledge in diverse local contexts. In the next section, we provide a brief overview of policies that have influenced the assessment landscape and we highlight the consequences—both intended and unanticipated—and lessons learned from those policies.

• Policies That Influenced the Current SEL Assessment Landscape

As we stated earlier, policies are typically designed to produce or prevent social outcomes—the outcomes are intentional but sometimes have unanticipated consequences. In this section, we describe the policies that have influenced the SEL assessment landscape, highlighting the shifts in foci and priorities in federal policy first, and how those shape local-level policy decisions and implementation.

Assessment to Understand Competence Development

The No Child Left Behind (NCLB) Act of 2002 served as the legislative update to the Elementary and Secondary Education Act (Klein, 2015; U.S. Department of Education, n.d.). The NCLB era, from 2002 to 2015, was characterized by increased federal accountability at all levels of the education system—starting with the Department of Education and trickling down to local-level implementation in school districts and schools. The intention of this increased accountability was originally to ensure equitable access to high-quality education to close the achievement gap, and to ensure U.S. competitiveness in a global economy. The NCLB Act was initially drafted with bipartisan support and backed by many civil rights organizations after earlier efforts at securing "opportunity to learn" standards to complement academic standards had failed (O'Day & Smith, 2019; Rebell, 2008).

One major outcome of NCLB was a rise in state-developed student learning standards that specified what youth should know and be able to do at each grade, and one major consequence of NCLB was a focus on student-level outcome assessments of math and English language arts attainment for the purpose of school- or district-level accountability. Once educators and schools were held accountable for student performance on standardized tests, teaching practices moved away from student-centered instruction to a "teach to the test" mentality (Walker, 2014). Although NCLB did not realize its intended outcomes of increasing school performance and reducing achievement gaps, it did lay a foundation for greater emphasis on learning standards that spanned beyond math and English language arts to include science, social studies, and, eventually, SEL.

Although the original point is not explicitly clear, we note that the SEL movement was gaining momentum at the same time, with policy gains (Illinois State Board of Education, n.d.; Kress, Norris, Schoenholz, Elias, & Seigle, 2004), the release of foundational research (Durlak, Weissberg, Dymnicki, Taylor, & Schellinger, 2011; Jones, Greenberg, & Crowley, 2015; Osher et al., 2016; Kendziora & Osher, 2016), and increasing concern that education should address 21st-century skills (National Research Council, 2012) and return to teaching the whole child (Darling-Hammond & Cook-Harvey, 2018).

The emergence of state-developed SEL standards was one of the first major actions that brought together the accountability era of NCLB and the SEL movement. The first SEL standards were established in 2003 with the passage of the Illinois Children's Mental Health Act, and they specified a set of core competency areas as well as what the expression of those competencies would look like for each grade (Gordon, Ji, Mulhall, Shaw, & Weissberg, 2016). As the NCLB era came to an end, and the high-stakes testing lost public appeal, states started using lower-stakes strategies and language, such as social and emotional "competencies" or "guidance" as opposed to "standards." Currently, and largely with the support of the Collaborative for Academic, Social, and Emotional Learning (CASEL)'s Collaborating States Initiative, 18 states have state-level SEL standards or competencies and 21 states have some level of educator guidance on implementing SEL (Yoder, Dusenbury, Martinez-Black, & Weissberg, 2020).

The next update of the Elementary and Secondary Education Act, in 2015, was the aptly named Every Student Succeeds Act (ESSA). This marked a clear shift from what had become a seemingly standardized and singularly focused approach to education systems and educators to a more autonomous and context-driven approach, with significant flexibility that allowed state and local agencies to shape decision making. Under the guidance of the ESSA, state and local education agencies could determine their own plans for enacting the legislation—including one set of accountability metrics defined by the state called "the fifth indicator." At the same time, the ESSA included language that called for supports for the whole child and for student engagement (and for the teacher preparation to do so) but did not explicitly reference "SEL." SEL was becoming an area of increased interest in states, districts, and schools and, as SEL implementation increased—with many educators learning new methods and adapting their teaching practice—the debates about how to measure SEL and for what purpose continued.

The debates largely focused on ESSA's fifth indicator—the indicator, to be chosen by the state or local education agency, gave them the most flexibility in determining what metrics they wanted to use to demonstrate success. SEL advocates, measurement experts, and policymakers explored the relative merits of assessing student SECs for accountability purposes and elevated the role of SEL assessment and the fifth indicator (Blad, 2015; Schachat, 2016; West, 2016). Some of the early fifth indicators state teams considered were chronic absenteeism, student discipline, and school climate, for example (Child Trends, 2017). Although we do not know the impetus for these decisions, we note that not a single state in the country chose a measure of student SEC for its fifth indicator, although some states did consider measures of school climate—in other words, the conditions that support SEL and the development of competence.

A Shift: From Competence Assessment to Assessing the Conditions That Support the Development of Competence

As the SEL movement gained speed, so too did discussions about the importance of understanding and improving school climate and conditions for learning for effective SEL. The ways in which we process information, focus our attention, remember new facts and skills, and make meaning from what we learn are greatly influenced by our culture, context, environment, and relationships with others (e.g., Jagers, William, & Osher, 2019; Lacy, 2014; Rogoff et al., 2017; Sternberg & Grigorenko, 2000)—what we refer to as school climate (along with the aspects of school climate that are most proximal to learning, which we refer to as conditions for learning).

In 2016, supported by the Robert Wood Johnson Foundation, American Institutes for Research (AIR) convened a group of practice, policy, and research leaders, to explore and describe the intersection between SEL and school climate. One outgrowth was a report validated through a combination of face-to-face meetings and a modified Delphi process (a multistage group communication and consensus process; Hsu & Sandford, 2007) that involved 67 practitioners and researchers in SEL, school climate, developmental science, school leaders, and funders. The report concluded that there was an inextricable link between climate and the development of SEL, and that link was best represented by the *conditions for learning,* which were the Venn intercept between climate and SEL (as shown in Figure 14.1; Berg, Osher, Moroney, & Yoder, 2017).

A second outgrowth was a collaborative effort, led by Tim Shriver, one of the expert practitioners, and David Osher, principal investigator for the project. This effort developed a consensus statement on: (1) whether and how assessments of SEC should be used in accountability, (2) the merits of employing measures of conditions for learning and school climate to ensure the conditions for SEL are met before assessing student-level SECs, and (3) the inherent challenges in using assessments of SECs in accountability systems (Osher & Shriver, 2016).

Ultimately, the consensus statement concluded that it is important to assess what is actionable, what is doable, and what matters and that this is usually school climate and/or conditions for learning, and rarely individual-level competencies. Although the discourse related to measuring individual-level competence was ongoing, there was increasing recognition and acceptance of the critical role climate measures could and should play.

Another Shift: A Renewed Interest in Competence Assessment

Stakeholder interest grew out of and fueled the federal policy discourse on whether and how to assess student SEC, but the same issues and concerns about this type of assessment were still prevalent. Philanthropy responded with the formation of the Funders' Collaborative for Innovative Measurement to ensure interoperability between multiple endeavors intended to describe, define, and develop strategies for the assessment of SECs. One funding endeavor was to support three major institutions that had existing projects or were leading voices in the SEL assessment space, including CASEL, the Ecological Approaches to Social and Emotional Learning (EASEL) Lab at Harvard University, and the RAND Corporation.

In 2015, the CASEL expanded an advisory group with the name of Establishing Practical Social-Emotional Competence Assessments of Preschool to High School Students. The group comprised SEL researchers and select research leads from "SEL-forward" districts. Their aim was to "advance progress toward establishing practical SEL assessments that are scientifically sound, feasible to use, and actionable as a key priority for the field" (Measuring SEL, n.d.). A year into the work, the group identified a need for an associated group of practice leaders (i.e., those individuals who are tasked with implementing policy at local levels). Led by 30 leaders from the education and out-of-school time fields, the National Practitioner Advisory Group was formed.

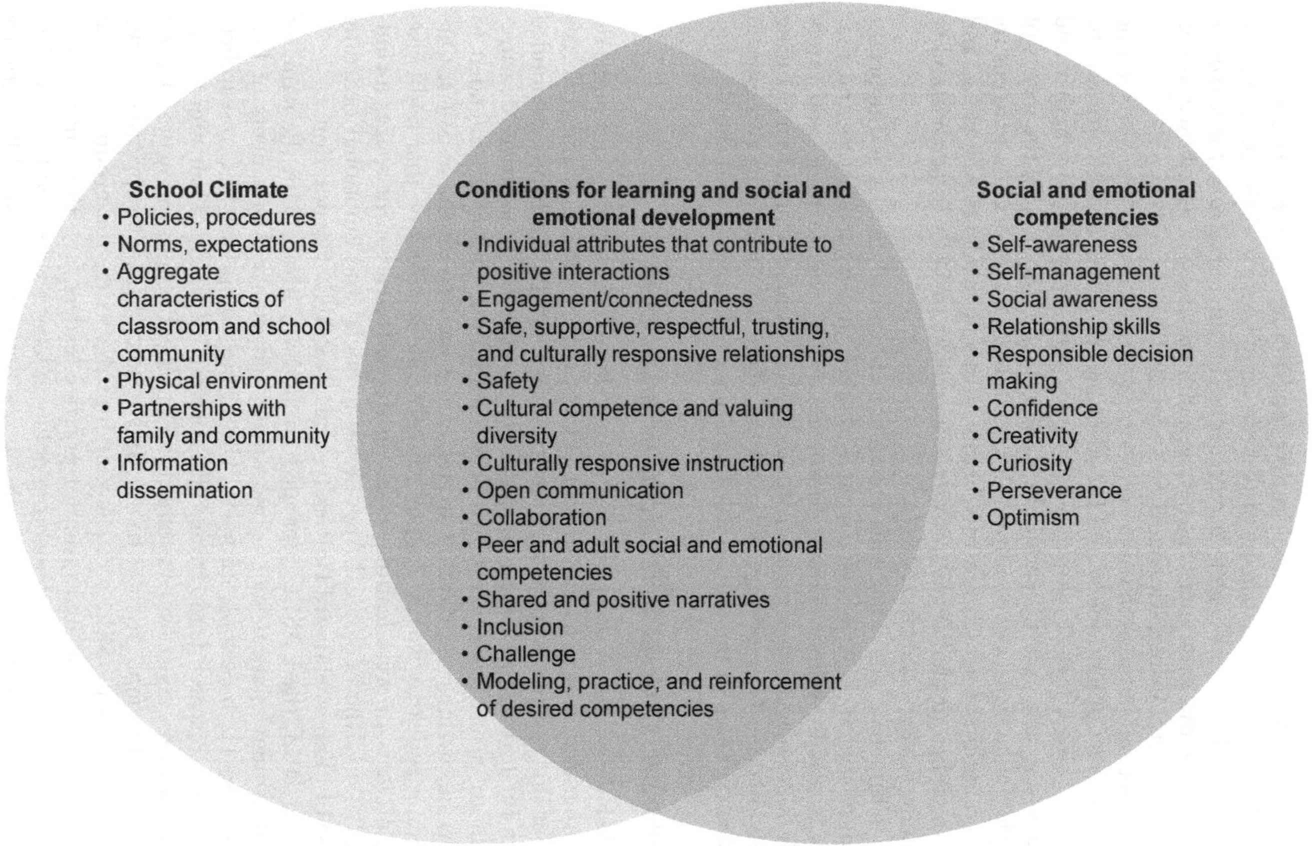

School Climate
- Policies, procedures
- Norms, expectations
- Aggregate characteristics of classroom and school community
- Physical environment
- Partnerships with family and community
- Information dissemination

Conditions for learning and social and emotional development
- Individual attributes that contribute to positive interactions
- Engagement/connectedness
- Safe, supportive, respectful, trusting, and culturally responsive relationships
- Safety
- Cultural competence and valuing diversity
- Culturally responsive instruction
- Open communication
- Collaboration
- Peer and adult social and emotional competencies
- Shared and positive narratives
- Inclusion
- Challenge
- Modeling, practice, and reinforcement of desired competencies

Social and emotional competencies
- Self-awareness
- Self-management
- Social awareness
- Relationship skills
- Responsible decision making
- Confidence
- Creativity
- Curiosity
- Perseverance
- Optimism

FIGURE 14.1. A model of the overlap between conditions for learning and SECs with illustrative components.

Each of the two groups authored guidance on the field of SEL assessment as a final product, summarizing its internal discourse and the shared conclusions its members had reached. In 2019 the Assessment Work Group produced "Student Social and Emotional Competence Assessment: The Current State of the Field and a Vision for the Future" (Assessment Work Group, 2019), a review of the state of assessments of SEC. The authors suggested that, as of 2019, there was an increased number of rigorous assessments and there was greater agreement on what constitutes a sound assessment, but that the field has work to do to ensure assessments are meaningfully employed for practical use. The piece articulated a vision for the future of SEL assessment, including considerations for policy, practice, the development of new assessments, and professional learning on the use of practical assessment. Also in 2019, the National Practitioner Advisory Group produced "Making SEL Assessment Work: Ten Practitioner Beliefs" (summarized in Figure 14.2).

By the conclusion of 2019, there was widespread recognition that guidance was needed for successful implementation of assessment of SECs at the local level. Each of the three organizations supported by the Funders' Collaborative on Innovative Measurement (CASEL, the EASEL Lab at Harvard University, and the RAND Corporation) produced practice-facing tools for measuring student SEC. In addition, AIR updated its 2015

---

1. Effective assessment begins with a strong vision and intentionality.

2. Assess SECs on the basis of strengths, not deficits.

3. A positive organizational culture and climate is foundational to social and emotional assessment.

4. When implemented and assessed through an equity lens, SEL can mitigate bias and promote appreciation of diversity.

5. Recognizing and promoting adult SEC is essential to thoughtful, sustainable assessment.

6. SECs evolve over time. Therefore, assess for growth, rather than finite outcomes.

7. Fostering adult capacity to assess SECs and interpret data can improve SEL practice.

8. Use SEL data to continuously improve practice.

9. Authentically engage and collaborate with stakeholders about assessment.

10. Practical SEL requires both universal and differentiated approaches informed by data.

FIGURE 14.2. Practitioner beliefs about SEL assessment (National Practitioner Advisory Group, 2019).

suite of SEL assessment resources, *Ready to Assess* (American Institutes for Research, 2019), which emphasized SEL assessment types including climate/conditions for learning and student competence measures. These resources provided guidance for local leaders regarding not only which SEL assessment tools to choose, but how, why, and under what conditions.

● Practical Considerations for SEL-Related Assessment in Context

Suffice it to say that SEL practices are most effective when they are systemic and coordinated; contextually relevant and culturally competent; implemented in a safe and supportive environment; active and engaging for all children and youth; and supported through ongoing formative assessment and reflection that drives continuous improvement (Newman et al., 2018). Measurement work should follow accordingly. Sound policy can support all of this.

In 2019, with the newest edition of *Ready to Assess*, staff at AIR suggested that those doing SEL work "stop and think" by asking themselves, "are we ready to assess?"[1] Whereas the original guidance had been "stop and think so you can choose the right SEL assessment tool for measuring youth competence," the new resources asked readers to consider whether they were *ready* for SEL implementation and assessment—whether they were creating the conditions conducive to social and emotional development and implementing SEL practices with quality—before deciding on the kind of SEC assessment that would best fit their needs.

From Readiness to Implementation Quality to Outcomes

Implementation readiness is having the motivation (and subsequent momentum), capacity, and knowledge to implement something new (Scaccia et al., 2015). Although the term *readiness* would imply something linear and final—you are ready or you are not; once you are ready, you are good to go—readiness is not linear nor is it a one-time checkpoint. It requires ongoing attention and recalibration, because the conditions that make an organization ready (less ready, more ready) are ever changing. Capacity is a good example. Consider a district that is implementing SEL practices and chooses to adopt a new assessment. That assessment requires training for district and school staff in how to use it and how to derive meaning from its data; time to attend said trainings and complete the assessment; and systems for data entry and management; and there is likely a cost associated with all of this. Perhaps the district and school leaders and staff have the

---

[1] Available at *https://measuringsel.casel.org/stop-and-think-before-you-act-are-you-ready-to-assess*.

motivation to use this assessment, but do they have the time or funds and resources to do so? Or perhaps they have that capacity in the beginning, but then funding cuts happen, and the resources to support the assessment are gone—what then? Alternatively, district leadership may be motivated and willing to devote resources but school leaders and teachers are not and this mismatch impedes implementation. For these reasons, it is essential to monitor readiness in an ongoing way—a dynamic, current state of readiness underpins implementation quality, and ultimately success.

There are measures to understand readiness (i.e., to use an SEL assessment or to implement SEL programs or strategies) that support understanding and improvement in this area. It stands to reason that, if implementation is bolstered by readiness, policies that promote understanding, measuring, building, and sustaining readiness would be beneficial. Promoting readiness also ensures that SEL efforts take into account elements that underpin equitable SEL practice, such as context and conditions as well as the inherent challenges of measuring SEL that we described earlier, such as bias and unintended consequences. As an assessor, are you ready to assess people who are different from you, for example, or settings that are different from what you have experienced? It is important to remember that SEL is a process—an active process of developing social and emotional attitudes, mindsets, behaviors, and skills. A district that is ready to support its schools to support SEL assessment is more likely to successfully create—and maintain—the conditions that support SEL and more likely to achieve overall implementation quality.

Creating positive conditions for learning (including SEL) is critical for growth and development along with SEL (Berg et al., 2017; Cantor et al., 2018). For example, if a student does not feel safe—physically, emotionally, and in terms of his or her identity—at school, his or her ability to focus on and contextualize content is severely limited; if a student fears humiliation (does not feel emotionally safe), his or her likelihood of raising a hand to ask a clarifying question is limited. In the same way that positive conditions for learning are critical for academic development, positive conditions for learning are necessary to support social and emotional development for young people. When students feel physically and emotionally safe, have supportive relationships with adults and their peers, and are engaged in meaningful learning activities, they are able to grow socially and emotionally. Positive conditions for learning are foundational—they contribute to social and emotional thriving (Osher et al., 2020).

Assessing the conditions for learning in a school can provide rich data to inform continuous improvement efforts, including those related to whether there are positive and culturally responsive conditions for SEL. As with assessments that measure student SEC, conditions for learning assessments can be completed by students (when developmentally appropriate), teachers, and families and should be employed to drive improvement.

When educators focus on measuring and improving conditions for learning, they receive concrete and actionable information, as they are hearing firsthand about students' experiences and perceptions of the conditions for learning as experienced by students and are inherently supporting young people's social and emotional growth by using this information to improve and create safe supportive spaces. It is important to keep in mind that any assessment of school climate or conditions for learning provides a snapshot; this type of measurement should be a repeated long-term endeavor as well as elaborated upon through intentional focus groups, interviews, and quick and regular check-ins with students. Climate and conditions for learning are malleable, as are students' perceptions of their conditions for learning. These data can best be employed for continuous improvement when students are involved in helping interpret these results (Osher, Cantor, Berg, Steyer, & Rose, 2018). The continuous improvement work spearheaded by the Nevada Department of Education's Office for a Safe and Respectful Learning Environment (OSRLE) provides an example of this practice. In response to a highly visible racist post on social media, OSRLE, in collaboration with the school district where the post occurred, gathered students from each high school in the rural county, who reviewed and interpreted their schools' results on the Nevada School Climate/Social Emotional Learning survey for their school administrators and spoke in depth about what it felt like day to day at school, prompting a greater understanding for these administrators and a driver of continued improvement in the conditions for learning at these schools. Understanding conditions for learning is particularly important when individuals are experiencing high levels of social and/or emotional need, which may be exacerbated by, for example, COVID-19-related changes and elevated discourse around racial equity and social issues. Researchers and practitioners have started addressing this. For example, AIR and Communities in Schools have developed tools to learn about how students are or are not engaging in learning (emotionally, socially, cognitively, and behaviorally) and what factors are limiting their engagement (*www.communitiesinschools.org/k12*). Another example is Nevada's OSRLE, which in partnership with AIR, developed and administered a voluntary well-being survey for students, staff, and families, addressing supports needed for mental health, basic needs, and conditions for learning during the pandemic.

Getting Ready to Assess: Decisions and Implications for Local Policy Implementation

Policymaking involves addressing key strategic questions that directly influence on-the-ground decision making, including purpose, quality, practicality, ethics, and alignment. *Purpose* is a foundational assessment-related decision. Why are you engaging in SEL assessment? There are many reasons for SEL assessment; however, the three most common reasons are for information sharing, for communication/storytelling, and for accountability purposes (American Institutes for Research, 2019). Accountability is often what we think of in the discussion of policy and its relation to practice—but it is information sharing and subsequent meaning-making that make assessment so valuable.

In addition to propelling purpose-aligned action, policy can also be a powerful tool to ward against misuse and misalignment with purpose. Well-designed policy can mitigate factors that have contributed to past inequities such as privileging and universalizing specific groups' norms and not others, elevating certain culturally grounded behaviors and not others, and minimizing the ways in which competencies and behaviors are demonstrated in different cultural contexts. Effective policy recognizes that our contextual and cultural lenses influence what we prioritize and how we measure our success against those priorities and serves to mitigate that influence by raising awareness of these issues and building in the necessary flexibility and guidance to authentically adapt to context and culture.

Another consideration is the *quality* (goodness) of the assessment approaches and instruments. Quality includes the potential value of the assessment, its validity and methodological soundness (including psychometric qualities of quantitative assessments), its helpfulness, limits, and relative advantages to alternative approaches. These considerations include how comprehensive the assessment will be and how it is intended (and not intended) to be used. Quality is not synonymous with intentionality and appropriate use of the assessment, although ease of implementing with quality can contribute to the value of a particular approach or tool. It is important to implement any measure as it was intended, unless there is evidence that the assessment cannot be used successfully with particular groups or in particular contexts. When modifications are necessary to adapt cultural and contextual factors, it is important to collect and assess data to ensure quality.

The third consideration is one of *practicality*—how much burden will using this assessment place on the user, and are there resources available for the assessment (think back to the discussion of readiness earlier in this chapter)? As we noted earlier, it is imperative to consider and have respect for the time, perspective, and experiences of those who will use the assessment and those who are assessed.

A fourth consideration when selecting an assessment approach or tool is *ethics*. Ethical considerations are perhaps the most important issue, but they are often overlooked. We tend to focus on whether the assessment measures the specific practices or outcomes we intend, and whether we have the resources available, but as we noted previously, we must take responsibility to avoid potentially negative consequences that stem from assessment in this area. We pose the following questions that warrant consideration:

- Does the benefit of collecting these data outweigh the burden and any risks?
- Is there evidence and a history of using this measure successfully with the population it is intended for?
- Are we using the data in a way that is intended by the measure developer and aligned with our planned administration?
- Do we have the knowledge and resources needed to interpret and derive meaning from the data in equitable and strengths-aligned ways?

The final consideration is *alignment*. This means reflecting on what it is that is being implemented and what can reasonably be expected in terms of observed practice and measurable outcomes. As the adage goes, "you get out what you put in," and this applies to assessment considerations as well.

Framework Alignment and Equitable Assessment

Implementation of SEL practice is typically driven by policy in the form of standards and frameworks. Although synergies exist across SEL standards (because they are typically derived from the CASEL framework) and other frameworks (Osher et al., 2016), they vary in their goals, focus, theoretical underpinnings, and coverage (Berg et al., 2017). For example, a study by Berg and colleagues identified and examined 136 frameworks in English-speaking countries that focused on SECs. This study found variation at the level of global focus (e.g., 21st-century skills or SEL), as well as at the domain, subdomain, and skill level. The authors determined that, among other things:

- Frameworks do not apply uniformly across individuals, groups, and systems.
- Fewer than 20% of frameworks consider culturally and linguistically diverse individuals and groups.
- Fewer than 20% of frameworks consider the experiences of youth with disabilities.
- Just under 6% of frameworks acknowledge trauma experiences.

Some of this variance may be explained by the sources used to develop the standards or frameworks. States and districts are often guided by the SEL framework from CASEL. Many frameworks are then adaptations, expansions, or derivations from the CASEL framework, created to fit a particular purpose or align with a different focus that is not always explicitly "SEL." Stephanie Jones and her colleagues at the EASEL Lab have developed an online database and set of visual tools called Explore SEL *(http://exploresel.gse.harvard.edu)*, which is designed to describe, connect, and communicate about SEL frameworks drawn from a wide array of U.S.-based and global organizations.

Regardless, this variance is important: Equitable assessment systems should reflect as well as address culture, disability, adversity, and resilience. This will not be easy, as frameworks and assessment choices are often driven by external sources, from funding requirements to administrative priorities, rather than the concerns and goals of students and families. They are also based on research, input, and a psychometric legacy that underrepresents or even ignores communities of color. Choices often reflect dominant values and beliefs that are baked into supposedly "color blind" research, and methodological paradigms that strip out or undervalue context along with the experience of minoritized groups. For example, in the same study, Berg and colleagues found that most frameworks did not address communalism—outcomes that are valued among many cultural communities of color (e.g., Alcalá, Rogoff, & Fraire, 2018). Similarly, the frameworks studied rarely addressed coping with racism and skills for fighting racism, which are particularly salient experiences of many people of color. These gaps are also reflected at the skill and mindset level. For example, the same study determined that most of the frameworks did not address the need for perspective taking and cultural competence (e.g., code switching), and only the frameworks that came from disability or racial perspectives addressed matters of privilege. These gaps are pronounced, given the need in both the United States and the world to address inequity and promote positive intercultural relationships and collaboration.

Clearly, identifying a SEL framework that is aligned with SEL practices, reflective of the culture and context of the student population, and reliable and useful for practice and improvement is primary. Earlier in the chapter we reference engaging a stakeholder team to define SEL policy assessment, and that team should also be involved in exploring the framework that most aligns with these critically important factors and using that framework to help them select an assessment. One of the conundra of practice is that the frameworks define youth-level competencies, but not the conditions for teaching and learning that underpin the development of those competencies, often leaving policymakers and practitioners left with the "What do I DO?" question even after the arduous stakeholder-involved task of choosing an aligned framework is complete. So, having an aligned framework is an important step, but it is not the end of the journey in designing a comprehensive policy agenda that supports the implementation, assessment, and improvement of SEL practices and competencies.

• Measurement Considerations That Matter for People

Policy influences what skills, competencies, and dispositions to assess; what data should inform the assessment; why we are assessing; how the data can be analyzed, assessed, and reported out; and the time horizon of focus—for example, in the moment, over a term, or over multiple years. This is no simple matter, as there are many social and emotional skills, competencies, and dispositions, many contexts in which they are utilized, and natural raters, with different implicit standards, who judge behavior (Kellam & Van Horn, 1997).

Assessment policy should address the individualized, developmental, jagged, culturally embedded (e.g., Arauz, Deter, Rogoff, & Aceves-Azuara, 2019; Gutiérrez & Rogoff, 2003), and contextually and situationally dependent nature of SEC (Cantor et al., 2018; Doebel, 2020; Rogoff, 2003). At the same time, policy also needs to address the fact that some competencies (e.g., self-regulation) and some competency subdomains (e.g., emotional self-regulation) may affect the ability to learn, develop, and express certain competencies, and may influence assessment results. This means that all people who develop a strong array of SECs over their life course will not look the same at any one point in their journey, or across all contexts at any one point in their journey. This also means that we need to engage the voices and perspectives of researchers and stakeholders from the diversity of communities to identify which competencies matter and how those competencies are successfully demonstrated within diverse, culturally rich contexts.

If the goal of assessment policy at every level is to promote the development of SEC, we need to ensure those that develop and those that implement policy address this dynamic complexity with humility, curiosity, and social responsibility:

• *Humility* includes an awareness that all people who are relevant to assessing a young person's SEC do not value or reinforce the same skills and competencies. In addition, the person who is being assessed must live with as well as apply the competencies they develop in their own cultural context. Humility also includes an awareness that any assessment is a snapshot or a series of snapshots of dynamic properties that can always be altered. For educators this means checking and understanding biases, recognizing cultural lenses, and a clear knowledge that competencies are malleable and individual (so one should not compare or make judgments based on other experiences or individuals).

• *Curiosity* involves wanting to learn what is behind the assessment data collected, as well as learning about how the individual who is being assessed makes sense of their skills and of the assessment process. There is a tension with the value in supporting individual competence development and the general recommendation that assessment data can be collected and used in a de-identified manner. When they are de-identified, these data can be combined with other data for research that enhances our understanding of development broadly (e.g., how SECs are fostered, how this process varies by individual and context, how we can emphasize the conditions that support SEL and address the factors that attenuate SECs) but this de-identification then inhibits one's ability to provide individualized supports that foster growth and development.

• *Responsibility* involves focusing on the equifinality (i.e., there are several means to the same end) of good outcomes and reducing the risks of inappropriate or premature conclusions, which can lead to harmful impacts (e.g., by creating self-fulfilling prophecies). Responsibility entails ensuring that the burden of assessment is worth it. Responsibility also involves addressing inequities, including victim-blaming thinking and interventions. For policymakers this means ensuring the assessment policy doesn't have unintended consequences (remember NCLB) and for educators and their stakeholders, this means ensuring assessment of SEC is responsible from a measurement perspective (i.e., does it measure what you hope to move in SEL practice?) and outcome perspective (i.e., is it universal and not targeted, useful for improvement?), and reflective of the student body culture and context. Importantly, since assessment of SECs is not yet quick and easy, is the burden on practitioners and students worth the benefit of the assessment findings? The irresponsible situation is when stakeholders (sometimes policymakers) demand assessment of SECs, practitioners scramble to respond and use ill-fitting assessment measures for the practice, and then the assessment findings sit unused for lack of interest or capacity to analyze and apply the data in a way that is useful.

Policy should focus on both assessing individuals and assessing the conditions that support the development of SEC. Given our current knowledge of assessment and the currently available assessment technologies—and the potential for assessment to have harmful effects—individual SEL assessment should be formative, not summative; that no consequences be tied to individual and school aggregate assessment; that individual data be provided to the student and staff who work with the student in support of SEL with support for applying the information; that aggregate data be provided to school, district, and state leadership for continuous quality improvement.

What we know about climate and the conditions for learning and the tools for measuring them are more advanced, and the risk of iatrogenic effects (i.e., inadvertent but caused by the assessor) are less than they are for measures of competence. In other words, it is harder to do harm with assessment of climate and conditions for learning. Hence, it may make sense to assess conditions for learning both formatively and summatively and, if there are accountability or performance monitoring systems, to include the assessment of conditions for learning within the systems, with a particular focus on them as leading indicators both in the short and long term. Federal and state policy can include guidance for the assessment of climate and conditions for learning at the local levels.

Evaluation and research should attend to the specificity of effects by individual and context, while attending to the dynamic of ecologies of schools and communities, which affect SEL. This responsibility can be enhanced when research about the assessment of SECs includes within-person SECs. In addition, research should address cultural diversity as well as the development of SECs in diverse social and cultural contexts, including:

- jaggedness of SECs that can still lead to similar outcomes as well as how culture and context affects individual trajectories and outcomes;
- the impact of culture, professional socialization, and social position of the researcher on SEL assessment-related research; and
- the factors that affect individual SEL, such as teacher cultural responsiveness and peer effects.

To summarize: People and their individual and collective thriving matter. If the goal, as we have suggested, is to create conditions for equity and thriving, then assessment and assessment policy that undergirds it must follow suit and be done in a way that enables educators to create the conditions for equity and thriving. Policies matter because they influence implementation, and measurement matters because it helps us to understand implementation. Ultimately, all of this happens because people matter—people in the assessment setting, in the community, and the people who will come later. Policies and assessment must put people first if we are to create conditions for equity and thriving.

REFERENCES

Alcalá, L., Rogoff, B., & López Fraire, A. (2018). Sophisticated collaboration is common among Mexican-heritage U.S. children. *Proceedings of the National Academy of Science, 115,* 11377–11384.

American Institutes for Research—AIR. (2019). *Ready to assess.* AIR.

Artiles, A. J., Kozleski, E. B., Trent, S. C., Osher, D., & Ortiz, A. (2010). Justifying and explaining disproportionality, 1968–2008: A critique of underlying views of culture. *Exceptional Children, 76*(3), 279–299.

Arauz, R. M., Dexter, A. L., Rogoff, B., & Aceves-Azaura, I. (2019). Children's management of attention as cultural practice. In T. Tulviste, D. L. Best, & J. L. Gibbons (Eds.), *Children's Social Worlds in Cultural Context* (pp. 23–39). Springer.

Assessment Work Group. (2019). *Student social and emotional competence assessment: The current state of the field and a vision for its future.* Collaborative for Academic, Social, and Emotional Learning.

Barbour, C., LaTurner, R. J., & Osher, D. (2018). Guiding and planning improvement for equity with excellence. In D. Osher, D. Moroney, & S. Williamson (Eds.), *Creating safe, equitable, engaging schools: A comprehensive, evidence-based approach to supporting students* (pp. 35–50). Harvard Education Press.

Berg, J., Osher, D., Moroney, D., & Yoder, N. (2017). *The intersection of school climate and social and emotional development.* Washington, DC: American Institutes for Research.

Blad, E. (2015). Accountability measures for traits like "grit" questioned. EdWeek. Retrieved from *www.edweek.org/leadership/accountability-measures-for-traits-like-grit-questioned/2015/05.*

Broadfoot, P. (1986). Assessment policy and inequality: The United Kingdom experience. *British Journal of Sociology of Education, 7*(2), 205–224.

Butler, A. R., Katz, J., Johnson, J., Osher, D., Pentimonti, J., & Neiman, S. (2018). Continuous improvement. In D. Osher, D. Moroney, & S. Williamson (Eds.), *Creating safe, equitable, engaging schools: A comprehensive, evidence-based approach to supporting students* (pp. 253–266). Harvard Education Press.

Cantor, P., Osher, D., Berg, J., Steyer, L., & Rose, T. (2018). Malleability, plasticity, and individuality: How children learn and develop in context. *Applied Developmental Science.*

Child Trends. (2017). Analysis of ESSA state plans "school quality or student success indicator." Author. Retrieved from *www.childtrends.org/wp-content/uploads/2017/09/ESSA-Fifth-Indicator-Coding-Child-Trends-9-20-2017.pdf.*

Chudnovsky, M., & Espinosa Trujillo, N. (2019). Conflict between formal and informal rules in policy coordination: The case of child homelessness in Mexico City. *Latin American Policy, 10*(1), 120–143.

Coppens, A. D., Corwin, A. I., & Alcalá, L. (2020). Beyond behavior: Linguistic evidence of cultural variation in parental ethnotheories of children's prosocial helping. *Frontiers in Psychology, 11,* 307.

Correa-Chávez, M., Rogoff, B., & Mejía Arauz, R. (2005). Cultural patterns in attending to two events at once. *Child Development, 76*(3), 664–678.

Curtin, A., Cahill, K., Hall, K., O'Sullivan, D., & Özerk, K. (2019). *Explorations in identity, culture, policy and inclusion.* Google Books.

Darling-Hammond, L., & Cook-Harvey, C. M. (2018). *Educating the whole child: Improving school climate to support student success.* Learning Policy Institute.

Doebel, S. (2020). Rethinking executive function and its development. *Perspectives on Psychological Science, 15*(4), 942–956.

Durlak, J. A., Weissberg, R. P., Dymnicki, A. B., Taylor, R. D., & Schellinger, K.

B. (2011). The impact of enhancing students' social and emotional learning: A meta-analysis of school-based universal interventions. *Child Development, 82*(1), 405–432.

Dymnicki, A., Wandersman, A., Osher, D., Grigorescu, V., & Huang, L. (2014). *Willing, able, ready: Basics and policy implications of readiness as a key component for implementation of evidence-based interventions*. Office of the Assistant Secretary for Planning and Evaluation, Office of Human Services Policy, U.S. Department of Health and Human Services. Office of the Assistant Secretary for Planning and Evaluation, Office of Human Services Policy, U.S. Department of Health and Human Services.

Fernández, D. L. (2015). Children's everyday learning by assuming responsibility for others: Indigenous practices as a cultural heritage across generations. *Advances in Child Development and Behavior, 49*, 53–89.

Gaylord-Harden, N. K., Barbarin, O., Tolan, P. H., & Murry, V. M. (2018). Understanding development of African American boys and young men: Moving from risks to positive youth development. *American Psychologist, 73*(6), 753.

Goffman, E. (1974). *Frame analysis: An essay on the organization of experience*. Harvard University Press.

Gordon, R., Ji, P., Mulhall, P., Shaw, W., & Weissberg, R. (2016). Social and emotional learning for Illinois: Policy, practice, and progress. CASEL. Retrieved from *https://casel.org/wp-content/uploads/2016/06/social-and-emotional-learning-for-illinois-students-policy-practice-and-progress-ilovepdf-compressed.pdf*.

Greenblatt, S. H. (1995). Phrenology in the science and culture of the 19th century. *Neurosurgery, 37*(4), 790–804; discussion 804–805.

Gutiérrez, K. D., & Rogoff, B. (2003). Cultural ways of learning: Individual traits or repertoires of practice. *Educational Researcher, 32*, 19–25.

Helms, J. E. (2006). Fairness is not validity or cultural bias in racial-group assessment: A quantitative perspective. *American Psychologist, 61*(8), 845–859.

Helms, J. E. (2007). Implementing fairness in racial-group assessment requires assessment of individuals. *American Psychologist, 62*(9), 1083–1085.

Hsu, C., & Sandford, B. A. (2007). The Delphi Technique: Making sense of consensus. *Practical Assessment, Research, & Evaluation, 12*(10), 1–8.

Illinois State Board of Education. (n.d.). Social/emotional learning standards. Retrieved from *www.isbe.net/Pages/Social-Emotional-Learning-Standards.aspx*.

Jagers, R. J., Williams, B., & Osher, D. (2019). Exploring the role of family socialization and parenting practices in promoting the social and emotional learning of children and youth. In D. Osher, M. J. Mayer, R. J. Jagers, K. Kendziora, & L. Wood (Eds.), *Keeping students safe and helping them thrive: A collaborative handbook on school safety, mental health, and wellness* (pp. 317–341). Praeger/ABC-CLIO.

Jones, D. E., Greenberg, M., & Crowley, M. (2015). Early social–emotional functioning and public health: The relationship between kindergarten social competence and future wellness. *American Journal of Public Health, 105*(11), 2283–2290.

Kellam, S. G., & Rebok, G. W. (1992). Building developmental and etiological theory through epidemiologically based preventive intervention trials. In J. McCord & R. E. Tremblay (Eds.), *Preventing antisocial behavior: Interventions from birth through adolescence* (pp. 162–195). Guilford Press.

Kellam, S. G., & Van Horn, Y. V. (1997). Life course development, community epidemiology, and preventive trials: A scientific structure for prevention research. *American Journal of Community Psychology, 25*(2), 177.

Kendziora, K., & Osher, D. (2016). Promoting children's and adolescents' social and emotional development: District adaptations of a theory of action. *Journal of Clinical Child & Adolescent Psychology, 45*(6), 797–811.

Klein, A. (2015, April 10). No Child Left Behind: An overview. Retrieved from *www.edweek.org/ew/section/multimedia/no-child-left-behind-overview-definition-summary.html.*

Kress, J. S., Norris, J. A., Schoenholz, D. A., Elias, M. J., & Seigle, P. (2004). Bringing together educational standards and social and emotional learning: Making the case for educators. *American Journal of Education, 111*(1), 68–89.

Kumkale, G. T., & Albarracín, D. (2004). The sleeper effect in persuasion: A meta-analytic review. *Psychological Bulletin, 130*(1), 143.

Lipsky, M. (1980). *Street-level bureaucracy: Dilemmas of the individual in public services.* Russell Sage Foundation.

May, P. J., & Winter, S. C. (2009). Politicians, managers, and street-level bureaucrats: Influences on policy implementation. *Journal of Public Administration Research and Theory, 19*(3), 453–476.

Maynard-Moody, S., & Musheno, M. (2000). State agent or citizen agent: Two narratives of discretion. *Journal of Public Administration Research and Theory, 10*(2), 329–358.

Mayo, R., Moroney, D. A., & Huff, B. (2019). Practical guidance for policy and practice: Strategies and tools for assessing and building readiness and for launching local efforts. In D. Osher, K. Kendziora, R. Jagers, L. Wood, & M. Mayer (Eds.), *Keeping students safe and helping them thrive: A collaborative handbook for education, safety, and justice professionals, families, and communities* (vol. 2, pp. 389–412). Praeger.

Measuring SEL. (n.d.). *Our initiative.* Retrieved from *https://measuringsel.casel.org/our-initiative.*

Merton, R. K. (1957). *Social theory and social structure* (rev. ed.). Free Press.

Mills, C. W. (1959). *The sociological imagination.* Oxford University Press.

National Practitioner Advisory Group. (2019). *Making SEL assessment work: Ten practitioner beliefs.* Collaborative for Academic, Social, and Emotional Learning and the American Institutes for Research.

National Research Council. (2012). *Education for life and work: Developing transferable knowledge and skills in the 21st century.* National Academies Press.

Nesselroade, J. R., & Molenaar, P. C. M. (2016). Some behavioral science measurement concerns and proposals. *Multivariate Behavioral Research, 51,* 396–412.

Newman, J. Z., Dymnicki, A., Fergus, E., Weissberg, R. P., & Osher, D. (2018). Social and emotional learning matters. In D. Osher, D. A. Moroney, & S.

Williamson (Eds.), *Creating safe, equitable, engaging schools: A comprehensive, evidence-based approach to supporting students* (pp. 213–222). Harvard Education Press.

O'Day, J. A., & Smith, M. S. (2019). *Opportunity for all: A framework for quality and equality in education.* Harvard Education Press.

Osher, D. (2014). The implementation of inclusive education in Beijing: Exorcizing the haunting specter of meritocracy. *Frontiers of Education in China, 9*(3), 461–463.

Osher, D., Pittman, K., Young, J., Smith, H., Moroney, D., & Irby, M. (2020). *Thriving, robust equity, and transformative learning & development: A more powerful conceptualization of the contributors to youth success.* Washington, DC: American Institutes for Research and Forum for Youth Investment.

Osher, D. (2018). Building readiness and capacity. In D. Osher, D. A. Moroney, & S. Williamson (Eds.), *Creating safe, equitable, engaging schools: A comprehensive, evidence-based approach to supporting students* (pp. 15–24). Harvard Education Press.

Osher, D., & Cantor, P. (in press). *The science of learning & development.* Taylor Francis.

Osher, D., Cantor, P., Berg, J., Steyer, L., & Rose, T. (2018). Drivers of human development: How relationships and context shape learning and development. *Applied Developmental Science.*

Osher, D., Kidron, Y., Brackett, M., Dymnicki, A., Jones, S., & Weissberg, R. (2016). Advancing the science and practice of social and emotional learning: Looking back and moving forward. *Review of Research in Education, 40,* 644–681.

Osher, D., Pittman, K., Young, J., Smith, H., Moroney, D., & Irby, M. (2020). *Thriving, robust equity, and transformative learning & development: A more powerful conceptualization of the contributors to youth success.* Washington, DC: American Institutes for Research and Forum for Youth Investment.

Osher, D., & Shriver, T. (2016). A call to action for inspiring and motivating our children and teachers to learn and grow in social, emotional, and cognitive arenas. Retrieved from *www.cfchildren.org/Portals/1/Advcy/advcy_doc/2016/essa-consensus-letter-secretary-king.pdf.*

Pas, E. T., & Bradshaw, C. P. (2014). What affects teacher ratings of student behaviors? The potential influence of teachers' perceptions of the school environment and experiences. *Prevention Science, 15*(6), 940–950.

Rebell, M. A. (2008). *Moving every child ahead: From NCLB hype to meaningful educational opportunity.* Teachers College Press.

Rogoff, B. (2003). *The cultural nature of human development.* Oxford University Press.

Rogoff, B., Coppens, A. D., Alcalá, L., Aceves-Azuara, I., Ruvalcaba, O., López, A., & Dayton, A. (2017). Noticing learners' strengths through cultural research. *Perspectives on Psychological Science, 12*(5), 876–888.

Rose, T. (2016). *The end of average: How we succeed in a world that values sameness.* Harper Collins.

Salinger, T., & Osher, D. (2018). Academic interventions—Use with care. In D.

Osher, D. Moroney, & S. Williamson (Eds.), *Creating safe, equitable, engaging schools: A comprehensive, evidence-based approach to supporting students*. Harvard Education Press.

Scaccia, J. P., Cook, B. S., Lamont, A., Wandersman, A., Castellow, J., Katz, J., & Beidas, R. S. (2015). A practical implementation science heuristic for organizational readiness: R= MC2. *Journal of Community Psychology, 43*(4), 484–501.

Schachat, A. (2016, July 25). *Why the buzz around ESSA's fifth indicator worries me as a teacher* [Blog post]. Retrieved from *www.aypf.org/blog/why-the-buzz-around-essas-fifth-indicator-worries-me-as-a-teacher*.

Sliwinski, M. J. (2008). Measurement-burst designs for social health research. *Social and Personality Psychology Compass, 2*(1), 245–261.

Spencer, M. B., Offidani-Bertrand, C., Harris, K., & Velez, G. (2020). Examining links between culture, identity, and learning. In N. S. Nasir, C. D. Lee, R. Pea, & M. M. de Royston (Eds.), *Handbook of the cultural foundations of learning* (pp. 44–61). Routledge.

Sternberg, R. J., & Grigorenko, E. L. (2000). *Practical intelligence and its development*. In R. Bar-On & J. D. A. Parker (Eds.), *The handbook of emotional intelligence: Theory, development, assessment, and application at home, school, and in the workplace* (pp. 215–243). Jossey-Bass.

U.S. Department of Education. (n.d.). No Child Left Behind Act of 2001. Retrieved from *www2.ed.gov/policy/elsec/leg/esea02/index.html*.

Walker, T. (2014). The testing obsession and the disappearing curriculum. National Education Association. Retrieved from *http://neatoday.org/2014/09/02/the-testing-obsession-and-the-disappearing-curriculum-2*.

Watts, T. W., Duncan, G. J., & Quan, H. (2018). Revisiting the marshmallow test: A conceptual replication investigating links between early delay of gratification and later outcomes. *Psychological Science, 29*(7), 1159–1177.

West, M. R. (2016, March 17). Should non-cognitive skills be included in school accountability systems? Preliminary evidence from California's CORE districts. Retrieved from *www.brookings.edu/research/should-non-cognitive-skills-be-included-in-school-accountability-systems-preliminary-evidence-from-californias-core-districts*.

Yoder, N., Dusenbury, N., Martinez-Black, T., & Weissberg, R. (2020). From insights to action: Redefining state efforts to support social and emotional learning. Collaborative for Academic, Social, and Emotional Learning. Retrieved from *https://casel.org/wp-content/uploads/2020/04/CASEL-CSI-Emerging-Insights-Brief-2020.pdf*.

Index